Middle School 2-2

기말고사 완벽대비

적중 100

영어 기출 문제집

중**2**

시사 | 송미정

Best Collection

구성과 특징

교과서의 주요 학습 내용을 중심으로 학습 영역별 특성에 맞춰 단계별로 다양한 학습 기회를 제공하여 단원별 학습능력 평가는 물론 중간 및 기말고사 시험 등에 완벽하게 대비할 수 있도록 내용을 구성

Words & Expressions

Step1 Key Words 단원별 핵심 단어 설명 및 풀이
Key Expression 단원별 핵심 숙어 및 관용어 설명
Word Power 반대 또는 비슷한 뜻 단어 배우기
English Dictionary 영어로 배우는 영어 단어

Step2 실력평가 단원별 수시평가 대비 주관식, 객관식 문제풀이

Step3 서술형 대비 학업성취도 및 수행능력평가 대비 서술형 문제풀이

Conversation

Step1 핵심 의사소통 의사소통에 필요한 주요 표현 방법 요약
핵심 Check 기본적인 표현 방법 및 활용능력 확인

Step2 대화문 익히기 상황에 따른 대화문 활용 및 연습

Step3 기본평가 시험대비 기초 학습 능력 평가

Step4 실력평가 단원별 수시평가 대비 주관식, 객관식 문제풀이

Step5 서술형 대비 학업성취도 및 수행능력평가 대비 서술형 문제풀이

Grammar

Step1 주요 문법 단원별 주요 문법 사항과 예문을 알기 쉽게 설명
핵심 Check 기본 문법사항에 대한 이해 여부 확인

Step2 기본평가 시험대비 기초 학습 능력 평가

Step3 실력평가 단원별 수시평가 대비 주관식, 객관식 문제풀이

Step4 서술형 대비 학업성취도 및 수행능력평가 대비 서술형 문제풀이

Reading

Step1 구문 분석 단원별로 제시된 문장에 대한 구문별 분석과 내용 설명
확인문제 문장에 대한 기본적인 이해와 인지능력 확인

Step2 확인학습A 빈칸 채우기를 통한 문장 완성 능력 확인

Step3 확인학습B 제시된 우리말을 영어로 완성하여 작문 능력 키우기

Step4 실력평가 단원별 수시평가 대비 주관식, 객관식 문제풀이

Step5 서술형 대비 학업성취도 및 수행능력평가 대비 서술형 문제풀이
교과서 구석구석 교과서에 나오는 기타 문장까지 완벽 학습

Composition

|영역별 핵심문제|

단어 및 어휘, 대화문, 문법, 독해 등 각 영역별 기출문제의 출제 유형을 분석하여 실전에 대비하고 연습할 수 있도록 문제를 배열

|서술형 실전 및 창의사고력 문제|

학교 시험에서 점차 늘어나는 서술형 시험에 집중 대비하고 고득점을 취득하는데 만전을 기하기 위한 학습 코너

|단원별 예상문제|

기출문제를 분석한 후 새로운 시험 출제 경향을 더하여 새롭게 출제될 수 있는 문제를 포함하여 시험에 완벽하게 대비할 수 있도록 준비

|단원별 모의고사|

영역별, 단계별 학습을 모두 마친 후 실전 연습을 위한 모의고사

INSIGHT
on the textbook

교과서 파헤치기

- **단어Test1~2** 영어 단어 우리말 쓰기와 우리말을 영어 단어로 쓰기

- **대화문Test1~2** 대화문 빈칸 완성 및 전체 대화문 쓰기

- **본문Test1~5** 빈칸 완성, 우리말 쓰기, 문장 배열연습, 영어 작문하기 복습 등 단계별 반복 학습을
  통해 교과서 지문에 대한 완벽한 습득

- **구석구석지문Test1~2** 지문 빈칸 완성 및 전문 영어로 쓰기

Contents

Lesson 7

Living in the AI World

의사소통 기능

- 의견 표현하기
  A: I'm going to fly a drone.
  B: That sounds like fun.

- 가능 여부 표현하기
  A: Is it possible for you to text with your eyes closed?
  B: Sure. I can do that.

언어 형식

- 지각동사
  I **see** a cat **crossing** the street.

- 가주어 'it'
  It is hard **to believe** that you can understand us.

Words & Expressions

Key Words

- **AI** 인공지능(artificial intelligence)
- **amusement** [əmjúːzmənt] 명 즐거움, 오락
- **animated** [ǽnəmèitid] 형 동영상의, 생기 있는
- **beat** [biːt] 동 이기다
- **beatbox** [bíːtbɑks] 동 비트박스를 하다
- **bedroom** [bédrùːm] 명 침실
- **burn** [bəːrn] 동 불타다
- **chance** [tʃæns] 명 기회
- **check** [tʃek] 동 확인하다, 점검하다
- **closet** [klázit] 명 옷장
- **cloudy** [kláudi] 형 구름의, 흐린
- **cross** [krɔːs] 동 건너다
- **danger** [déindʒər] 명 위험
- **dictionary** [díkʃənèri] 명 사전
- **easily** [íːzili] 부 쉽게
- **else** [els] 부 그 밖의
- **exciting** [iksáitiŋ] 형 흥미진진한, 신나는
- **freeze** [friːz] 동 얼리다, 얼다
- **impossible** [impásəbl] 형 불가능한
- **intelligent** [intélədʒənt] 형 똑똑한
- **interesting** [íntərəstiŋ] 형 재미있는, 흥미로운
- **like** [laik] 전 ~ 같이, ~처럼
- **lucky** [lʌ́ki] 형 행운의
- **machine** [məʃíːn] 명 기계
- **mean** [miːn] 동 의미하다
- **off** [ɔːf] 부 할인되어
- **perfect** [pə́ːrfikt] 형 완벽한
- **point** [pɔint] 동 돌리다, 향하게 하다
- **possible** [pásəbl] 형 가능한
- **predict** [pridíkt] 동 예측하다
- **project** [prádʒekt] 명 과제
- **replace** [ripléis] 동 대체하다
- **select** [silékt] 동 선택하다
- **sense** [sens] 동 감지하다
- **situation** [sìtʃuéiʃən] 명 상황
- **space** [speis] 명 공간, 우주
- **strange** [streindʒ] 형 이상한
- **take** [teik] 동 선택하다, 사다
- **teleport** [téləpɔ̀ːrt] 동 순간 이동하다
- **text** [tekst] 동 (휴대전화로) 문자를 보내다
- **theater** [θíːətər] 명 극장
- **through** [θruː] 부 ~을 통해, ~ 사이로
- **translate** [trænsléit] 동 번역하다
- **translator** [trænsléitər] 명 번역가
- **unbelievable** [ʌnbilívəbəl] 형 믿기 어려운, 놀랄만한
- **without** [wiðáut] 전 ~ 없이

Key Expressions

- **based on** ~에 근거하여
- **be able to 동사원형** ~할 수 있다
- **because of** ~ 때문에
- **by the way** 그런데, 그건 그렇고
- **by 동사ing** ~함으로써
- **don't have to** ~할 필요가 없다(need not)
- **face to face** (~와) 서로 얼굴을 맞대고
- **free from** ~의 염려가 없는
- **get in** ~에 타다
- **get off** ~에서 내리다, ~에서 떨어지다
- **get to** ~에 도착하다
- **get 비교급** 점점 더 ~해지다
- **go with** 같이 가다, 어울리다
- **in danger** 위험에 처한, 위험에 빠진
- **Is it possible (for 목적격) to 동사원형 ~?** (…가) ~하는 것이 가능할까?
- **keep 동사ing** 계속 ~하다
- **look for** ~을 찾다
- **look ~ up** (사전·참고 자료·컴퓨터 등에서 정보를) 찾아보다
- **look 형용사** ~하게 보이다
- **move on** ~로 이동하다
- **not just** 단지 ~뿐이 아니다
- **no longer** 더 이상 ~하지 않다
- **out of** (원천·출처) ~에서, ~으로부터
- **over there** 저쪽에
- **see if 주어 동사** ~인지 아닌지 확인하다
- **slow down** 속도를 늦추다
- **sound like 명사** ~처럼 들리다
- **sound 형용사** ~하게 들리다
- **try to 동사원형** 노력하다
- **watch out** 조심하다

Word Power

※ 명사 + 접미사 -y → 형용사

- □ **dust**(먼지) – **dusty**(먼지가 많은)
- □ **ease**(쉬움) – **easy**(쉬운)
- □ **fun**(재미) – **funny**(재미있는)
- □ **greed**(욕심) – **greedy**(욕심 많은)

- □ **health**(건강) – **healthy**(건강한)
- □ **luck**(행운) – **lucky**(운이 좋은)
- □ **noise**(소음) – **noisy**(시끄러운)
- □ **sleep**(잠) – **sleepy**(졸린)

※ 날씨 관련 명사에 **y**가 붙어 형용사가 되는 경우

- □ **cloud**(구름) – **cloudy**(흐린)
- □ **rain**(비) – **rainy**(비가 오는)
- □ **snow**(눈) – **snowy**(눈이 내리는)

- □ **sun**(태양) – **sunny**(맑은)
- □ **wind**(바람) – **windy**(바람이 부는)
- □ **fog**(안개) – **foggy**(안개가 낀)

※ 음식 관련 명사에 **y**가 붙어 형용사가 되는 경우

- □ **oil**(기름) – **oily**(기름기가 있는)
- □ **salt**(소금) – **salty**(짠)

- □ **taste**(맛) – **tasty**(맛있는)

English Dictionary

- □ **amusement** 즐거움, 오락
  → the enjoyment that you get from being entertained
  즐겁게 되는 것에서 얻는 기쁨
- □ **beat** 이기다
  → to defeat someone in a game
  경기에서 누군가를 패배시키다
- □ **beatbox** 비트박스를 하다
  → to create the sounds of powerful rhythm with the voice and the hands
  목소리와 손으로 강력한 리듬의 소리를 만들다
- □ **burn** 불타다
  → to be destroyed by fire 불에 의해서 파괴되다
- □ **closet** 옷장
  → a large piece of furniture with a door used for storing clothes 의복을 저장하기 위해 만들어진 문이 있는 큰 가구
- □ **cloudy** 구름의, 흐린
  → when the sky is covered with a lot of clouds
  하늘이 많은 구름으로 덮인
- □ **cross** 건너다
  → to go from one side to the other side of an area
  한 지역의 한쪽에서 다른 쪽으로 가다
- □ **dictionary** 사전
  → a book that contains a list of words and phrases alphabetically with their meanings or their translations in another language
  알파벳순으로 그것의 의미 또는 다른 언어로의 번역이 있는 일련의 단어와 구를 포함하는 책

- □ **lucky** 행운의
  → having desirable things unexpectedly happen to you
  바람직한 상황이 예기치 않게 일어난
- □ **perfect** 완벽한
  → the best possible 가능한 최고의
- □ **possible** 가능한
  → able to happen or be done
  일어나거나 발생할 수 있는
- □ **predict** 예측하다
  → to say that an event will happen in the future
  미래에 어떤 일이 발생할 것이라고 말하다
- □ **replace** 대체하다
  → to take the place of …에 대신하다, …을 대리하다
- □ **select** 선택하다
  → to choose something from a number of things
  많은 것들 중에서 어떤 것을 고르다
- □ **sense** 감지하다
  → to perceive or realize something
  어떤 것을 인지하거나 깨닫다
- □ **situation** 상황
  → what is happening at a particular time and place
  특정한 시간과 장소에서 발생하는 것
- □ **translate** 번역하다
  → to change words in another language
  말들을 다른 언어로 바꾸다

01 다음 중 밑줄 친 부분의 뜻풀이가 바르지 <u>않은</u> 것은?

① Some animals have the ability to <u>predict</u> earthquakes. (예측하다)

② I hope my water pipes in the house don't <u>freeze</u>. (얼다)

③ I can <u>teleport</u> through time and space. (전화하다)

④ Please <u>check</u> the password and try again. (확인하다)

⑤ I <u>selected</u> a toy for a child. (선택했다)

서답형
02 주어진 단어를 이용해 빈칸을 완성하시오.

> Your story is so _____ that I can't stop laughing. (fun)

[03~04] 다음 빈칸에 알맞은 것을 고르시오.

03
> Do you know anyone who can _____ French into English?

① translate　② transform　③ prevent
④ select　　　⑤ mean

중요
04
> In the first match against Greece, the South Korean team _____ the Greek team.

① fell　　② hit　　③ beat
④ broke　⑤ predicted

05 다음 밑줄 친 단어의 성격이 <u>다른</u> 하나를 고르시오.

① Doesn't it sound <u>like</u> fun to learn in a forest?

② You look <u>like</u> a totally new person in that suit.

③ Why do you <u>like</u> it so much?

④ Doesn't it seem <u>like</u> a chess game of some sort?

⑤ They are sad for a long time <u>like</u> humans.

중요
06 다음 밑줄 친 부분과 의미가 가장 가까운 것은?

> After the test, the people were asked if they saw anything <u>strange</u>.

① natural　　　② unusual
③ expected　　④ familiar
⑤ necessary

서답형
07 다음 주어진 우리말에 맞게 빈칸을 채우시오. (철자가 주어진 것도 있음)

(1) 우리는 Oliver가 이 마을에 더 이상 살지 않기 때문에 그를 자주 볼 수 없다.

➡ We cannot see Oliver very often because he _____ _____ lives in this town.

(2) 더 이상 저를 걱정할 필요 없어요. 전 괜찮아요.

➡ You _____ h_____ to worry about me. I'm fine.

01 다음 〈보기〉의 단어를 골라 문맥에 맞게 고쳐 쓰시오.

┌ 보기 ┐
cloud   fun   greed   luck   sun

(1) Scrooge was a _____ old man.
(2) I like this book because the story is _____.
(3) It was _____ today, but it will be _____ tomorrow. You will have to bring your umbrella.
(4) I met my favorite movie star by chance. It's my _____ day!

02 두 문장이 같은 의미가 되도록 빈칸을 채우시오. (주어진 철자로 시작할 것)

The new cells take the place of the old cells.
= The new cells r_____ the old cells.

03 다음 빈칸에 공통으로 들어갈 말을 쓰시오.

• _____ the way, are you still working at the public library?
• You can learn time management skills _____ doing it.

04 다음 우리말에 맞도록 빈칸에 알맞은 말을 쓰시오. (철자가 주어진 경우 주어진 철자로 시작할 것)

(1) 영어를 한국어로 번역할 수 있나요?
➡ Can you _____ English into Korean?
(2) 마감 시간 전에 숙제를 끝내는 것이 가능한가요?
➡ Is it p_____ to _____ your homework before deadline?
(3) 그 밖에 또 필요한 것이 있나요?
➡ Do you need anything e_____?
(4) 그것은 완벽할 필요는 없다.
➡ It doesn't h_____ to be _____.

05 다음 빈칸에 들어갈 말을 〈보기〉에서 찾아 쓰시오.

┌ 보기 ┐
in   off   to

(1) Get _____ the car right now, or you'll be late.
(2) When I got _____ the top of the mountain, it was very dark.
(3) We will see him soon. Passengers are getting _____ the plane now.

06 다음 우리말에 맞게 주어진 단어를 바르게 배열하시오.

(1) 나는 그가 길을 건너는 것을 봤다.
(saw, the, crossing, I, him, street)
➡ _____
(2) 그는 국내 총 생산량이 오를 것이라고 예측했다.
(he, up, go, that, would, the, predicted, GDP)
➡ _____

Conversation

① 의견 표현하기

> **A** I'm going to fly a drone. 난 드론을 날릴 거야.
> **B** That sounds like fun. 그거 재미있겠다.

■ 의견을 물어 보는 질문에 대한 답으로 동사 'sound(~하게 들리다)'를 사용해 의견을 표현할 수 있다. 'sound+형용사'를 사용하거나, 'sound+like+명사'를 이용하여 말할 수 있다.

- It sounds interesting. 그거 재미있겠다.
- It sounds like fun. 그거 재미있겠다.

■ 'It'이나 'That'을 생략해서 'Sounds interesting/good/terrible.'로도 말할 수 있다.

■ 의견을 나타내는 다른 표현들로는 'I think ~.', 'It seems that ~.', 'In my opinion, ~.' 등이 있다.

■ 자신의 의견을 나타낸 뒤, 자신의 생각을 뒷받침하는 이유나 근거를 함께 언급하기도 한다. 또는 'How about you?(너는 어때?)'를 사용해 상대방의 의견을 다시 물어볼 수도 있다.

의견 표현하기

- (That) Sounds (very) interesting.
- How interesting!
- I think (that) it's interesting.
- In my opinion, it's interesting.

핵심 Check

1. 다음 우리말과 일치하도록 빈칸에 알맞은 말을 쓰시오.

A: I will go swimming with my friends. (내 친구들과 수영하러 갈 거야.)

B: _____ like fun. (재미있겠다.)

2. 다음 우리말과 일치하도록 주어진 단어를 바르게 배열하시오.

A: Why don't we make a movie together? (함께 영화를 만드는 것은 어때?)

B: _____ _____ _____. (good, that, sounds) How about you? (좋아. 너는 어때?)

C: _____ _____ _____ _____. (exciting, it's, I, think)
(나는 그것이 재미있다고 생각해.)

② 가능 여부 표현하기

A Is it possible for you to text with your eyes closed?

눈 감고 문자 메시지 보내는 것이 가능하니?

B Sure. I can do that. 물론이지. 할 수 있어.

■ 'Is it possible for 목적격 to 동사원형 ~?'은 상대방에게 어떤 것을 하는 것이 가능한지 물어볼 때 쓰는 표현이다. 여기서 it은 가주어이며 to 동사원형이 to부정사로 진주어이며 for 목적격은 to부정사의 의미상 주어이다. to부정사 대신에 that절을 사용해서 말할 수도 있다.

• Is it possible for you to text with your eyes closed?
   = Is it possible that you text with your eyes closed?

■ possible 대신에 likely(~할 것 같은)나 probable((현실로) 있음직한, 가망이 있는)을 사용할 수도 있다.

■ 조동사 'can(~할 수 있다)'을 사용해서 'Can+주어+동사원형 ~?(~을 할 수 있니?)'으로 질문할 수 있다.

가능 여부 표현하기

• Is it possible[probable/likely] that 주어 동사 ~?

• Is it possible[probable/likely] for 목적격 to 동사원형 ~?

• Can 주어 동사원형 ~?

핵심 Check

3. 다음 우리말과 일치하도록 빈칸에 알맞은 말을 쓰시오.

A: _____ _____ _____ _____ I can carry that box?

(제가 저 상자를 운반할 수 있을까요?)

B: I think it's possible with some help. I'll help you.

(전 약간의 도움으로 가능하다고 생각해요. 제가 도와드릴게요.)

A: Thanks. (고마워요.)

4. 다음 대화에서 밑줄 친 부분과 같은 의미가 되도록 주어진 단어를 이용해 문장을 만드시오.

A: Is it possible that he can finish this marathon?
B: Yes, it's possible.

➡ _____ (possible, to)

➡ _____ (can)

5. 다음 우리말과 일치하도록 주어진 어구를 빈칸에 알맞게 배열하시오.

A: _____ (a cake, it, you, to, is, possible, for, make)

(케이크를 만들 수 있니?)

B: Yes, it is. (응. 할 수 있어.)

Listen & Speak 1 B-1

B: Do you have any ideas for our group project?

G: No. What about you?

B: ❶I'm thinking we should talk about future jobs. ❷What do you think?

G: ❸That sounds perfect for our project. ❹Let's look for some information on the Internet.

B: 우리 조별 프로젝트에 대한 좋은 생각이 있니?

G: 아니. 너는 어때?

B: 나는 미래 직업에 대해 이야기하면 좋겠다고 생각하고 있어. 너는 어떻게 생각해?

G: 우리 프로젝트에 완벽한 것 같아. 인터넷에서 정보를 찾아보자.

❶ 'we should talk about future jobs'는 think의 목적어이며 앞에 접속사 that이 생략되어 있다. talk about: ∼에 대해서 이야기하다

❷ 'What do you think?'는 자신의 의견을 말한 뒤, 상대방의 의견을 물어볼 때 쓰며 '너는 어떻게 생각하니?'의 의미이다. 바꿔서 쓸 수 있는 표현으로 'How about you?', 'What about you?' 등이 있다.

❸ sound 형용사: ∼하게 들리다 perfect: 완벽한

❹ 'Let's 동사원형'은 '∼하자'라는 의미로 어떤 것을 제안하고자 할 때 사용한다. 'Why don't we ∼?'로 바꿔 쓸 수 있다.

Check(√) True or False

(1) They are going to look for some information for their group project in the book. T ☐ F ☐

(2) They will look for some information about future jobs. T ☐ F ☐

Listen & Speak 2 B-1

G: This computer ❶looks nice. ❷How much is it?

M: ❸It's 500 dollars. It's ❹the newest one.

G: ❺Is it possible to use this coupon?

M: Let me ❻check. Yes, you can. So, you'll get 30 dollars ❼off.

G: Perfect. I'll ❽take it.

G: 이 컴퓨터가 좋아 보이네요. 얼마예요?

M: 500달러예요. 가장 최신 컴퓨터예요.

G: 이 쿠폰을 사용하는 것이 가능한가요?

M: 확인해 볼게요. 네, 사용할 수 있어요. 그러면, 30달러 할인 돼요.

G: 좋아요. 이걸로 살게요.

❶ look 형용사: ∼하게 보이다

❷ 가격을 묻고자 할 때 'How much ∼?(∼은 얼마인가요?)' 표현을 사용한다.

❸ 'How much ∼?'의 질문에 'It's+가격.'으로 대답한다.

❹ the newest는 형용사 new의 최상급으로 '가장 최신의'의 의미이다. one = computer

❺ 'Is it possible to+동사원형 ∼?'은 '∼하는 것이 가능한가요?'라는 의미로 가능 여부를 물을 때 사용하는 표현이다. 이때 it은 가주어이고 to부정사구가 진주어이다.

❻ check: 확인하다, 점검하다

❼ off: 할인되어

❽ take: 선택하다, 사다

Check(√) True or False

(3) The girl has a coupon which cannot be used. T ☐ F ☐

(4) The girl will buy the newest computer. T ☐ F ☐

Listen & Speak 1 A

B: ❶Why don't we try a new VR game?
G: ❷That sounds interesting.

❶ '~을 하자'라는 제안을 하고자 할 때 'Why don't we ~?' 외에도 'Let's ~'의 표현을 쓸 수 있다.
❷ 'That sounds interesting.' 상대방이 한 말에 대하여 '재미있겠다'라는 표현으로 'How interesting!'이나 'Sounds interesting!'으로 바꾸어 사용할 수 있다.

Listen & Speak 1 B-2

G: The Robot Expo begins next week. ❶Why don't you go with me?
B: ❷Yes, I'd love to. ❸That sounds exciting.
G: We'll have ❹a chance to meet robotics engineers.
B: ❺That'll be great.

❶ Why don't you ~?: ~하는 게 어때? (= What about ~? = How about ~?) go with: 같이 가다, 어울리다
❷ 상대방의 제안에 응할 때는 'Yes, I'd love to.', 그렇지 않을 때는 'Sorry, but I can't.'로 대답할 수 있다.
❸ sound 형용사: ~하게 들리다 exciting: 흥미진진한
❹ to meet이 a chance(기회)를 수식하는 형용사적 용법으로 사용되고 있다. robotics: 로봇 공학 engineer: 기술자
❺ That'll be great.: 그러면 아주 좋겠다.

Listen & Speak 2 A

G: ❶Is it possible for you to live without your smartphone?
B: No, it's ❷not possible.

❶ Is it possible (for 목적격) to 동사원형 ~?: (…가) ~하는 것이 가능할까? without: ~ 없이
❷ 'not possible'을 'impossible(불가능한)'로 바꿔 쓸 수 있다.

Listen & Speak 2 B-2

B: ❶We took lots of pictures during our trip.
G: We sure ❷did. We have more than 500 pictures.
B: ❸Is it possible to make an animated photo album out of them?
G: Yes, it's ❹possible. I have an app for that.

❶ take a picture: 사진을 찍다 lots of: 많은 during: ~ 동안
❷ did는 'took lots of pictures'를 의미한다.
❸ Is it possible (for 목적격) to 동사원형 ~?: (…가) ~하는 것이 가능할까? 'it'은 가주어, 'to make an animated photo album out of them'은 진주어이다. out of: (원천 · 출처) ~에서, ~으로부터
❹ possible: 가능한

Listen & Speak 2 C-1

A: ❶Is it possible for you to text ❷with your eyes closed?
B: Sure. I can ❸do that.

❶ Is it possible (for 목적격) to 동사원형 ~?: (…가) ~하는 것이 가능할까? text: (휴대전화로) 문자를 보내다
❷ with+명사구(your eyes)+과거분사(closed): 너의 눈을 감은 채로 / 명사구가 과거분사된 채로(부대상황)
❸ do = text with my eyes closed

Real-Life Zone

G: Look at those words on the board.
B: ❶What do they mean? Let's ❷look them up in the dictionary.
G: ❸What about using the AI translator?
B: How do I use ❹it?
G: ❺You point your smartphone camera at the words and ask AI to translate. You will get an answer.
B: ❻Is it possible for AI to read those words?
Speaker: Sure. I can read any language and translate it.
B: ❼Wow, that sounds unbelievable. So, AI, what do those words mean?
Speaker: ❽They mean "Dreams come true!"
B: ❾That's amazing.

❶ 'What do they mean?'은 '그 말들은 무슨 뜻이지?'란 의미로 의미를 묻는 말이다.
❷ look ~ up: (사전 · 참고 자료 · 컴퓨터 등에서 정보를) 찾아보다
❸ What about 동명사 ~?: ~하는 게 어때? translator: 번역가
❹ it은 앞에 나온 'the AI translator'를 가리킨다.
❺ point: 돌리다, 향하게 하다 point와 ask는 접속사 and로 연결된 병렬 관계이다. translate: 번역하다
❻ Is it possible (for 목적격) to 동사원형 ~?: (…가) ~하는 것이 가능할까?
❼ sound 형용사: ~하게 들리다 unbelievable: 믿기 어려운, 놀랄만한
❽ 'What does[do] it[they] mean?'으로 의미를 물었을 때 'mean(의미하다)'을 이용해 'It/They mean(s) ~.(~라는 뜻이에요.)'로 대답할 수 있다.
❾ 놀람을 표현할 때는 'That's surprising.', 'That's amazing.', 'I can't believe it.' 등으로 말할 수 있다.

교과서 확인학습

● 다음 우리말과 일치하도록 빈칸에 알맞은 말을 쓰시오.

Listen & Speak 1 A

B: Why _____ we try a new VR game?

G: That _____ interesting.

B: 우리 새로운 VR 게임을 해 보는 게 어때?
G: 그거 재미있겠다.

Listen & Speak 1 B

1. B: Do you _____ _____ ideas _____ our group _____?

   G: No. _____ _____ you?

   B: I'm thinking we should _____ _____ _____ jobs. _____ do you _____?

   G: That _____ _____ for our project. Let's _____ _____ some information on the Internet.

2. G: The Robot Expo _____ next week. _____ don't you go _____ me?

   B: Yes, I'd love _____. That _____ exciting.

   G: We'll have a _____ _____ _____ _____ engineers.

   B: That'll be _____.

1. B: 우리 조별 프로젝트에 대한 좋은 생각이 있니?
   G: 아니. 너는 어때?
   B: 나는 미래 직업에 대해 이야기하면 좋겠다고 생각하고 있어. 너는 어떻게 생각해?
   G: 우리 프로젝트에 완벽한 것 같아. 인터넷에서 정보를 찾아보자.

2. G: 로봇 박람회가 다음 주에 시작돼. 나와 함께 가는 게 어때?
   B: 응, 가고 싶어. 그거 재미있겠는데.
   G: 우리는 로봇 공학자를 만날 기회가 있을 거야.
   B: 그거 아주 좋겠다.

Listen & Speak 1 C

1. A: I'm _____ to fly a _____.

   B: That sounds _____ _____.

2. A: I'm _____ to _____ a model car.

   B: That sounds _____ _____.

1. A: 난 드론을 날릴 거야.
   B: 그거 재미있겠다.

2. A: 난 모형 자동차를 조립할 거야.
   B: 그거 재미있겠다.

Listen & Speak 2 A

G: It is _____ for you _____ _____ _____ your smartphone?

B: No, it's not _____.

G: 네가 스마트폰 없이 사는 것이 가능할까?
B: 아니, 그건 불가능해.

Listen & Speak 2 B

1. **G:** This computer _____ nice. _____ _____ is it?

   M: It's 500 dollars. It's the _____ one.

   G: _____ _____ _____ _____ _____ this coupon?

   M: Let me _____. Yes, you can. So, you'll get 30 dollars _____.

   G: _____. I'll take it.

2. **B:** We _____ lots of _____ _____ our trip.

   G: We sure _____. We have more _____ 500 pictures.

   B: Is _____ _____ _____ _____ an animated photo album _____ _____ them?

   G: Yes, it's possible. I _____ an app for that.

Listen & Speak 2 C

1. **A:** _____ _____ _____ for you _____ _____ _____ your eyes _____?

   B: Sure. I can do that.

2. **A:** Is it _____ _____ _____ to travel around Gangwondo _____ bicycle?

   B: Sure. I can do that.

Real-Life Zone A

G: Look _____ those words on the board.

B: _____ do _____ _____? Let's _____ _____ _____ in the _____.

G: What _____ _____ the AI translator?

B: _____ do I use it?

G: You _____ your smartphone camera at the words and ask AI to _____. You will _____ an answer.

B: Is it _____ _____ _____ _____ _____ those words?

Speaker: Sure. I can _____ any language and _____ it.

B: Wow, that sounds _____. So, AI, what do those words _____?

Speaker: They mean "Dreams come true!"

B: That's _____.

해석

1. G: 이 컴퓨터가 좋아 보이네요. 얼마예요?
   M: 500달러예요. 가장 최신 컴퓨터예요.
   G: 이 쿠폰을 사용하는 것이 가능한가요?
   M: 확인해 볼게요. 네, 사용할 수 있어요. 그러면, 30달러 할인돼요.
   G: 좋아요. 이걸로 살게요.

2. B: 우리는 여행 동안 사진을 많이 찍었어.
   G: 진짜 그랬어. 500장 넘게 있어.
   B: 그 사진들로 동영상 앨범을 만드는 것이 가능하니?
   G: 응, 가능해. 나는 그것을 위한 앱이 있어.

1. A: 눈 감고 문자 메시지 보내는 것이 가능하니?
   B: 물론이지. 할 수 있어.

2. A: 자전거로 강원도를 여행하는 것이 가능하니?
   B: 물론이지. 할 수 있어.

G: 저기 칠판에 있는 글자 좀 봐.
B: 무슨 뜻이지? 사전에서 찾아보자.
G: AI 번역기를 사용하는 게 어때?
B: 어떻게 사용하는 거니?
G: 스마트폰 카메라를 글자 위에 댄 후에 AI에게 번역해 달라고 해 봐. 아마 답을 해 줄 거야.
B: AI가 저런 글자를 읽는 것이 가능해?
Speaker: 물론이에요. 저는 어떤 언어도 읽을 수 있고 번역할 수 있어요.
B: 오, 정말 놀라워. 그럼 AI, 이 글자는 뜻이 뭐니?
Speaker: "꿈은 이루어진다."라는 뜻이에요.
B: 정말 대단하구나.

01 다음 대화의 밑줄 친 부분과 바꿔 쓸 수 있는 것을 고르시오.

> A: <u>Is it possible for you to read 50 novels during summer vacation?</u>
> B: Sure. I can do that.

① Should you read 50 novels during summer vacation?
② Are you going to read 50 novels during summer vacation?
③ Is it possible that you read 50 novels during summer vacation?
④ Is it unlikely for you to read 50 novels during summer vacation?
⑤ Are you thinking of reading 50 novels during summer vacation?

02 다음 대화의 빈칸에 알맞은 것을 고르시오.

> B: Do you have any ideas for our group project?
> G: No. What about you?
> B: I'm thinking we should talk about future jobs. What do you think?
> G: _____ Let's look for some information on the Internet.

① That sounds perfect for our project.
② I have a different idea about our project.
③ I think it's too small for us.
④ In my opinion, that's not true.
⑤ I agree with you. That sounds bad.

03 주어진 문장 뒤에 올 대화의 순서가 바르게 배열된 것을 고르시오.

> The Robot Expo begins next week. Why don't you go with me?

> (A) We'll have a chance to meet robotics engineers.
> (B) Yes, I'd love to. That sounds exciting.
> (C) That'll be great.

① (A) – (C) – (B)   ② (B) – (A) – (C)
③ (B) – (C) – (A)   ④ (C) – (A) – (B)
⑤ (C) – (B) – (A)

[01~02] 다음 대화를 읽고 물음에 답하시오.

> G: The Robot Expo begins next week. Why don't you go with me?
> B: Yes, I'd love to. _____(A)_____
> G: We'll have a chance to meet robotics engineers.
> B: That'll be great.

01 위 대화의 빈칸 (A)에 알맞은 말을 고르시오.

① I think it's very boring.
② That sounds exciting.
③ In my opinion, it will be crowded.
④ It doesn't sound like fun.
⑤ I'm not interested in robots.

02 위 대화를 읽고 답할 수 <u>없는</u> 질문은?

① What does the boy think about the Robot Expo?
② Who can they meet at the Robot Expo?
③ Where does the girl want to go with the boy?
④ Where will they meet to go to the Robot Expo?
⑤ When does the Robot Expo begin?

[03~04] 다음 대화를 읽고 물음에 답하시오.

> G: Look at those words on the board.
> B: What do they mean? Let's look them up in the dictionary. (①)
> G: What about using the AI translator?
> B: How do I use it? (②)
> G: You point your smartphone camera at words and ask AI to translate. (③) You will get an answer. (④)
> B: Is it possible for AI to read those words?
> Speaker: Sure. I can read any language and translate it.
> B: Wow, that sounds unbelievable. So, AI! (⑤)
> Speaker: They mean "Dreams come true!"
> B: That's amazing.

03 위 대화의 ①~⑤ 중 주어진 문장이 들어갈 곳은?

> What do those words mean?

① ② ③ ④ ⑤

04 위 대화의 내용과 일치하지 <u>않는</u> 것을 고르시오.

① AI 번역기는 모든 언어를 읽을 수 있고 번역할 수 있다.
② 여자아이는 AI 번역기를 사용하는 방법을 알고 있다.
③ 칠판에 있는 글자는 "꿈은 이루어진다."라는 뜻을 가지고 있다.
④ 여자아이와 남자아이는 칠판 위의 모르는 글자를 사전에서 찾아봤다.
⑤ AI 번역기를 사용하기 위해서 먼저 스마트폰 카메라를 글자 위에 대야 한다.

[05~07] 다음 대화를 읽고 물음에 답하시오.

> G: Minseok, there is a smart food-ordering machine over there. (①) Why don't we try it?
> B: _____ (A) _____ We'll be able to order easily and fast by using it.
> G: I hope so. (②) By the way, do you think maybe it will be possible for robots to replace humans someday?
> B: I'm not sure. (③) But we will be free from danger because of robots.
> G: What do you mean?
> B: (④) Robots can do the dangerous work so humans don't have to.
> G: You're right. We should always try to look on the bright side. (⑤)

05 위 대화의 ①~⑤ 중 주어진 문장이 들어갈 곳은?

> Robots can help people in danger.

①   ②   ③   ④   ⑤

06 위 대화의 빈칸 (A)에 알맞은 말을 고르시오.

① I think that it is delicious.
② In my opinion, robots are necessary in our lives.
③ I don't want to try it.
④ We don't have to use it.
⑤ That sounds interesting.

07 위 대화의 내용과 일치하지 <u>않는</u> 것을 고르시오.

① 민석이는 로봇 덕분에 사람들이 위험한 일을 하지 않을 것이라고 생각한다.
② 민석이는 로봇이 인간을 대체할 수 있을 거라고 생각한다.
③ 민석이는 스마트 음식 주문 자판기가 주문을 쉽고 빠르게 해 줄 것이라고 생각한다.
④ 여자아이는 항상 좋은 면을 봐야 한다고 말하고 있다.
⑤ 그들은 스마트 음식 주문 자판기를 사용할 것이다.

[08~09] 다음 중 짝지어진 대화가 <u>어색한</u> 것은?

08
① A: I go to the farm with my family on weekends.
　 B: That sounds interesting.
② A: Is it possible that I finish my homework by tomorrow?
　 B: Sure. You can.
③ A: Is it possible that I keep a pet?
　 B: Yes, I can.
④ A: Do you know that ice cream is from China?
　 B: No. That sounds interesting.
⑤ A: Is it possible that you go abroad alone?
　 B: Of course. I can.

09
① A: Is it possible to drink juice in space?
　 B: Sure, it's possible.
② A: What do you think about this place?
　 B: I like it. I think it's very comfortable.
③ A: Why don't we join the Mozart Club?
　 B: That sounds like fun. I love music.
④ A: Why don't we watch a movie tonight?
　 B: I don't think so. It sounds like fun.
⑤ A: Is it possible that a dog solves a math problem?
　 B: No. That sounds impossible.

01 다음 대화의 밑줄 친 문장과 의미가 같도록 빈칸에 알맞은 말을 쓰시오.

> G: Is it possible for you to live without your smartphone?
> B: No, it's not possible.

> _____ _____ live without your smartphone?

[02~03] 다음 대화를 읽고 물음에 답하시오.

> G: This computer looks nice. How much is it?
> M: It's 500 dollars. It's the newest one.
> G: 이 쿠폰을 사용하는 것이 가능한가요?
> M: Let me check. Yes, you can. So, you'll get 30 dollars off.
> G: Perfect. I'll take it.

02 다음 밑줄 친 우리말을 주어진 단어를 이용해 영작하시오.

> (possible, use)

➡ _____

03 다음 질문에 주어진 단어를 이용해 완전한 문장으로 대답하시오.

> How much will the girl pay for the computer?

➡ _____ (will)

[04~05] 다음 대화를 읽고 물음에 답하시오.

> G: Look at those words on the board.
> B: What do they mean? Let's look them __(A)__ in the dictionary.
> G: What __(B)__ using the AI translator?
> B: How do I use it?
> G: You point your smartphone camera at the words and ask AI to translate. You will get an answer.
> B: Is it possible for AI to read those words?
> Speaker: Sure. I can read any language and translate it.
> B: Wow, that sounds (C)believe. So, AI, what do those words mean?
> Speaker: They mean "Dreams come true!"

04 위 대화의 빈칸 (A)와 (B)에 알맞은 것을 쓰시오.

(A) _____ (B) _____

05 위 대화의 밑줄 친 believe를 알맞은 형으로 고치시오.

➡ _____

06 다음 괄호 안에 주어진 단어를 알맞게 배열하시오.

> G: _____
> (Gangwondo, travel, is, bicycle, for, to, possible, you, it, by, around)
> B: Sure. I can do that.

➡ _____
_____

Grammar

1 지각동사

- **I see** a cat **crossing** the street. 고양이가 길을 건너고 있는 게 보여.
- **I heard** him **sing**. 나는 그가 노래하는 소리를 들었다.

■ 지각동사는 감각 기관을 통하여 인지하는 것을 나타내는 동사로, '보다, 듣다, 느끼다' 등의 의미를 갖는 see, look at, watch, hear, listen to, feel 등의 동사를 말한다. 'see/hear/feel+목적어+원형부정사/현재분사'의 형태로 '목적어가 ~하는 것을[~하는 중인 것을] 보다/듣다/느끼다'라는 의미를 갖는다. 목적격보어 자리에 원형부정사와 현재분사를 모두 사용할 수 있으나 의미상 그 동작이 진행 중인 것을 나타낼 때에는 주로 현재분사를 사용한다.

- They **saw** him **read** a book. 그들은 그가 책을 읽는 것을 보았다.
- Did you **hear** the baby **crying**? 너는 그 아기가 울고 있는 소리를 들었니?

■ '지각동사+목적어+원형부정사[현재분사]'로 쓰이는 경우, 목적어와 목적격보어는 능동 관계가 된다. '지각동사+목적어+과거분사'로 쓰이는 경우 목적어와 목적격보어의 관계는 수동 관계이다.

- She **felt** him **touch** her hand. 그녀는 그가 손을 만지는 것을 느꼈다.
- I **heard** my name **called**. 나는 내 이름이 불리는 소리를 들었다.

■ 사역동사 make, have, let과 혼동하지 않도록 한다. 사역동사도 5형식 동사로 목적어와 목적격보어를 취하지만, 사역동사의 목적격보어로는 동사원형이 나온다. have나 make는 목적격보어로 과거분사를 취할 때도 있다.

- The teacher **made** me **do** my homework. 선생님은 나에게 숙제를 하도록 시키셨다.
- I **had** my computer **fixed** yesterday. 나는 어제 내 컴퓨터가 수리되도록 했다.

핵심 Check

1. 다음 괄호 안에서 알맞은 말을 고르시오.

(1) She saw him (to do / doing) his homework.

➡ _____

(2) I heard my sister (sing / sang) in her room.

➡ _____

(3) He had his car (washing / washed).

➡ _____

② 가주어 'it'

- **It** is hard **to believe** that you can understand us.
  네가 우리를 이해할 수 있다는 것을 믿기 힘들어.

- **It** is interesting **to play** soccer. 축구하는 것은 재미있다.

■ 비교적 긴 to부정사 부분이 문장의 주어로 쓰일 때 그 to부정사 부분을 보통의 주어 자리인 문장의 맨 앞에 두지 않고 문장 뒤에 두고, 대신 그 주어 자리에 it을 넣어주는데 그것이 가주어 it이며 뒤로 간 to 부정사 부분은 진주어라고 한다. 이때 쓰인 가주어 'it'은 해석하지 않는다.

- **It** is not easy **to study** hard every day. 매일 열심히 공부하는 것은 쉽지 않다.
  = **To study** hard every day is not easy.
- **It** is a lot fun **to draw** cartoons. 만화를 그리는 것은 아주 재미있다.
  = **To draw** cartoons is a lot fun.

■ to부정사의 의미상 주어

'to부정사'가 행하는 동작의 주체를 to부정사의 의미상 주어라고 한다. to부정사의 의미상 주어를 나타 낼 때는 to부정사 바로 앞에 'for+목적격'의 형태로 쓴다. 문장에 쓰인 형용사가 kind, foolish, rude, careless, wise 등과 같이 사람의 성질을 나타내는 말일 때는 'of+목적격'을 쓴다. 또한 to부정사의 부정 은 to부정사 앞에 not[never]을 써서 'not[never]+to V'로 나타낸다.

- **It** is necessary **for you to be** careful all the time. 너는 항상 조심할 필요가 있다.
- **It** is kind **of you to show** me the way. 길을 가르쳐 주셔서 감사합니다.
- **It** was difficult **for him not to smoke**. 그가 담배를 피우지 않는 것은 힘들었다.

■ 주어로 쓰인 'that'절의 경우에도 보통 가주어 'it'을 쓰고 'that'절을 문장 뒤로 보낸다.

- **That** he should attend the meeting every day is important. 그가 매일 회의에 참석하는 것이 중요하다.
  = **It** is important **that** he should attend the meeting every day.

핵심 Check

2. 다음 괄호 안에서 알맞은 말을 고르시오.

(1) It is fun (play / to play) basketball.

➡ _____

(2) It was hard for him (solve / to solve) the problem.

➡ _____

(3) (It / That) is necessary for you to exercise.

➡ _____

01 다음 문장에서 어법상 <u>어색한</u> 부분을 바르게 고쳐 쓰시오.

(1) The girl heard the birds sang.

_____ ➡ _____

(2) He saw a drone to fly.

_____ ➡ _____

(3) It is important choose good friends.

_____ ➡ _____

(4) That is necessary to learn a new language.

_____ ➡ _____

02 주어진 단어를 어법에 맞게 빈칸에 쓰시오.

(1) I heard her _____ in the room. (cry)
(2) They saw the room _____. (clean)
(3) People came to watch them _____ the game. (play)
(4) Helen felt the water _____ with her hands. (flow)

03 다음 우리말을 영어로 바르게 옮긴 것은?

> 그 여행 가방들을 들고 다니는 것은 불가능하다.

① That is impossible to carry the suitcases.
② That is impossible carrying the suitcases.
③ It is impossible carry the suitcases.
④ It is impossible to carry the suitcases.
⑤ It is impossible carries the suitcases.

04 주어진 어구를 바르게 배열하여 다음 우리말을 영어로 쓰시오. 필요하다면 단어를 추가하거나 변형하시오.

> 당신은 쉬는 것이 필요하다.
> (a rest, you, it, take, is, necessary, to)

➡ _____

중요

01 다음 빈칸에 알맞은 말이 순서대로 바르게 짝지어진 것은?

> • I saw a cat _____ the street.
> • It is a lot of fun _____ cartoons.

① cross – drawing
② crossed – draw
③ crossed – to draw
④ crossing – draw
⑤ crossing – to draw

02 다음 빈칸에 들어갈 말로 가장 적절한 것은?

> David felt the dog _____ his clothes.

① pulls   ② pulled
③ pulling   ④ to pull
⑤ to pulling

03 다음 빈칸에 알맞은 말로 바르게 짝지어진 것을 고르시오.

> _____ is very exciting _____ the soccer game in the stadium.

① It – to watch
② It – watch
③ That – watching
④ That – watch
⑤ That – to watch

서답형

04 주어진 단어를 이용하여 다음 우리말을 영어로 쓰시오. (10 단어)

> 주말에 재미로 자전거를 타는 것은 좋다. (it, for fun, good, ride bicycles)

➡ _____

중요

05 다음 중 어법상 바르지 <u>않은</u> 것은?

① I saw a boy helping an old lady cross the road.
② They listened to Michelle singing on the stage.
③ Jekyll heard someone coming up the stairs.
④ At times, Nora felt him to stare at her.
⑤ She watched her father come toward her.

서답형

06 다음 괄호 안에서 알맞은 말을 고르시오.

(1) Did you see many people (to wait / waiting) in a line?
(2) I heard Jack (played / playing) the guitar.
(3) I watched the game (played / playing) from beginning to end.
(4) Why are you making him (listening / listen) to Wayne?
(5) (That / It) is not easy to speak in front of many people.
(6) It is dangerous (swims / to swim) in the sea.
(7) It's so kind (for / of) you to show me the way to the station.

07 다음 중 어법상 바르지 <u>않은</u> 것은?

> Max ①sat ②in front of the oven and ③ watched her ④to bake ⑤the cookies.

①   ②   ③   ④   ⑤

08 다음 문장에서 어법상 <u>틀린</u> 부분을 찾아 바르게 고쳐 쓰시오.

> This isn't true that Ella likes to speak in front of people.

_____ ➡ _____

[09~10] 다음 우리말을 영어로 바르게 옮긴 것을 <u>모두</u> 고르시오.

09

> 나는 누군가 내 어깨를 만지는 것을 느꼈다.

① I felt someone touches my shoulder.
② I felt someone touched my shoulder.
③ I felt someone touch my shoulder.
④ I felt someone touching my shoulder.
⑤ I felt someone to touch my shoulder.

10

> 여름에 선글라스를 쓰는 것은 도움이 된다.

① It is helpful wears sunglasses in summer.
② It is helpful wore sunglasses in summer.
③ It is helpful wear sunglasses in summer.
④ It is helpful to wear sunglasses in summer.
⑤ It is helpful to wearing sunglasses in summer.

11 다음 대화의 빈칸에 알맞은 말을 4단어로 쓰시오.

> A: It is cold here. Who turned off the stove?
> B: Bill did. I saw _____.

➡ _____

12 다음 중 어법상 올바른 문장을 <u>모두</u> 고르시오.

① Jane heard the dog barking at a stranger.
② I saw a boy to solve math problems.
③ By the way, do you think it will be possible of robots to replace humans someday?
④ Is it possible to flying through a rainbow?
⑤ It is not dangerous to do bungee jumping.

13 다음 중 (A)~(C)에서 어법상 옳은 것끼리 바르게 짝지은 것은?

> • I heard the boy (A)(shouting / to shout).
> • We can see the sky (B)(turn / turned) yellow with dust.
> • He was almost asleep when he heard his name (C)(calling / called).

① to shout – turn – calling
② to shout – turned – called
③ shouting – turn – called
④ shouting – turn – calling
⑤ shouting – turned – calling

14 다음 중 밑줄 친 부분의 쓰임이 <u>다른</u> 하나는?

① Is <u>it</u> possible for AI to read those words?

② Look! <u>It</u> is going up that tree.

③ <u>It</u> is hard to believe that you can understand us.

④ <u>It</u> is difficult to remember all my friends' birthdays.

⑤ Of course <u>it</u> was not easy to break my old habit.

15 다음 주어진 문장의 밑줄 친 부분과 쓰임이 같은 것은?

> Jekyll's friend saw Jekyll <u>drinking</u> strange water.

① <u>Watching</u> the movie, we had some popcorn.

② The smell was from the soup that she was <u>cooking</u> for us.

③ We all heard a baby <u>crying</u> loudly.

④ <u>Driving</u> a smart car was not so difficult.

⑤ When I was standing in front of the screen on the smart closet door, my clothes kept <u>changing</u>.

서답형

16 다음 문장을 it을 이용하여 바꿔 쓰시오.

(1) To make her laugh is not easy.

➡ _____

(2) To read 10 books during winter vacation is my plan.

➡ _____

서답형

17 다음 문장에서 어법상 어색한 부분을 바르게 고치시오.

(1) Stephanie watched her husband to paint the wall.

_____ ➡ _____

(2) It is safer wears a helmet when riding a bike.

_____ ➡ _____.

(3) Is it possible of you to live without your smartphone?

_____ ➡ _____.

서답형

18 다음 괄호 안에 주어진 단어를 이용하여 우리말을 영어로 옮기시오.

(1) 민수는 그 집을 지나갈 때마다 개가 짖는 소리를 듣는다. (Minsu로 시작할 것)
(a dog, bark, hear, pass by, whenever)

➡ _____

_____

(2) 나는 새가 하늘 높이 나는 것을 봤다.
(see, a bird, fly, high)

➡ _____

(3) 내가 친구들과 함께 야구 경기를 관람하는 것은 재미있다.
(my friends, exciting, watch, baseball games, it) (12 단어)

➡ _____

_____

(4) 종이를 불 근처에 두는 것은 위험하다.
(dangerous, near the fire, put, it) (9 단어)

➡ _____

01 다음 문장에서 어법상 어색한 부분을 찾아 바르게 고쳐 다시 쓰시오.

(1) I saw them to play soccer in the playground.

➡ _____

(2) Barbara felt her heart beaten faster.

➡ _____

(3) Aaron looked at Sylvia came with Alex hand in hand.

➡ _____

_____

(4) A farmer bought 43 sheep at the market and saw them steal 24 hours later.

➡ _____

_____

(5) It is hard take care of a baby.

➡ _____

(6) That is a lot of fun to go on a picnic.

➡ _____

(7) It is difficult of me to learn a new language.

➡ _____

02 〈보기〉와 같이 다음 두 문장을 하나의 문장으로 쓰시오.

┌─ 보기 ─┐
• I saw a boy.　• He was reading a book.
➡ I saw a boy reading a book.
└────────┘

• I heard Sam.
• Sam was baking some cookies.

➡ _____

03 다음 문장을 It으로 시작하여 다시 쓰시오.

(1) To answer the math questions was very difficult.

➡ _____

(2) To swim in the blue sea was a great experience.

➡ _____

(3) To exercise regularly is good for your health.

➡ _____

(4) To learn English is not easy for me.

➡ _____

(5) That a friend in need is a friend indeed is true.

➡ _____

04 〈보기〉에서 의미상 적절한 단어를 골라 빈칸에 알맞은 형태로 쓰시오.

┌─ 보기 ─┐
pull / stay / take / sing
└────────┘

(1) The doctor told me _____ _____ in bed for one more day.

(2) He saw the building _____ down by the workers.

(3) Can you hear my sister _____ upstairs?

(4) She made him _____ off his shirt.

05 다음 빈칸에 적절한 말을 쓰시오.

Is it possible for you _____ _____ _____ _____ during summer vacation? (50 novels)

06 두 문장이 같은 뜻이 되도록 (1)~(3)은 to부정사를 이용하여, (4)는 that절을 이용하여 빈칸을 완성하시오.

(1) I have difficulty in passing the driver's test.
➡ It is difficult _____.

(2) Watching the view as we went higher and higher was so exciting.
➡ It was so exciting _____
_____.

(3) You are kind to help that old woman.
➡ It is kind _____.

(4) In fact, Annabelle didn't tell him a lie.
➡ It is true _____.

07 다음 빈칸에 적절한 말을 쓰시오.

I saw Jane _____ a website.

08 다음 두 문장을 〈보기〉와 같이 한 문장으로 고쳐 쓰시오.

┌── 보기 ──┐
I saw him. + He was running with his dog.
= I saw him running with his dog.
└──────────┘

(1) He heard them.
+ They were playing the drums.
➡ _____

(2) Suhan looked at AI Speaker.
+ AI Speaker was playing a movie.
➡ _____

09 to부정사를 진주어로 하여 주어진 문장과 같은 의미가 되도록 쓰시오.

(1) She is very smart to solve that problem.
➡ _____

(2) This river is not safe to swim in as it is very deep.
➡ _____
_____

A Day at the AI Expo

Jina and Suhan are at the World AI Expo. They <u>are entering</u> the AI
현재진행형(be+~ing): ~하고 있다
home.

Suhan: Look at this! It's a house of the future.

Jina: Let's go <u>into</u> the bedroom first. Look, there's a smart closet.
~으로 들어가다

Suhan: I'm standing <u>in front of</u> this screen on the closet door and my
~ 앞에
clothes <u>keep changing</u>.
keep -ing: 계속 ~하다

Jina: The screen suggests clothes <u>that</u> suit the weather.
주격 관계대명사

Suhan: That's amazing! We <u>no longer</u> have to <u>worry about</u> dressing for
더 이상 ~하지 않다　　　~에 대해 걱정하다
the weather.

Jina: Right. Let's <u>move on</u> to the living room.
~로 이동하다

Suhan: Oh, I like this music speaker.

AI Speaker: I'm <u>not just</u> a music speaker. I can do <u>more than</u> you can
단지 ~이 아닌　　　　　　~ 이상
imagine.

Jina: <u>It's</u> hard <u>to believe</u> that you can understand us. What can you do?
가주어　　　진주어

AI Speaker: <u>How about</u> watching a movie? I'll play <u>one</u> for you.
제안, 권유: ~하는 것이 어때?　　　　　　　= a movie

Suhan: Look, those smart windows are <u>getting darker</u>. I <u>feel like</u> I'm in
get+비교급: 점점 ~해지다　　~인 것 같다
a movie theater.

📎 **확인문제**

● 다음 문장이 본문의 내용과 일치하면 T, 일치하지 <u>않으면</u> F를 쓰시오.

1 Jina and Suhan are at the World AI Expo. ☐

2 Suhan actually keeps changing his clothes. ☐

3 AI Speaker can do more than people can imagine. ☐

4 Jina and Suhan are in a movie theater now. ☐

AI 인공 지능

Expo 박람회

enter 들어가다

future 미래

bedroom 침실

closet 옷장

suggest 제안하다

dress 옷을 입다; 옷, 드레스

imagine 상상하다

window 창문

theater 극장

dark 어두운

Jina: What else can you do?
그 밖의

AI Speaker: I can beatbox, too. Here comes, "cats and boots and cats and boots."

Suhan: You're funny. Good job!
잘했어!

Jina: Hurry! There's a smart car station outside! Let's go and ride in that red car.

Suhan: This car is so cool. Let's get in.
타다

AI Car: Welcome. Are you ready to go?
be ready to: ~할 준비가 되다

Jina: Yes, what should we do now? It's my first time to ride in a smart car.
to부정사의 형용사적 용법

AI Car: You don't need to do anything. I will drive and take you to the
~할 필요가 없다   아무것도   데리고 가다
next station.

Suhan: Watch out! I see a cat crossing the street.
조심해!   지각동사+목적어+목적격보어(원형부정사/현재분사)

AI Car: Don't worry. I have just sensed it. When I sense dangerous
have+pp: 현재완료의 완료 용법(막 ~했다)
situations, I slow down or stop.
속도를 늦추다

Jina: How can you do that?
= slow down or stop

AI Car: I'm a very intelligent robotic car. I know all about driving. I can predict danger based on knowledge and experience.
~에 근거하여

Suhan: How smart! You think and act like a person. You are really like
감탄문 How+형용사(+주어+동사)!   ~처럼   ~와 같은
a human.

else 그 밖의	
beatbox 비트박스를 하다	
boot 부츠, 목이 긴 신발	
funny 재미있는	
station 정류장	
outside 밖에	
cross 건너다	
sense 감지하다	
dangerous 위험한	
situation 상황	
intelligent 지능적인, 똑똑한	
predict 예측하다	
person 사람, 개인	
human 인간, 인간의	

확인문제

● 다음 문장이 본문의 내용과 일치하면 T, 일치하지 않으면 F를 쓰시오.

1   AI Speaker can beatbox, too. ☐

2   Jina has ridden in a smart car before. ☐

3   When AI Car senses dangerous situations, it slows down or stops. ☐

4   AI Car can't drive as well as humans. ☐

● 우리말을 참고하여 빈칸에 알맞은 말을 쓰시오.

1 A Day _____ the AI Expo

2 Jina and Suhan are _____ _____ _____ _____ _____.

3 They are _____ the AI home.

4 Suhan: Look at this! It's a house _____ _____ _____.

5 Jina: Let's _____ _____ the bedroom first. Look, there's a smart closet.

6 Suhan: I'm standing in front of this screen _____ _____ _____ _____ and my clothes _____ _____.

7 Jina: The screen suggests clothes _____ _____ _____.

8 Suhan: That's amazing! We _____ _____ have to worry about _____ _____ _____ _____.

9 Jina: Right. Let's _____ _____ _____ the living room.

10 Suhan: Oh, I like _____ _____ _____.

11 AI Speaker: _____ _____ _____ a music speaker.

12 I can do _____ _____ you can imagine.

13 Jina: _____ _____ _____ _____ that you can understand us. What can you do?

14 AI Speaker: _____ _____ watching a movie?

15 I'll _____ _____ for you.

16 Suhan: Look, those smart windows are _____ _____.

17 I _____ _____ I'm in a movie theater.

1	인공 지능 박람회에서의 하루
2	진아와 수한이가 세계 인공 지능 박람회에 있다.
3	그들은 인공 지능 집으로 들어가고 있다.
4	수한: 이것 봐! 미래의 집이야.
5	진아: 침실 먼저 들어가 보자. 이거 봐, 스마트 옷장이 있어.
6	수한: 옷장 문에 있는 스크린 앞에 서 있으니까 내 옷이 계속해서 바뀌어.
7	진아: 스크린이 날씨에 적합한 옷을 제안하는 거야.
8	수한: 놀라워! 우린 더 이상 날씨 때문에 무슨 옷을 입을지 걱정할 필요가 없겠다.
9	진아: 맞아. 이제 거실로 가 보자.
10	수한: 오, 이 음악 스피커 마음에 들어.
11	인공 지능 스피커: 저는 그냥 음악 스피커가 아니에요.
12	저는 당신이 상상하는 것 이상의 것을 할 수 있어요.
13	진아: 네가 우리를 이해한다니 믿기 어려운 걸! 넌 뭘 할 수 있어?
14	인공 지능 스피커: 영화 보는 건 어때요?
15	하나 틀어 줄게요.
16	수한: 이것 봐, 스마트 창문이 점점 어두워지고 있어.
17	마치 내가 영화관 안에 있는 것 같아.

18 Jina: _____ _____ can you do?

19 AI Speaker: I can beatbox, too. _____ _____, "cats and boots and cats and boots."

20 Suhan: You're funny. _____ _____!

21 Jina: _____! There's a smart car station outside!

22 Let's go and _____ _____ that red car.

23 Suhan: This car is _____ _____. Let's _____ _____.

24 AI Car: Welcome. Are you _____ _____ _____?

25 Jina: Yes, _____ _____ we do now?

26 It's _____ _____ _____ to ride in a smart car.

27 AI Car: You _____ _____ _____ do anything.

28 I will drive and _____ _____ _____ the next station.

29 Suhan: Watch out! I see a cat _____ the street.

30 AI Car: Don't worry. I _____ _____ _____ it.

31 When I _____ _____ _____, I slow down or stop.

32 Jina: _____ can you do that?

33 AI Car: I'm a very _____ _____ car.

34 I know _____ _____ _____.

35 I can predict danger _____ _____ knowledge and experience.

36 Suhan: _____ smart! You think and act _____ a person.

37 You are really _____ a human.

18 진아: 또 뭘 할 수 있어?

19 인공 지능 스피커: 비트박스도 할 수 있어요. "북치기 박치기 북치기 박치기."

20 수한: 넌 정말 재미있구나. 잘했어!

21 진아: 서둘러! 밖에 스마트 자동차 정류장이 있어.

22 가서 저 빨간 차를 타 보자.

23 수한: 이 차 정말 멋지다. 차에 타자.

24 인공 지능 자동차: 어서 오세요. 갈 준비 됐나요?

25 진아: 응, 우린 이제 뭘 해야 하지?

26 스마트 자동차에 타는 건 처음이야.

27 인공 지능 자동차: 아무 것도 하지 않아도 돼요.

28 제가 운전해서 다음 정류장까지 데려다줄 거니까요.

29 수한: 조심해! 고양이가 길을 건너고 있는 게 보여.

30 인공 지능 자동차: 걱정 말아요. 이미 감지했어요.

31 저는 어떤 위험 상황을 감지하면 속도를 늦추거나 멈춰요.

32 진아: 어떻게 그렇게 할 수 있어?

33 인공 지능 자동차: 전 아주 지능적인 로봇 차예요.

34 저는 운전에 대한 모든 걸 알고 있어요.

35 저는 제 지식과 경험을 바탕으로 위험을 예측할 수 있어요.

36 수한: 정말 똑똑하구나! 사람처럼 생각하고 행동하는구나.

37 정말 인간 같아.

• 우리말을 참고하여 본문을 영작하시오.

1 인공 지능 박람회에서의 하루

➡ _____

2 진아와 수한이가 세계 인공 지능 박람회에 있다.

➡ _____

3 그들은 인공 지능 집으로 들어가고 있다.

➡ _____

4 수한: 이것 봐! 미래의 집이야.

➡ _____

5 진아: 침실 먼저 들어가 보자. 이거 봐, 스마트 옷장이 있어.

➡ _____

6 수한: 옷장 문에 있는 스크린 앞에 서 있으니까 내 옷이 계속해서 바뀌어.

➡ _____

7 진아: 스크린이 날씨에 적합한 옷을 제안하는 거야.

➡ _____

8 수한: 놀라워! 우린 더 이상 날씨 때문에 무슨 옷을 입을지 걱정할 필요가 없겠다.

➡ _____

9 진아: 맞아. 이제 거실로 가 보자.

➡ _____

10 수한: 오, 이 음악 스피커 마음에 들어.

➡ _____

11 인공 지능 스피커: 저는 그냥 음악 스피커가 아니에요.

➡ _____

12 저는 당신이 상상하는 것 이상의 것을 할 수 있어요.

➡ _____

13 진아: 네가 우리를 이해한다니 믿기 어려운 걸! 넌 뭘 할 수 있어?

➡ _____

14 인공 지능 스피커: 영화 보는 건 어때요?

➡ _____

15 하나 틀어 줄게요.

➡ _____

16 수한: 이것 봐, 스마트 창문이 점점 어두워지고 있어.

➡ _____

17 마치 내가 영화관 안에 있는 것 같아.

➡ _____

18 진아: 또 뭘 할 수 있어?

➡ _____

19 인공 지능 스피커: 비트박스도 할 수 있어요. "북치기 박치기 북치기 박치기."

➡ _____

20 수한: 넌 정말 재미있구나. 잘했어!

➡ _____

21 진아: 서둘러! 밖에 스마트 자동차 정류장이 있어.

➡ _____

22 가서 저 빨간 차를 타 보자.

➡ _____

23 수한: 이 차 정말 멋지다. 차에 타자.

➡ _____

24 인공 지능 자동차: 어서 오세요. 갈 준비 됐나요?

➡ _____

25 진아: 응, 우린 이제 뭘 해야 하지?

➡ _____

26 스마트 자동차에 타는 건 처음이야.

➡ _____

27 인공 지능 자동차: 아무 것도 하지 않아도 돼요.

➡ _____

28 제가 운전해서 다음 정류장까지 데려다줄 거니까요.

➡ _____

29 수한: 조심해! 고양이가 길을 건너고 있는 게 보여.

➡ _____

30 인공 지능 자동차: 걱정 말아요. 이미 감지했어요.

➡ _____

31 저는 어떤 위험 상황을 감지하면 속도를 늦추거나 멈춰요.

➡ _____

32 진아: 어떻게 그렇게 할 수 있어?

➡ _____

33 인공 지능 자동차: 전 아주 지능적인 로봇 차예요.

➡ _____

34 저는 운전에 대한 모든 걸 알고 있어요.

➡ _____

35 저는 제 지식과 경험을 바탕으로 위험을 예측할 수 있어요.

➡ _____

36 수한: 정말 똑똑하구나! 사람처럼 생각하고 행동하는구나.

➡ _____

37 정말 인간 같아.

➡ _____

[01~03] 다음 글을 읽고 물음에 답하시오.

Jina and Suhan are at the World AI Expo. ⓐ They are entering the AI home.

Suhan: Look at this! It's a house of the future.

Jina: Let's go into the bedroom first. Look, there's a smart closet.

Suhan: I'm ⓑstanding in front of this screen on the closet door and my clothes keep changing.

Jina: The screen suggests clothes that suit the weather.

Suhan: That's amazing! We no longer have to worry about dressing for the weather.

Jina: Right. Let's move on to the living room.

서답형

01 위 글의 밑줄 친 ⓐThey가 가리키는 것을 본문에서 찾아 쓰시오.

➡ _____

02 위 글의 밑줄 친 ⓑstanding과 문법적 쓰임이 같은 것을 고르시오. (3개)

① You must stop smoking for your health.

② I smelled something burning.

③ My plan is going to Paris.

④ Kids are playing on the sand.

⑤ I saw him playing tennis.

03 위 글의 내용과 일치하지 않는 것은?

① 진아와 수한이는 세계 인공 지능 박람회에 있다.

② 수한이는 침실에 먼저 들어가 보자고 말한다.

③ 옷장 문에 있는 스크린 앞에 서 있으면 옷이 계속해서 바뀐다.

④ 옷장 문에 있는 스크린이 날씨에 적합한 옷을 제안해 준다.

⑤ 수한이는 더 이상 날씨 때문에 무슨 옷을 입을지 걱정할 필요가 없겠다고 말한다.

[04~06] 다음 글을 읽고 물음에 답하시오.

Suhan: Oh, I like this music speaker. (①)

AI Speaker: (②) I'm not just a music speaker. (③) I can do more than you can imagine. (④)

Jina: (⑤) What can you do?

AI Speaker: How about watching a movie? I'll play (A)[it / one] for you.

Suhan: Look, those smart windows are getting darker. ⓐ마치 내가 영화관 안에 있는 것 같아.

Jina: (B)[What / What else] can you do?

AI Speaker: I can beatbox, too. Here (C)[come / comes], "cats and boots and cats and boots."

Suhan: You're funny. Good job!

04 위 글의 흐름으로 보아, 주어진 문장이 들어가기에 가장 적절한 곳은?

> It's hard to believe that you can understand us.

①　　　②　　　③　　　④　　　⑤

서답형

05 위 글의 괄호 (A)~(C)에서 문맥이나 어법상 알맞은 낱말을 골라 쓰시오.

(A) _____ (B) _____ (C) _____

서답형

06 위 글의 밑줄 친 ⓐ의 우리말에 맞게 주어진 어휘를 이용하여 8단어로 영작하시오.

> feel like

➡ _____

[07~09] 다음 글을 읽고 물음에 답하시오.

Jina: Hurry! There's a smart car station outside! Let's go and ride in that red car.

Suhan: This car is so ⓐcool. Let's get in.

AI Car: Welcome. Are you ready to go?

Jina: Yes, what should we do now? It's my first time to ride in a smart car.

AI Car: You don't need to do anything. I will drive and take you to the next station.

Suhan: Watch out! I see a cat ____(A)____ the street.

AI Car: Don't worry. I have just sensed it. When I sense dangerous situations, I slow down or stop.

Jina: How can you do that?

AI Car: I'm a very intelligent robotic car. I know all about driving. I can predict danger based on knowledge and experience.

Suhan: How smart! You think and act like a person. You are really like a human.

07 위 글의 빈칸 (A)에 들어갈 알맞은 말을 고르시오. (2개)

① cross
② to cross
③ crosses
④ crossing
⑤ crossed

08 위 글의 밑줄 친 ⓐcool과 같은 의미로 쓰인 것을 모두 고르시오.

① I like a cool breeze in autumn.
② You look pretty cool with that new haircut.
③ How did you keep cool in the moment of danger?
④ Store lemons in a cool dry place.
⑤ How cool my new smart phone is!

09 위 글의 제목으로 가장 알맞은 것을 고르시오.

① Let's Go and Ride in a Smart Car
② My First Time to Ride in a Smart Car
③ Don't Worry! I Know All about Driving
④ Watch Out! A Cat Is Crossing the Street
⑤ I've Already Sensed a Dangerous Situation!

[10~12] 다음 글을 읽고 물음에 답하시오.

Jina and Suhan are at the World AI Expo. They are entering the AI home.

Suhan: Look at this! It's a house of the future.

Jina: Let's go into the bedroom first. Look, there's a smart closet.

Suhan: I'm standing in front of this screen on the closet door and my clothes keep ____ⓐ____.

Jina: The screen suggests clothes that suit the weather.

Suhan: That's amazing! We no longer have to ⓑworry about dressing for the weather.

Jina: Right. Let's move on to the living room.

10 위 글의 빈칸 ⓐ에 change를 알맞은 형태로 쓰시오.

➡ _____

11 위 글의 밑줄 친 ⓑworry about과 바꿔 쓸 수 없는 것을 모두 고르시오.

① be concerned about
② be anxious for
③ be worried about
④ be anxious about
⑤ be concerned with

12 위 글을 읽고 대답할 수 <u>없는</u> 질문은?

① Where are Jina and Suhan entering?

② Where do Jina and Suhan enter first at the AI home?

③ Where is Suhan standing?

④ How does Suhan's clothes keep changing?

⑤ What does the screen on the closet door suggest?

[13~16] 다음 글을 읽고 물음에 답하시오.

> Suhan: Oh, I like this music speaker.
>
> AI Speaker: I'm not just a music speaker. ①I can do more than you can imagine.
>
> Jina: It's hard to believe that you can understand us. What can ②you do?
>
> AI Speaker: How about watching a movie? I'll play one for ③you.
>
> Suhan: Look, those smart windows are getting darker. I feel ⓐlike I'm in a movie theater.
>
> Jina: What else can you do?
>
> AI Speaker: ④I can beatbox, too. Here comes, "cats and boots and cats and boots."
>
> Suhan: ⑤You're funny. Good job!

13 다음 밑줄 친 ①~⑤ 중에서 가리키는 대상이 나머지 넷과 <u>다른</u> 것은?

①   ②   ③   ④   ⑤

14 위 글의 밑줄 친 ⓐlike와 문법적 쓰임이 같은 것을 고르시오. (2개)

① No one sings the blues <u>like</u> she did.

② I <u>like</u> my coffee strong.

③ Cut the cabbage <u>like</u> this.

④ It looks <u>like</u> her bed wasn't slept in.

⑤ She responded in <u>like</u> manner.

15 위 글의 주제로 알맞은 것을 고르시오.

① the speaker that Suhan likes most at the World AI Expo

② the reason why Jina can't believe that the speaker can understand them

③ how to watch a movie using AI Speaker

④ AI Speaker that can beatbox

⑤ what AI Speaker can do besides playing its original role

서답형

16 본문의 내용과 일치하도록 다음 빈칸 (A)와 (B)에 알맞은 단어를 쓰시오.

> AI Speaker not only is a (A)_____ _____ but also can play a movie and (B)_____.

[17~19] 다음 글을 읽고 물음에 답하시오.

> Jina: Hurry! There's a smart car station outside! Let's go and ride in that red car.
>
> Suhan: This car is so cool. Let's get in.
>
> AI Car: Welcome. Are you ready ⓐto go?
>
> Jina: Yes, what should we do now? It's my first time to ride in a smart car.
>
> AI Car: You don't need to do anything. I will drive and take you ____(A)____ the next station.
>
> Suhan: Watch out! I see a cat crossing the street.
>
> AI Car: Don't worry. I have just sensed it. When I sense dangerous situations, I slow down or stop.

Jina: How can you do that?

AI Car: I'm a very intelligent robotic car. I know all about driving. I can ___(B)___ based ___(C)___ knowledge and experience.

Suhan: How smart! You think and act like a person. You are really like a human.

17 위 글의 빈칸 (A)와 (C)에 들어갈 전치사가 바르게 짝지어진 것은?

① to – on
② in – by
③ in – from
④ to – by
⑤ for – on

18 위 글의 빈칸 (B)에 들어갈 알맞은 말을 고르시오.

① predict safety
② protect cats
③ decide routes
④ predict danger
⑤ generate danger

19 위 글의 밑줄 친 ⓐto go와 to부정사의 용법이 다른 것을 고르시오. (2개)

① I have nothing particular to do today.
② He must be a liar to say such a thing.
③ He is rich enough to buy large house.
④ I told him to clean the room.
⑤ I am sorry to have to leave so early.

[20~23] 다음 글을 읽고 물음에 답하시오.

DAILY NEWS

AI Beats Human!

An AI program has ___(A)___ a human in a baduk match. The AI had a match with Lee Sedol, ⓐ그는 가장 위대한 바둑기사들 중의 한 명이다. Baduk is a board game, and the rules are difficult to understand. Many people believed ___(B)___ would be impossible for an AI to beat a human player. However, the AI was able to predict Lee's play, and it finally won the game. People are shocked that an AI can be more intelligent than a human.

서답형

20 본문의 한 단어를 변형하여 위 글의 빈칸 (A)에 들어갈 알맞은 말을 쓰시오.

➡ _____

서답형

21 위 글의 빈칸 (B)에 들어갈 알맞은 말을 쓰시오.

➡ _____

서답형

22 위 글의 밑줄 친 ⓐ의 우리말에 맞게 주어진 어휘를 이용하여 8단어로 영작하시오.

who, baduk players

➡ _____

23 위 글의 내용과 일치하지 않는 것은?

① 바둑 대국에서 AI 프로그램이 인간을 이겼다.
② 바둑은 보드 게임이고, 그 규칙은 이해하기 어렵다.
③ 많은 사람들은 AI가 인간 기사를 이기는 것은 불가능할 것이라고 믿었다.
④ 이세돌은 경기를 예측할 수 있었고, 그리고 마침내 AI와의 경기에서 이겼다.
⑤ 사람들은 AI가 인간보다 더 똑똑할 수 있다는 것에 충격을 받았다.

[01~03] 다음 글을 읽고 물음에 답하시오.

Jina and Suhan are at the World AI Expo. ⓐ They are entering into the AI home.

Suhan: Look at this! It's a house of the future.

Jina: Let's go into the bedroom first. Look, there's a smart closet.

Suhan: I'm standing in front of this screen on the closet door and my clothes keep changing.

Jina: (A)The screen suggests clothes that suit the weather.

Suhan: That's amazing! ⓑ우린 더 이상 날씨 때문에 무슨 옷을 입을지 걱정할 필요가 없겠다.

Jina: Right. Let's move on to the living room.

01 위 글의 밑줄 친 ⓐ에서 어법상 틀린 부분을 찾아 고치시오.

_____ ➡ _____

02 위 글의 밑줄 친 ⓑ의 우리말에 맞게, 주어진 어휘를 알맞게 배열하시오.

the weather / dressing / have to / we / about / no longer / for / worry

➡ _____

_____

03 다음 빈칸 (a)와 (b)에 알맞은 단어를 넣어 위 글의 밑줄 친 (A)The screen에 대한 소개를 완성하시오.

It is the screen on the smart (a)_____ _____ and suggests clothes that suit (b)_____ _____ to the person who is standing in front of it.

[04~07] 다음 글을 읽고 물음에 답하시오.

Suhan: Oh, I like this music speaker.

AI Speaker: I'm not just a music speaker. I can do more ___ⓐ___ you can imagine.

Jina: It's hard to believe that you can understand us. What can you do?

AI Speaker: ⓑHow about watching a movie? I'll play one for you.

Suhan: Look, those smart windows are ⓒgetting darker. I feel like I'm in a movie theater.

Jina: What else can you do?

AI Speaker: I can beatbox, too. Here comes, "cats and boots and cats and boots."

Suhan: You're funny. Good job!

04 위 글의 빈칸 ⓐ에 들어갈 알맞은 말을 쓰시오.

➡ _____

05 위 글의 밑줄 친 ⓑ를 다음과 같이 바꿔 쓸 때 빈칸에 들어갈 알맞은 말을 쓰시오.

_____ _____ watching a movie?
= _____ _____ _____ watch a movie?

06 위 글의 밑줄 친 ⓒgetting과 바꿔 쓸 수 있는 단어를 쓰시오.

➡ _____

07 위 글을 읽고 '음악 스피커의 역할' 외에 AI Speaker가 할 수 있는 일 두 가지를 우리말로 쓰시오.

(1) _____
(2) _____

[08~11] 다음 글을 읽고 물음에 답하시오.

Jina: Hurry! There's a smart car station outside! Let's go and ride in that red car.

Suhan: This car is so cool. Let's get in.

ⓐAI Car: Welcome. Are you ready to go?

Jina: Yes, what should we do now? It's my first time to ride in a smart car.

AI Car: ⓑYou don't need to do anything. I will drive and take you to the next station.

Suhan: Watch out! I see a cat crossing the street.

AI Car: ⓒDon't worry. I have just sensed ⓓit. When I sense dangerous situations, I slow down or stop.

Jina: How can you do that?

AI Car: I'm a very intelligent robotic car. I know all about driving. I can predict danger based on knowledge and experience.

Suhan: How smart! You think and act like a person. You are really like a human.

08 다음 빈칸에 본문의 한 단어를 알맞은 형태로 바꿔 넣어, 위 글의 밑줄 친 ⓐAI의 줄이지 않은 형태를 완성하시오.

Artificial _____

09 위 글의 밑줄 친 ⓑ를 다음과 같이 바꿔 쓸 때 빈칸에 들어갈 알맞은 말을 쓰시오.

(1) You _____ _____ _____ do anything.

(2) You _____ _____ do anything.

10 위 글에서 AI Car가 밑줄 친 ⓒ처럼 말한 이유를 우리말로 쓰시오.

➡ _____

_____

_____

11 위 글의 밑줄 친 ⓓit이 가리키는 것을 본문에서 찾아 쓰시오.

➡ _____

[12~14] 다음 글을 읽고 물음에 답하시오.

Jina and Suhan are at the World AI Expo. They are entering the AI home.

Suhan: Look at this! It's a house of the future.

Jina: Let's go into the bedroom first. Look, there's a smart closet.

Suhan: I'm standing in front of this screen on the closet door and my clothes keep changing.

Jina: The screen suggests clothes that suit the weather.

Suhan: ⓐThat's amazed! We no longer have to worry about dressing for the weather.

Jina: Right. Let's move on to the living room.

12 위 글의 본문의 내용과 일치하도록 다음 빈칸 (A)와 (B)에 알맞은 단어를 쓰시오.

(A)_____ doesn't actually keep changing his clothes. He is only standing in front of the screen on the closet door and (B)_____ _____ keep changing.

13 위 글의 밑줄 친 ⓐ에서 어법상 틀린 부분을 찾아 고치시오.

_____ ➡ _____

14 Why does Suhan say that they no longer have to worry about dressing for the weather? Fill in the blanks with suitable words.

Because the screen on the closet door _____ _____ that suit the weather.

구석구석

Before You Read

DAILY NEWS

AI Beats Human!

An AI program has beaten a human in a baduk match. The AI had a match
beat–beat–beaten
with Lee Sedol, who is one of the greatest baduk players.
one+of+the+복수명사: ~ 중의 하나
Baduk is a board game, and the rules are difficult to understand. Many people
to부정사의 부사적 용법(형용사 수식)
believed it would be impossible for an AI to beat a human player. However,
가주어   의미상 주어   진주어
the AI was able to predict Lee's play, and it finally won the game.
= AI   win the game: 시합에 이기다
People are shocked that an AI can be more intelligent than a human.
감정을 나타내는 동사는 수식받는 명사가 감정을 느끼게 되는 경우에 과거분사를 쓴다.

구문해설 ・**beat**: 이기다 ・**match**: 경기, 시합 ・**board game**: 보드 게임(판을 놓고 그 위에서 말을 이
동시켜 가며 하는 모든 게임) ・**intelligent**: 총명한, 똑똑한 ・**shocked**: 충격을 받은

Focus on Expressions

In 2099, people get in a flying car to get to the moon. Kids love to go to the
날아다니는   목적어로 쓰인 부정사(= going)
moon because the greatest amusement park is there. Above all, horse-riding is
최상급   = in the moon   동명사(주어)
their favorite activity. They don't want to get off the horses.
목적어로 쓰인 부정사

구문해설 ・**get in**: ~에 들어가다, ~에 타다 ・**get to**: ~에 도착하다 ・**above all**: 다른 무엇보다도 특
히, 우선 첫째로 ・**get off**: ~에서 내리다, ~에서 떨어지다

Wrap Up 1-2

G: Minseok, there is a smart food-ordering machine over there. Why don't we
there is 단수명사: ~가 있다   Why don't we+동사 ~?: 함께 ~하자, ~하지 않을래?
try it?

B: That sounds interesting. We'll be able to order easily and fast by using it.
sound 형용사: ~하게 들리다   order(동사)를 수식하고 있으므로 부사를 사용   by 동사ing: ~함으로써

G: I hope so. By the way, do you think maybe it will be possible for robots to

replace humans someday?

B: I'm not sure. But we will be free from danger because of robots.

G: What do you mean?
'무슨 뜻이야?'(의미를 물을 때 사용)

B: Robots can help people in danger. Robots can do the dangerous work so
위험에 처한, 위험에 빠진   그래서
humans don't have to.
~할 필요가 없다(= need not). 뒤에 do the dangerous work가 생략되었음

G: You're right. We should always try to look on the bright side.

구문해설 ・**machine**: 기계 ・**over there**: 저쪽에 ・**be able to**: ~할 수 있다(= can) ・**by the
way**: 그런데, 그건 그렇고 (대화에서 화제를 바꿀 때 씀) ・**possible**: 가능한 ・**replace**: 대체
하다 ・**free from**: ~이 없는 ・**danger**: 위험 ・**because of**: ~ 때문에

데일리 뉴스
AI가 인간을 이기다!
바둑 대국에서 AI 프로그램이
인간을 이겼다. AI가 이세돌과
대국을 벌였는데, 그는 가장
위대한 바둑기사들 중의 한 명
이다.
바둑은 보드 게임이고, 그 규
칙은 이해하기 어렵다. 많은
사람들은 AI가 인간 기사를 이
기는 것은 불가능할 것이라고
믿었다. 그러나, AI는 이세돌의
경기를 예측할 수 있었고, 그
리고 마침내 경기에서 이겼다.
사람들은 AI가 인간보다 더 똑
똑할 수 있다는 것에 충격을
받았다.

2099년에 사람들은 달에 가
기 위해 날아다니는 차를 탑
니다. 아이들은 가장 멋진 놀
이공원이 그곳에 있기 때문에
달에 가는 것을 좋아합니다.
다른 무엇보다도, 말타기는
그들이 가장 좋아하는 활동입
니다. 그들은 말에서 내리기
를 원하지 않습니다.

G: 민석아, 저쪽에 스마트 음
식 주문 자판기가 있어.
가서 해 보지 않을래?
B: 재미있겠다. 저걸 사용하
면 우린 쉽고 빠르게 주문
할 수 있을 거야.
G: 그러길 바라. 그건 그렇
고, 너는 로봇이 언젠가
인간을 대체할 수 있을 거
라고 생각하니?
B: 잘 모르겠어. 하지만 우리
는 로봇 덕분에 위험이 없
어질 거야.
G: 무슨 뜻이야?
B: 로봇은 위험에 처한 사람
들을 도울 수 있어. 로봇
이 위험한 일을 할 수 있
어서 사람들이 그 일을 하
지 않아도 되지.
G: 네 말이 맞아. 우리는 항상
좋은 면을 보도록 해야 해.

영역별 핵심문제

Words & Expressions

01 다음 빈칸에 공통으로 들어갈 말을 쓰시오.

> • He will give you enough time to _____ them up on the Internet.
> • These whales _____ for their food as a team.

02 다음 빈칸에 알맞은 말을 고르시오.

> She is never free _____ worry.

① from   ② for   ③ at
④ in   ⑤ on

03 다음 문장의 빈칸에 알맞은 것을 〈보기〉에서 찾아 쓰시오.

> ┤ 보기 ├
> if   just   longer   on

(1) The movie is based _____ a famous novel.
(2) It's not _____ about the money.
(3) She is no _____ a child.
(4) Go and see _____ the door is locked.

04 다음 우리말에 맞도록 빈칸에 알맞은 말을 쓰시오. (주어진 철자로 시작할 것.)

(1) 이 경기에선 우리 팀이 너희 팀을 이길 것이다.
➡ Our team will b_____ your team in this match.

(2) Dave는 잘생겼을 뿐만 아니라 똑똑하기까지 하다.
➡ Dave is not only handsome but also i_____.

(3) 너는 쉽게 전구를 교체할 수 있다.
➡ You can easily r_____ the bulb.

Conversation

[05~06] 다음 대화를 읽고 물음에 답하시오.

> B: We took lots of pictures during our trip.
> G: We sure ___(A)___ . We have more than 500 pictures.
> B: Is it possible ___(B)___ an animated photo album out of them?
> G: _____(C)_____ I have an app for that.

05 빈칸 (A)와 (B)에 들어갈 말이 순서대로 바르게 짝지어진 것은?

① do – making   ② do – to make
③ did – make   ④ did – to make
⑤ can – making

06 빈칸 (C)에 알맞은 말을 고르시오.

① No, I think it's impossible.
② Yes, I am able to take many pictures.
③ Yes, it's possible.
④ Yes, it sounds interesting.
⑤ That sounds perfect.

07 다음 대화의 빈칸 (A)와 (B)에 들어갈 말이 순서대로 바르게 짝지어진 것은?

> B: ___(A)___ don't we try a new VR game?
> G: That ___(B)___ interesting.

① What – sounds   ② What – was
③ Why – thinks   ④ Why – was
⑤ Why – sounds

[08~10] 다음 대화를 읽고 물음에 답하시오.

> B: Do you have any ideas for our group project? (①)
> G: No. (②) What about you?
> B: I'm thinking we should talk about future jobs. (③)
> G: That sounds perfect ___(A)___ our project. (④) Let's look ___(B)___ some information on the Internet. (⑤)

08 ①~⑤ 중 주어진 문장이 들어갈 알맞은 곳은?

> What do you think?

①   ②   ③   ④   ⑤

09 다음 빈칸 (A)와 (B)에 공통으로 들어갈 말을 쓰시오.

➡ _____

10 위 대화의 내용과 일치하지 않는 것을 고르시오.

① The girl doesn't have any ideas about the group project.
② Their group project will be about future jobs.
③ The girl disagrees with the boy's idea about the group project.
④ They are talking about their group project.
⑤ They will use the Internet to find some information.

11 다음 대화의 빈칸에 들어갈 말을 고르시오.

> G: The Robot Expo begins next week. Why don't you go with me?
> B: _____ That sounds exciting.
> G: We'll have a chance to meet robotics engineers.
> B: That'll be great.

① Yes, I'd love to.
② Really? Me, too.
③ That's too bad.
④ I think it's not perfect.
⑤ I don't want to go with you.

12 다음 대화의 빈칸에 들어갈 말을 고르시오.

> A: Is it possible (A)[for / of] you to read 50 novels during summer vacation?
> B: (B)[Sure not / Sure]. I can (C)[do / be] that.

(A) _____ (B) _____ (C) _____

Grammar

[13~14] 다음 빈칸에 알맞은 말이 순서대로 짝지어진 것은?

13

• I can smell the bread _____.
• I watched the people _____ in the river.

① bake – to swim
② bakes – swimming
③ baked – swam
④ to bake – swims
⑤ baking – swim

14

_____ is good for both body and mind _____ every day.

① This – exercising
② That – exercise
③ That – to exercise
④ It – exercise
⑤ It – to exercise

15 다음 그림을 보고 괄호 안에 주어진 어휘를 이용하여 빈칸에 알맞은 말을 쓰시오.

(1)   (2)   (3)

(1) I saw a person _____ badminton. (play)
(2) I saw a person _____ in the pool. (swim)
(3) I saw a person _____ a horse. (ride)

16 다음 중 어법상 올바르지 <u>않은</u> 것은?

① It is impossible to finish the work in time.
② It was interesting that compare their situation and ours.
③ It is hard to believe that he knows all the answers to the problems.
④ It is true that nature itself is a teacher and a school.
⑤ Is it possible to make energy from waste?

17 다음 중 어법상 올바르지 <u>않은</u> 것은?

① She had him throw away the trash yesterday.
② I often watch her talking on the phone.
③ It is important to wash your hands before doing an experiment.
④ Now it is not hard to see AI robots to serve dishes in the school cafeteria.
⑤ Is it possible to drink while standing on your head?

18 괄호 안에 주어진 어휘를 이용하여 다음을 영작하시오.

(1) 나는 그가 공원에서 자전거를 타고 있는 것을 보았다. (ride, see, a bike)

➡ _____

(2) 나는 부엌에서 무언가가 타고 있는 냄새를 맡았다. (smell, something, burn)

➡ _____

(3) 달에서 말하는 것은 가능하지 않다. (not, talk, the moon, it)

➡ _____

(4) 친구들과 농구하는 것은 흥미롭다. (it, exciting, with friends)

➡ _____

19 다음 문장에서 어법상 어색한 부분을 바르게 고치시오.

(1) We saw him danced on the street.

_____ ➡ _____

(2) Hyde smells something burns in the room.

_____ ➡ _____

(3) I felt my heart tearing to pieces by regret.

_____ ➡ _____

(4) It is dangerous of you to swim in the sea.

_____ ➡ _____

(5) Many people believed it would be impossible for an AI beating a human player.

_____ ➡ _____

(6) Is it possible make an animated photo album out of them?

_____ ➡ _____

Reading

[20~22] 다음 글을 읽고 물음에 답하시오.

Jina and Suhan are at the World AI Expo. They are entering the AI home.

Suhan: Look at this! It's a house of the future.

Jina: Let's go into the bedroom first. Look, there's a smart closet.

Suhan: I'm standing in front of this screen on the closet door and my clothes keep changing.

Jina: The screen suggests clothes ___ⓐ___ suit the weather.

Suhan: That's amazing! We no longer have to worry about dressing for the weather.

Jina: Right. Let's move on to the living room.

20 위 글의 빈칸 ⓐ에 들어갈 알맞은 말을 모두 고르시오.

① that　　　　② who
③ what　　　　④ whom
⑤ which

21 위 글의 제목으로 가장 알맞은 것을 고르시오.

① The World AI Expo
② The House of the Future
③ There's a Screen on the Closet Door!
④ The Screen Which Suggests Clothes
⑤ How to Wear Clothes Suitable for the Weather

22 주어진 영영풀이에 해당하는 단어를 위 글에서 찾아 쓰시오.

a small room or cabinet used for storage space

➡ _____

[23~24] 다음 글을 읽고 물음에 답하시오.

Suhan: Oh, I like this music speaker.

AI Speaker: I'm not just a music speaker. ⓐ저는 당신이 상상하는 것 이상의 것을 할 수 있어요.

Jina: ⓑIt's hard to believe that you can understand us. What can you do?

AI Speaker: How about watching a movie? I'll play one for you.

Suhan: Look, those smart windows are getting darker. I feel like I'm in a movie theater.

Jina: What else can you do?

AI Speaker: I can beatbox, too. Here comes, "cats and boots and cats and boots."

Suhan: You're funny. Good job!

23 위 글의 밑줄 친 ⓐ의 우리말에 맞게 주어진 어휘를 알맞게 배열하시오.

> more / can / you / do / than / imagine / can / I

➡ _____

24 위 글의 밑줄 친 ⓑIt과 문법적 쓰임이 같은 것을 고르시오.

① It was raining this morning.
② It's impossible to get there in time.
③ I find it strange that she doesn't want to go.
④ It's two miles from here to the beach.
⑤ Look! It's going up that tree.

[25~27] 다음 글을 읽고 물음에 답하시오.

Jina: Hurry! There's a smart car station outside! Let's go and ride in that red car.
Suhan: This car is so cool. Let's get in.
AI Car: Welcome. Are you ready to go?
Jina: Yes, what should we do now? It's my first time to ride in a smart car.
AI Car: You don't need to do anything. I will drive and take you to the next station.
Suhan: ⓐWatch out! I see a cat crossing the street.
AI Car: Don't worry. I ⓑhave just sensed it. When I sense dangerous situations, I slow down or stop.
Jina: How can you ⓒdo that?
AI Car: I'm a very intelligent robotic car. I know all about driving. I can predict danger based on knowledge and experience.
Suhan: How smart! You think and act like a person. You are really like a human.

25 위 글의 밑줄 친 ⓐWatch out과 바꿔 쓸 수 있는 말을 쓰시오.

➡ _____

26 아래 〈보기〉에서 위 글의 밑줄 친 ⓑhave just sensed와 현재완료의 용법이 다른 것의 개수를 고르시오.

> ① We <u>have</u> already <u>done</u> it.
> ② I <u>have</u> never <u>read</u> the book.
> ③ They <u>have lived</u> in Seoul for ten years.
> ④ He <u>has gone</u> to Busan.
> ⑤ She <u>has waited</u> for you since last night.

① 1개　② 2개　③ 3개　④ 4개　⑤ 5개

27 위 글의 밑줄 친 ⓒdo that이 가리키는 것을 본문에서 찾아 영어로 쓰시오.

➡ _____
_____

[28~29] 다음 글을 읽고 물음에 답하시오.

> **Messi Is Playing at Our School!**
> Scientists have developed a soccer robot _____ⓐ_____ "Alpha-Foot." Alpha-Foot is almost human looking and is programmed as Messi. Next week, Alpha-Foot will play in his first soccer match with our soccer team. We are all excited to see the AI robot play for our school.

28 위 글의 빈칸 ⓐ에 call을 알맞은 형태로 쓰시오.

➡ _____

29 위 글의 종류로 알맞은 것을 고르시오.

① review　　　② book report
③ essay　　　④ diary
⑤ a school paper article

✏️ 출제율 90%

01 제시된 영영풀이의 단어로 빈칸을 채우시오. (주어진 철자로 시작할 것)

> b_____ : to be destroyed by fire

> Lower the heat, or it'll _____.

✏️ 출제율 95%

02 다음 밑줄 친 부분을 알맞은 형태로 고치시오.

> The next night was dark and <u>cloud</u>.

➡ _____

✏️ 출제율 100%

03 다음 중 〈보기〉에 있는 단어를 사용하여 자연스러운 문장을 만들 수 없는 것은?

> ┌ 보기 ┐
> point take text freeze

① It takes all day just to _____ a tray of ice cubes.

② It is widely used to _____ down aging.

③ Do you like _____ or talking to your friends online?

④ It's not polite to _____ at strangers in public.

⑤ I'll _____ two adult tickets, please.

✏️ 출제율 95%

04 주어진 우리말에 맞게 빈칸을 채우시오.

(1) 얼마나 많은 공장 노동자들이 일자리를 잃을 위험에 처해 있는가?

➡ How many factory workers are _____ _____ of losing their jobs?

(2) 너의 성적은 네 개의 과제물과 기말 고사를 기준으로 매겨질 것이다.

➡ Your grade will be _____ _____ four papers and a final exam.

[05~08] 다음 대화를 읽고 물음에 답하시오.

G: Look at those words on the board.

B: What do they mean? Let's look them up in the dictionary.

G: What about using the AI ___(A)___?

B: _____(B)

G: You point your smartphone camera at the words and ask AI to translate. You will get an answer.

B: AI가 저 글자들을 읽는 것이 가능해?

Speaker: Sure. I can read any language and translate it.

B: Wow, that sounds unbelievable. So, AI, what do those words mean?

Speaker: They mean "Dreams come true!"

B: That's amazing.

✏️ 출제율 90%

05 위의 대화에 나온 단어를 이용해 빈칸 (A)에 알맞은 말을 쓰시오. (주어진 철자로 시작할 것)

➡ t_____

✏️ 출제율 95%

06 위 대화의 빈칸 (B)에 알맞은 말을 고르시오.

① What do you think?

② Why don't you use those words?

③ What about you?

④ Do you have any ideas for those words?

⑤ How do I use it?

07 밑줄 친 우리말과 일치하도록 주어진 단어를 이용해 문장을 만드시오.

> (AI, possible, those)

➡ _____

출제율 85%

08 위 대화에서 다음 영영풀이에 해당하는 단어를 찾아 쓰시오.

> a book that contains a list of words and phrases alphabetically with their meanings or their translations in another language

➡ _____

[09~10] 문장을 대화의 흐름에 맞게 배열하시오.

출제율 95%

09

> (A) That sounds perfect for our project. Let's look for some information on the Internet.
> (B) I'm thinking we should talk about future jobs. What do you think?
> (C) Do you have any ideas for our group project?
> (D) No. What about you?

➡ _____

출제율 100%

10

> (A) We sure did. We have more than 500 pictures.
> (B) Yes, it's possible. I have an app for that.
> (C) Is it possible to make an animated photo album out of them?
> (D) We took lots of pictures during our trip.

➡ _____

[11~12] 다음 대화를 읽고 물음에 답하시오.

> A: Let's see (A)[which / if / what] we can answer these science questions.
> B: That sounds like fun.
> A: 불을 얼리는 것이 가능할까?
> B: Yes, I think it's possible.

출제율 85%

11 위 대화의 괄호 (A)에서 적절한 것을 고르시오.

➡ _____

출제율 85%

12 밑줄 친 우리말과 일치하도록 주어진 단어를 이용하여 영작하시오. (6단어)

> (possible)

➡ _____

출제율 90%

13 다음 빈칸에 들어갈 말이 바르게 짝지어진 것은?

> _____ is possible _____ a robot _____ me how to play the piano.

① It – of – teach
② It – for – to teach
③ That – of – teach
④ That – for – to teach
⑤ This – of – to teach

14 다음 빈칸에 들어갈 말이 바르게 짝지어진 것은?

- I noticed the man _____ slowly toward me.
- It is fun _____ together with Ella and Jaden every day.

① coming – get ② coming – to get
③ to come – get ④ to come – to get
⑤ come – get

[15~16] 다음 중 어법상 올바른 문장을 <u>모두</u> 고르시오.

15 ① Alice saw him running toward her.
② I heard my name calling repeatedly.
③ Jenny felt somebody pulling her hair.
④ Mick watched them fought each other.
⑤ He was looking at the dog to eat the bones.

16 ① That is necessary to come early in the morning.
② It is good to go for a walk on holidays.
③ It is helpful read many kinds of books.
④ It was really boring of me to memorize English words.
⑤ It is important that you follow the rules.

[17~19] 다음 글을 읽고 물음에 답하시오.

Jina and Suhan are at the World AI Expo. They are entering the AI home.
Suhan: Look at this! It's a house of the future.
Jina: Let's go into the bedroom first. Look, there's a smart closet.
Suhan: I'm standing in front of this screen on the closet door and my clothes keep changing.

Jina: ⓐThe screen suggests clothes that suits the weather.
Suhan: That's amazing! We no longer have to worry ___(A)___ dressing ___(B)___ the weather.
Jina: Right. Let's move on to the ⓑliving room.

17 위 글의 빈칸 (A)와 (B)에 들어갈 전치사가 바르게 짝지어진 것은?

① for – from ② about – for
③ at – for ④ for – to
⑤ about – to

18 위 글의 밑줄 친 ⓐ에서 어법상 틀린 부분을 찾아 고치시오.

_____ ➡ _____

19 위 글의 밑줄 친 ⓑliving과 문법적 쓰임이 <u>다른</u> 것을 <u>모두</u> 고르시오.

① a sleeping car ② a waiting lady
③ a walking stick ④ a waiting room
⑤ a walking dictionary

[20~22] 다음 글을 읽고 물음에 답하시오.

Suhan: Oh, I like this music speaker.
AI Speaker: I'm not just a music speaker. I can do more than ⓐyou can imagine.
Jina: It's hard (A)to believe that ⓑyou can understand ⓒus. What can you do?
AI Speaker: How about watching a movie? ⓓI'll play one for you.

Suhan: Look, those smart windows are getting darker. I feel like I'm in a movie theater.

Jina: What else can ⓔyou do?

AI Speaker: How

Suhan: You're funny. Good job!

출제율 95%

20 위 글의 밑줄 친 ⓐ~ⓔ 중 가리키는 대상이 같은 것끼리 짝 지어진 것은?

① ⓐ – ⓑ ② ⓐ – ⓓ ③ ⓑ – ⓒ

④ ⓑ – ⓓ ⑤ ⓒ – ⓔ

출제율 90%

21 아래 보기에서 위 글의 밑줄 친 (A)to believe와 to부정사의 용법이 다른 것의 개수를 고르시오.

① This plan leaves nothing to be desired.

② To read these books is important.

③ He was too foolish to solve it.

④ Would you like to leave a message?

⑤ To read is to feed the mind.

① 1개 ② 2개 ③ 3개 ④ 4개 ⑤ 5개

출제율 100%

22 위 글의 내용과 일치하지 않는 것은?

① 수한이는 음악 스피커가 마음에 든다.

② 인공 지능 스피커는 사람들이 상상하는 것 이상의 것을 할 수 있다고 말한다.

③ 화면이 점점 어두워지고 있다.

④ 수한이는 마치 영화관 안에 있는 것 같이 느낀다.

⑤ 인공 지능 스피커는 비트박스도 할 수 있다.

[23~25] 다음 글을 읽고 물음에 답하시오.

Jina: Hurry! There's a smart car station outside! Let's go and ride in that red car.

Suhan: This car is so cool. Let's get in.

AI Car: Welcome. Are you ready to go?

Jina: Yes, what should we do now? It's my first time to ride in a smart car.

AI Car: You don't need to do anything. I will drive and take you to the next station.

Suhan: Watch out! I see a cat crossing the street.

AI Car: Don't worry. (①) I have just sensed it. (②)

Jina: How can you do that? (③)

AI Car: I'm a very intelligent robotic car. (④) I know all about driving. (⑤) I can predict danger based on knowledge and experience.

Suhan: How smart! You think and act like a person. You are really like a human.

출제율 95%

23 위 글의 흐름으로 보아, 주어진 문장이 들어가기에 가장 적절한 곳은?

When I sense dangerous situations, I slow down or stop.

①   ②   ③   ④   ⑤

출제율 100%

24 위 글의 주제로 알맞은 것을 고르시오.

① People want to ride in a cool smart car.

② People share the experience to ride in a smart car.

③ What should we do to ride in a smart car?

④ The AI car knows all about driving.

⑤ How does a smart car sense dangerous situations?

출제율 90%

25 다음 빈칸 (A)와 (B)에 알맞은 단어를 넣어 '인공 지능 자동차'에 대한 소개를 완성하시오.

It's a very intelligent (A)_____ _____ which knows all about driving. People don't need to (B)_____ _____ while they are riding in this smart car.

01 대화의 흐름상 또는 어법상 <u>어색한</u> 것을 하나 찾아서 고치시오.

> **A:** Do you have any questions?
> **B:** Yes. Is that possible to communicate face to face with other people without speaking?
> **A:** Not now. But maybe someday.

_____ ➡ _____

02 대화의 밑줄 친 부분과 같은 뜻이 되도록 주어진 단어를 이용하여 문장을 완성하시오.

> **B:** Do you have any ideas for our group project?
> **G:** No. What about you?
> **B:** I'm thinking we should talk about future jobs. What do you think?
> **G:** <u>That sounds perfect for our project.</u> Let's look for some information on the Internet.

➡ _____ (think)

03 밑줄 친 우리말과 일치하도록 주어진 단어를 이용하여 문장을 만드시오.

> **A:** <u>눈 감고 문자 메시지 보내는 것이 가능하니?</u>
> **B:** Sure. I can do that.

> (it. for, close, with)

➡ _____

04 주어진 어휘를 이용하여 다음 우리말을 (1) to부정사 주어를 써서, (2) 가주어를 써서 영작하시오.

> 우리 일상생활에서 에너지를 절약하는 것이 중요하다. (save, our daily lives)

(1) _____
(2) _____

> 퇴근 후 피곤함을 느끼는 것은 당연하다.
> (natural, tired, after work)

(1) _____
(2) _____

05 다음 그림을 보고 괄호 안에 주어진 어휘를 이용하여 빈칸을 알맞게 채우시오.

> I watched Jane _____ _____ _____.
> (ride)

Jina and Suhan are at the World AI Expo. They are entering the AI home.

Suhan: Look at this! It's a house of the future.

Jina: Let's ⓐgo into the bedroom first. Look, there's a smart closet.

Suhan: I'm standing in front of this screen on the closet door and my clothes keep changing.

Jina: ⓑ스크린이 날씨에 적합한 옷을 제안하는 거야.

Suhan: That's amazing! ⓒWe no longer have to worry about dressing for the weather.

Jina: Right. Let's move on to the living room.

06 위 글의 밑줄 친 ⓐgo into와 바꿔 쓸 수 있는 한 단어를 본문에서 찾아 알맞은 형태로 쓰시오.

➡ _____

07 위 글의 밑줄 친 ⓑ의 우리말에 맞게 주어진 어휘를 이용하여 8단어로 영작하시오.

suggests, suit, weather

➡ _____

_____

08 위 글의 밑줄 친 ⓒ를 다음과 같이 바꿔 쓸 때 빈칸에 들어갈 알맞은 말을 쓰시오.

We don't have to worry about dressing for the weather _____ _____.

Jina: Hurry! There's a smart car station outside! Let's go and ride in that red car.

Suhan: This car is so cool. Let's get in.

AI Car: Welcome. Are you ready to go?

Jina: Yes, (A)[how / what] should we do now? It's my first time to ride in a smart car.

AI Car: You don't need to do anything. I will drive and take you to the next station.

Suhan: Watch out! I see a cat crossing the street.

AI Car: Don't worry. I have just sensed it. ⓐWhen I sense dangerous situations, I speed up or stop.

Jina: (B)[How / What] can you do that?

AI Car: I'm a very intelligent robotic car. I know all about driving. I can predict danger (C)[basing / based] on knowledge and experience.

Suhan: ⓑHow smart! You think and act like a person. You are really like a human.

09 위 글의 괄호 (A)~(C)에서 어법상 알맞은 낱말을 골라 쓰시오.

(A) _____ (B) _____ (C) _____

10 위 글의 밑줄 친 ⓐ에서 흐름상 어색한 부분을 찾아 고치시오.

_____ ➡ _____

11 위 글의 밑줄 친 ⓑHow smart!를 What을 사용하여 고치시오.

➡ _____

01 가능 여부를 묻고 대답하는 다음 대화를 완성하시오.

조건

• 더운 날 길 위에서 계란을 부치는 것이 가능한지에 대해 이야기할 것.

• possible을 이용할 것.

A: _____

B: _____

02 지각동사 see를 이용하여 다음 그림을 묘사하는 문장을 완성하시오. (괄호 안에 주어진 어휘를 이용할 것.)

(1) I can see a man and a woman _____ a song together. (sing)

(2) I can see _____ an ice corn with her left arm raised. (girl, eat)

(3) I can see _____ the shirts in the store. (boy, look)

03 다음 내용을 바탕으로 기획한 제품을 쇼핑 호스트가 되어 홍보하는 대본을 쓰시오.

AI Cook

- It selects vegetables and meat from the refrigerator.

- It cooks a delicious meal with these vegetables and meat.

 Today, I'll tell you about the "(A)_____." It can select (B)_____ from the refrigerator for you. It can cook (C)_____ with these (D)_____. When the meal is ready, it'll let you know. Now, please call 800-1234-8282 if you'd like to buy one of these AI Cooks.

단원별 모의고사

01 다음 문장에 공통으로 들어갈 말을 고르시오.

> • The story is _____ more and more interesting.
>
> • He is _____ in the front seat of the taxi.

02 다음 빈칸에 알맞은 말을 〈보기〉에서 골라 쓰시오.

> ┌─ 보기 ─────────────────┐
>
> of   on   to
>
> └───────────────────────┘

(1) They are sitting face _____ face and looking at each other.

(2) Now, let's move _____ to the next story.

(3) They make plastics out _____ plant materials such as corn and soybeans.

03 다음 빈칸에 알맞은 말을 고르시오.

> We are offering 25% _____ all furniture purchased on the day of our grand opening.

① on   ② in   ③ off

④ from   ⑤ to

[04~05] 다음 대화를 읽고 물음에 답하시오.

> G: 네가 스마트폰 없이 사는 것이 가능할까?
>
> B: No, it's (A)not possible.

04 밑줄 친 우리말과 일치하도록 주어진 단어를 이용하여 영작하시오.

> (possible)

➡ _____

05 위 대화의 밑줄 친 (A)를 한 단어로 바꾸시오.

➡ _____

[06~08] 다음 대화를 읽고 물음에 답하시오.

> G: This computer looks nice. How much is ⓐit?
>
> M: ⓑIt's 500 dollars. ⓒIt's the newest one.
>
> G: Is ⓓit possible to use this coupon?
>
> M: Let me check. Yes, you can. ___(A)___, you'll get 30 dollars off.
>
> G: Perfect. I'll take ⓔit.

06 위 대화의 ⓐ~ⓔ 중 대상이 다른 하나를 고르시오.

① ⓐ   ② ⓑ   ③ ⓒ   ④ ⓓ   ⑤ ⓔ

07 위 대화의 빈칸 (A)에 알맞은 말을 고르시오.

① So   ② However

③ Unfortunately   ④ Also

⑤ In addition

08 위 대화를 읽고 대답할 수 없는 질문을 고르시오.

① Is the coupon which the girl has available to use?

② Will the girl pay in cash or credit card?

③ Where are they?

④ How much discount does the girl get?

⑤ What does the girl want to buy?

[09~12] 다음 대화를 읽고 물음에 답하시오.

> G: Minseok, there is a smart food-ordering machine over there. ⓐWhy don't we try it?
>
> B: That sounds ___(A)___ (interest). ⓑWe'll be able to order easily and fast by using it.
>
> G: ⓒI hope so. By the way, do you think maybe it will be possible for robots ___(B)___ (replace) humans someday?
>
> B: I'm not sure. But we will be free ___(C)___ danger because ___(D)___ robots.
>
> G: ⓓWhat do you mean?
>
> B: Robots can help people in danger. Robots can do the dangerous work so humans don't have to.
>
> G: You're right. ⓔWe should always try to look on the dark side.

09 위 대화의 괄호 안에 주어진 단어를 이용하여 빈칸 (A)와 (B)를 채우시오.

(A) _____ (B) _____

10 위 대화의 빈칸 (C), (D)에 알맞은 전치사를 쓰시오.

(C) _____ (D) _____

11 위 대화의 문맥상 어색한 것을 고르시오.

① ⓐ   ② ⓑ   ③ ⓒ   ④ ⓓ   ⑤ ⓔ

12 위 대화에서 다음 영영풀이에 해당하는 단어를 찾아 쓰시오.

> able to happen or be done

➡ _____

13 다음 문장을 it을 주어로 하여 다시 쓰시오.

(1) To eat a lot of vegetables is good for your health.

➡ _____

(2) That people may not want to talk to each other anymore is possible.

➡ _____
_____

14 다음 중 어법상 어색한 것은?

① Mike heard his phone ringing.
② It is my plan to read 10 books during the winter vacation.
③ It was exciting to watch them singing and dancing to the music.
④ She watched him to cut the paper.
⑤ Is it possible for you to text with your eyes closed?

15 다음 중 어법상 어색한 것은?

① She heard someone crying.
② I saw the boy singing in the classroom.
③ She watched him helping the lady get into the bus.
④ Is it possible to freeze fire?
⑤ It is very kind for you to help us.

16 주어진 단어를 이용하여 다음 우리말을 영어로 쓰시오.

(1) 민아는 양파가 튀겨지는 냄새를 맡았다.
(smell, fry)

➡ _____

(2) 우리는 그들이 서로에게 속삭이고 있는 것을 들었다. (whisper, each other)

➡ _____

(3) 새로운 것들을 찾아서 만드는 것은 흥미롭다.
(new things, interesting, find and create, it)

➡ _____

(4) 당신이 이메일을 보내는 것은 쉽다.
(it, send e-mails)

➡ _____

17 다음 어법상 틀린 문장의 개수는?

> ⓐ I saw my brother singing a song.
> ⓑ We heard Yena played the violin.
> ⓒ She noticed him shaking his head.
> ⓓ Jeniffer felt him came closer.
> ⓔ It is good to volunteer at the community center.
> ⓕ I think it's possible that a spacecraft can be controlled by a computer program.
> ⓖ Is it safe swim in this river?

① 1개　② 2개　③ 3개　④ 4개　⑤ 5개

[18~20] 다음 글을 읽고 물음에 답하시오.

> Jina and Suhan are at the World AI Expo. They are entering the AI home.
> Suhan: Look at this! It's a house of the future.
> Jina: Let's go into the bedroom first. Look, there's a smart closet.
> Suhan: I'm standing in front of this screen on the closet door and my clothes keep changing.
> Jina: The screen suggests clothes ⓐthat suit the weather.
> Suhan: ⓑThat's amazing! We no longer have to worry about dressing for the weather.
> Jina: ⓒRight. Let's move on to the living room.

18 아래 보기에서 위 글의 밑줄 친 ⓐthat과 문법적 쓰임이 다른 것의 개수를 고르시오.

> ① I believe that you'll pass the exam.
> ② He is the only man that I love.
> ③ I'm glad that you like it.
> ④ I was so busy that I could not help him.
> ⑤ This is the pen that he bought yesterday.

① 1개　② 2개　③ 3개　④ 4개　⑤ 5개

19 위 글의 밑줄 친 ⓑThat이 가리키는 것을 본문에서 찾아 쓰시오.

➡ _____

20 위 글의 밑줄 친 ⓒRight.과 바꿔 쓸 수 없는 말을 고르시오.

① You got it.
② You can say that again.
③ I agree with you.
④ That's all right.
⑤ You said it.

[21~22] 다음 글을 읽고 물음에 답하시오.

Suhan: Oh, I ___(A)___ this music speaker.

AI Speaker: I'm not just a music speaker. I can do more than you can imagine.

Jina: It's hard to believe that you can understand us. What can you do?

AI Speaker: How about watching a movie? I'll play one for you.

Suhan: Look, ⓐthat smart windows are getting darker. I feel ___(B)___ I'm in a movie theater.

Jina: What else can you do?

AI Speaker: I can beatbox, too. Here comes, "cats and boots and cats and boots."

Suhan: You're funny. Good job!

21 위 글의 빈칸 (A)와 (B)에 공통으로 들어갈 알맞은 말을 쓰시오.

➡ _____

22 위 글의 밑줄 친 ⓐ에서 어법상 틀린 부분을 찾아 고치시오.

_____ ➡ _____

[23~25] 다음 글을 읽고 물음에 답하시오.

Jina: Hurry! There's a smart car station outside! Let's go and ride in that red car.

Suhan: This car is so cool. Let's get in.

AI Car: Welcome. Are you ready to go?

Jina: Yes, what should we do now? It's my first time ⓐto ride in a smart car.

AI Car: You don't need to do anything. I will drive and take you to the next station.

Suhan: Watch out! I see a cat crossing the street.

AI Car: Don't worry. I have just sensed it. When I sense dangerous situations, I slow down or stop.

Jina: How can you do that?

AI Car: I'm a very intelligent robotic car. I know all about driving. ⓑ저는 제 지식과 경험을 바탕으로 위험을 예측할 수 있어요.

Suhan: How smart! You think and act like a person. You are really like a human.

23 위 글의 밑줄 친 ⓐto ride와 to부정사의 용법이 같은 것을 모두 고르시오.

① I don't know when to begin the work.

② Does she have a house to live in?

③ I had an opportunity to see him last year.

④ It is best not to make him angry.

⑤ You must work hard to succeed in the examination.

24 위 글의 밑줄 친 ⓑ의 우리말에 맞게 한 단어를 보충하여, 주어진 어휘를 알맞게 배열하시오.

and / predict / experience / can / based / I / knowledge / danger

➡ _____

_____

25 위 글의 내용과 일치하지 않는 것은?

① 진아는 스마트 자동차 정류장에 가서 빨간 차를 타 보기를 원한다.

② 진아는 스마트 자동차에 처음 타 본다.

③ 인공 지능 자동차는 고양이가 길을 건너고 있는 것을 감지했다.

④ 인공 지능 자동차는 어떤 위험 상황을 감지하면 속도를 늦추거나 멈춘다.

⑤ 인공 지능 자동차는 자신의 학습 능력을 바탕으로 위험을 예측할 수 있다.

Lesson 8

The Unknown Hero

🎙 의사소통 기능

- 알고 있는지 묻기
  A: Do you know anything about King Sejong?
  B: No, I don't.

- 설명 요청하기
  A: Could you explain the rules of *bisachigi*?
  B: Each player throws a stone at another stone.

🎙 언어 형식

- 동사+목적어+to부정사
  Japanese officials **pressed** him **to build** Japanese houses.

- 과거분사
  Through his efforts, we now have Bukchon **filled** with its beautiful hanoks.

Words & Expressions

Key Words

- **affair** [əféər] 몡 사건, 일
- **alive** [əláiv] 휑 살아 있는
- **another** [ənʌ́ðər] 휑 또 다른, 다른 하나의
- **architecture** [áːrkrtèktʃər] 몡 건축
- **businessman** [bíznəsmæn] 몡 사업가
- **collect** [kəlékt] 동 모으다, 수집하다
- **community** [kəmjúːnəti] 몡 지역사회, 주민
- **dynasty** [dáinəsti] 몡 왕조, 시대
- **explain** [ikspléin] 동 설명하다
- **fan** [fæn] 몡 부채, 선풍기
- **fit** [fit] 동 적합하다
- **found** [faund] 동 설립하다
- **hometown** [hóumtaun] 몡 고향
- **independence** [ìndipéndəns] 몡 독립
- **interest** [íntərəst] 몡 관심, 흥미
- **land** [lænd] 몡 땅, 토지
- **meaning** [míːniŋ] 몡 의미
- **modern** [mάdərn] 휑 현대의
- **movement** [múːvmənt] 몡 운동
- **nature** [néitʃər] 몡 자연
- **novel** [nάvəl] 몡 소설
- **official** [əfíʃəl] 몡 공무원, 당국

- **part** [pɑːrt] 몡 부분, 일부
- **poem** [póuəm] 몡 시
- **pottery** [pάtəri] 몡 도자기
- **press** [pres] 동 압박하다
- **property** [prάpərti] 몡 재산
- **royal** [rɔ́iəl] 휑 왕의, 왕실의
- **rule** [ruːl] 동 통치하다 몡 규칙, 원칙
- **society** [səsáiəti] 몡 사회, 단체
- **Spanish** [spǽniʃ] 휑 스페인의
- **stone** [stoun] 몡 돌
- **store** [stɔːr] 동 저장하다, 보관하다
- **suffer** [sʌ́fər] 동 고통 받다, 시달리다
- **support** [səpɔ́ːrt] 동 지원하다
- **taste** [teist] 몡 맛, 취향
- **through** [θruː] 전 ~을 통하여
- **tourist** [túərist] 몡 여행객
- **tradition** [trədíʃən] 몡 전통
- **unknown** [ənnóun] 휑 알려지지 않은
- **village** [vílidʒ] 몡 마을
- **waste** [weist] 동 낭비하다
- **Western** [wéstərn] 휑 서양의

Key Expressions

- **a lot** 많이
- **be famous for** ~으로 유명하다
- **be filled with** ~으로 가득하다
- **be in harmony with** ~와 조화를 이루다
- **be interested in** ~에 흥미를 가지다
- **be known as** ~으로 알려지다
- **care for** ~을 돌보다
- **fall off** (사업, 세력 등이) 쇠퇴하다

- **hundreds of** 수백의, 수많은
- **in danger** 위험에 빠진
- **in need** 어려움에 처한
- **in part** 부분적으로는
- **rise up** 일어서다
- **set foot** 발을 들여놓다
- **take care of** ~을 돌보다
- **thanks to** ~ 덕분에

Word Power

※ 국가와 관련된 여러 가지 어휘

☐ **Korea**(한국) – **Korean**(한국어; 한국의)

☐ **China**(중국) – **Chinese**(중국어; 중국의)

☐ **Japan**(일본) – **Japanese**(일본어; 일본의)

☐ **Vietnam**(베트남) – **Vietnamese**(베트남어; 베트남의)

☐ **England**(영국) – **English**(영어; 영국의)

☐ **France**(프랑스) – **French**(프랑스어; 프랑스의)

☐ **Spain**(스페인) – **Spanish**(스페인어; 스페인의)

☐ **Germany**(독일) – **German**(독일어; 독일의)

English Dictionary

☐ **alive** 살아 있는
→ not dead
죽지 않은

☐ **architecture** 건축, 건축학
→ the art of planning, designing and constructing buildings
건물을 계획하고, 설계하고 짓는 기술

☐ **businessman** 사업가, 실업가
→ a man who works in business
사업에 종사하는 사람

☐ **explain** 설명하다
→ to give details about something or describe it so that it can be understood
어떤 것이 이해될 수 있도록 그것에 관해 상세히 기술하거나 묘사하다

☐ **found** 설립하다
→ to get an institution, company, or organization started, often by providing the necessary money
종종 필요한 돈을 제공해서, 어떤 단체, 회사, 조직이 시작되게 하다

☐ **hometown** 고향
→ the place where someone lives or the town that they come from 어떤 사람이 살거나 그들이 출생한 장소

☐ **land** 토지, 땅
→ an area of ground, especially one that is used for a particular purpose such as farming or building
특히 농사나 건축과 같은 특별한 목적을 위해 사용되는 지역

☐ **nature** 자연
→ all the animals, plants, and other things in the world that are not made by people, and all the events and processes that are not caused by people
사람들에 의해 만들어지지 않은 모든 동물, 식물, 그리고 자연의 사물들과 사람들에 의해 일어나지 않은 모든 사건과 과정

☐ **novel** 소설
→ a long written story about imaginary people and events
상상의 사람들이나 사건들에 관해 쓰인 긴 이야기

☐ **property** 재산
→ all the things that belong to someone or something that belongs to them
어떤 사람에게 속해 있는 모든 것들 또는 그들에게 속해 있는 어떤 것

☐ **stone** 돌, 석조
→ a hard solid substance found in the ground and often used for building houses 땅에서 발견되며 종종 집들을 짓는 데 사용되는 딱딱한 고체의 물질

☐ **store** 저장하다
→ to put things in a container or other places and leave them there until they are needed
물건들을 용기나 다른 장소에 넣고 나중에 필요할 때까지 그곳에 두다

서답형

01 다음 〈보기〉와 같은 관계가 되도록 빈칸에 알맞은 말을 써 넣으시오.

┌─ 보기 ─┐

Korea – <u>Korean</u>

(1) China – _____
(2) Span – _____

중요

02 다음 중 밑줄 친 부분의 의미로 알맞지 <u>않은</u> 것은?

① My hobby is to <u>collect</u> stamps. (수집하다)
② Do you mean I didn't practice <u>enough</u>? (충분히)
③ Why <u>waste</u> money on clothes you don't need? (저축하다)
④ The colour and style is a matter of personal <u>taste</u>. (취향)
⑤ Be careful not to damage other people's <u>property</u>. (재산)

03 다음 빈칸에 알맞은 전치사로 짝지어진 것은?

┌─────────────────────────┐
The place is famous _____ its beauty.
I will take care _____ the patient.
└─────────────────────────┘

① for – of   ② of – with
③ to – with   ④ in – of
⑤ at – from

중요

04 다음 빈칸에 알맞은 단어를 고르시오.

┌─────────────────────────┐
We _____ goods in a warehouse.
└─────────────────────────┘

① save   ② waste
③ allow   ④ store
⑤ decide

05 다음 중 밑줄 친 부분이 <u>어색한</u> 것을 고르시오.

① We don't know whether he's <u>alive</u> or dead.
② There is no <u>loyal</u> road to learning.
③ I need <u>another</u> computer.
④ The burglar got in <u>through</u> the window.
⑤ The company will <u>support</u> customers in Europe.

서답형

06 다음 주어진 우리말에 맞게 빈칸을 채우시오.

(1) 우리는 다른 사람들과 조화를 이루며 살 수 있기를 원한다.
➡ We want to be able to live in _____ with other people.

(2) 그녀의 발명 덕분에 많은 사람들이 더 나은 생활을 하고 있다.
➡ _____ to her invention, many people live better lives.

01 다음 괄호 안의 단어를 문맥에 맞게 고쳐 쓰시오.

(1) Jackson is so _____ in fine arts. (interest)

(2) We were all _____ at the news. (amaze)

02 다음 두 문장이 같은 의미가 되도록 빈칸을 채우시오.

> She moved back home to _____ for her elderly parents.
> = She moved back home to _____ care of her elderly parents.

03 다음 우리말에 맞도록 빈칸에 알맞은 말을 쓰시오.

(1) 허리케인 시즌만 되면 수백 명의 사람들이 목숨을 잃습니다.
➡ _____ of people lose their lives every hurricane season.

(2) 네가 싫다. 그러니까 내 땅에 발을 들여놓지 마라.
➡ I hate you. So don't _____ foot on my property.

(3) 나는 새해가 행복으로 가득 차기를 바란다.
➡ I hope the New Year will be _____ with happiness!

04 다음 빈칸에 공통으로 들어갈 말을 쓰시오.

> • Mr. Smith will _____ a company next year.
> • Mike _____ something to eat in the room.

05 다음 빈칸에 들어갈 말을 〈보기〉에서 찾아 쓰시오.

> ┌ 보기 ┐
> as   at   for   in

(1) _____ last we won the game.

(2) The children are _____ danger now.

(3) He can't wait _____ the party.

(4) Ann's father is known _____ a great scientist.

06 다음 우리말에 맞게 주어진 단어를 바르게 배열하시오.

(1) 올해에 기쁨이 가득하길 바란다.
(be, joy, hope, I, of, will, this, full, year)
➡ _____

(2) 나는 그 드레스를 입어 보았지만 맞지가 않았다.
(I, it, the, on, fit, tried, didn't, dress, but)
➡ _____

Conversation

교과서

1 알고 있는지 묻기

> A: Do you know anything about King Sejong? (너는 세종대왕에 대해 아는 것이 있니?)
> B: No, I don't. (아니, 없어.)

■ 어떤 것에 관해 알고 있는지 물을 때는 'Do you know ~?'를 이용해 표현한다.

알고 있는지 묻기

- Do you know anything about that singer? (너는 저 가수에 대해 아는 것이 있니?)
- Do you know who Jane Goodall is? (Jane Goodall이 누구인지 알고 있니?)
- Do you know that Ann's father is an actor? (너는 Ann의 아버지가 배우라는 것을 알고 있니?)
- What do you know about BTS? (너는 BTS에 대해 무엇을 알고 있니?)
- Can you guess what it is? (이게 무엇인지 추측할 수 있겠니?)

알고 있는지 답하기

- No, I don't. (아니, 몰라.)
- Yes, I do. (응, 알아.)
- Yes, a little. (응, 조금 알아.)
- Sure, I do. They're famous singers. (물론, 알지. 그들은 유명한 가수야.)

A: Do you know anything about Changdeoggung? (너는 창덕궁에 대해 아는 것이 있니?)
B: Yes, a little. It's famous for its beautiful garden. (응, 조금. 그것은 아름다운 정원으로 유명해.)

핵심 Check

1. 다음 우리말과 일치하도록 빈칸에 알맞은 말을 쓰시오.

    A: _____ the musical *Cats*? (너는 뮤지컬 Cats에 대해 아는 것이 있니?)

    B: Yes. It's famous for the song "Memory". (응. 그것은 Memory라는 노래로 유명해.)

    A: _____ giraffes sleep only about 2 hours a day? (너는 기린이 하루에 겨우 2시간만 자는 것을 아니?)

    B: No, I don't. That's surprising! (아니, 몰라. 그거 참 놀랍구나!)

2 설명 요청하기

> A: Could you explain the rules of *bisachigi*? (너 비사치기의 규칙에 대해 설명해 줄 수 있니?)
>
> B: Each player throws a stone at another stone. (각 경기자가 돌을 던져 다른 돌에 맞히는 거야.)

■ 'Can[Could] you explain ~?'은 '너는 ~을 설명해 줄 수 있니?'라는 뜻으로, 상대방에게 설명을 요청할 때 쓰는 표현이다. 공손하게 표현할 때는 can 대신 could를 쓰며 explain 대신 tell을 쓸 수 있다.

설명 요청하기

- Can you explain this painting? (이 그림을 설명해 줄 수 있니?)
- Could you explain what this meaning is? (이 의미가 무엇인지 설명해 주실 수 있나요?)
- I don't get it. Can you explain why? (이해가 안 가요. 이유를 설명해 줄 수 있나요?)
- Can you tell me how to use the buttons? (버튼 사용법을 말해 줄 수 있니?)
- Can you show me how to use this machine? (어떻게 이 기계를 사용하는지 알려줄 수 있나요?)

핵심 Check

2. 다음 우리말과 일치하도록 빈칸에 알맞은 말을 쓰시오.

   A: Can you _____ this poem? (이 시를 설명해 줄 수 있니?)

   B: Sure. (물론이지.)

   A: _____ you _____ this painting? (이 그림에 대해 설명을 해 주시겠습니까?)

   B: Sure. It's *the Two Sisters* by Renoir. (물론이죠. 이 그림은 르누아루의 "두 자매"예요.)

3. 다음 우리말과 일치하도록 주어진 단어를 배열하여 문장을 만드시오.

   A: _____ (you, your, to, plan, save, money, could, explain) (돈을 절약할 너의 계획에 대해 설명해 줄 수 있니?)

   B: I won't waste my money on snacks. (간식에 돈을 낭비하지 않을 거야.)

Listen & Speak 1 B-1

B: ❶Do you know anything about Korean history?

G: ❷I don't know much about it but I'm interested in it.

B: ❸Can you help me with my history homework?

G: Sure. ❹No problem.

B: 너는 한국 역사에 대해 아는 것이 있니?

G: 그것에 대해 많이 알지는 못하지만, 관심은 있어.

B: 내 역사 숙제를 도와 줄 수 있니?

G: 물론이지. 문제없어.

❶ Do you know anything about ~?은 어떤 것에 대해 알고 있는지 묻는 표현이다.
❷ it=Korean history / be interested in: ~에 관심이 있다
❸ help A with ~: A가 ~하는 것을 돕다
❹ No problem.: 문제없어. (상대방의 제안에 승낙하는 표현)

Check(√) True or False

(1) The boy knows much about Korean history.   T ☐ F ☐

(2) The girl will help the boy with his history homework.   T ☐ F ☐

Wrap Up

B: Do you know anything about a *dol* party?

G: Yes. ❶It's the birthday party for a one-year-old baby.

B: ❷Could you tell me more about it?

G: ❸Well, the family members get together for the party, and the birthday baby wears a *hanbok*.

B: ❹That sounds interesting.

G: ❺The family members share food and wish for a long life for the baby. It's a Korean tradition.

B: 넌 돌잔치에 대해 아는 것이 있니?

G: 응. 그건 한 살 먹은 아기를 위한 생일잔치야.

B: 그것에 대해 더 말해 줄 수 있니?

G: 음. 그 잔치를 위해 가족들이 함께 모이고 생일을 맞은 아기는 한복을 입어.

B: 그거 재미있구나.

G: 가족들은 음식을 함께 나누어 먹고 아기가 오래 살기를 바라. 그건 한국의 전통이야.

❶ a one-year-old baby: 한 살 먹은 아기
❷ Could you tell me more about it?: 그것에 대해 더 말해 줄 수 있니? (상대방에게 설명을 요청하는 표현이다.)
❸ get together: 함께 모이다
❹ That은 지시대명사로 앞 문장의 내용을 가리킨다.
❺ share food: 음식을 나누어 먹다 wish for: ~을 바라다

Check(√) True or False

(3) The *dol* party is the birthday party for a one-year-old baby.   T ☐ F ☐

(4) The boy has attended the *dol* party before.   T ☐ F ☐

Listen & Speak 1 B-3

B: Do you know anything about this writer?

G: Yes. ❶I've read some of his novels. Why?

B: ❷How were they? ❸I'm thinking of buying his books.

G: ❹You shouldn't. ❺I didn't enjoy his books that much.

❶ I've read=I have read 'have+p.p.'의 현재완료 구문이다.

❷ they=his novels

❸ think of ~ing: ~할 생각이다

❹ shouldn't=should not: 금지를 나타낸다.

❺ that much: 그렇게 많이 that은 지시부사로 쓰여 '그렇게, 그만큼'의 뜻을 나타낸다.

Listen & Speak 2 C

A: ❶Could you explain your plan to save money?

B: ❷I won't waste my money on snacks.

❶ to save money는 plan을 수식하는 형용사적 용법이다.

❷ waste one's money on: ~에 돈을 낭비하다

Listen & Speak 2 B-1

G: ❶Can you explain this poem?

B: Sure. ❷It was written by Yun Dongju.

G: What's it about?

B: It's about him missing his hometown.

❶ Can you explain ~?은 어떤 것에 대해 설명을 요청하는 표현이다. Can 대신에 Could를 쓰면 더 정중한 요청이 된다.

❷ It=this poem / was written은 과거형 수동태이다.

Real-Life Zone

G: What are *hanoks*? Do you know anything about them?

M: *Hanoks* are traditional Korean houses. ❶They are designed to be in harmony with nature.

G: ❷Could you explain a little more about them?

M: *Hanoks* are cool in the summer and warm in the winter.

W: ❸That sounds interesting. Where can I see these traditional houses?

M: There's a *hanok* village near here.

G: ❹How about going there and seeing the *hanoks*?

W: Good idea! ❺How can we get there?

M: ❻You can take Bus Number 5 over there at the bus stop.

Listen & Speak 2 B-2

B: ❶Could you explain what Helping Hands is?

G: ❷It's a volunteer group in our community.

B: Could you tell me more about it?

G: ❸Well, they take care of children in need.

❶ what Helping Hands is는 간접의문문으로 explain의 목적어이다.

❷ community: 지역 사회

❸ take care of: ~을 돌보다 in need: 어려움에 처한

❶ be designed to ~: ~하도록 설계되다 be in harmony with: ~와 조화를 이루다

❷ a little more: 좀 더 많이

❸ That은 지시대명사로 앞 문장의 내용을 가리킨다.

❹ How about ~ing?: ~하는 게 어때?

❺ get there=get to the *hanok* village

❻ over there at the bus stop: 저기 버스 정류장에서

● 다음 우리말과 일치하도록 빈칸에 알맞은 말을 쓰시오.

Listen & Speak 1 B-2

G: _____ you know _____ about Changdeokgung?

B: Yes, a _____. It's _____ _____ its beautiful garden.

G: I'm _____ _____ go there _____ my Chinese friend.

B: I _____ you'll _____ it.

Listen & Speak 2 A

B: Could you _____ this _____?

W: Sure. It's the *Two Sisters* by Renoir. He _____ it in 1881.

Listen & Speak 2 B-1

1. G: Can you _____ this poem?

   B: Sure. It _____ _____ by Yun Dongju.

   G: What's it _____?

   B: It's _____ him _____ his hometown.

2. B: Could you _____ what Helping Hands is?

   G: It's a _____ _____ in our community.

   B: Could you _____ me _____ about it?

   G: Well, they _____ _____ of children in need.

Listen & Speak 2 C

A: _____ you _____ your plan to save money?

B: I won't _____ my money _____ snacks.

Real-Life Zone A

G: _____ are *hanoks*? Do you know _____ _____ them?

M: *Hanoks* are traditional _____ _____. They _____ _____ to be _____ _____ with nature.

G: Could you explain _____ _____ more about them?

M: *Hanoks* are _____ in the summer and _____ in the winter.

W: That _____ interesting. _____ can I _____ these traditional houses?

M: There's a *hanok* village _____ _____.

G: How _____ _____ there and _____ the *hanoks*?

W: Good _____! _____ can we _____ there?

M: You can _____ Bus Number 5 _____ _____ at the bus stop.

W: 그거 재미있네요. 이 전통 가옥을 어디에서 볼 수 있어요?
M: 이 근처에 한옥 마을이 있어요.
G: 거기 가서 한옥들을 보는 게 어때요?
W: 좋은 생각이구나! 그곳에 어떻게 갈 수 있죠?
M: 저기 버스 정류장에서 5번 버스를 타시면 돼요.

Real-Life Zone B

1. A: Do you _____ _____ about the Great Wall of China?

   B: Yes. It is one of the _____ _____ in the world.

   A: Can you explain _____ it is _____?

   B: It's _____ it is the _____ _____ in the world.

2. A: Do you know anything _____ the _____ *The Old Man and the Sea*?

   B: Yes. It is a _____ _____ written by Ernest Hemingway.

   A: Can you _____ _____ it is famous?

   B: It's because Hemingway _____ the Pulitzer Prize in 1953 _____ this novel.

1. A: 중국의 만리장성에 대해 아는 것이 있나요?
   B: 네. 그것은 세계에서 멋진 광경들 중의 하나예요.
   A: 그것이 왜 유명한지 설명해 줄 수 있나요?
   B: 세계에서 가장 긴 성벽이기 때문이죠.

2. A: '노인과 바다'라는 소설에 대해 아는 것이 있나요?
   B: 네. 그것은 어니스트 헤밍웨이가 쓴 소설이에요.
   A: 그것이 왜 유명한지 설명해 줄 수 있나요?
   B: 헤밍웨이가 이 책으로 1953년 풀리쳐상을 받았기 때문이죠.

Real-Life Zone B e.g.

A: Do you _____ _____ about the Eiffel Tower?

B: Yes. It _____ _____ in 1889 by Gustave Eiffel.

A: Can you _____ _____ it is famous?

B: _____ _____ it was the _____ _____ in the world at that time.

A: 너는 에펠탑에 대해 아는 것이 있니?
B: 응. 그것은 1889년에 Gustave Eiffel에 의해 세워졌어.
A: 그것이 왜 유명한지 설명할 수 있니?
B: 그것은 그 당시 그 탑이 세계에서 가장 높은 탑이었기 때문이야.

Wrap Up

B: Do you _____ _____ about a *dol* party?

G: Yes. It's the _____ party for a one-year-old baby.

B: Could you _____ me _____ about it?

G: Well, the family members _____ _____ for the party, and the birthday baby _____ a *hanbok*.

B: That sounds _____.

G: The family members _____ _____ and _____ _____ a long life for the baby. It's a _____ _____.

B: 넌 돌잔치에 대해 아는 것이 있니?
G: 응. 그건 한 살 먹은 아기를 위한 생일잔치야.
B: 그것에 대해 더 말해 줄 수 있니?
G: 음, 그 잔치를 위해 가족들이 함께 모이고 생일을 맞은 아기는 한복을 입어.
B: 그거 재미있구나.
G: 가족들은 음식을 함께 나누어 먹고 아기가 오래 살기를 바라. 그건 한국의 전통이야.

01 다음 대화의 빈칸에 알맞은 것을 고르시오.

> B: _____
>
> G: I don't know much about it but I'm interested in it.
>
> B: Can you help me with my history homework?
>
> G: Sure. No problem.

① Are you interested in Korean history?

② What do you know about Korean history?

③ Have you ever studied Korean history?

④ Do you know anything about Korean history?

⑤ May I help you with your history homework?

02 다음 대화의 순서를 바르게 배열하시오.

> (A) I'm going to go there with my Chinese friend.
>
> (B) Yes, a little. It's famous for its beautiful garden.
>
> (C) Do you know anything about Changdeokgung?
>
> (D) I think you'll like it.

➡ _____

03 다음 대화의 밑줄 친 부분의 의도로 알맞은 것을 고르시오.

> B: <u>Could you explain what Helping Hands is?</u>
>
> G: It's a volunteer group in our community.
>
> B: Could you tell me more about it?
>
> G: Well, they take care of children in need.

① 안부 묻기　　　　② 설명 요청하기

③ 충고 구하기　　　　④ 직업 묻기

⑤ 취미 말하기

[01~03] 다음 대화를 읽고 물음에 답하시오.

> G: (A) _____
> B: Sure. It (B) (wrote / was written) by Yun Dongju.
> G: What's it about?
> B: It's about him missing his hometown.

01 위 대화의 빈칸 (A)에 알맞은 말을 고르시오.

① Who wrote this poem?
② Can you explain this poem?
③ Why do you like this poem?
④ Do you like poems?
⑤ Do you know that Yun Donju wrote many poems?

 서답형
02 위 대화의 괄호 (B)에 알맞은 것을 고르시오.

➡ _____

03 위 대화를 읽고 답할 수 있는 질문은?

① Does the girl like poems?
② What is the title of this poem?
③ Does the boy like Yun Dongju?
④ What is this poem about?
⑤ Why is the girl interested in this poem?

04 다음 중 짝지어진 대화가 <u>어색한</u> 것은?

① A: Could you explain the rules of *bisachigi*?
B: Sure. Each player throws a stone at another stone.
② A: How was the English test today?
B: I didn't do well. I was sleepy during the test.
③ A: Do you know anything about your sister's interest?
B: Yes. She's into making pottery.
④ A: Do you know anything about King Sejong?
B: No, I don't. He is the king who invented Hangeul.
⑤ A: How do you like this restaurant?
B: The food is okay, but the service is terrible.

05 다음 대화의 순서를 바르게 배열한 것을 고르시오.

> (A) It's because it was the tallest tower in the world at that time.
> (B) Can you explain why it is famous?
> (C) Do you know anything about the Eiffel Tower?
> (D) Yes. It was built in 1889 by Gustave Eiffel.

① (B) - (A) - (C) - (D)
② (B) - (C) - (A) - (D)
③ (C) - (A) - (B) - (D)
④ (C) - (B) - (A) - (D)
⑤ (C) - (D) - (B) - (A)

[06~09] 다음 대화를 읽고 물음에 답하시오.

B: Do you know anything about a *dol* party?
G: Yes. It's the birthday party for a one-year-old baby.
B: (A) _____
G: Well, the family members get together for the party, and the birthday baby wears a *hanbok*.
B: (B)That sounds interesting.
G: The family members (C)_____ food and wish for a long life for the baby. It's a Korean tradition.

06 위 대화의 빈칸 (A)에 알맞은 것은?

① Could you tell me more about it?
② Why do they have a *dol* party?
③ Do your family members get together often?
④ Shall I tell you about the *dol* party?
⑤ When do your family members get together?

서답형
07 위 대화의 밑줄 친 (B)가 가리키는 것을 우리말로 쓰시오.

➡ _____

_____

서답형
08 위 대화의 빈칸 (C)에 다음 정의에 해당하는 단어를 써 넣으시오.

to have something, use it, or occupy it with another person

➡ _____

중요
09 위 대화의 내용으로 보아 알 수 없는 것은?

① The boy knows about a *dol* party.
② A *dol* party is the birthday party for a one-year-old baby.
③ The birthday baby wears a hanbok at a *dol* party.
④ The boy wants to attend a *dol* party.
⑤ A *dol* party is a Korean tradition.

[10~12] 다음 대화를 읽고 물음에 답하시오.

A: Do you know anything about the novel *The Old Man and the Sea*?
B: Yes. It is a short novel (A)write by Ernest Hemingway.
A: Can you (B)_____ why it is famous?
B: It's because Hemingway won the Pulitzer Prize in 1953 for this novel.

서답형
10 위 대화의 밑줄 친 (A)를 알맞은 형으로 고치시오.

➡ _____

중요
11 위 대화의 빈칸 (B)에 알맞은 것은?

① know   ② explain
③ think   ④ imagine
⑤ suggest

서답형
12 What did Hemingway win in 1953? Answer in English.

➡ _____

[01~05] 다음 대화를 읽고 물음에 답하시오.

G: What are *hanoks*? Do you know anything about them?

M: *Hanoks* are traditional Korean houses. They are designed to be (A)_____ harmony with nature.

G: Could you explain a little more about them?

M: *Hanoks* are (B)_____ in the summer and warm in the winter.

G: That sounds (C)_____(interest). Where can I see these traditional houses?

M: There's a *hanok* village near here.

G: (D)How about going there and seeing the *hanoks*?

W: Good idea! (E)How can we get there?

M: You can take Bus Number 5 over there at the bus stop.

01 위 대화의 빈칸 (A)에 알맞은 전치사를 쓰시오.

➡ _____

02 위 대화의 빈칸 (B)에 흐름상 알맞은 말을 쓰시오.

➡ _____

03 빈칸 (C)를 괄호 안에 주어진 단어를 이용하여 채우시오.

➡ _____

04 위 대화의 밑줄 친 (D)와 같은 뜻이 되도록 다음 문장의 빈칸에 알맞은 말을 쓰시오.

➡ _____ we go there and see the *hanoks*?

05 위 대화의 밑줄 친 (E)와 같은 뜻이 되도록 다음 문장의 빈칸에 알맞은 말을 쓰시오.

➡ Do you know _____ _____ get there?

[06~07] 다음 대화를 읽고 물음에 답하시오.

A: Do you know anything about the Great Wall of China?

B: Yes. (A)It is one of the greatest sight in the world.

A: Can you explain (B)_____ it is famous?

B: It's (C)_____ it is the longest wall in the world.

06 위 대화의 밑줄 친 (A)에서 어법상 어색한 것을 고치시오.

_____ ➡ _____

07 위 대화의 빈칸 (B)와 (C)에 각각 알맞은 말을 쓰시오.

(B) _____ (C) _____

Grammar

① 목적격보어로 to부정사를 취하는 동사

> • Japanese officials **pressed** him to **build** Japanese houses.
> 일본인 관리들은 그에게 일본식 가옥을 지으라고 압박했다.
>
> • The woman **asked** me **to wait** for her at the hall.
> 그 여인은 내게 홀에서 자기를 기다리라고 요청했다.

■ 형태: want/ask/tell/advise/order 등 + 목적어 + to부정사

■ 의미: ~가 …하기를 바라다, ~에게 …하기를 요청하다, ~에게 …하라고 말하다, ~에게 …하라고 충고하다, ~에게 …하라고 명령하다

  • I **want** you **to finish** your homework first. 나는 네가 숙제를 먼저 끝내길 원해.

  • Mom **told** me **to put** out the trash. 엄마는 나에게 쓰레기를 내놓으라고 말씀하셨다.

■ to부정사를 목적격보어로 취하는 동사에는 want, ask, tell 외에도 advise, allow, beg, cause, enable, encourage, expect, force, get, order, persuade, press 등이 있다.

  • They **advised** him **to leave** the place as soon as possible.
  그들은 그에게 가능한 한 빨리 그곳을 떠나라고 조언했다.

■ to부정사의 부정형은 'not[never]+to 동사원형'이다.

  • She **asked** me **not to say** anything. 그녀는 나에게 아무 말도 하지 말라고 요청했다.

  • The doctor **ordered** me **not to drink** alcohol. 의사는 나에게 술을 마시지 말라고 명령했다.

핵심 Check

1. 다음 괄호 안에서 알맞은 것을 고르시오.

   (1) She wanted me (to buy / buy) her a bag.

   (2) I expected him (to be / being) a soccer player.

   (3) He asked them (be / to be) quiet.

2. 다음 우리말과 일치하도록 빈칸에 알맞은 말을 쓰시오. (철자가 주어진 것도 있음.)

   (1) 우리는 그녀가 늦을 것이라고 예상했다.

   ➡ We _____ her _____ _____ late.

   (2) 갑작스런 굉음 때문에 나는 펄쩍 뛰었다.

   ➡ A sudden noise c_____ me _____ j_____.

   (3) 그들은 그에게 서류에 서명하도록 강요했다.

   ➡ They f_____ him _____ _____ the paper.

2 명사를 수식하는 현재분사와 과거분사

> • Jeong Segwon wanted to help the **suffering** people.
> 정세권은 고통 받는 사람들을 돕기를 원했다.
>
> • Through his efforts, we now have Buckchon **filled** with its beautiful *hanoks*.
> 그의 노력으로 우리에게는 지금 아름다운 한옥으로 가득 차 있는 북촌이 있다.

■ 분사는 Ving 형태를 취하는 **현재분사**와, p.p. 형태를 취하는 **과거분사**로 나뉘며, 모두 명사를 수식하거나 설명하는 형용사 역할을 한다. **현재분사**는 '~하는'이라는 의미로 **능동**이나 **진행**의 의미를 나타내고, **과거분사**는 '~된'이라는 의미로 **수동**이나 **완료**의 의미를 나타낸다.

  • I saw a **crying** baby. 나는 우는 아기를 봤어.

  • Look at the water **polluted** by the waste. 쓰레기로 오염된 물을 보세요.

■ 분사가 단독으로 명사를 수식할 때에는 일반적으로 명사 앞에서 수식하지만, 다른 어구와 함께 명사를 수식할 때에는 명사 뒤에서 수식한다.

  • Look at the **laughing** children. 웃고 있는 아이들을 보아라.

  • People **living** in the village felt happy. 그 마을에 사는 사람들은 행복했다.

  • I found a **broken** vase. 나는 깨진 꽃병을 발견했다.

  • Kevin found a letter **written** on his notebook. Kevin은 자신의 공책 위에 쓰여진 편지를 발견했다.

■ **have[get]+목적어+과거분사**', '**지각동사+목적어+과거분사**'는 목적어와 목적격보어의 관계가 수동인 경우 쓰인다.

  • Jason **had** the man **repair** his car. Jason은 그 남자가 자신의 차를 수리하게 했다.

  = Jason **had** his car **repaired** by the man. Jason은 그의 차가 그 남자에 의해 수리되게 했다.

■ 'Ving'로 형태가 같은 현재분사와 동명사의 차이를 구별하자. 현재분사는 '~하는', '~하는 중인'이라고 해석되고, 동명사는 '~하는 것'이라고 해석되거나 'V를 용도로 하는 명사'로 해석된다.

  • There is a **sleeping** baby. [현재분사] 잠자는 아기가 있다.

  • Did you find your **sleeping** bag? [동명사] 너의 침낭을 찾았니? (잠자는 데 쓰이는 가방 – 침낭)

핵심 Check

3. 다음 주어진 동사를 어법에 맞게 빈칸에 쓰시오.

   (1) 너는 그 노래 부르는 소녀를 보았니?

   ➡ Did you see the _____ girl? (sing)

   (2) 나는 John에 의해 쓰여진 책을 읽었어.

   ➡ I read the book _____ by John. (write)

   (3) 너는 무언가를 쓰고 있는 그 소녀를 아니?

   ➡ Do you know the girl _____ something? (write)

01 다음 빈칸에 알맞은 것은?

| I asked him _____ off the TV. |

① turn   ② turns   ③ turned

④ turning   ⑤ to turn

02 다음 괄호 안에서 알맞은 것을 고르시오.

(1) The girl (eating / eaten) cookies is Susan.

(2) We want to find the treasure (hiding / hidden) in the ocean.

(3) The two boys (talking / talked) to each other are Tom and Sam.

(4) All the people (inviting / invited) to the party are enjoying themselves.

03 다음 문장에서 어법상 <u>어색한</u> 것을 찾아 바르게 고쳐 다시 쓰시오.

(1) I want you clean the windows.

➡ _____

(2) Timothy got an email sending by a stranger this morning.

➡ _____

(3) Who are the boys played soccer on the ground?

➡ _____

(4) Tell her buying a comfortable pair of shoes!

➡ _____

04 다음 우리말에 맞게 주어진 어구를 바르게 배열하시오.

(1) Jack은 그의 아내에게 진주로 만든 목걸이를 주었다.

(Jack, pearls, his wife, made, gave, a, necklace, of)

➡ _____

(2) 칼로 소고기 샌드위치를 자르고 있는 남자는 누구니? (the beef sandwiches, knife, the man, a, who, cutting, is, with)

➡ _____

(3) Mike는 그녀에게 일찍 잠자리에 들라고 충고했다. (Mike, go, her, advised, early, to, to, bed)

➡ _____

01 다음 중 빈칸에 들어갈 말로 가장 적절한 것은?

My dad had his shoes _____ .

① to shine
② shining
③ shined
④ to shining
⑤ shine

02 다음 중 어법상 올바른 것은?

① Do you want me clean your house for you?
② He told Perry putting on a yellow shirt.
③ She didn't allow us to play the piano.
④ The doctor advised Ted stopped smoking.
⑤ Ms. Green asked him carried the boxes.

03 다음 밑줄 친 부분의 쓰임이 나머지 넷과 다른 하나는?

① The girl walking in the park is my sister.
② Do you know the woman talking to Tom?
③ The alarm clock ringing noisily is Jason's.
④ The boy singing on the stage is my best friend.
⑤ I started taking the chess class on weekends.

04 다음 빈칸에 알맞은 말이 바르게 짝지어진 것은?

• Who is the girl _____ beside the piano?
• Frank expected Jane _____ him.

① singing – helped
② singing – to help
③ sang – helped
④ sang – to help
⑤ sings – helping

05 다음 빈칸에 공통으로 들어갈 수 있는 것을 고르시오.

• Kirk _____ Jenny to take part in the party.
• Harold _____ to know what was in the box.

① asked
② wanted
③ invited
④ told
⑤ advised

06 다음 괄호 안에서 알맞은 말을 고르시오.

(1) Who is the girl (carries / carrying) a basket?
(2) I got an e-mail (written / writing) in Chinese.
(3) Look at the (cat sleeping / sleeping cat).

07 다음 빈칸에 들어갈 말로 알맞게 짝지어진 것은?

> • Kate warned her son _____ fast food.
> • Jerome asked me _____ the TV volume.

① not to eat – to turn down
② not eating – to turn down
③ to not eat – turning down
④ not eating – turning down
⑤ not eat – turn down

 다음 밑줄 친 부분이 어법상 어색한 것을 고르시오.

① The boy <u>played</u> soccer on the ground is my brother.
② The man <u>driving</u> the red car almost hit my sister.
③ He bought a cell phone <u>made</u> in Korea.
④ Who is the boy <u>drinking</u> milk at the table?
⑤ This is the picture <u>painted</u> by Gogh.

서답형
09 주어진 동사를 어법에 맞게 빈칸에 쓰시오.

(1) My best friend Bill often asks me _____ him. (help)
(2) My dad doesn't allow me _____ out at night. (go)
(3) Marianne ordered him _____ with her. (stay)
(4) The manager warned him _____ any pictures here. (take, not)

서답형
10 다음 문장에서 어법상 어색한 부분을 바르게 고쳐 쓰시오.

(1) I know the boy kick a ball there.
_____ ➡ _____
(2) Who is the playing badminton man?
_____ ➡ _____
(3) The baby crying is Kate's son.
_____ ➡ _____

11 다음 빈칸에 들어갈 괄호 안에 주어진 동사의 형태가 <u>다른</u> 하나는?

① I want you _____ the dishes. (wash)
② Mom made me _____ playing the computer games. (stop)
③ They got him _____ a new contract. (sign)
④ She asked him _____ to the movies together. (go)
⑤ He didn't allow me _____ camping. (go)

12 다음 밑줄 친 부분의 쓰임이 어색한 것은?

① I'm reading a play <u>written</u> by Shakespeare.
② You can see many people <u>dancing</u> to the music.
③ Who is the man <u>playing</u> the piano?
④ I found a cat <u>lie</u> in the sun.
⑤ Do you know the boy <u>sitting</u> next to David?

 다음 중 어법상 어색한 부분을 찾아 바르게 고친 것은?

> Mom wants Tom come home by 5:30.

① wants → want   ② Tom → Tom's
③ come → to come   ④ home → to home
⑤ by → to

14 다음 빈칸에 들어갈 말이 바르게 짝지어진 것은?

> • The man _____ the phone is my uncle.
> • The boys _____ to dinner were two hours late.

① answering – inviting
② answers – invited
③ answering – invited
④ answers – inviting
⑤ answering – to invite

15 다음 중 어법상 올바르지 <u>않은</u> 것은?

① They asked me to stay there.
② Susan, do you want me to dance?
③ I made her clean her room.
④ Tell her to come to my office.
⑤ Dad didn't allow me going to the dance party.

서답형

16 동사 write를 어법에 맞게 빈칸에 쓰시오.

> • My cousin is the boy _____ something on his notebook.
> • Did you see the letter _____ in Korean?

➡ _____, _____

17 다음 문장의 빈칸에 알맞지 <u>않은</u> 것은?

> Yuna _____ him to follow her advice.

① made   ② wanted
③ asked   ④ expected
⑤ advised

18 다음 우리말에 맞게 영작한 것을 고르시오.

> 너는 태권도를 배우고 있는 저 여자아이를 아니?

① Do you know that girl learn *taekwondo*?
② Do you know that girl learns *taekwondo*?
③ Do you know that girl to learn *taekwondo*?
④ Do you know that girl learning *taekwondo*?
⑤ Do you know that girl to learning *taekwondo*?

서답형

19 주어진 어구를 활용하여 다음 우리말을 영어로 쓰시오.

(1) 나의 부모님은 항상 내게 학교에서 최선을 다하라고 말씀하신다. (always, do, best, in school)
➡ _____

(2) 건강했기 때문에 그는 그 계획을 수행할 수 있었다. (good health, carry out, enable)
➡ _____

20 다음 밑줄 친 부분의 쓰임이 나머지와 <u>다른</u> 것은?

① Look at the woman <u>walking</u> down the road.
② Do you know the boy <u>wearing</u> a mask?
③ Jenny loves <u>going</u> hiking.
④ My brother is <u>washing</u> the dishes.
⑤ The girls <u>dancing</u> to the music are my friends.

01 다음 문장에서 어법상 어색한 부분을 바르게 고쳐 쓰시오.

(1) She asked her brother helping her with her homework.

_____ ➡ _____

(2) Jim wanted her go shopping with him.

_____ ➡ _____

(3) They advised him left the place as soon as possible.

_____ ➡ _____

(4) I watched the excited bowling game on TV.

_____ ➡ _____

(5) Who is the boy throws a ball?

_____ ➡ _____

(6) Nancy had his husband to repair their car.

_____ ➡ _____

02 주어진 어휘를 어법에 맞게 빈칸에 쓰시오.

(1) The name of a fruit _____ with "m" is melon. (begin)

(2) It looks like a person _____ with open arms. (dance)

(3) The woman _____ at the news started to cry. (frighten)

(4) They are the photos _____ there. (take)

03 다음 괄호 안에서 알맞은 것을 고르시오.

(1) He told me (came / to come) home before 9 o'clock.

(2) Harry wanted me (doing / to do) it at once.

(3) My mom (expects / hopes) me to be a teacher.

(4) She allowed her daughter (go / to go) to the K-pop concert.

04 주어진 어휘를 이용하여 다음 우리말을 영작하시오.

(1) 선생님은 내게 문을 닫아달라고 부탁하셨다. (the teacher, ask, the door)

➡ _____

(2) 엄마는 내게 그 개를 산책시키라고 말씀하셨다. (mom, walk the dog)

➡ _____

(3) Kate는 눈으로 덮인 산을 올라갔다. (climb, cover)

➡ _____

(4) 언제 깨진 창문을 고칠 거예요? (going, fix, break)

➡ _____

(5) Mariko는 공원에서 그녀의 딸이 놀고 있는 것을 바라보았다. (look, play)

➡ _____

05 다음 두 문장을 같은 뜻을 갖는 한 문장으로 바꿔 쓰시오.

(1) • The business woman is Sophie.
   • She is running a big company.
➡ _____
  _____

(2) • There is a bridge in our village.
   • It was built long time ago.
➡ _____

06 다음 상황에 알맞은 말을 어법에 맞게 빈칸에 쓰시오.

(1) The driver drove the car very fast. He said to his driver, "Don't drive so fast."
➡ He ordered his driver _____
_____ _____ _____.

(2) Paul is good at playing the guitar. So Bella said to him, "Will you play the piano for us?"
➡ Bella asked Paul _____ _____
_____ _____ _____.

07 다음 주어진 단어를 어법에 맞게 빈칸에 쓰시오.

> hit / excite / play / amaze / repair

(1) The girl _____ badminton is my sister.
(2) I have an _____ story to tell you.
(3) We had the car _____ by Potter and Parker.
(4) Jina is an _____ basketball player.
(5) Did you see the building _____ by a dump truck?

08 다음 괄호 안에 주어진 단어를 사용해 다음을 영작하시오.

(1) 그 여자는 그 남자에게 자기의 가방을 들어달라고 요청했다. (ask, carry)
➡ _____

(2) Emma는 나에게 내일까지 기다리라고 충고했다. (advise, till)
➡ _____

(3) Peter는 Sylvia에게 자기와 함께 춤을 추자고 말했다. (tell, dance)
➡ _____

(4) 그들은 그가 축제에 참가할 것으로 기대했다. (expect, participate, the festival)
➡ _____

(5) 좋은 건강이 그가 그 계획을 마칠 수 있도록 했다. (good, enable, finish)
➡ _____

09 다음 우리말의 의미에 맞게 빈칸에 알맞은 말을 쓰시오.

(1) 그 어린 주자들은 응원하는 군중 옆을 지나갔다.
➡ The young runners passed by the _____ crowd.

(2) 그 요리사는 얇게 잘린 양파를 차가운 물에 넣었다.
➡ The chef put the _____ onions in cold water.

10 다음 밑줄 친 부분이 동명사인지 현재분사인지 구별하고, 그 이유를 서술하시오.

> (1) They are underline{waiting} for you.
> (2) The underline{waiting} room is full of people.

(1) _____ ➡ 이유: _____
(2) _____ ➡ 이유: _____
_____
_____

Reading

The King of Architecture in Gyeongseong

Have you been to Bukchon? There is a beautiful *hanok* village in
Bukchon. It is popular with tourists who want to see Korea's past.

However, not many people know that Bukchon was created through one man's efforts. That man was Jeong Segwon, known as the King of Architecture in Gyeongseong.

Jeong Segwon was a businessman who founded Geonyangsa in 1920. At the time, Korea was ruled by Japan, and the Japanese were changing Gyeongseong to fit their taste. Many Japanese moving into Gyeongseong were building Japanese or Western houses. Jeong Segwon wanted to protect the *hanok* and help the suffering people. He said, "People are power. We Joseon people should keep Jongno and not let the Japanese set foot here." He bought the land between Gyeongbokgung and Changdeokgung.

There he built small, modern *hanoks* for the people. Through his efforts, we now have Bukchon filled with its beautiful *hanoks*.

architecture: 건축
popular: 인기 있는
tourist: 여행객
past: 과거
create: 만들다
effort: 노력
businessman: 사업가
rule: 지배하다, 통치하다
fit: ~에 맞추다
taste: 맛, 취향
move into: ~으로 이사 오다
set foot: 발을 들여놓다
modern: 현대적인

📎 **확인문제**

● 다음 문장이 본문의 내용과 일치하면 T, 일치하지 않으면 F를 쓰시오.

1 Tourists who want to see Korea's past go to Bukchon. ☐

2 Bukchon was created through many people's efforts. ☐

3 Japanese people who moved into Gyeongseong built Japanese or Western houses. ☐

4 Jeong Segwon built ancient *hanoks* to protect the *hanok*. ☐

Jeong Segwon helped the independence movement <u>in many ways</u>.
여러 방법으로

<u>For example</u>, he built the office building <u>for</u> the Joseon Language
예를 들면 ~을 위한
Society and supported its efforts <u>to keep</u> the Joseon language alive.
efforts를 수식하는 형용사적 용법 목적격보어
When the Joseon Language Affair <u>happened</u>, he <u>was caught</u> by the
was happend (x) 과거형 수동태
police and suffered <u>a lot</u>. Japanese officials <u>pressed</u> him to build
많이 press A to ~: ~하도록 A에게 압박을 가하다
Japanese houses. He said, "I don't know <u>how to build</u> Japanese
~하는 방법(know의 목적어)
houses." An official said, "You know <u>how to build</u> *hanoks*, so you can
=how you should build 그래서
build Japanese houses, too." But he did not do <u>what the Japanese told</u>
명사절로 do의 목적어
<u>him to do</u>. The cost was high. His business fell off, and he <u>lost</u> his
lose(잃다)의 과거형
property. <u>However</u>, in part, thanks to Jeong Segwon, the traditions of
그러나
Korea still live with us today.

independence: 독립
movement: 운동
office: 사무실
language: 언어
society: 사회, 학회
support: 지원하다
affair: 사건, 사태
happen: 일어나다, 발생하다
police: 경찰
suffer: 고통을 겪다
official: 관리
press: 압박을 가하다
cost: 비용, 대가
business: 사업
fall off: 쇠퇴하다
property: 재산
in part: 부분적으로는
thanks to: ~ 덕분에
tradition: 전통
still: 아직도, 여전히

 확인문제

● 다음 문장이 본문의 내용과 일치하면 T, 일치하지 <u>않으면</u> F를 쓰시오.

1 Jeong Segwon didn't participate in the independence movement. ☐

2 Jeong Segwon made an effort to keep the Joseon language alive. ☐

3 Jeong Segwon was caught by the police after the Joseon Language Affair. ☐

4 A Japanese official told Jeong Segwon to build Korean houses. ☐

5 Jeong Segwon lost his property because he didn't follow the Japanese official's order. ☐

● 우리말을 참고하여 빈칸에 알맞은 말을 쓰시오.

1 The King of _____ in Gyeongseong

2 _____ you _____ to Bukchon?

3 _____ _____ a beautiful *hanok* village in Bukchon.

4 It is _____ with tourists _____ want to see Korea's _____.

5 However, not many people _____ that Bukchon _____ _____ through one man's _____.

6 That man was Jeong Segwon, _____ _____ the King of Architecture in Gyeongseong.

7 Jeong Segwon was a businessman _____ _____ Geonyangsa in 1920.

8 At the _____, Korea _____ _____ by Japan, and the Japanese were changing Gyeongseong to _____ their _____.

9 Many Japanese _____ _____ Gyeongseong were building _____ or _____ houses.

10 Jeong Segwon _____ to _____ the *hanok* and help the _____ people.

11 He said, "People are _____. We Joseon people should _____ Jongno and not _____ the Japanese _____ _____ here."

12 He bought the land _____ Gyeongbokgung _____ Changdeokgung.

13 There he built small, _____ *hanoks* for the _____.

14 Through his _____, we now have Bukchon _____ _____ its beautiful *hanoks*.

1	경성의 건축왕
2	당신은 북촌에 다녀온 적이 있는가?
3	북촌에는 아름다운 한옥 마을이 있다.
4	그곳은 한국의 과거를 보고 싶어 하는 관광객들에게 인기가 있다.
5	그러나 북촌이 한 사람의 노력으로 만들어졌다는 것을 아는 사람은 많지 않다.
6	그 사람은 경성의 건축왕으로 알려진 정세권이었다.
7	정세권은 **1920**년에 건양사를 설립한 사업가였다.
8	그 당시 한국은 일본의 지배를 받았고, 일본인들은 경성을 그들의 취향에 맞게 바꾸고 있었다.
9	경성으로 이주하는 많은 일본인들은 일본식이나 서양식 집들을 짓고 있었다.
10	정세권은 한옥을 지키고 고통받는 사람들을 돕기를 원했다.
11	그는 말했다. "사람이 힘이다. 우리 조선 사람들은 종로를 지켜야 하며, 일본인들이 이곳에 발을 붙이지 못하게 해야 한다."
12	그는 경복궁과 창덕궁 사이의 땅을 샀다.
13	거기에 그는 사람들을 위해 작은 현대식 한옥들을 지었다.
14	그의 노력으로 북촌은 현재 아름다운 한옥으로 가득 차 있다.

15 Jeong Segwon helped the _____ _____ in many _____.

16 For _____, he built the office building for the Joseon Language Society and _____ its efforts to _____ the Joseon language _____.

17 When the Joseon Language Affair _____, he was _____ by the police and _____ a lot.

18 Japanese officials _____ him to _____ Japanese houses.

19 He said, "I don't know _____ _____ build Japanese houses."

20 An _____ said, "You _____ how to build *hanoks*, _____ you can _____ Japanese houses, too."

21 But he did not do _____ the Japanese _____ him to do.

22 The _____ was _____.

23 His business _____ off, and he lost his _____.

24 However, in _____, thanks _____ Jeong Segwon, the _____ of Korea _____ live with us today.

---

15 정세권은 여러 방법으로 독립운동을 도왔다.

16 예를 들면, 그는 조선어 학회를 위한 회관을 지었고 조선어를 지키려는 그들의 노력을 지원했다.

17 조선어 학회 사건이 발생했을 때 그는 경찰에 잡혀 많은 고통을 겪었다.

18 일본인 관리들은 그에게 일본식 가옥을 지으라고 압박했다.

19 그는 말했다. "나는 일본식 가옥을 지을 줄 모르오."

20 한 관리가 말했다. "당신은 한옥을 지을 줄 아오. 그러니 일본식 가옥도 지을 수 있소."

21 그러나 그는 그 일본인이 그에게 요구한 것을 하지 않았다.

22 그 대가는 컸다.

23 그의 사업은 쇠퇴했고, 그는 재산을 잃었다.

24 그러나 부분적으로나마, 정세권 덕분에 한국의 전통이 오늘날 여전히 우리와 함께 살아 있다.

● 우리말을 참고하여 본문을 영작하시오.

1 경성의 건축왕

➡ _____

2 당신은 북촌에 다녀온 적이 있는가?

➡ _____

3 북촌에는 아름다운 한옥 마을이 있다.

➡ _____

4 그곳은 한국의 과거를 보고 싶어 하는 관광객들에게 인기가 있다.

➡ _____

5 그러나 북촌이 한 사람의 노력으로 만들어졌다는 것을 아는 사람은 많지 않다.

➡ _____

6 그 사람은 경성의 건축왕으로 알려진 정세권이었다.

➡ _____

7 정세권은 1920년에 건양사를 설립한 사업가였다.

➡ _____

8 그 당시 한국은 일본의 지배를 받았고, 일본인들은 경성을 그들의 취향에 맞게 바꾸고 있었다.

➡ _____

9 경성으로 이주하는 많은 일본인들은 일본식이나 서양식 집들을 짓고 있었다.

➡ _____

10 정세권은 한옥을 지키고 고통받는 사람들을 돕기를 원했다.

➡ _____

11 그는 말했다. "사람이 힘이다. 우리 조선 사람들은 종로를 지켜야 하며, 일본인들이 이곳에 발을 붙이지 못하게 해야 한다."

➡ _____

➡ _____

12 그는 경복궁과 창덕궁 사이의 땅을 샀다.

➡ _____

13 거기에 그는 사람들을 위해 작은 현대식 한옥들을 지었다.

➡ _____

14 그의 노력으로 북촌은 현재 아름다운 한옥으로 가득 차 있다.

➡ _____

15 정세권은 여러 방법으로 독립운동을 도왔다.

➡ _____

16 예를 들면, 그는 조선어 학회를 위한 회관을 지었고 조선어를 지키려는 그들의 노력을 지원했다.

➡ _____

_____

17 조선어 학회 사건이 발생했을 때 그는 경찰에 잡혀 많은 고통을 겪었다.

➡ _____

18 일본인 관리들은 그에게 일본식 가옥을 지으라고 압박했다.

➡ _____

19 그는 말했다. "나는 일본식 가옥을 지을 줄 모르오."

➡ _____

20 한 관리가 말했다. "당신은 한옥을 지을 줄 아오. 그러니 일본식 가옥도 지을 수 있소."

➡ _____

21 그러나 그는 그 일본인이 그에게 요구한 것을 하지 않았다.

➡ _____

22 그 대가는 컸다.

➡ _____

23 그의 사업은 쇠퇴했고, 그는 재산을 잃었다.

➡ _____

24 그러나 부분적으로나마, 정세권 덕분에 한국의 전통이 오늘날 여전히 우리와 함께 살아 있다.

➡ _____

[01~05] 다음 글을 읽고 물음에 답하시오.

Jeong Segwon was a businessman ⓐ founded Geonyangsa in 1920. At the time, Korea was ruled by Japan, and the Japanese were changing Gyeongseong to fit their taste. ⓑMany Japanese moved into Gyeongseong were building Japanese or Western houses. Jeong Segwon wanted to ⓒ the hanok and help the suffering people. He said, "People are power. ⓓWe Joseon people should keep Jongno and not let the Japanese set foot here."

서답형

01 위 글의 빈칸 ⓐ에 알맞은 말을 쓰시오.

➡ _____

서답형

02 위 글의 밑줄 친 ⓑ의 문장에서 어법상 어색한 것을 고치시오.

➡ _____

중요

03 위 글의 빈칸 ⓒ에 알맞은 것은?

① found ② protect
③ invent ④ exchange
⑤ destroy

서답형

04 위 글의 밑줄 친 ⓓ를 우리말로 옮기시오.

➡ _____
_____

중요

05 위 글의 내용과 일치하지 않는 것은?

① 정세권은 1920년에 건양사를 설립했다.
② 그 당시 일본인들은 경성을 그들의 취향에 맞게 바꾸고 있었다.
③ 많은 일본인들이 경성으로 이주해 왔다.
④ 일본인들은 일본식 가옥과 서양식 가옥을 짓고 있었다.
⑤ 정세권은 일본인들이 종로에 발을 들여놓는 것에 신경 쓰지 않았다.

[06~08] 다음 글을 읽고 물음에 답하시오.

Have you been ⓐ Bukchon? There is a beautiful hanok village in Bukchon. ⓑ그곳은 한국의 과거를 보기를 원하는 사람들에게 인기가 있다. However, not many people know that Bukchon was created ⓒ one man's efforts. That man was Jeong Segwon, ⓓknow as the King of Architecture in Gyeongseong.

중요

06 위 글의 빈칸 ⓐ와 ⓒ에 들어갈 전치사가 바르게 짝지어진 것은?

① from – by ② in – by
③ for – from ④ to – through
⑤ for – through

서답형

07 위 글의 밑줄 친 ⓑ의 우리말에 맞게 주어진 어휘를 이용하여 11단어로 영작하시오.

| with, tourists, who |

➡ _____

서답형

08 위 글의 밑줄 친 ⓓ를 알맞은 어형으로 고치시오.

➡ _____

[09~12] 다음 글을 읽고 물음에 답하시오.

Jeong Segwon helped the independence movement ⓐ many ways. For example, he built the office building for the Joseon Language Society and supported its efforts ⓑto keep the Joseon language alive. When the Joseon Language Affair happened, he was caught by the police and suffered a lot. Japanese officials pressed him ⓒ Japanese houses. He said, "I don't know how to build Japanese houses."

09 위 글의 빈칸 ⓐ에 알맞은 전치사는?

① in   ② to

③ at   ④ from

⑤ with

10 위 글의 밑줄 친 ⓑto keep과 같은 용법으로 쓰인 것을 고르시오.

① I want to learn Chinese culture.

② Is there anything to eat in the fridge?

③ Were you glad to hear the news?

④ Love is to trust each other.

⑤ Her daughter grew up to be an actress.

11 위 글의 빈칸 ⓒ에 알맞은 것은?

① build   ② built

③ to build   ④ building

⑤ to building

12 위 글의 내용으로 보아 대답할 수 없는 것은?

① Why did Jeong Segwon help the independence movement?

② Who built the office building for the Joseon Language Society?

③ Did Jeong Segwon make an effort to keep the Joseon language alive?

④ When was Jeong Segwon caught by the police?

⑤ Did Jeong Segwon build Japanese houses?

[13~14] 다음 글을 읽고 물음에 답하시오.

An official said, "You know how to build *hanoks*, so you can build Japanese houses, too." But he did not do ⓐwhat the Japanese told him to do. The cost was high. His business fell ⓑ , and he lost his property. However, in part, thanks ⓒ Jeong Segwon, the traditions of Korea still live with us today.

13 아래 보기에서 위 글의 밑줄 친 ⓐwhat과 문법적 쓰임이 같은 것의 개수를 고르시오.

┌─── 보기 ───┐
① Guess what is in this box.
② He spent what he had earned.
③ What you must do is very important.
④ I gave her what she needed.
⑤ Ask her what she wants.
└───────────┘

① 1개   ② 2개   ③ 3개   ④ 4개   ⑤ 5개

14 위 글의 빈칸 ⓑ와 ⓒ에 알맞은 것으로 짝지어진 것은?

① of – to   ② from – in

③ with – of   ④ from – of

⑤ off – to

[15~18] 다음 글을 읽고 물음에 답하시오.

① Jeong Segwon said, "People are power. ② We Joseon people should keep Jongno and not ⓐ____ the Japanese set foot here." ③ He bought the land between Gyeongbokgung and Changdeokgung. ④ ⓑThrough his efforts, we now have Bukchon filled ⓒ____ its beautiful *hanoks*. ⑤

15 위 글의 흐름으로 보아, 주어진 문장이 들어가기에 가장 적절한 곳은?

There he built small, modern *hanoks* for the people.

① ② ③ ④ ⑤

16 위 글의 빈칸 ⓐ에 알맞은 것은?

① get
② make
③ let
④ take
⑤ allow

17 위 글의 밑줄 친 ⓑ와 같은 뜻으로 쓰인 것은?

① The doctor pushed his way through the crowd.
② The Charles River flows through Boston.
③ The children are too young to sit through a concert.
④ I couldn't hear their conversation through the wall.
⑤ You can only achieve success through hard work.

18 위 글의 빈칸 ⓒ에 알맞은 것은?

① of
② with
③ for
④ from
⑤ along

[19~21] 다음 글을 읽고 물음에 답하시오.

Have you been to Bukchon? There is a beautiful *hanok* village in Bukchon. ⓐIt is popular with tourists who want to see Korea's ⓑ____. However, not many people know that Bukchon was created through one man's efforts. That man was Jeong Segwon, known ⓒas the King of Architecture in Gyeongseong.

서답형
19 위 글의 밑줄 친 ⓐIt이 가리키는 것을 영어로 쓰시오.

➡ _____

서답형
20 위 글의 빈칸 ⓑ에 다음 정의에 해당하는 단어를 쓰시오.

the time before the present, and the things that have happened

➡ _____

21 위 글의 밑줄 친 ⓒas와 같은 뜻으로 쓰인 것은?

① My mother often sings as she works.
② I wish to work as an interpreter.
③ As it rained too much, we couln't go hiking.
④ Can you run as fast as Mike?
⑤ As we go higher, the air gets colder.

[22~25] 다음 글을 읽고 물음에 답하시오.

ⓐJeong Segwon was a businessman. He founded Geonyangsa in 1920. At the time, Korea was ruled by Japan, and the Japanese were changing Gycongseong ⓑto fit their taste. Many Japanese moving into Gyeongseong were building Japanese or Western houses. Jeong Segwon wanted to protect the *hanok* and help the suffering people. He said, "People are power. We Joseon people should keep Jongno and not let the Japanese set foot here."

서답형

22 위 글의 밑줄 친 ⓐ를 관계대명사를 써서 한 문장으로 만드시오.

➡ _____

_____

23 위 글의 밑줄 친 ⓑ와 용법이 같은 것은?

① My hope is to work as a doctor in Africa.

② It's time to go to bed now.

③ My job is to report the news.

④ The boys hoped to find the hidden treasure.

⑤ Kate went to a shopping mall to buy clothes.

중요

24 위 글의 내용으로 보아 정세권에 대한 묘사로 가장 알맞은 것을 고르시오.

① creative   ② negative

③ patriotic   ④ friendly

⑤ passionate

서답형

25 What houses were many Japanese building? Answer in English. (7 words)

➡ _____

[26~28] 다음 글을 읽고 물음에 답하시오.

Jeong Segwon helped the independence movement in many ways. ⓐ example, he built the office building for the Joseon Language Society and supported its efforts to keep the Joseon language ⓑlive. ⓒWhen the Joseon Language Affair was happened, he was caught by the police and suffered a lot. Japanese officials pressed him to build Japanese houses.

26 위 글의 빈칸 ⓐ에 들어갈 알맞은 것은?

① For   ② In

③ At   ④ With

⑤ From

서답형

27 위 글의 밑줄 친 ⓑ를 알맞은 어형으로 고치시오.

➡ _____

서답형

28 위 글의 밑줄 친 ⓒ에서 어법상 어색한 것을 고치시오.

_____ ➡ _____

[01~04] 다음 글을 읽고 물음에 답하시오.

Japanese officials pressed Jeong Segwon to build Japanese houses. ⓐHe said, "I don't know how to build Japanese houses." An official said, "You know how to build *hanoks*, ⓑ[so / for] you can build Japanese houses, too." But he did not do ⓒ[that / what] the Japanese told him to do. The cost was high. His business fell off, and he lost his property. However, in part, thanks ⓓ[to / of] Jeong Segwon, the traditions of Korea still live with us today.

01 위 글의 밑줄 친 ⓐ를 간접화법의 문장으로 바꿔 쓰시오.

➡ _____

_____

02 위 글의 괄호 ⓑ~ⓒ에서 문맥이나 어법상 알맞은 낱말을 골라 쓰시오.

➡ ⓑ _____ ⓑ _____ ⓒ _____

03 위 글의 내용과 일치하도록 다음 빈칸 (A)와 (B)에 알맞은 단어를 쓰시오.

Despite a Japanese official's pressure, Jeong Segwon didn't (A)_____ Japanese houses. As the result, he lost his (B)_____.

04 What houses did Japanese officials press Jeong Segwon to build? Answer in English. (7 words)

➡ _____

[05~07] 다음 글을 읽고 물음에 답하시오.

Jeong Segwon said, "People are power. We Joseon people should keep Jongno and not ⓐ let the Japanese set foot here." He bought the ⓑ_____ between Gyeongbokgung (A)[or / and] Changdeokgung. There he built small, modern *hanoks* for the people. (B)[Until / Through] his efforts, we now have Bukchon filled (C)[with / of] its beautiful *hanoks*.

05 위 글의 밑줄 친 ⓐ와 같은 뜻이 되도록 다음 문장의 빈칸에 알맞은 말을 쓰시오.

allow the Japanese _____ _____ foot here

06 위 글의 빈칸 ⓑ에 다음 정의에 해당하는 말을 쓰시오.

an area of ground, especially one that is used for a particular purpose such as farming or building

➡ _____

07 위 글의 괄호 (A)~(C)에서 어법상 알맞은 낱말을 골라 쓰시오.

➡ (A) _____ (B) _____ (C) _____

[08~12] 다음 글을 읽고 물음에 답하시오.

Jeong Segwon helped the ⓐdepend movement in many ways. ⓑ_____ example, he built the office building for the Joseon Language Society and supported its efforts to keep the Joseon language alive. ⓒ조선어 학회 사건이 일어났을 때, 그는 경찰에 잡혀 많은 고통을 겪었다. Japanese officials pressed him (A)[building / to build] Japanese houses. He said, "I don't know (B) [how / what] to build Japanese houses."

08 위 글의 밑줄 친 ⓐ를 문맥상 알맞은 말로 어형을 바꾸시오.

➡ _____

09 위 글의 빈칸 ⓑ에 알맞은 말을 쓰시오.

➡ _____

10 (중요) 위 글의 밑줄 친 ⓒ의 우리말에 맞게 한 단어를 보충하여, 주어진 어구를 알맞게 배열하시오. (when으로 시작할 것.)

was / the police / happened / he / when / and / suffered / caught / a lot / the Choseon Language Affair

➡ _____

_____

11 위 글의 괄호 (A)~(B)에서 어법상 알맞은 낱말을 골라 쓰시오.

➡ (A) _____ (B) _____

12 What did the Joseon Language Society make an effort to do? Answer in English.

➡ _____

[13~15] 다음 글을 읽고 물음에 답하시오.

Have you been (A)[for / to] Bukchon? ⓐ There is a beautiful *hanok* village in Bukchon. It is popular (B)[with / from] tourists who want to see Korea's past. However, not many people know that Bukchon was created (B)[among / through] one man's efforts. That man was Jeong Segwon, ⓑknow as the King of Architecture in Gyeongseong.

13 (중요) 위 글의 괄호 (A)~(C)에서 어법상 알맞은 낱말을 골라 쓰시오.

➡ (A) _____ (B) _____ (C) _____

14 (고난이도) 위 글의 밑줄 친 ⓐ와 같은 뜻이 되도록 다음 문장의 빈칸에 알맞은 말을 쓰시오.

➡ Bukchon _____ a beautiful *hanok* village.

15 위 글의 밑줄 친 ⓑ를 알맞은 어형으로 고치시오.

➡ _____

Before You Read

Japanese officials pressed the Joseon people to use the Japanese language.
목적격보어

The Joseon people tried to keep the Joseon language alive.
명사적 용법(tried의 목적어)   살아 있는

The Joseon people wanted to protect the country. Soon, the independence

movement rose up.
rise의 과거형

구문해설 • alive: 살아 있는 • protect: 지키다 • rise up: 일어나다, 봉기하다

일본 관리들은 조선 사람들에게 일본어를 쓰도록 압박했다. 조선 사람들은 조선어를 살아 있게 지키려고 노력했다.

조선 사람들은 나라를 지키기를 원했다. 이윽고, 독립운동이 일어났다.

Language in Use

A woman moved into the building next to Joe's store. She opened up a new
building을 수식하는 형용사구

store. Many people started to go to the woman's new store instead of Joe's
~하기 시작했다.   ~ 대신에

store. Few people set foot in Joe's store. His food business fell off.
~에 발을 들여 놓았다

구문해설 • next to: ~ 옆에 open up: 열다, 개점하다 • few: 거의 ~ 않는 • fall off: 쇠퇴하다

한 여인이 Joe의 가게 옆에 있는 건물로 이사 왔다. 그녀는 새로운 가게를 열었다. 많은 사람들이 Joe의 가게 대신에 그 여인의 새 가게로 가기 시작했다. Joe의 가게에 들어오는 사람들은 거의 없었다. 그의 음식 장사는 쇠퇴했다.

Writing Workshop

Who is An Yongbok?

He lived during the Joseon Dynasty, and his job was catching fish. When he
~ 중에. ~ 동안(during+특정한 기간)

was fishing, he saw the Japanese people fishing near Ulleungdo. He visited
지각동사   목적격보어(현재분사)

Japan twice and said that Ulleungdo and Dokdo were part of Korea. In 1696,
be part of: ~의 일부이다

the Japanese ruler officially told the Japanese people not to fish near Ulleugdo
물고기를 잡지 말라고(to부정사의 부정)

and Dokdo. He did his best to protect Ulleungdo and Dokdo.

구문해설 • dynasty: 왕조 • twice: 두 번 • officially: 공식적으로 • do one's best: 최선을 다하다

안용복은 누구인가?
그는 조선왕조 시대에 살았으며, 그의 직업은 물고기를 잡는 것이었다. 그가 물고기를 잡고 있었을 때 그는 일본 사람들이 울릉도 근처에서 물고기를 잡는 것을 보았다. 그는 일본을 두 번 방문해서 울릉도와 독도는 한국에 속해 있다고 말했다. 1696년에 일본인 통치자는 일본인들에게 울릉도와 독도 근처에서 물고기를 잡지 말라고 공식적으로 말했다. 그는 울릉도와 독도를 지키기 위해 최선을 다했다.

01 다음 짝지어진 단어의 관계가 같도록 빈칸에 알맞은 말을 쓰시오.

(1) China – Chinese : France : _____
(2) poem – poet : architecture : _____

02 다음 우리말에 맞도록 빈칸에 알맞은 말을 쓰시오

(1) 그녀는 실내에서 할 수 있는 일에 관심이 있다.
➡ She is _____ in working indoors.
(2) 우리가 그 일의 힘든 부분은 다 했다.
➡ We've done the difficult _____ of the job.
(3) 내 방은 현대식 스타일로 꾸며져 있다.
➡ My room is decorated in a _____ style.

03 다음 빈칸에 알맞은 말을 고르시오.

The city is famous _____ its scenery.

① from　　② for
③ with　　④ in
⑤ by

04 다음 영영풀이가 나타내는 말을 고르시오.

a long written story about imaginary people and events

① novel　　② article
③ report　　④ essay
⑤ diary

05 다음 대화의 빈칸에 들어갈 말을 고르시오.

B: Could you _____ this painting? W: Sure. It's *the Two Sisters* by Renoir. He painted it in 1881.

① view　　② tell
③ show　　④ excuse
⑤ explain

06 다음 대화가 자연스럽게 이어지도록 순서대로 배열하시오.

(A) It's a volunteer group in our community. (B) Well, they take care of children in need. (C) Could you tell me more about it? (D) Could you explain what Helping Hands is?

➡ _____

07 다음 대화의 흐름상 어색한 것을 고르시오.

B: ⓐDo you know anything about this writer? G: Yes. ⓑI've read some of his novels. Why? B: ⓒHow were they? I'm thinking of buying his books. G: ⓓYou should. ⓔI didn't enjoy his books that much.

① ⓐ　　② ⓑ　　③ ⓒ　　④ ⓓ　　⑤ ⓔ

[08~11] 다음 대화를 읽고 물음에 답하시오.

G: What are *hanoks*? ①

M: Hanoks are traditional Korean houses. ② ⓐ <u>They design to be in harmony with nature.</u>

G: Could you explain a little more about them? ③

M: *Hanoks* are cool in the summer and warm in the winter. ④

G: That sounds interesting. ⑤ Where can I see these traditional houses?

M: There's a *hanok* village near here.

G: How about going there and seeing the hanoks?

W: Good idea! ⓑ can we get there?

M: You can take Bus Number 5 over there at the bus stop.

08 ①~⑤ 중 주어진 문장이 들어갈 곳은?

> Do you know anything about them?

① ② ③ ④ ⑤

09 위 대화의 밑줄 친 ⓐ에서 어법상 어색한 것을 고쳐 다시 쓰시오.

➡ _____

10 위 대화의 빈칸 ⓑ에 알맞은 것은?

① What ② When
③ How ④ Why
⑤ Where

11 위 대화의 내용과 일치하지 <u>않는</u> 것을 고르시오.

① 소녀는 한옥이 무엇인지 모른다.
② 한옥은 자연과 조화를 이루도록 설계되었다.
③ 소녀는 한국의 전통 마을을 방문하기를 원한다.
④ 전통 마을은 대화자들이 이야기하는 장소에서 멀리 있다.
⑤ 소녀와 여인은 버스를 타고 전통 마을에 갈 것이다.

Grammar

12 다음 중 주어진 문장의 밑줄 친 부분과 쓰임이 <u>다른</u> 하나는?

> Did you see the <u>swimming</u> pool?

① Kevin was not interested in <u>fishing</u>.
② My hobby is <u>taking</u> pictures.
③ The boys are <u>riding</u> bikes together.
④ They enjoyed <u>cooking</u> with her.
⑤ Tanya focused on <u>studying</u> English.

13 다음 문장에서 어법상 잘못된 것을 고치시오.

(1) They asked him give a speech.

_____ ➡ _____

(2) Clara made him to wait for her for an hour outside.

_____ ➡ _____

(3) I will have Mike to repair my cellphone.

_____ ➡ _____

(4) I saw the boys played soccer at the park.

_____ ➡ _____

(5) He was reading a letter writing in English.

_____ ➡ _____

14 다음 우리말을 올바르게 영작한 것은?

> 그는 Christine에게 집에 조금 일찍 도착하라고 요청했다.

① He asked Christine arrive home a little early.

② He asked Christine arrives home a little early.

③ He asked Christine arrived home a little early.

④ He asked Christine to arrive home a little early.

⑤ He asked Christine arriving home a little early.

15 다음 중 어법상 어색한 문장은?

① I liked the pictures painted by Mike.

② He knows the girl dancing on the stage.

③ I saw the dog sleeping on the sofa.

④ The baby smiled at me is very cute.

⑤ They watched the birds singing on the tree.

16 다음 중 빈칸에 들어갈 말이 바르게 짝지어진 것은?

> • Did you find your (A)[breaking / broken] camera?
> • I saw an (B)[exciting / excited] movie yesterday.
> • I can't open the (C)[locking / locked] door.

	(A)	(B)	(C)
①	breaking	–	exciting	–	locked
②	breaking	–	excited	–	locked
③	breaking	–	excited	–	locking
④	broken	–	exciting	–	locking
⑤	broken	–	exciting	–	locked

17 다음 중 어법상 어색한 부분을 찾아 바르게 고쳐 다시 쓰시오.

(1) Lucy's dad wants her being a police officer.

➡ _____

(2) My mother asked me buy some milk on my way home.

➡ _____

(3) The teacher told the students bringing some water.

➡ _____

(4) She got her two sons divided a cake exactly in half.

➡ _____

18 주어진 단어를 활용하여 다음 우리말을 영어로 쓰시오.

(1) 우리는 낙엽 위를 걷는 것을 좋아합니다. (like / on / fall / leaves)

➡ _____

(2) 그는 그 날아오는 공을 쳤다. (hit / fly)

➡ _____

19 다음 두 문장의 해석을 쓰고 밑줄 친 부분의 어법상 차이를 설명하시오.

> (1) Jane likes sliced cheese.
> (2) Jane likes slicing cheese.

(1) 해석: _____

(2) 해석: _____

(3) 어법상 차이: _____

_____

Reading

[20~23] 다음 글을 읽고 물음에 답하시오.

(①) An Yongbok lived during the Joseon Dynasty, and his job was ⓐcatching fish. (②) When he was fishing, he saw the Japanese people fishing near Ulleungdo. (③) In 1696, the Japanese _____ⓑ_____ officially told the Japanese people not to fish near Ulleugdo and Dokdo. (④) He did his best to protect Ulleungdo and Dokdo. (⑤)

20 위 글의 흐름으로 보아, 주어진 문장이 들어가기에 가장 적절한 곳은?

> He visited Japan twice and said that Ulleungdo and Dokdo were part of Korea.

① ② ③ ④ ⑤

21 위 글의 밑줄 친 ⓐ와 같은 용법으로 쓰인 것은?

① Barking dogs seldom bite.
② Working in the field was very interesting.
③ The girl reading a book is Mary.
④ We saw Mike climbing the mountain alone.
⑤ Turning to the left, you will find a hotel.

22 위 글의 빈칸 ⓑ에 다음 정의에 해당하는 단어를 쓰시오.

> the person who rules a country

➡ _____

23 위 글을 읽고 대답할 수 없는 질문은?

① Did An Yongbok live during the Joseon Dynasty?
② What did he do for a living?
③ Was he good at catching fish?
④ How many times did he visit Japan?
⑤ Could the Japanese people fish near Dokdo after 1696?

[24~26] 다음 글을 읽고 물음에 답하시오.

ⓐHave you ever seen this kind of pot? It is an onggi. People in the old times used it for storing rice for a long time.
We have designed a modern onggi with flowers ⓑpaint on it, and it even has handles.

24 위 글의 밑줄 친 ⓐ를 우리말로 옮기시오.

➡ _____

25 위 글의 밑줄 친 ⓑpaint를 알맞은 형으로 고치시오.

➡ _____

26 Why did people in the old times use this kind of pot? Answer in English. (6 words)

➡ _____

[27~30] 다음 글을 읽고 물음에 답하시오.

ⓐHow about learning *taegwondo* at the Buckon *Hanok* Village? People can experience the Korean ⓑnation sport. They will learn that *taegwondo* is a sport ⓒthat trains both the spirit and the ____ⓓ____ .

27 위 글의 밑줄 친 ⓐ를 다음과 같이 바꿔 쓸 때 빈칸에 들어갈 알맞은 말을 쓰시오.

➡ _____ don't you learn *taegwondo* at the Buckon *Hanok* Village?

28 위 글의 밑줄 친 ⓑnation을 알맞은 형으로 고치시오.

➡ _____

29 위 글의 밑줄 친 ⓒthat와 용법이 같은 것은? (2개)

① It is strange that she doesn't come.
② I know that you don't like cats.
③ Look at the trees that stand on the hill.
④ It was here that she first met Mike.
⑤ This is the doll that my mother made for me.

30 위 글의 빈칸 ⓓ에 다음 정의에 해당하는 단어를 쓰시오.

> all your physical parts, including your head, arms, and legs

➡ _____

[31~33] 다음 글을 읽고 물음에 답하시오.

Jeong Segwon was a businessman who founded Geonyangsa in 1920. At the time, Korea was ruled by Japan, and the Japanese were changing Gyeongseong to fit their taste. Many Japanese moving into Gyeongseong were building Japanese or ⓐWest houses. Jeong Segwon wanted to protect the *hanok* and help the suffering people. He said, "People are power. We Joseon people should keep Jongno and not let the Japanese ____ⓑ____ foot here."

31 위 글의 밑줄 친 ⓐWest를 알맞은 형으로 고치시오.

➡ _____

32 위 글의 빈칸 ⓑ에 알맞은 것은?

① get   ② set
③ fix   ④ put
⑤ take

33 위 글을 읽고 대답할 수 없는 질문은?

① What did Jeong Segwon do for a living?
② When did Jeong Segwon found Geonyangsa?
③ Why were the Japanese changing Gyeongseong?
④ What did Jeong Segwon want to do?
⑤ How did Jeong Segwon keep Jongno?

01 다음 두 문장이 같은 뜻이 되도록 빈칸에 알맞은 것은?

> Who's taking care of the children while you're away?
> = Who's caring _____ the children while you're away?

① of　　② to　　③ at
④ for　　⑤ with

02 다음 빈칸에 공통으로 들어갈 말을 쓰시오.

> • He sensed that his life was _____ danger.
> • Jake is interested _____ chess.

03 다음 중 〈보기〉에 있는 단어를 사용하여 자연스러운 문장을 만들 수 없는 것은?

> ┌─ 보기 ─┐
> abroad　known　explain　meaning waste

① What's the _____ of this word?
② First, I'll _____ the rules of the game.
③ Why did you _____ money on clothes you didn't need?
④ I'm planning to travel _____.
⑤ The boy was trying, for some _____ reason, to count the stars.

04 다음 영영풀이에 해당하는 단어를 고르시오.

> to feel pain in your body or in your mind

① store　　② require
③ suffer　　④ expect
⑤ endure

[05~08] 다음 대화를 읽고 물음에 답하시오.

> B: Do you know anything about a *dol* party?
> G: Yes. ⓐIt's the birthday party for a one-year-old baby.
> B: Could you tell me more about it?
> G: Well, the family members get together for the party, and the birthday baby wears a *hanbok*.
> B: That sounds interesting.
> G: The family members share food and wish _____ⓑ_____ a long life for the baby. It's a Korean _____ⓒ_____.

05 위 대화의 밑줄 친 It이 가리키는 것을 우리말로 쓰시오.

➡ _____

06 위 대화의 빈칸 ⓑ에 알맞은 것은?

① to　　② for
③ of　　④ with
⑤ from

07 위 대화의 빈칸 ⓒ에 다음 영영풀이에 해당하는 단어를 쓰시오.

> a custom or belief that has existed for a long time

➡ _____

08 위 대화를 읽고 대답할 수 <u>없는</u> 질문은?

① Does the boy know much about a *dol* party?

② What is a *dol* party?

③ Can the girl tell the boy about a *dol* party?

④ How many family members get together for the party?

⑤ What do family members do at the *dol* party?

[09~12] 다음 대화를 읽고 물음에 답하시오.

Reporter: You founded Geonyangsa. What does Geonyangsa do?

Jeong: We build houses. We build *hanoks* on the land between Gyeongbokgung and Changdeokgung.

Reporter: Why did you build *hanoks* ⓐ<u>there</u>?

Jeong: Many Japanese are moving into Gyeongseong and changing ⓑ<u>it</u> to fit their taste. So I want to protect the *hanok*.

Reporter: You are also helping the independence ⓒ_____ (move) in many ways. How have you helped?

Jeong: I know a lot about architecture, so I have built the office building for the Joseon Language Society.

09 위 대화의 밑줄 친 ⓐthere가 가리키는 것을 영어로 쓰시오.

➡ _____
_____

10 위 대화의 밑줄 친 ⓑ가 가리키는 것을 영어로 쓰시오.

➡ _____

11 괄호 안에 주어진 단어를 이용해 빈칸 ⓒ를 채우시오.

➡ _____

12 위 대화의 내용으로 보아 알 수 <u>없는</u> 것은?

① A reporter is interviewing Jeong.

② Jeong founded Geonyangsa.

③ There are a lot of *hanoks* between Gyeongbokgung and Changdeokgung.

④ Many Japanese are changing Gyeongseong to fit their taste.

⑤ Jeong wants to protect the *hanok*.

13 다음 빈칸에 들어갈 말이 바르게 짝지어진 것은?

> • The girl _____ a book is my sister.
> • There was a _____ window.

① read – breaking
② read – broken
③ reading – broken
④ read – break
⑤ reading – break

14 다음 우리말에 맞도록 빈칸에 알맞은 말을 차례대로 쓰시오.

(출제율 95%)

(1) 그가 돌아오면 저를 도와주라고 부탁해 주시겠
어요?

= Will you ask him _____ me when
he _____ back?

(2) 그녀는 자기 딸에게 고양이에게 밥을 주라고 말
했다.

= She told her daughter _____ the
cat.

15 다음 중 어법상 어색한 것을 고르시오.

(출제율 100%)

① Is snow falling?

② I met a girl naming Kate in the park.

③ There was a fence painted green.

④ Who is the man cooking *bibimbap*?

⑤ A spectator is someone watching a game
or a play.

16 다음 중 밑줄 친 부분의 쓰임이 바르지 못한 것은?

(출제율 95%)

① Jack wants Jane to water the plants.

② He asked her teach math to his son.

③ He made her do her work right now.

④ We saw him singing in the rain.

⑤ He advised me not to smoke.

17 다음 문장의 빈칸에 알맞은 것은?

(출제율 90%)

> She told me _____ careful when I
> crossed the road.

① be ② was

③ is ④ being

⑤ to be

[18~20] 다음 글을 읽고 물음에 답하시오.

When the Joseon Language Affair (A)
[happened / was happened], Jeong Segwon was
caught by the police and suffered a lot. Japanese
officials pressed him (B)[building / to build]
Japanese houses. He said, "I don't know how to
build Japanese houses." An official said, "You
know how to build hanoks, so you can build
Japanese houses, too." But he did not do (C)
[what / that] the Japanese told him to do. (D)대
가는 컸다. His business fell off, and he lost his
property.

18 위 글의 괄호 (A)~(C)에서 문맥이나 어법상 알맞은 낱말을
골라 쓰시오.

(출제율 100%)

➡ (A)_____ (B)_____ (C)_____

19 위 글의 밑줄 친 (D)를 영어로 옮길 때 빈칸에 알맞은 것은?

(출제율 90%)

> The cost was _____.

① much ② many

③ high ④ large

⑤ expensive

20 위 글의 내용과 일치하지 않는 것은?

(출제율 95%)

① 조선어 학회 사건이 발생했을 때 정세권은 경찰
에 체포되었다.

② 일본인 관리들은 정세권에게 일본식 집을 짓도
록 강요했다.

③ 정세권은 일본식 집을 짓기로 마음먹었다.

④ 정세권은 일본식 집을 짓지 않았다.

⑤ 정세권은 일본인 관리의 말을 듣지 않은 결과 재
산을 잃게 되었다.

[21~23] 다음 글을 읽고 물음에 답하시오.

The woman ⓐwear a pink dress opens the window. The sun is shining in the sky. Johnsy looks at a leaf (A)[painted / painting] on the wall. Johnsy looks happy. The man (B)[held / holding] a brush sees the happy face.

21 위 글의 밑줄 친 ⓐwear를 알맞은 형으로 고치시오.

➡ _____

22 위 글의 괄호 (A), (B)에서 어법상 알맞은 낱말을 골라 쓰시오.

➡ (A) _____ (B) _____

23 위 글의 분위기로 가장 알맞은 것은?
① exciting   ② sad
③ scary   ④ hopeful
⑤ lonely

[24~26] 다음 글을 읽고 물음에 답하시오.

Have you been to Bukchon? ⓐThere is a beautiful *hanok* village in Bukchon. It is ___ⓑ___ with tourists who want to see Korea's past. ⓒHowever, not many people know that Bukchon created through one man's efforts. That man was Jeong Segwon, known as the King of Architecture in Gyeongseong.

24 위 글의 밑줄 친 ⓐ와 같은 뜻이 되도록 다음 문장의 빈칸에 알맞은 말을 쓰시오.

➡ Bukchon _____ a beautiful *hanok* village.

25 위 글의 빈칸 ⓑ에 알맞은 것은?
① known   ② well
③ popular   ④ familiar
⑤ unknown

26 위 글의 밑줄 친 ⓒ에서 어법상 어색한 것을 고치시오.

_____ ➡ _____

[27~28] 다음 글을 읽고 물음에 답하시오.

(①) A woman moved into the building next to Joe's store. (②) She opened up a new store. (③) Many people started to go to the woman's new store instead of Joe's store. (④) ___ⓐ___ people set foot in Joe's store. (⑤)

27 위 글의 ①~⑤ 중 주어진 문장이 들어갈 곳은?

His food business fell off.

①   ②   ③   ④   ⑤

28 위 글의 빈칸 ⓐ에 알맞은 것은?
① Few   ② A few
③ Many   ④ Much
⑤ A little

01 다음 대화의 흐름상 어색한 것을 하나 찾아서 고치시오.

> B: Do you know anything about Korean history?
> G: I don't know much about it and I'm interested in it.
> B: Can you help me with my history homework?
> B: Sure. No problem.

➡ _____

_____

[02~03] 다음 대화를 읽고 물음에 답하시오.

> G: Do you know anything about Changdeokgung?
> B: ⓐYes, a little. It's famous for its beautiful garden.
> G: I'm going to go ⓑthere with my Chinese friend.
> B: I think you'll like it.

02 위 대화의 밑줄 친 ⓐ를 생략되지 않은 문장으로 쓰시오.

➡ _____

03 위 대화의 밑줄 친 ⓑ가 가리키는 것을 영어로 쓰시오.

➡ _____

04 다음 대화의 빈칸에 알맞은 단어를 쓰시오.

> A: Could you _____ your plan to save money?
> B: I won't waste my money on snacks.

➡ _____

05 괄호 안의 동사를 어법에 맞게 고쳐 쓰시오.

(1) The policeman asked her (tell) him the truth.

➡ _____

(2) Her parents encouraged her (study) hard.

➡ _____

(3) Please help me (push) the boat.

➡ _____

06 주어진 단어를 어법에 맞게 빈칸에 쓰시오.

(1) A girl _____ Jiho called you an hour ago. (name)

(2) The _____ robot is really expensive. (talk)

07 다음 상황에 알맞은 말을 어법에 맞게 빈칸에 쓰시오.

(1) This morning he was late for school. The teacher said to him, "Don't be late."

➡ The teacher told him _____ late for school.

(2) Mr. White said to me, "Don't give up."

➡ Mr. White encouraged me _____ up.

08 다음 우리말에 맞게 주어진 어구를 배열하시오.

(1) 이것은 그에 의해서 쓰인 유일한 책이다.
(the / him / only / by / book / written / this / is)

➡ _____

(2) 이 집에 사는 소년은 Andy이다.
(house / living / the / in / is / Andy / this / boy)

➡ _____

(3) 선생님은 우리에게 체육관에 모이라고 말씀하셨다. (the teacher / the gym / us / gather / told / at / to)

➡ _____

(4) 지호는 도훈이에게 창문을 닦아 달라고 부탁했다. (Jiho / Dohun / the window / clean / asked / to)

➡ _____

10 위 글의 밑줄 친 ⓑ에서 어법상 어색한 것을 고치시오.

_____ ➡ _____

11 What did An Yongbok do for a living? Answer in English. (4 words)

➡ _____

[09~11] 다음 글을 읽고 물음에 답하시오.

Who is An Yongbok?
He lived ____ⓐ____ the Joseon Dynasty, and his job was catching fish. When he was fishing, he saw the Japanese people fishing near Ulleungdo. He visited Japan twice and said that Ulleungdo and Dokdo were part of Korea. ⓑIn 1696, the Japanese ruler officially told the Japanese people to not fish near Ulleugdo and Dokdo. He did his best to protect Ulleungdo and Dokdo.

[12~13] 다음 글을 읽고 물음에 답하시오.

Have you ever seen this kind of pot? It is an onggi. People in the old times used it for ⓐstore rice for a long time.
We have designed a modern onggi with flowers painted on ⓑit, and it even has handles.

12 위 글의 밑줄 친 ⓐ를 알맞은 형으로 고치시오.

➡ _____

09 위 글의 빈칸 ⓐ에 알맞은 전치사를 쓰시오.

➡ _____

13 위 글의 밑줄 친 ⓑ가 가리키는 것을 우리말로 쓰시오.

➡ _____

01 다음 주어진 동사와 to부정사를 이용하여 보기와 같이 여러 가지 문장을 쓰시오.

---
order want ask tell allow advise force persuade

보기

My boss ordered me to go to London.

(1) _____

(2) _____

(3) _____

(4) _____

(5) _____

(6) _____

(7) _____

02 다음 대화를 읽고 대화의 내용을 요약한 문장을 완성하시오.

Reporter: You founded Geonyangsa. What does Geonyangsa do?

Jeong: We build houses. We build *hanoks* on the land between Gyeongbokgung and Changdeokgung.

Reporter: Why did you build *hanoks* there?

Jeong: Many Japanese are moving into Gyeongseong and changing it to fit their taste. So I want to protect the *hanok*.

Reporter: You are also helping the independence movement in many ways. How have you helped?

Jeong: I know a lot about architecture, so I have built the office building for the Joseon Language Society.

This is a dialogue (A)_____ Jeong Segwon and a reporter. His job is (B)_____ houses. Many Japanese (C)_____ into Gyeongseong are changing it to fit their (D)_____. So he wants to (E)_____ the *hanok*. He is also helping the (F)_____ movement in many ways. For (G)_____, he has built the office (H)_____ for the Joseon Language Society.

단원별 모의고사

01 다음 문장의 빈칸에 알맞은 것으로 짝지어진 것은?

> • Hundreds _____ people lose their lives every hurricane season.
> • Thanks _____ her invention, many people live better lives.

① of - for
② of - to
③ at - for
④ from - to
⑤ with - from

02 다음 우리말을 영어로 옮길 때 빈칸에 알맞은 것으로 짝지어진 것은?

> • 그 물고기는 아직 살아 있니?
> ➡ Is the fish still _____?
> • 커피 한 잔 더 드시겠어요?
> ➡ Won't you have _____ cup of coffee?

① live - other
② living - other
③ living - another
④ alive - other
⑤ alive - another

03 다음 밑줄 친 단어의 뜻이 잘못된 것을 고르시오.

① Don't <u>waste</u> your time and money. (낭비하다)
② He got the job <u>through</u> a friend of his. (~을 통하여)
③ Mike read a historical <u>novel</u>. (소설)
④ The house is made of <u>stone</u>. (흙)
⑤ Ants <u>store up</u> food for winter. (저장하다)

[04~06] 다음 대화를 읽고 물음에 답하시오.

> B: Do you know anything about a *dol* party?
> G: Yes. It's the birthday party for a one-year-old baby.
> B: Could you tell me more about ⓐit?
> G: Well, the family members get together for the party, and the birthday baby _____ⓑ_____ a *hanbok*.
> B: That sounds interesting.
> G: The family members share food and wish for a long life for the baby. It's a Korean tradition.

04 위 대화의 밑줄 친 ⓐit이 가리키는 것을 우리말로 쓰시오.

➡ _____

05 위 대화의 빈칸 ⓑ에 다음 정의에 해당하는 단어를 쓰시오.

> to have something such as clothes, shoes, or gloves on your body or on part of your body

➡ _____

06 위 대화의 내용으로 보아 대답할 수 <u>없는</u> 질문은?

① Does the boy know a lot about a *dol* party?
② What is a *dol* party?
③ Do the family members get together for the party?
④ What food the family members eat at the *dol* party?
⑤ Do the family members wish for a long life for the baby?

07 다음 대화를 순서대로 바르게 배열한 것은?

> (A) Yes. It is one of the greatest sights in the world.
> (B) Can you explain why it is famous?
> (C) Do you know anything about the Great Wall of China?
> (D) It's because it is the longest wall in the world.

① (B) – (A) – (C) – (D) ② (B) – (C) – (D) – (A)
③ (C) – (A) – (B) – (D) ④ (C) – (B) – (A) – (D)
⑤ (C) – (D) – (B) – (A)

[08~11] 다음 대화를 읽고 물음에 답하시오.

> Reporter: You founded Geonyangsa. What does Geonyangsa do?
> Jeong: We build houses. (①) We build *hanoks* on the land between Gyeongbokgung and Changdeokgung. (②)
> Reporter: Why did you build hanoks ⓐthere?
> Jeong: (③) Many Japanese are moving into Gyeongseong and changing it to fit their taste. (④)
> Reporter: ⓑ당신은 또한 여러 방법으로 독립 운동을 도와주고 있습니다. How have you helped?
> Jeong: I know a lot about architecture, so I have built the office building for the Joseon Language Society. (⑤)

08 ①~⑤ 중 주어진 문장이 들어갈 곳은?

> So I want to protect the *hanok*.

①   ②   ③   ④   ⑤

09 밑줄 친 ⓐthere가 가리키는 것을 우리말로 쓰시오.

➡ _____

10 밑줄 친 ⓑ를 괄호 안에 주어진 단어를 이용하여 영작하시오. (also, way)

➡ _____
_____

11 위 대화의 내용으로 보아 알 수 없는 것을 고르시오.

① Jeong founded Geonyangsa.
② Jeong builds *hanoks*.
③ Jeong doesn't know how to build Japanese houses.
④ Many Japanese are changing Gyeongseong to fit their taste.
⑤ Jeong has built the office building for the Joseon Language Society.

12 다음 빈칸에 들어갈 동사 do의 형태가 다른 하나는?

① Jim wanted me _____ the dishes.
② She advised him _____ some exercise regularly.
③ Our teacher told us _____ our homework.
④ Did you expect him _____ his best?
⑤ My mom made us _____ it.

13 다음 중 빈칸에 들어갈 단어 use의 형태가 <u>다른</u> 하나는?

① I found her _____ my pen.
② The boy _____ your computer is my son.
③ David is _____ the copy machine.
④ They bought a _____ car.
⑤ Ann is _____ a special knife to cut meat.

14 다음 중 어법상 올바른 것을 고르시오.

① The typhoon caused the old bridge to fall.
② They expect her participating in the ceremony.
③ Judy asked him make sandwiches.
④ Do you want me waking you up tomorrow morning?
⑤ The math teacher told us solved 10 problems every day.

15 다음 두 문장을 관계대명사를 사용하지 않고 하나의 문장으로 바꿔 쓰시오.

> • She bought a smartphone.
> • The smartphone was made in Korea.

➡ _____

16 다음 빈칸에 알맞은 말을 쓰시오.

> 그는 충격을 받은 것처럼 보인다.
> He looks _____.

17 다음 빈칸에 적절하지 <u>않은</u> 것은?

> I _____ her to take part in the party.

① watched ② wanted
③ told ④ persuaded
⑤ expected

[18~19] 다음 글을 읽고 물음에 답하시오.

> ⓐHave you been to Bukchon? There is a beautiful hanok village in Bukchon. It is popular with tourists who want to see Korea's past. However, not many people know that Bukchon was created through one man's efforts. That man was Jeong Segwon, known ⓑas the King of Architecture in Gyeongseong.

18 위 글의 밑줄 친 ⓐ와 용법이 같은 것은?

① I <u>have been</u> in this country since last month.
② Yumi <u>has seen</u> this movie many times.
③ Mike <u>has just cleaned</u> his room.
④ Lisa <u>has had</u> this cat for ten years.
⑤ She <u>has gone</u> out and this room is cold.

19 위 글의 밑줄 친 ⓑas와 의미가 같은 것은?

① He came up <u>as</u> I was speaking.
② When in Rome, do <u>as</u> the Romans do.
③ He is famous <u>as</u> an artist.
④ <u>As</u> it rained, they stopped the game.
⑤ <u>As</u> we go higher, the air gets colder.

[20~22] 다음 글을 읽고 물음에 답하시오.

When the Joseon Language Affair happened, ⓐ Jeong Segwon caught by the police and suffered a lot. Japanese officials pressed him to build Japanese houses. He said, "I don't know how to build Japanese houses." An official said, "You know how to build *hanoks*, ⓑ you can build Japanese houses, too." But he did not do what the Japanese told him to do. The cost was high. His business fell off, and he lost his property. _____ⓑ_____, in part, thanks to Jeong Segwon, the traditions of Korea still live with us today.

20 위 글의 밑줄 친 ⓐ에서 어법상 어색한 것을 고치시오.

_____ ➡ _____

21 위 글의 빈칸 ⓑ에 알맞은 것은?

① so
② or
③ for
④ but
⑤ though

22 위 글의 빈칸 ⓑ에 알맞은 것은?

① Though
② However
③ Besides
④ Furthermore
⑤ Therefore

[23~25] 다음 글을 읽고 물음에 답하시오.

An Yongbok lived during the Joseon Dynasty, and his ⓐ was catching fish. When he was fishing, he saw the Japanese people fishing near Ulleungdo. He visited Japan twice and said that Ulleungdo and Dokdo were part of Korea. In 1696, the Japanese ruler ⓑofficial told the Japanese people not to fish near Ulleugdo and Dokdo. He did his best to protect Ulleungdo and Dokdo.

23 위 글의 빈칸 ⓐ에 다음 정의에 해당하는 단어를 쓰시오.

the work that someone does to earn money

➡ _____

24 위 글의 밑줄 친 ⓑ를 알맞은 형으로 고치시오.

➡ _____

25 위 글의 내용과 일치하지 <u>않는</u> 것은?

① 안용복은 조선 왕조 시대에 살았다.
② 안용복의 직업은 어부였다.
③ 안용복은 일본인들이 울릉도 부근에서 고기를 잡는 것을 보았다.
④ 안용복은 일본을 한 번 방문했다.
⑤ 안용복은 울릉도와 독도를 지키려고 노력했다.

Lesson 9

Manners Make the Man

🎙 의사소통 기능

- 약속 정하기
  A: How about going to the hot spring on Thursday at 2:00? Can you make it?

  B: Yes. That would be great.

- 상기시키기
  A: Don't forget to turn off your cellphone in the theater.
  B: Okay, I won't.

🎙 언어 형식

- 관계부사
  Today's quiet concerts began in the 19th century **when** many big concert halls were built.

- 간접의문문
  We do not know **what concerts will look like in the future**.

Words & Expressions

Key Words

- **actually** [ǽktʃuəli] 부 사실은
- **appear** [əpíər] 동 나타나다
- **audience** [ɔ́ːdiəns] 명 관객
- **between** [bitwíːn] 전 (위치가) ~ 사이[중간]에
- **blame** [bleim] 동 비난하다
- **book fair** 도서 박람회
- **bright** [brait] 형 밝은
- **century** [séntʃəri] 명 세기, 100년
- **clap** [klæp] 동 박수치다
- **classical** [klǽsikəl] 형 고전의, 클래식 음악의
- **concerto** [kəntʃéərtou] 명 협주곡
- **correct** [kərékt] 형 올바른, 정확한
- **dependent** [dipéndənt] 형 의존적인, 의존하는
- **disturb** [distə́ːrb] 동 방해하다
- **enjoyable** [indʒɔ́iəbl] 형 즐거운, 즐길 수 있는
- **event** [ivént] 명 행사
- **familiar** [fəmíljər] 형 익숙한
- **forget** [fərgét] 동 잊다
- **freely** [fríːli] 부 자유롭게
- **healthy** [hélθi] 형 건강한
- **imagine** [imǽdʒin] 동 상상하다
- **increased** [inkríːst] 형 증가된
- **inside** [ìnsáid] 전 ~ 안에
- **manners** [mǽnərz] 명 예절
- **memorable** [mémərəbl] 형 기억에 남을, 기억할 만한
- **mostly** [móustli] 부 주로
- **movement** [múːvmənt] 명 움직임, (큰 교향곡 따위의) 악장[부분]
- **nobleman** [nóublmən] 명 귀족
- **noise** [nɔiz] 명 소음, 잡음
- **orchestra** [ɔ́ːrkəstrə] 명 오케스트라
- **pause** [pɔːz] 명 정지, 멈춤 동 정지하다
- **performance** [pərfɔ́ːrməns] 명 공연
- **place** [pleis] 명 장소
- **quiet** [kwáiət] 형 조용한
- **remember** [rimémbər] 동 기억하다
- **result** [rizʌ́lt] 명 결과
- **return** [ritə́ːrn] 동 돌려주다, 반납하다
- **scene** [siːn] 명 장면
- **secret** [síːkrit] 명 비밀
- **serious** [síəriəs] 형 심각한, 진지한
- **silent** [sáilənt] 형 조용한
- **social** [sóuʃəl] 형 사회적인, 사교적인
- **surprisingly** [sərpráiziŋli] 부 놀랍게도
- **trash can** 쓰레기통
- **volunteer work** 자원봉사
- **whistle** [hwísl] 동 휘파람을 불다
- **work** [wəːrk] 명 작품

Key Expressions

- **after some time** 얼마 후
- **as a result** 그 결과(=consequently)
- **at any time** 아무 때나
- **dependent on** ~에 의존하는
- **be on time** 제시간에 오다, 시간을 맞추다
- **blame A for B** B 때문에 A를 비난하다
- **by the way** 그건 그렇고
- **for example** 예를 들면(=for instance)
- **for now** 우선은, 현재로는, 지금은
- **go back in time** 과거로 거슬러 올라가다
- **no longer** 더 이상 ~하지 않는
- **part of** ~의 부분
- **take a look at** ~을 보다
- **take care of** ~을 돌보다
- **with time** 시간이 지남에 따라

Word Power

※ '~하는 사람'의 뜻을 갖는 '-ist'

□ **art** (예술) → **artist** (예술가)

□ **tour** (관광) → **tourist** (관광객)

□ **journal** (저널, 신문[잡지]) → **journalist** (기자)

□ **piano** (피아노) → **pianist** (피아노 연주자)

□ **novel** (소설) → **novelist** (소설가)

□ **science** (과학) → **scientist** (과학자)

□ **medal** (메달) → **medalist** (메달 딴 선수)

□ **violin** (바이올린) → **violinist** (바이올린 연주자)

※ 서로 반대되는 뜻을 가진 어휘

□ **dark** (어두운) ↔ **bright** (밝은)

□ **familiar** (익숙한) ↔ **unfamiliar** (익숙하지 않은)

□ **increase** (증가하다) ↔ **decrease** (감소하다)

□ **appear** (나타나다) ↔ **disappear** (사라지다)

□ **dependent** (의존적인) ↔ **independent** (독립적인)

□ **blame** (비난하다) ↔ **praise** (칭찬하다)

English Dictionary

□ **appear**: 나타나다
→ to start to be seen
보이기 시작하다

□ **blame**: 비난하다
→ to think or say that someone or something is responsible for something bad
누군가 또는 무언가가 나쁜 일에 책임이 있다고 생각하거나 말하다

□ **clap**: 박수치다
→ to hit your open hands together
두 손뼉을 마주 치다

□ **concerto**: 협주곡
→ a piece of music for one or more solo instruments playing with an orchestra
오케스트라와 연주하는 하나 이상의 독주 악기를 위한 음악

□ **disturb**: 방해하다
→ to interrupt someone when they are trying to work, sleep, etc.
일을 하거나 잠을 자려고 할 때 누군가를 방해하다

□ **nobleman**: 귀족
→ a man from a family of high social rank; a female member of the nobility 신분이 높은 집안의 남자; 귀족 출신의 여자

□ **noise**: 소음, 잡음
→ a loud or unpleasant sound
크거나 불쾌한 소리

□ **orchestra**: 오케스트라
→ a group of musicians who play usually classical music together and who are led by a conductor
대개 고전 음악을 함께 연주하며 지휘자가 이끄는 음악가 모임

□ **pause**: 정지하다, 멈추다
→ to stop talking or doing something for a short time before continuing
계속하기 전에 잠시 말하거나 무언가를 하는 것을 멈추다

□ **performance**: 공연
→ the act of performing a play, concert, or some other form of entertainment
연극, 콘서트 또는 다른 형태의 오락물을 공연하는 행위

□ **result**: 결과
→ something that is caused by something else that happened or was done before 이전에 발생하거나 행해진 다른 것에 의해 유발된 것

□ **return**: 돌려주다, 반납하다
→ to bring something to the place that it came from or the place where it should go
어떤 것을 원래 있던 곳이나 가야 할 곳으로 가져가다

□ **secret**: 비밀
→ a fact or piece of information that is kept hidden from other people
남들에게 숨겨진 사실이나 정보

□ **whistle**: 휘파람을 불다
→ to make a high sound by blowing air through your lips or teeth
입술이나 치아 사이로 공기를 내보내어 고음을 내다

□ **work**: 작품
→ something such as a book, song, or painting that is produced by a writer, musician, artist, etc.
작가, 음악가, 화가 등이 만든 책, 노래, 그림 같은 것

01 다음 짝지어진 단어의 관계가 같도록 빈칸에 알맞은 말을 쓰시오.

> library : librarian = tour : _____

02 다음 중 밑줄 친 단어의 우리말 뜻이 잘못된 것은?

① He has good manners. 예절
② They look serious nowadays. 심각한
③ Let's clap along to the music. 박수치다
④ The number of students increased last year. 감소했다.
⑤ They blamed each other for the failure. 비난했다.

03 다음 중 밑줄 친 단어와 의미가 같은 것은?

> Don't disturb Jane. She's studying for her exam.

① pause
② appear
③ whistle
④ interrupt
⑤ depend

04 다음 영영풀이에 해당하는 단어는?

> to think or say that someone or something is responsible for something bad

① connect
② worry
③ blame
④ cause
⑤ predict

05 다음 중 〈보기〉의 밑줄 친 단어와 같은 의미로 쓰인 것은?

> ┤ 보기 ├
> Their dancing was a <u>work</u> of art.

① He's still looking for <u>work</u>.
② She goes to <u>work</u> at 8 o'clock.
③ Taking care of a baby is hard <u>work</u>.
④ When do you leave for <u>work</u>?
⑤ She put her <u>works</u> on display in the art gallery.

06 다음 빈칸에 들어갈 말이 바르게 짝지어진 것은?

> • You must be _____ time.
> • Take a look _____ her old picture.

① in - to
② on - at
③ at - in
④ of - by
⑤ in - with

07 다음 우리말에 맞게 빈칸에 알맞은 말을 쓰시오.

(1) 그녀는 밝은 색을 좋아한다.
　➡ She likes _____ colors.
(2) 그 새는 하늘에서 자유롭게 날고 있다.
　➡ The bird is flying _____ in the sky.
(3) 이것은 유명한 피아노 협주곡이다.
　➡ This is a famous piano _____.

01 다음 빈칸에 들어갈 말을 〈보기〉에서 골라 알맞은 형태로 쓰시오.

┌─ 보기 ─┐
novel tour science art
└────────┘

(1) A figure skater is an _____ on the ice.

(2) Sumi wants to be a _____ who studies the stars.

(3) Emily Bronte is an English female _____.

(4) Please tell me the way to the _____ information center.

02 다음 영영풀이에 해당하는 말을 한 단어로 쓰시오.

┌────────────────────────────────┐
│ to hit your open hands together │
└────────────────────────────────┘

➡ _____

03 다음 문장의 빈칸에 들어갈 말을 〈보기〉에서 골라 쓰시오.

┌─ 보기 ─┐
mostly serious blame audience
└────────┘

(1) Don't _____ him. He did his best.

(2) The _____ was moved by the play.

(3) The consequences were _____.

(4) The readers are _____ women and children.

04 다음 밑줄 친 부분과 의미가 같은 단어를 주어진 철자로 시작하여 쓰시오.

┌────────────────────────────┐
│ As a result, my team lost. │
└────────────────────────────┘

➡ C_____

05 다음 우리말과 같도록 빈칸에 알맞은 말을 써 넣으시오.

(1) 나는 더 이상 오래 머물 수 없다.
➡ I can stay _____ _____.

(2) 아이는 부모에 의존한다.
➡ A child is _____ _____ his parents.

(3) 그들은 아무 때나 휘파람을 불고 박수를 친다.
➡ They whistle and clap _____ _____ _____.

06 다음 우리말에 맞게 주어진 단어를 바르게 배열하시오.

(1) 나는 작은 쓰레기통이 필요하다. (need / can / a / I / trash / small)
➡ _____

(2) 소음은 단지 콘서트의 일부였다. (just / noise / concert / of / was / the / part)
➡ _____

(3) 모차르트 시대의 콘서트는 주로 사교적 행사였다. (time / mostly / in / events / concerts / social / Mozart's / were)
➡ _____

Conversation

1 약속 정하기

> A: How about going to the hot spring on Thursday at 2:00? Can you make it?
> (목요일 2시에 온천에 가는 게 어때? 갈 수 있니?)
>
> B: Yes. That would be great. (응. 그거 좋겠다.)

- 'Can you make it?'은 '갈 수 있니?'라는 뜻으로 약속을 정할 때 쓰는 표현이다. 'make it'은 '해내다, 성공하다'라는 의미를 갖고 있지만, 시간이나 장소의 표현과 함께 쓰여 '시간에 맞춰 가다' 또는 '도착하다'라는 의미를 갖는다.

약속 정하기 표현

- Can you make it at six? 6시에 올 수 있니?
- Why don't we meet at the park? 공원에서 만나는 게 어떠니?
- How[What] about meeting at six? 6시에 만나는 게 어떠니?
- Shall we meet after school? 방과 후에 만날까?
- Let's meet at ten on Saturday. 토요일 10시에 만나자.

약속 정하기에 답하는 표현

〈승낙하기〉

That would be great. / That's fine with me. / No problem. / Why not? / Sure, I'd love to. / That's a good idea. / (That) Sounds great.

〈거절하기〉

I'm sorry, I can't. / I'm afraid not. / I'd love to, but I can't. / Not this time, thanks. / Maybe next time.

핵심 Check

1. 다음 우리말과 일치하도록 빈칸에 알맞은 말을 쓰시오.

(1) A: Can you _____ _____ at five? (5시에 올 수 있니?)

　 B: That's _____ with me. (난 괜찮아.)

(2) A: How _____ _____ to the movie theater tomorrow?

　 (우리 내일 영화관에 가는 게 어때?)

　 B: No _____. (문제없어.)

2 상기시키기

A: Don't forget to turn off your cellphone in the theater. (너의 휴대 전화를 극장에서 끄는 것을 잊지 마.)

B: Okay, I won't. (알았어. 잊지 않을게.)

■ 'Don't forget to ~'는 상대방에게 어떤 일을 해야 한다고 알려 주거나 해야 할 일을 상기시켜 주기 위해 사용하는 표현으로 'Remember to+동사원형 ~' 또는 'Make sure that 주어+동사 ~' 또는 'Make sure to+동사원형 ~'으로 바꾸어 쓸 수 있다.

어떤 일을 해야 한다고 알려 주기

- Don't forget to bring your lunch box. 도시락을 가져오는 것을 잊지 마라.
- Remember to bring your lunch box. 도시락을 가져와야 한다는 것을 기억해라.
- Make sure that you should bring your lunch box. 도시락을 가져와야 함을 명심해라.
- Make sure to bring your lunch box. 도시락을 가져와야 함을 명심해라.
- Keep in mind that you should bring your lunch box. 도시락을 가져와야 한다는 것을 명심해라.

■ forget이나 remember 뒤에 -ing를 쓰면 '(과거에) ~했던 것을 잊다[기억하다]'라는 의미가 되고, 'to+동사원형'을 쓰면 '(미래에) ~해야 할 것을 잊다[기억하다]'라는 의미를 나타낸다.

- forget + -ing: (과거에) ~한 것을 잊다
- forget + to 동사원형: (미래에) ~해야 할 것을 잊다
- remember + -ing: (과거에) ~한 것을 기억하다
- remember + to 동사원형: (미래에) ~해야 할 것을 기억하다

핵심 Check

2. 다음 우리말과 일치하도록 빈칸에 알맞은 말을 쓰시오.

(1) A: _____ _____ _____ bring your umbrella. (너의 우산을 가져올 것을 잊지 마라.)

   B: Okay, I see. (네. 알겠어요.)

(2) A: It looks like it's going to rain soon. _____ _____ close the windows.

   (창문을 닫아야 한다는 것을 기억해라.)

   B: Okay, I will. (네. 그럴게요.)

(3) A: I'm going skating tomorrow. (나는 내일 스케이트를 타러 갈 거야.)

   B: _____ _____ _____ put your gloves on. (장갑 끼는 것을 명심해라.)

(4) A: Don't forget to turn off the light before you leave. (떠나기 전에 불을 끌 것을 잊지 마라.)

   B: Okay, I _____. (알았어. 잊지 않을게.)

Listen & Speak 1 B-1

B: ❶Are you interested in going to an opera? I have two tickets.

G: Yes, I love opera. When is ❷it?

B: It's this Saturday at 5:00. ❸Can you make it?

G: Yes, ❹thanks so much for asking me.

B: 너 오페라에 가는 것에 관심이 있니? 내게 표가 두 장 있어.

G: 응, 나 오페라 아주 좋아해. 언제야?

B: 이번 주 토요일 5시야. 갈 수 있니?

G: 응. 나한테 물어봐 줘서 정말 고마워.

❶ be interested in: ~에 관심이 있다
❷ it=the opera
❸ Can you make it?: 갈 수 있니?
❹ thanks so much=thank you so much

Check(√) True or False

(1) The boy isn't interested in going to an opera.　　　　T ☐ F ☐

(2) The girl will go to the opera with the boy.　　　　T ☐ F ☐

Wrap Up

G: Yunho! ❶Have you heard about the Christmas concert at the city hall?

B: Yes. ❷I heard that a famous opera singer will be on the stage.

G: Oh, ❸then why don't we go on Christmas Day? Can you make it?

B: Sure. ❹Do you know what time the concert starts?

G: It starts at 5:30. Let's meet at the bus stop at 4:00.

B: Good. ❺Don't forget to dress up.

G: Okay. I won't.

G: 윤호야! 너 시청에서 하는 크리스마스 콘서트에 대해 들어 봤어?

B: 응. 유명한 오페라 가수가 무대에 오를 것이라고 들었어.

G: 오, 그러면 크리스마스 날에 가는 게 어때? 갈 수 있니?

B: 물론이지. 너는 콘서트가 언제 시작하는지 아니?

G: 5시 30분에 시작해. 버스 정류장에서 4시에 만나자.

B: 좋아. 옷을 차려 입는 것 잊지 마.

G: 알았어. 잊지 않을게.

❶ Have you heard about ~?: ~에 대해 들어 봤니? (경험을 나타내는 현재완료이다.)
❷ that은 접속사로 heard의 목적어가 되는 명사절을 이끈다. be on the stage: 무대에 오르다
❸ why don't we ~?: 우리 ~하는 게 어때? (제안을 나타내는 표현이다.)
❹ what time the concert starts는 간접의문문으로 know의 목적어이다.
❺ Don't forget to ~.: ~하는 것을 잊지 마. (상기시키는 표현이다.) dress up: 옷을 갖춰[격식을 차려] 입다

Check(√) True or False

(3) The Christmas concert will be held at the city hall.　　　　T ☐ F ☐

(4) The girl won't dress up when she goes to the oprea.　　　　T ☐ F ☐

Listen & Speak 1 B-2

B: ❶Why don't we go to the new shoe shop this weekend?

G: Okay. ❷What about at 2:00 on Saturday?

B: ❸Can you make it at 1:00? ❹I have to take care of my sister at 3:00.

G: Sure. ❺See you then.

❶ Why don't we go ～?=Shall we go ～?
❷ What about ～?: ～은 어때?
❸ Can you make it at 1:00?: 1시에 올 수 있니?
❹ take care of: ～을 돌보다
❺ See you then.: 그때 보자.

Listen & Speak 2 B-1

B: ❶We're going to Hangang this weekend. Do you remember?

G: Of course. ❷Don't forget to bring your camera.

B: Okay. ❸I won't. I'll bring some snacks, too.

G: ❹Sounds great.

❶ We're going to Hangang=We're going to go to Hangang
❷ Don't forget to ～: ～할 것을 잊지 마. (상기시키는 표현이다.)
❸ I won't.=I won't forget to bring my camera.
❹ Sounds great.: 그거 좋은데.

Listen & Speak 2 B-2

G: You look healthy. What's your secret?

B: Thanks. ❶Well, I go swimming every day. You should go with me sometime.

G: ❷That sounds like fun. ❸Any other things I should do?

B: ❹Don't forget to eat many kinds of fruits and vegetables, too.

❶ go swimming: 수영하러 가다
❷ That sounds like fun.: 그거 재미있는 것 같구나. fun이 명사이므로 앞에 like를 붙인다.
❸ Any other things I should do?=Are there any other things (which) I should do?
❹ many kinds of fruits: 많은 종류의 과일 (fruit은 보통 단수형으로 쓰이지만, 과일의 종류를 나타낼 때는 복수형을 취한다.)

Real-Life Zone A

G: What are you listening to?

B: Classical music. ❶I'm going to a concert tomorrow and I'd like to know about the music before I go.

G: ❷I guess it's more enjoyable if you know the music.

B: ❸Actually, I don't want to clap at the wrong time.

G: Don't you just clap when the music stops?

B: No. ❹In classical music, one piece of music may have several pauses. ❺You should wait and clap at the very end.

G: I see. ❻Make sure you don't forget to clap at the real ending. ❼By the way, can you make it to our soccer practice tomorrow at 4:00?

B: Sure. ❽I'll come to the practice after the concert finishes.

G: Okay. See you then.

❶ I'm going to a concert tomorrow=I'm going to go to a concert tomorrow / I'd like to: ～하고 싶다
❷ I guess=I think
❸ at the wrong time: 잘못된 때에
❹ may: ～일지도 모른다 (추측을 나타내는 조동사)
❺ at the very end: 맨 마지막에
❻ Make sure (that) you don't forget to ～: ～할 것을 잊지 말도록 해라.
❼ by the way: 그런데 / can you make it to ～: ～에 올 수 있니?
❽ after the concert finishes: 콘서트가 끝난 후에 (때를 나타내는 부사절은 현재형으로 미래의 일을 나타낸다.)

● 다음 우리말과 일치하도록 빈칸에 알맞은 말을 쓰시오.

Listen & Speak 1 B

1. B: Are you _____ _____ going to an opera? I have two
    _____.

   G: Yes, I love opera. _____ is it?

   B: It's _____ Saturday _____ 5:00. Can you _____ _____?

   G: Yes, _____ so much for _____ me.

2. B: _____ _____ we go to the new shoe shop _____
    weekend?

   G: Okay. _____ _____ at 2:00 on Saturday?

   B: Can you _____ _____ at 1:00? I _____ _____ take
    care of my sister at 3:00.

   G: Sure. _____ you then.

Listen & Speak 2 B

1. B: We're _____ _____ Hangang this weekend. Do you _____?

   G: Of course. _____ _____ to bring your camera.

   B: Okay. I _____. I'll bring some snacks, too.

   G: _____ great.

2. G: You _____ healthy. What's your _____?

   B: Thanks. Well, I _____ _____ every day. You should go with
    me _____.

   G: That _____ _____ fun. _____ things I should do?

   B: Don't _____ _____ eat _____ _____ of fruits and
    vegetables, too.

해석

1. B: 너 오페라에 가는 것에 관심이 있
    니? 내게 표가 두 장 있어.
   G: 응, 나 오페라 아주 좋아해. 언제
    야?
   B: 이번 주 토요일 5시야. 갈 수 있
    니?
   G: 응. 나한테 물어봐 줘서 정말 고마
    워.

2. B: 우리 이번 주말에 새로 생긴 신발
    가게에 가는 거 어때?
   G: 좋아. 토요일 2시 어때?
   B: 1시에 가능하니? 난 3시에 여동생
    을 돌봐야 해.
   G: 당연하지. 그때 보자.

1. B: 우리 이번 주말에 한강 가잖아. 기
    억하니?
   G: 물론이지. 카메라 가져 오는 것 잊
    지 마.
   B: 알았어. 잊지 않을게. 나는 약간의
    간식도 가져올게.
   G: 아주 좋아.

2. G: 너 건강해 보여. 비결이 뭐니?
   B: 고마워. 음, 나는 매일 수영하러
    가. 너도 언젠가 나와 함께 가는 게
    좋겠어.
   G: 재밌을 것 같은데. 내가 또 해야
    하는 다른 것들이 있니?
   B: 다양한 종류의 과일과 채소를 먹
    는 것도 잊지 마.

Real-Life Zone A

G: What are you _____ _____?

B: Classical music. I'm _____ _____ a concert tomorrow and I'd _____ _____ know about the music _____ I go.

G: I _____ it's _____ enjoyable _____ you know the music.

B: Actually, I don't want to _____ at the _____ time.

G: Don't you just clap _____ the music _____?

B: No. In classical music, one piece of music _____ have several _____. You should _____ and clap at the _____ _____.

G: I _____. _____ _____ you don't _____ _____ clap at the _____ _____. By the _____, can you _____ _____ to our soccer _____ tomorrow at 4:00?

B: Sure. I'll come to the practice _____ the concert _____.

G: Okay. _____ you then.

Real-Life Zone B

A: _____ _____ we go to the library on Monday _____ school? Can you _____ it?

B: Sorry, but I _____. How _____ on Tuesday?

A: Okay. _____ _____ to bring your library card.

B: All _____. I _____.

Wrap Up

G: Yunho! _____ you _____ about the Christmas concert at the city hall?

B: Yes. I heard _____ a famous opera singer _____ _____ on the stage.

G: Oh, then _____ _____ we go on Christmas Day? Can you _____ _____?

B: Sure. Do you know _____ _____ the concert starts?

G: It starts _____ 5:30. _____ _____ at the bus stop at 4:00.

B: Good. Don't _____ _____ dress up.

G: Okay. I _____.

G: 무엇을 듣고 있니?

B: 클래식 음악. 나 내일 콘서트에 가는데 가기 전에 음악에 대해 알고 싶어.

G: 음악을 알면 더 즐길 수 있겠지.

B: 사실 박수를 잘못된 때에 치고 싶지 않아.

G: 그냥 음악이 멈추었을 때 박수를 치지 않니?

B: 아니야. 클래식 음악에선 음악 한 곡에 여러 번 멈춤이 있을 수가 있어. 기다렸다가 맨 마지막에 박수를 쳐야 해.

G: 그렇구나. 진짜 마지막에 박수를 치는 것을 잊지 마. 그건 그렇고, 내일 4시 축구 연습에 올 수 있니?

B: 물론이지. 콘서트가 끝난 후 연습에 갈게.

G: 좋아. 그때 보자.

A: 월요일 방과 후에 도서관에 가는 게 어때? 갈 수 있니?

B: 미안하지만, 못 가. 화요일은 어때?

A: 좋아. 도서관 카드 가져오는 걸 잊지 마.

B: 알았어. 잊지 않을게.

G: 윤호야! 너 시청에서 하는 크리스마스 콘서트에 대해 들어 봤어?

B: 응. 유명한 오페라 가수가 무대에 오를 것이라고 들었어.

G: 오, 그러면 크리스마스 날에 가는 게 어때? 갈 수 있니?

B: 물론이지. 너는 콘서트가 언제 시작하는지 아니?

G: 5시 30분에 시작해. 버스 정류장에서 4시에 만나자.

B: 좋아. 옷을 차려입는 것 잊지 마.

G: 알았어. 잊지 않을게.

01 다음 대화의 빈칸에 알맞은 것을 고르시오.

> B: Are you interested in going to an opera? I have two tickets.
>
> G: Yes, I love opera. When is it?
>
> B: It's this Saturday at 5:00. _____
>
> G: Yes, thanks so much for asking me.

① Do you like operas?

② What opera are you interested in?

③ Let's go to an opera.

④ Can you make it?

⑤ How can you go there?

02 다음 대화의 순서를 바르게 배열하시오.

> (A) Sure. See you then.
>
> (B) Okay. What about at 2:00 on Saturday?
>
> (C) Why don't we go to the new shoe shop this weekend?
>
> (D) Can you make it at 1:00? I have to take care of my sister at 3:00.

➡ _____

03 다음 대화의 밑줄 친 부분의 의도로 알맞은 것을 고르시오.

> B: We're going to Hangang this weekend. Do you remember?
>
> G: Of course. <u>Don't forget to bring your camera.</u>
>
> B: Okay. I won't. I'll bring some snacks, too.
>
> G: Sounds great.

① 계획 묻기   ② 상기시키기

③ 충고 구하기   ④ 문제점 제안하기

⑤ 약속 정하기

[01~03] 다음 대화를 읽고 물음에 답하시오.

> G: You look ⓐ<u>health</u>. What's your secret?
> B: Thanks. Well, I go swimming every day. You should go with me sometime.
> G: That sounds like fun. ⓑ<u>Any other things I should do?</u>
> B: Don't forget to eat many kinds of fruits and vegetables, too.

01 위 대화의 밑줄 친 ⓐ를 알맞은 형으로 고치시오.

➡ _____

02 위 대화의 밑줄 친 ⓑ를 괄호 안에 주어진 단어를 보충하여 다시 쓰시오. (are, that)

➡ _____

03 위 대화의 내용과 일치하는 것은?

① 소녀는 소년이 건강해 보이는 비결을 알고 있다.
② 소년은 매일 수영을 한다.
③ 소년은 소녀가 언젠가 함께 수영하러 가기를 원한다.
④ 소녀는 소년과 함께 수영하러 가는 것을 재미있게 생각한다.
⑤ 소년은 소녀에게 많은 과일과 채소를 먹으라고 충고한다.

04 다음 대화의 밑줄 친 부분과 의미가 같도록 한 단어로 바꾸어 쓰시오.

> A: Don't forget to look to the right before you cross the street in London.
> B: Okay, I see.

➡ _____

05 다음 대화의 순서를 바르게 배열한 것을 고르시오.

> (A) Okay. Don't forget to bring your library card.
> (B) All right. I won't.
> (C) Why don't we go to the library on Monday after school? Can you make it?
> (D) Sorry, but I can't. How about on Tuesday?

① (B) - (A) - (C) - (D)
② (B) - (C) - (A) - (D)
③ (C) - (A) - (B) - (D)
④ (C) - (B) - (A) - (D)
⑤ (C) - (D) - (A) - (B)

06 다음 밑줄 친 말과 바꾸어 쓸 수 있는 것을 고르시오. (2개)

> A: What time should we meet tomorrow?
> B: <u>Can you make it at five?</u>

① I need to meet you at five.
② Let's meet tomorrow.
③ Let's meet at five.
④ How about meeting at five?
⑤ I can't make it at five.

[07~12] 다음 대화를 읽고 물음에 답하시오.

G: What are you listening   ⓐ   ?

B: Classical music. I'm going to a concert tomorrow and I'd like to know about the music   (A)   I go.

G: I guess it's more enjoyable   (B)   you know the music.

B: Actually, I don't want to clap at the wrong time.

G: Don't you just clap when the music stops?

B: No. In classical music, one piece of music ⓑmay have several pauses. You should wait and clap at the very end.

G: I see. Make sure you don't forget to clap at the real ending. By the way, can you   ⓒ   it to our soccer practice tomorrow at 4:00?

B: Sure. ⓓI'll come to the practice after the concert will finish.

G: Okay. See you then.

07 위 대화의 빈칸 ⓐ에 알맞은 것은?

① at   ② to
③ of   ④ for
⑤ with

08 위 대화의 빈칸 (A)와 (B)에 알맞은 것은?

	(A)	(B)
①	before	if
②	after	if
③	after	when
④	before	until
⑤	before	after

09 위 대화의 밑줄 친 ⓑ와 용법이 같은 것은?

① You may come in if you wish.
② May she rest in peace!
③ The rumor may be false.
④ May I take a picture here?
⑤ You may stay at this hotel for a week.

10 위 대화의 빈칸 ⓒ에 알맞은 것은?

① do   ② let
③ get   ④ make
⑤ find

서답형
11 위 대화의 밑줄 친 ⓓ에서 어법상 어색한 것을 고쳐 다시 쓰시오.

➡ _____

12 위 대화의 내용으로 보아 알 수 없는 것은?

① The boy is listening to classical music.
② The boy often claps at the wrong time.
③ The girl advises the boy to clap at the real ending.
④ The girl knows that there is their soccer practice tomorrow at 4:00.
⑤ The boy will come to the soccer practice tomorrow.

[01~05] 다음 대화를 읽고 물음에 답하시오.

> G: Yunho! Have you heard about the Christmas concert at the city hall?
> B: Yes. I heard ⓐ a famous opera singer will be on the stage.
> G: ⓑOh, then why don't we go on Christmas Day? Can you make it?
> B: Sure. (A)
> G: It starts at 5:30. Let's meet at the bus stop at 4:00.
> B: Good. (B) 옷을 차려 입는 것을 잊지 마.
> G: Okay. I won't.

01 위 대화의 빈칸 ⓐ에 알맞은 말을 쓰시오.

➡ _____

02 위 대화의 밑줄 친 ⓑ와 같은 뜻이 되도록 다음 문장의 빈칸에 알맞은 말을 쓰시오.

➡ Oh, then _____ go on Christmas Day.

03 위 대화의 빈칸 (A)에 다음 두 문장을 한 문장으로 바꿔 채우시오.

> Do you know?+What time does the concert start?

➡ _____

04 위 대화의 밑줄 친 우리말 (B)를 주어진 단어를 이용하여 옮기시오. (5 words)

> forget / up

➡ _____

05 When and where will the girl and the boy meet?

➡ _____

[06~07] 다음 대화를 읽고 물음에 답하시오.

> A: (A)How don't we go to the library on Monday after school? Can you make it?
> B: Sorry, but I can't. (B)How about on Tuesday?
> A: Okay. Don't forget to bring your library card.
> B: All right. I won't.

06 위 대화의 밑줄 친 (A)에서 어법상 어색한 것을 고치시오.

_____ ➡ _____

07 위 대화의 밑줄 친 (B)와 같은 뜻이 되도록 빈칸에 알맞은 말을 쓰시오.

➡ _____ _____ go to the library on Tuesday?

Grammar

1 관계부사

> • Today's quiet concerts began in the 19th century **when** many big concert halls were built.
> 오늘날의 조용한 콘서트는 많은 대형 콘서트홀이 지어진 19세기에 시작되었다.
>
> • Leipzig is the city **where** Wagner was born in 1813.
> 라이프치히는 와그너가 1813년에 태어난 도시이다.

■ 관계부사는 접속사와 부사의 역할을 동시에 하며, 관계대명사처럼 선행사를 수식하는 형용사절을 이끈다. 선행사가 '때'를 나타낼 때는 when, '장소'는 where를 쓴다. 관계부사는 '전치사(at, in, on)+관계대명사(which)'로 바꿔 쓸 수 있다.

	선행사	종류	전치사+관계대명사
장소	the place, the city, the house 등	where	in[at/on] + which
때	the time, the day 등	when	in[at/on] + which
이유	the reason	why	for + which
방법	the way	how	in + which

• I remember the day. She left for Busan on the day.
= I remember the day **on which** she left for Busan. 난 그녀가 부산으로 떠난 날을 기억한다.
= I remember the day **when** she left for Busan.

• A desert is an amazing place **where** a variety of animals survive in their own way.
사막은 다양한 동물들이 그들만의 방식대로 살아가는 놀라운 장소이다.

• Do you know the reason **why**(= **for which**) Dan didn't come? 넌 Dan이 오지 않는 이유를 알고 있니?

■ 선행사가 방법을 나타내는 the way일 경우에는 the way와 how를 함께 쓸 수 없다.

• This is **the way** the man opened the door. 이것이 그 남자가 문을 연 방법이다.

• This is **how** the man opened the door.

• This is the way how the man opened the door. (×)

핵심 Check

1. 다음 문장의 괄호 안에서 알맞은 것을 고르시오.

(1) Sam knows the exact time (when / where) Kate will come.

(2) I'd like to visit the city (why / where) I was born.

(3) Tell me the reason (why / which) you were late for school.

(4) This is (the way how / how / the way) he killed the big bear.

② 간접의문문

> • We do not know **what concerts will look like in the future**.
> 우리는 콘서트가 미래에 어떤 모습일지 알지 못한다.
>
> • I remember **when I went to a concert for the first time**.
> 나는 내가 처음으로 콘서트에 갔던 때를 기억한다.

■ 간접의문문은 의문문이 '의문사+주어+동사' 형태로 문장 안에서 목적어의 역할을 하는 것을 말한다.

　• I don't know **why he was absent**. 〈목적어 역할〉 나는 그가 왜 결석했는지 모른다.

■ 의문사가 주어인 경우에는 의문사가 주어 역할을 동시에 하므로 직접의문문처럼 '의문사+동사'의 어순임에 유의한다.

　• Do you know **who wrote this book**? 너는 누가 이 책을 썼는지 아니?

■ 간접의문문으로 바꾸어 쓸 때에는 조동사 do를 삭제한다. 이때, 조동사 do의 시제를 간접의문문의 동사에 반영해야 한다는 점에 유의해야 한다.

　• Please tell me. + What did you do last night?
　→ Please tell me **what you did last night**. 너는 어젯밤 무엇을 했는지 내게 말해 줘.

■ 의문사가 없는 경우에는 의문사 대신에 if나 whether를 쓴다.

　• Will you tell me? + Are you hungry?
　→ Will you tell me **if[whether] you are hungry**? 배가 고픈지 내게 말해 줄래?

■ believe, imagine, suppose, consider, expect, think, guess 등과 같은 동사가 주절에 있을 경우 간접의문문의 의문사를 문장 맨 앞으로 배치한다.

　• Do you think? + Who is he?
　→ **Who** do you think **he is**? 너는 그가 누구라고 생각하니?
　→ Do you think who he is? (×)

핵심 Check

2. 다음 우리말과 일치하도록 빈칸에 알맞은 말을 쓰시오.

(1) 네가 무엇을 샀는지 말해 줄 수 있니?

➡ Can you tell me ＿＿＿＿ ＿＿＿＿ ＿＿＿＿?

(2) 나는 네가 그것을 좋아하는지 궁금해.

➡ I wonder ＿＿＿＿ ＿＿＿＿ ＿＿＿＿ it.

(3) 너는 누가 그 경기에서 이길 거라고 생각하니?

➡ ＿＿＿＿ ＿＿＿＿ ＿＿＿＿ ＿＿＿＿ ＿＿＿＿ win the game?

01 다음 두 문장을 한 문장으로 연결할 때 올바른 것은?

> • Do you know?
> • What is it famous for?

① Do you know what is it famous for?
② Do you know what it is famous for?
③ Do you know it is famous for what?
④ What do you know it is famous for?
⑤ What do you know is it famous for?

02 다음 괄호 안에서 알맞은 것을 고르시오.

(1) November is the month (when / where) I was born.

(2) This is the restaurant (when / where) I first met him.

(3) I can't forget the day (when / where) I arrived in Canada.

(4) That is the reason (which / why) I came back so soon.

03 우리말과 의미가 같도록 빈칸에 들어갈 말로 알맞은 것을 고르시오.

> • 나는 그가 내일 집으로 돌아올지 알 필요가 있어.
> ➡ I need to know _____ back home tomorrow.

① if he will come   ② he will come
③ will he come   ④ whether will he come
⑤ that he will come

04 다음 빈칸에 알맞은 말을 〈보기〉에서 골라 쓰시오.

> why   how   when   where

(1) This is the park _____ I often take a walk.

(2) I'll never forget the day _____ I met my favorite soccer player.

(3) I know the reason _____ Jack loves you.

(4) This is _____ Miss White could marry Johnson.

01 다음 빈칸에 알맞은 것을 고르시오.

> A: Do you know _____?
> B: It's on the desk.

① where does the book
② where the books are
③ where are the books
④ where is the book
⑤ where the book is

02 다음 문장의 빈칸에 알맞은 것은?

> I remember the day on _____ we started the work.

① which   ② when
③ that   ④ where
⑤ how

03 다음 우리말을 영어로 바르게 옮긴 것은?

> 너는 그의 생일이 언제인지 기억하니?

① When do you remember his birthday is?
② When do you remember is his birthday?
③ Do you remember when is his birthday?
④ Do you remember his birthday is when?
⑤ Do you remember when his birthday is?

04 다음 문장의 괄호 안에서 알맞은 것을 고르시오.

(1) I know the hotel (which / where) he is staying.

(2) This is (the way / the way how) she opened the door.

(3) Do you know the reason (which / for which) he didn't go to the meeting?

05 다음을 간접의문문을 이용하여 한 문장으로 쓰시오.

(1) Do you know? Who is that tall guy over there?

    ➡ _____

(2) Tell me. Who made this chocolate cake?

    ➡ _____

(3) I wonder. Did Marianne get married?

    ➡ _____

(4) Do you think? Where is Snow White?

    ➡ _____

06 다음 중 밑줄 친 부분의 쓰임이 나머지와 다른 하나는?

① Do you know when to stop?
② He forgot the day when he had first met her.
③ When does he go to the library?
④ I wonder when he will arrive at home.
⑤ When did you last see your friend Mike?

07 다음 중 어법상 바르지 <u>않은</u> 것은?

① Do you know where the first train station in Korea is?
② Tell me whether he is at home.
③ She wants to know who the winner is.
④ The woman is asking me where the library is.
⑤ I'm not sure if or not this answer is right.

08 다음 빈칸에 들어갈 말로 알맞게 짝지어진 것은?

• Tell me the reason _____ he came here.
• I will explain _____ the detective cleared up the mystery.

① why – how
② that – what
③ which – how
④ why – which
⑤ that – which

서답형

09 다음 두 문장을 간접의문문을 이용하여 한 문장으로 쓰시오.

(1) I know. + Who won the race?
➡ _____

(2) Do you know? + When will the bus come?
➡ _____

(3) The man is asking her. + How long does it take to get to TIG Market?
➡ _____
_____

(4) Do you think? + Who will win the game?
➡ _____

(5) Do you guess? + What does she want to buy?
➡ _____

10 다음 빈칸에 들어갈 말이 나머지와 <u>다른</u> 하나는?

① Today is the day _____ I have a test.
② This is the place _____ we held a party.
③ This is the room _____ I sleep every day.
④ This is the library _____ I read the book.
⑤ The town _____ I was born had a large river.

서답형

11 다음 중 어법상 <u>어색한</u> 것을 찾아 바르게 고치시오.

(1) Tell me when does the show start.
_____ ➡ _____

(2) Please let me know that does the bag have some pockets.
_____ ➡ _____

(3) Do you think who runs fastest?
_____ ➡ _____

12 다음 두 문장을 한 문장으로 바르게 연결한 것은? (2개)

• This is a famous restaurant.
• Many people go there in France.

① This is a famous restaurant many people go there in France.
② This is a famous restaurant to which many people go in France.
③ This is a famous restaurant which many people go in France.
④ This is a famous restaurant where many people go in France.
⑤ This is a famous restaurant where many people go there in France.

13 다음 두 문장을 간접의문문으로 바르게 바꾼 것은?

> • Do you know?
> • Who is Leonardo da Vinci?

① Who is Leonardo da Vinci do you know?
② Who do you know is Leonardo da Vinci?
③ Who do you know Leonardo da Vinci is?
④ Do you know who is Leonardo da Vinci?
⑤ Do you know who Leonardo da Vinci is?

서답형
14 다음 괄호 안의 말을 이용하여 우리말을 영작하시오.

(1) 나는 그녀가 그 문제를 푼 방법을 안다. (how, solve)

➡ _____

(2) 나는 Jerry가 화가 났던 이유를 안다. (why, angry)

➡ _____

(3) 이곳은 내가 집에 가는 길에 종종 들르는 도서관이다. (where, stop by, on)

➡ _____

15 다음 문장의 밑줄 친 when과 쓰임이 같은 것은?

> Tell me the day when he will come.

① When you go out, take your umbrella.
② I didn't have a bike when I was a kid.
③ I was sleeping when the phone rang.
④ I remember the day when I started the work.
⑤ She waved her hand at Tom when she saw him.

 16 다음 괄호 안의 단어를 바르게 배열할 때 다섯 번째로 오는 단어는?

> (is / house / this / live / with / I / parents / the / where / my)

① is   ② I
③ house   ④ where
⑤ live

17 다음 우리말을 영어로 바르게 옮긴 것은? (2개)

> 나는 프랑스를 방문했던 그 여름을 잊지 못한다.

① I can't forget the summer what I visited France.
② I can't forget the summer which I visited France.
③ I can't forget the summer when I visited France.
④ I can't forget the summer where I visited France.
⑤ I can't forget the summer in which I visited France.

서답형
18 다음 두 문장을 한 문장으로 만들었을 때, 나머지 한 문장을 쓰시오.

(1) • He is asking her.
  + • _____
    ➡ He is asking her how long it takes to reach the top.

(2) • The woman was not sure.
  + • _____
    ➡ The woman was not sure if the thief was a man or a woman.

(3) • Do you believe?
  + • _____
    ➡ What do you believe the secret of his success is?

01 다음 두 문장을 하나의 문장으로 바꿔 쓰시오.

(1) Tell me. + What do you want for Christmas?

➡ _____

(2) She asks me. + How much sugar is there in the bottle?

➡ _____

(3) Do you know? + Where is Greece on the map?

➡ _____

(4) I wonder. + Is he a singer?

➡ _____

(5) I have no idea. + Will he join us soon?

➡ _____

(6) Do you think? + Where does your soul go after you die?

➡ _____

02 다음 두 문장을 한 문장으로 바르게 연결하시오.

(1) This is the house. I was born in this house.

➡ _____

(2) December 25th is the day. Christmas is celebrated on that day.

➡ _____
_____

(3) There is a small bed. I always sleep on it.

➡ _____

(4) This is the way. I solved the problem in the way.

➡ _____

03 다음 괄호 안에서 알맞은 말을 고르시오.

(1) Mike asked me what (did I eat / I ate) for breakfast.

(2) We have no idea when (she left / did she leave).

(3) She knows who (is he / he is).

(4) I don't know (that / if) he will come here.

04 다음 문장의 밑줄 친 부분을 바르게 고쳐 쓰시오.

(1) I don't know the reason which my mom was angry.

➡ _____

(2) Write the name of the city where you live in.

➡ _____

(3) This is the way how we found the answers.

➡ _____

(4) He was born in the year which the war ended.

➡ _____

05 다음 문장을 어법에 맞게 고쳐 쓰시오.

(1) The doctor will ask you what did you eat for breakfast.

➡ _____

(2) Please let us know are you able to attend the meeting.

➡ _____

_____

(3) Do you suppose what they are thinking?

➡ _____

06 다음 우리말을 참고하여 빈칸에 알맞은 말을 쓰시오.

(1) 나는 그가 편지를 감춘 곳을 알고 있다.

➡ I know the place _____ he hid the letter.

(2) 너는 그가 너에게 돈을 준 이유를 아니?

➡ Do you know the reason _____ he gave you money?

(3) 너는 자동차가 없던 시절을 상상할 수 있니?

➡ Can you imagine the days _____ there were no cars?

07 괄호 안에 주어진 어휘를 이용하여 다음 우리말을 영작하시오.

(1) Daniel은 그가 어떻게 가수가 되었는지 우리에게 말해 주었다. (become, a singer)

➡ _____

(2) 그가 올지 안 올지 의심스럽다. (it, doubtful, whether, come, or)

➡ _____

08 다음 우리말과 같도록 주어진 단어를 배열하여 문장을 완성하시오.

(1) 너는 네 여동생을 처음 본 날을 기억하니?
(sister / you / little / first / you / remember / your / do / the / day / when / saw)?

➡ _____

(2) 공원은 사람들이 산책을 하는 곳이다.
(where / park / walk / take / people / a / place / a / is / a)

➡ _____

(3) Mariel은 자기가 아사코를 만나게 될지 어떨지 알고 싶어 한다.
(Mariel / to / to / is / know / wants / meet / he / whether / Asako / going)

➡ _____

09 다음 문장을 두 문장으로 나누어 쓰시오.

(1) Nobody knows why Lauren left the office early.

➡ _____

(2) It is difficult to understand what the teacher says.

➡ _____

(3) Steve didn't tell me when the movie began.

➡ _____

(4) What do you think the most typical Korean dish is?

➡ _____

(5) They wonder if they can borrow some books today.

➡ _____

Reading

The History of Classical Concert Manners

Imagine yourself at a classical music concert. The orchestra starts
재귀대명사(재귀 용법)   ~하기 시작하다
to play one of Mozart's piano concertos. The concert hall is dark and

silent. Nobody makes a sound. Everybody looks serious.
        누구도 ~하지 않는   단수 취급

The audiences only clap after the concerto finishes. This is a familiar
            부사절 after 이하를 수식

scene at concerts today.

Let's go back in time and take a look at one of Mozart's concerts in
                        go와 병렬 구조

the 18th century. You are in a bright hall inside a nobleman's house.

Mozart is playing the piano. Surprisingly, however, the audiences are
눈앞에 벌어지는 일을 나타내는 현재진행형   문장 전체를 수식하는 부사

eating, drinking, and talking freely. They whistle and clap at any time.

You are shocked by their bad manners, but Mozart himself would be
주어가 충격을 받는 입장을 나타내는 수동태   강조 용법의 재귀대명사(생략 가능)

surprised by today's quiet audiences.

Concerts in Mozart's time were mostly social events. They were

good places to meet people. Noise was just part of the concert.
     places를 수식하는 형용사적 용법의 부정사

imagine 상상하다
classical 고전적인
concerto 협주곡, 콘체르토
silent 조용한
look ~해 보이다
serious 진지한, 심각한
audience 청중, 관객
clap 박수를 치다
finish 끝나다
familiar 친숙한
scene 장면
nobleman 상류층, 귀족
surprisingly 놀랍게도
whistle 휘파람을 불다
mostly 주로
social 사교적인, 사회적인

 확인문제

● 다음 문장이 본문의 내용과 일치하면 T, 일치하지 <u>않으면</u> F를 쓰시오.

1 The concert hall is dark and silent. ☐

2 The audiences only clap after the concerto finishes. ☐

3 Mozart's concert hall in the 18th century was bright. ☐

4 Mozart wouldn't be surprised by today's quiet audiences. ☐

5 Concerts in Mozart's time weren't mostly social events. ☐

Today's quiet concerts began in the 19th century when many big
concert halls were built. More people, not just noblemen, went to
concerts. Artists were no longer dependent on noblemen for money.
The artists had more power over their works and started to use their
increased power. For example, Wagner blamed the audience for
making noise. After some time, a no-clapping-between-movements
rule appeared.

As a result, here we are today, very quiet and serious. We do not
know what concerts will look like in the future because manners
change with time. For now, however, if you want to enjoy classical
music concerts, just remember this: Enjoy the music, but do not
disturb those around you.

not just 단지 ~ 뿐만 아니라
no longer 더 이상 ~ 아닌
dependent 의존하는
increase 증가시키다
for example 예를 들면
blame 비난하다
movement 악장, 움직임
appear 나타나다
as a result 결과적으로
look like ~처럼 보이다
in the future 미래에
manners 예의범절
for now 지금은
disturb 방해하다

 확인문제

● 다음 문장이 본문의 내용과 일치하면 T, 일치하지 않으면 F를 쓰시오.

1 Today's quiet concerts began in the 19th century. ☐

2 Many big concert halls were built in the 18th century. ☐

3 Just noblemen, not most people, went to concerts in the 19th century. ☐

4 Artists were dependent on noblemen for money in the 19th century. ☐

5 The artists had less power over their works in the 19th century. ☐

6 We know what concerts will look like in the future because manners don't change
    with time. ☐

● 우리말을 참고하여 빈칸에 알맞은 말을 쓰시오.

1 The History of _____ Concert _____

2 _____ _____ at a _____ music concert.

3 The _____ starts to _____ _____ of Mozart's _____ concertos.

4 The concert _____ is _____ and _____ .

5 _____ makes a _____ .

6 _____ looks _____ .

7 The _____ only _____ after the concerto _____ .

8 This is a _____ _____ _____ concerts today.

9 Let's _____ _____ in _____ and _____ a _____ at one of Mozart's concerts in the 18th century.

10 You are in a _____ hall _____ a _____ house.

11 Mozart is _____ the _____ .

12 _____ , however, the _____ are eating, drinking, and _____ _____ .

13 They _____ and _____ at any time.

14 You are _____ by their _____ manners, but Mozart _____ would be _____ by today's _____ audiences.

15 Concerts in Mozart's time _____ _____ _____ events.

16 They were _____ _____ _____ people.

17 Noise was _____ _____ of the concert.

1 클래식 콘서트 관람 예절의 역사

2 당신이 클래식 공연장에 있다고 상상해 보아라.

3 오케스트라가 모차르트의 피아노 협주곡들 중 한 곡을 연주하기 시작한다.

4 콘서트장은 어둡고 조용하다.

5 아무도 소리를 내지 않는다.

6 모두가 진지하게 보인다.

7 청중은 오직 협주곡이 끝난 후에만 손뼉을 친다.

8 이것이 오늘날 콘서트에서 익숙한 장면이다.

9 과거로 거슬러 올라가서 18세기 모차르트의 콘서트들 중 하나를 살펴보자.

10 당신은 한 귀족의 집안 밝은 홀에 있다.

11 모차르트는 피아노를 치고 있다.

12 하지만 놀랍게도, 청중들은 먹고 마시며 자유롭게 대화하고 있다.

13 그들은 아무 때나 휘파람을 불고 박수를 친다.

14 당신은 그들의 나쁜 매너에 충격을 받지만, 모차르트 자신은 오늘날의 조용한 청중에게 놀랄지도 모른다.

15 모차르트 시대의 콘서트는 주로 사교적인 행사였다.

16 콘서트는 사람을 만나기에 좋은 장소였다.

17 소음은 그저 콘서트의 일부였다.

18 Today's _____ concerts began in the 19th _____ _____ many big concert halls _____ _____ .

19 More people, _____ _____ _____ , went to concerts.

20 Artists were _____ _____ _____ on noblemen for money.

21 The artists had _____ _____ over their works and started to _____ their _____ power.

22 _____ _____ , Wagner _____ the audience _____ making noise.

23 _____ some time, a no-clapping-between-movements _____ _____ .

24 _____ _____ _____ , here we are today, very _____ and serious.

25 We do not know _____ _____ will _____ _____ in the future _____ manners _____ with time.

26 For now, _____ , if you want to _____ _____ music concerts, _____ _____ this:

27 _____ the music, but do not _____ _____ around you.

18	오늘날의 조용한 콘서트는 많은 대형 공연장이 생긴 **19**세기에 시작됐다.
19	귀족뿐만 아니라 더 많은 사람들이 콘서트에 갔다.
20	예술가들은 더 이상 돈을 벌기 위해 귀족들에게 의존하지 않았다.
21	예술가들은 자신의 작품에 더 많은 권한이 생겼고 그 힘을 사용하기 시작했다.
22	예를 들어, 바그너는 소음을 낸다는 것 때문에 관객들을 비난했다.
23	얼마 후에 '악장 사이 박수 금지 규칙'이 생겼다.
24	그 결과, 오늘날 우리는, 매우 조용하고 진지하다.
25	예절은 시대에 따라 변하기 때문에 우리는 콘서트가 미래에는 어떤 모습일지 모른다.
26	하지만 지금은 당신이 클래식 음악 공연을 즐기고 싶다면 이것만은 기억해라:
27	음악은 즐기되 당신 주변의 다른 사람들을 방해하지 마라.

● 우리말을 참고하여 본문을 영작하시오.

1 클래식 콘서트 관람 예절의 역사
➡ _____

2 당신이 클래식 공연장에 있다고 상상해 보아라.
➡ _____

3 오케스트라가 모차르트의 피아노 협주곡들 중 한 곡을 연주하기 시작한다.
➡ _____

4 콘서트장은 어둡고 조용하다.
➡ _____

5 아무도 소리를 내지 않는다.
➡ _____

6 모두가 진지하게 보인다.
➡ _____

7 청중은 오직 협주곡이 끝난 후에만 손뼉을 친다.
➡ _____

8 이것이 오늘날 콘서트에서 익숙한 장면이다.
➡ _____

9 과거로 거슬러 올라가서 18세기 모차르트의 콘서트들 중 하나를 살펴보자.
➡ _____

10 당신은 한 귀족의 집안 밝은 홀에 있다.
➡ _____

11 모차르트는 피아노를 치고 있다.
➡ _____

12 하지만 놀랍게도, 청중들은 먹고 마시며 자유롭게 대화하고 있다.
➡ _____

13 그들은 아무 때나 휘파람을 불고 박수를 친다.
➡ _____

14 당신은 그들의 나쁜 매너에 충격을 받지만, 모차르트 자신은 오늘날의 조용한 청중에게 놀랄지도 모른다.
➡ _____

15 모차르트 시대의 콘서트는 주로 사교적인 행사였다.
➡ _____

16 콘서트는 사람을 만나기에 좋은 장소였다.
➡ _____

17 소음은 그저 콘서트의 일부였다.
➡ _____

18 오늘날의 조용한 콘서트는 많은 대형 공연장이 생긴 19세기에 시작됐다.

➡ _____

19 귀족뿐만 아니라 더 많은 사람들이 콘서트에 갔다.

➡ _____

20 예술가들은 더 이상 돈을 벌기 위해 귀족들에게 의존하지 않았다.

➡ _____

21 예술가들은 자신의 작품에 더 많은 권한이 생겼고 그 힘을 사용하기 시작했다.

➡ _____

22 예를 들어, 바그너는 소음을 낸다는 것 때문에 관객들을 비난했다.

➡ _____

23 얼마 후에 '악장 사이 박수 금지 규칙'이 생겼다.

➡ _____

24 그 결과, 오늘날 우리는, 매우 조용하고 진지하다.

➡ _____

25 예절은 시대에 따라 변하기 때문에 우리는 콘서트가 미래에는 어떤 모습일지 모른다.

➡ _____

26 하지만 지금은 당신이 클래식 음악 공연을 즐기고 싶다면 이것만은 기억해라.

➡ _____

27 음악은 즐기되 당신 주변의 다른 사람들을 방해하지 마라.

➡ _____

[01~03] 다음 글을 읽고 물음에 답하시오.

Imagine yourself at a classical music concert. The orchestra starts ⓐto play one of Mozart's piano concertos. The concert hall is dark and silent. Nobody makes a sound. Everybody looks serious. The audiences only clap after the concerto finishes. ⓑThis is a familiar scene at concerts today.

01 위 글의 밑줄 친 ⓐto play와 문법적 쓰임이 같은 것을 모두 고르시오.

① He wants to see the game this weekend.
② The old lady came here to meet you yesterday.
③ For the work, I need a pen to write with.
④ My sister hopes to be a doctor in the future.
⑤ We decided to finish the work.

서답형
02 위 글의 밑줄 친 ⓑThis가 가리키는 것을 본문에서 찾아 영어로 쓰시오.

➡ _____

_____

_____

중요
03 위 글의 내용과 일치하지 않는 것은?

① 오늘날의 콘서트홀은 밝다.
② 오늘날의 콘서트홀은 조용하다.
③ 연주회에서는 소음을 내지 않는다.
④ 관객의 표정은 진지하다.
⑤ 관객들은 연주 중간에 박수를 치지 않는다.

[04~06] 다음 글을 읽고 물음에 답하시오.

Let's go back in time and take a look ⓐ____ one of Mozart's concerts in the 18th century. You are in a bright hall inside a nobleman's house. Mozart is playing the piano. Surprisingly, however, the audiences are eating, drinking, and ⓑtalking freely. They whistle and clap at any time. You are shocked by their bad manners, but Mozart himself would be surprised ⓒ____ today's quiet audiences. Concerts in Mozart's time were mostly social events. They were good places to meet people. Noise was just part of the concert.

중요
04 위 글의 빈칸 ⓐ와 ⓒ에 들어갈 전치사가 바르게 짝지어진 것은?

① for - about   ② in - by
③ at - by   ④ at - about
⑤ by - on

서답형
05 By what would Mozart be surprised? Fill in the blanks with the suitable words.

➡ He would be surprised by _____

_____.

06 위 글의 밑줄 친 ⓑtalking과 문법적 쓰임이 다른 것을 모두 고르시오.

① He was talking with his friends.
② You must be proud of being a member of the team.
③ She will be listening to music.
④ They were playing basketball after the class.
⑤ He enjoyed watching the movie.

[07~09] 다음 글을 읽고 물음에 답하시오.

Today's quiet concerts began in the 19th century when many big concert halls were built. More people, not just noblemen, went to concerts. Artists were no longer dependent on noblemen for money. The artists had more power over their works and started to use their increased power. For example, Wagner blamed the audience for making noise. After some time, a no-clapping-between-movements rule appeared.

서답형

07 위 글의 밑줄 친 when과 바꿔 쓸 수 있는 두 단어를 쓰시오.

➡ _____

중요
08 위 글의 제목으로 알맞은 것을 고르시오.

① Today's Quiet Concerts
② How Today's Quiet Concerts Began
③ What Made Artists Dependent on Noblemen?
④ Why Wagner Blamed the Audience
⑤ How Did Artists Have More Power over Their Works?

09 위 글을 읽고 19세기의 Artists에 대해 알 수 있는 것을 모두 고르시오.

① They could use many big concerts halls.
② They made more money than before.
③ Their works were better than ever.
④ Wagner didn't like the audience making noise.
⑤ They made a no-clapping-between-movements rule.

[10~12] 다음 글을 읽고 물음에 답하시오.

As a result, here we are today, very quiet and serious. We do not know (A)[how / what] concerts will look like in the future because (B)[manners / manner] change with time. For now, ⓐ_____, if you want to enjoy classical music concerts, just remember this: Enjoy the music, but do not disturb (C)[that / those] ⓑ_____ you.

중요
10 위 글의 괄호 (A)~(C)에서 문맥이나 어법상 알맞은 낱말을 골라 쓰시오.

➡ (A)_____ (B)_____ (C)_____

중요
11 위 글의 밑줄 친 빈칸 ⓐ에 들어가기에 자연스러운 것은?

① however
② therefore
③ as a result
④ at last
⑤ for instance

12 위 글의 빈칸 ⓑ에 들어가기에 적절한 전치사는?

① with   ② around   ③ in
④ for   ⑤ over

[13~15] 다음 글을 읽고 물음에 답하시오.

Imagine ⓐyourself at a classical music concert. ⓑThe orchestra starts to play one of Mozart's piano concerto. The concert hall is dark and silent. Nobody makes a sound. Everybody looks serious. The audiences only clap after the concerto finishes. This is a familiar scene at concerts today.

13 위 글의 밑줄 친 문장 ⓐ에 나오는 yourself와 용법이 <u>다른</u> 것을 <u>모두</u> 고르시오.

① He <u>himself</u> drove the car in the rain yesterday.
② She prepared this food <u>herself</u> for her family.
③ He expresses <u>himself</u> in good clear English.
④ She watched <u>herself</u> in the mirror for a long time.
⑤ He will do the work <u>himself</u> after he comes home.

서답형
14 위 글의 밑줄 친 ⓑ에서 어법이 <u>어색한</u> 것을 찾아 올바른 형태로 바꾸어 쓰시오.

➡ _____

15 위 글을 읽고 대답할 수 <u>없는</u> 질문은?

① Does everybody look serious at the concert?
② How is the concert hall?
③ What is a familiar scene at concerts today?
④ When do the audiences clap?
⑤ Why did the orchestra play Mozart's piano concerto?

[16~18] 다음 글을 읽고 물음에 답하시오.

Let's go back in time and take a look at one of Mozart's concerts in the 18th century. You are in a bright hall inside a nobleman's house. Mozart is playing the piano. Surprisingly, however, the audiences are eating, drinking, and talking freely. They whistle and clap at any time. You are shocked by their bad manners, but Mozart himself would be surprised by today's quiet audiences. Concerts in Mozart's time were mostly social events. They were good places ⓐto meet people. Noise was just part of the concert.

16 What is the passage mainly talking about?

① What did Mozart play at the concert in the 18th century?
② When did the audiences clap at the concert?
③ By what was Mozart shocked at the concert?
④ What was the concert like in Mozart's time?
⑤ Why did the audiences make noise at the concert?

17 위 글의 밑줄 친 ⓐto meet과 to부정사의 용법이 <u>다른</u> 것을 <u>모두</u> 고르시오.

① The kind woman wants <u>to meet</u> you.
② She needs some friends <u>to help</u> her with the work.
③ His brother gave me some interesting books <u>to read</u>.
④ I am sorry <u>to hear</u> that.
⑤ He has some work <u>to finish</u> now.

18 위 글의 내용과 일치하지 <u>않는</u> 것은?

① In the 18th century, concerts were held in bright halls.
② A concert hall was inside a nobleman's house at the time.
③ The audiences were talking freely during the concert.
④ The audiences didn't whistle and clap at any time.
⑤ Concerts were good places to meet people.

[19~21] 다음 글을 읽고 물음에 답하시오.

ⓐ<u>Today's quiet concerts began in the 19th century when many big concert halls built.</u> More people, not just noblemen, went ① _____ concerts. Artists were no longer dependent ② _____ noblemen for money. The artists had more power ③ _____ their works and started to use their increased power. For example, Wagner blamed the audience ④ _____ making noise. ⑤ _____ some time, a no-clapping-between-movements rule appeared.

19 위 글의 빈칸 ①~⑤에 들어갈 단어 중 적절하지 <u>않은</u> 것은?

① to ② on ③ over
④ by ⑤ After

서답형
20 위 글의 밑줄 친 ⓐ에서 어법상 틀린 부분을 찾아 고치시오.

_____ ➡ _____

21 위 글의 내용과 일치하지 <u>않는</u> 것은?

① 오늘날의 조용한 콘서트는 18세기에 시작되었다.
② 19세기에는 많은 사람들이 콘서트에 갔다.
③ 예술가들이 귀족의 후원에서 벗어날 수 있었다.
④ 바그너는 소음을 내는 것을 싫어했다.
⑤ 악장 사이에 박수 치지 않는 규칙이 생겼다.

[22~23] 다음 글을 읽고 물음에 답하시오.

As a result, here we are today, very (A)[quiet / noisy] and serious. We do not know what concerts will look ⓐ _____ in the future (B)[because of / because] manners change with time. For now, however, if you want to enjoy classical music concerts, just remember this: Enjoy the music, but do not (C)[watch / disturb] those around you.

22 위 글의 빈칸 ⓐ에 들어가기에 알맞은 말을 고르시오.

① after ② into
③ at ④ like
⑤ out

23 위 글의 괄호 (A)~(C)에서 문맥이나 어법상 알맞은 것은?

	(A)	(B)	(C)
①	quiet	because	watch
②	quiet	because	disturb
③	quiet	because of	watch
④	noisy	because of	disturb
⑤	noisy	because	disturb

[01~03] 다음 글을 읽고 물음에 답하시오.

①Imagine yourself at a classical music concert. ②The orchestra starts to play one of Mozart's piano concertos. ③The concert hall is dark and silent. ④Nobody makes a sound. ⑤Everybody look serious. The audiences only clap after the concerto finishes. ⓐThis is a familiar scene at concerts today.

01 위 글의 밑줄 친 ①~⑤ 중에서 어법상 틀린 것을 찾아 번호를 쓰고, 고치시오.

➡ 번호: _____ 틀린 것: _____
올바른 형태: _____

02 위 글에서 다음 설명에 해당하는 단어를 찾아 쓰시오.

> a group of people who come to watch and listen to someone speaking or performing in public

➡ _____

03 밑줄 친 ⓐ가 가리키는 것을 우리말로 쓰시오.

➡ _____
_____
_____

[04~06] 다음 글을 읽고 물음에 답하시오.

Let's go back in time and (A)[take] a look at one of Mozart's concerts in the 18th century. You are in a bright hall inside a nobleman's house. Mozart is playing the piano. Surprisingly, however, the audiences are eating, drinking, and talking (B)[free]. They whistle and clap at any time. You are shocked by their bad manners, but Mozart himself would be surprised by today's quiet audiences. Concerts in Mozart's time were mostly social events. They were good places to meet people. Noise was just part of the concert.

04 위 글 (A)에 주어진 단어의 적절한 형태를 쓰시오.

➡ (A) _____

05 위 글에서 다음 영영사전의 뜻을 나타내는 단어를 찾아 쓰시오.

> a man who is a member of the highest social class and has a title such as 'Duke'

➡ _____

06 위 글 (B)에 주어진 단어의 적절한 형태를 쓰시오.

➡ (B) _____

[07~09] 다음 글을 읽고 물음에 답하시오.

Today's quiet concerts began in the 19th century when many big concert halls were built. More people, not just noblemen, went to concerts. ⓐArtists were no longer dependent on noblemen for money. The artists had more power over their works and started to use their increased power. For example, Wagner blamed the audience for making noise. After some time, a no-clapping-between-movements rule appeared.

07 Why did Wagner blame the audience? Fill in the blanks with suitable words.

➡ Wagner blamed the audience because they made _____ .

08 다음 문장에 적절한 말을 채워, 위 글 ⓐ와 같은 뜻의 문장을 완성하시오.

Artists _____ dependent on noblemen for money any longer.

09 위 글에 어울리도록 아래 주어진 문장의 빈칸에 적절한 말을 쓰시오.

Many big concerts hall began to (A)_____ _____ in the 19th century and artists had more (B)_____ over their works.

[10~12] 다음 글을 읽고 물음에 답하시오.

As a result, here we are today, very quiet and serious. We do not know (A)_____ concerts will look like in the future ⓐ[because / because of] manners change with time. For now, however, if you want to enjoy classical music concerts, just remember (B)this: Enjoy the music, but do not disturb ⓑ[ones / those] around you.

10 위 글의 빈칸 (A)에 들어가기에 적절한 단어를 쓰시오.

➡ _____

11 위 글 ⓐ와 ⓑ에 어법상 적절한 것을 고르시오.

➡ ⓐ _____ ⓑ _____

12 위 글의 밑줄 친 (B)의 this가 가리키는 것을 찾아 우리말로 쓰시오.

➡ _____

[13~15] 다음 글을 읽고 물음에 답하시오.

Imagine yourself at a classical music concert. The orchestra starts to play one of Mozart's piano concertos. The concert hall is dark and silent. ⓐ_____ makes a sound. ⓑ모두가 진지해 보인다. The audiences only clap after the concerto finishes. This is a familiar scene at concerts today.

13 위 글의 빈칸 ⓐ에 들어갈 알맞은 말을 쓰시오.

➡ _____

14 위 글의 밑줄 친 ⓑ의 우리말을 세 단어로 쓰시오.

➡ _____

15 다음 빈칸 (A)와 (B)에 알맞은 단어를 넣어 오늘날의 연주회장을 설명하시오.

Today the concert hall is (A)_____ and (B)_____ and the audiences (C)_____ only after the concerto is over.

구석구석

Before You Read B

A Guide to Good Concert Manners

Watching a classical music concert can be a memorable experience if you keep these tips in mind.
keep ~ in mind: ~을 명심하다

Before You Go In:
• Plan to arrive 20-30 minutes before concert time.
• Find out what music will be played.
~을 알아내다   미래 수동태: 조동사+be+과거분사(p.p.)

When Music Is Playing:
• Turn off your cellphone!
~을 끄다
• Stay quiet. No talking, whistling, singing along to the music.
No -ing: ~하지 마라(=Don't+동사원형 ~)
• Don't clap until the whole piece is over. It is safe to clap when the audience
starts clapping.   It 가주어 ~ to 동사원형 구문
=starts to clap

구문해설 • classical: 고전의, 클래식 음악의 • memorable: 기억에 남을 만한, 기억할 만한
• experience: 경험하다 • whistle: 휘파람을 불다 • clap: 박수치다 • audience: 관객

콘서트 예절에 대한 안내

당신이 이와 같은 조언들을 명심한다면 클래식 콘서트를 보는 것은 기억에 남는 경험이 될 것이다.

들어가기 전:
• 콘서트 시간 20–30분 전에 도착하기를 계획하라.
• 어떤 음악이 연주될지 알아보아라.

음악이 연주될 때:
• 휴대 전화를 꺼라.
• 조용히 있어라. 말하거나 휘파람을 불거나 음악에 따라 노래하지 말아라.
• 전체의 곡이 끝날 때까지 박수치지 말아라. 관객들이 박수 치기 시작할 때 박수를 치는 것이 안전하다.

Writing Workshop

Music Concert Review

On February 2, I went to a concert hall at the Seoul Arts Center where Jo
on+특정한 날   선행사   관계부사
Seongu's piano concert was held. It was a great opportunity to listen to him
수동태: be+p.p.   지각동사+목적어+목적격보어(동사원형 또는 현재분사)
play live. He played Chopin's Piano Concerto No. 1. I did not know how
beautiful the classical music was. I liked his live performance. I will not forget
간접의문문: 의문사+주어+동사
this experience.

구문해설 • review: 논평, 비평 • hold: 열다, 개최하다 • opportunity: 기회 • live: (공연이) 라이브의; 라이브로 • performance: 공연 • forget: 잊다 • experience: 경험

음악 콘서트 리뷰

2월 2일에 나는 조성우의 피아노 콘서트가 열린 서울 아트 센터의 콘서트홀에 갔다. 그가 라이브로 연주하는 것을 듣는 것은 훌륭한 기회였다. 그는 쇼팽의 피아노 협주곡 1번을 연주했다. 나는 클래식 공연이 얼마나 아름다운지 몰랐다. 나는 그의 라이브 공연이 아주 마음에 들었다. 나는 이 경험을 잊지 않을 것이다.

Wrap Up 7

Reporter: When is your new album coming out?
come out: 나오다
Justin Otter: It's coming out next month.
=my new album
Reporter: What are your plans for the new album?
Justin Otter: I'm planning to have a concert at the Super Stadium. My hero
be planning to: ~할 계획이다
Michael Johnson held one of his concerts during his world tour at the place.
one of+복수명사: ~ 중 하나

구문해설 • plan: 계획 • hero: 영웅 • tour: 순회공연 • place: 장소

기자: 당신의 새 앨범은 언제 나오나요?
저스틴 오터: 다음 달에 나옵니다.
기자: 새 앨범에 대한 계획은 무엇인가요?
저스틴 오터: 저는 수퍼 스타디움에서 콘서트를 가질 계획입니다. 저의 영웅인 마이클 존슨이 세계 공연 동안 콘서트들 중 하나를 그 장소에서 열었거든요.

01 다음 짝지어진 단어의 관계가 같도록 빈칸에 알맞은 말을 쓰시오.

appear : disappear = familiar : _____

02 다음 영영풀이에 해당하는 단어는?

to bring something to the place that it came from or the place where it should go

① free ② accept ③ gather
④ receive ⑤ return

03 다음 중 밑줄 친 단어의 뜻풀이가 바르지 않은 것은?

① Press pause to stop the tape. 멈춤
② That is not a correct answer. 정확한
③ This is a serious problem. 심각한
④ I am dependent on others. 독립적인
⑤ I don't want to disturb you. 방해하다

04 주어진 단어를 이용해서 다음 우리말에 맞게 빈칸에 알맞은 말을 쓰시오.

(1) 너는 아무 때나 도움을 요청해도 좋다.
➡ You can ask me for help _____ _____ _____. (time)
(2) 지금은 그가 혼자 있고 싶어 한다.
➡ He wants to be left alone _____ _____. (now)
(3) 그 결과 그녀는 무대 위에서 굉장히 잘했다.
➡ _____ _____ _____, she did a great job on stage. (result)

05 다음 대화의 빈칸에 들어갈 말을 고르시오.

A: How _____ going to the music festival on Friday at 5:00? Can you make it?
B: Yes. That would be great.

① to ② of
③ from ④ with
⑤ about

06 다음 대화가 자연스럽게 이어지도록 순서대로 배열하시오.

(A) Yes, I love opera. When is it?
(B) Yes, thanks so much for asking me.
(C) It's this Saturday at 5:00. Can you make it?
(D) Are you interested in going to an opera? I have two tickets.

➡ _____

07 다음 대화에서 어법이나 흐름상 어색한 것을 고르시오.

B: We're going to Hangang ⓐthis weekend. Do you remember?
G: Of course. Don't forget ⓑbringing your camera.
B: Okay. I ⓒwon't. I'll bring some snacks, ⓓtoo.
G: Sounds ⓔgreat.

① ⓐ ② ⓑ ③ ⓒ ④ ⓓ ⑤ ⓔ

[08~11] 다음 대화를 읽고 물음에 답하시오.

> G: What are you listening to?
>
> B: Classical music. I'm going to a concert tomorrow and I'd like to know about the music before I go.
>
> G: I guess it's more enjoyable ____ⓐ____ you know the music.
>
> B: ⓑActual, I don't want to clap at the wrong time.
>
> G: Don't you just clap when the music stops?
>
> B: No. In classical music, one piece of music may have several pauses. You should wait and clap at the very end.
>
> G: I see. ⓒMake sure you don't forget to clap at the real ending. By the way, can you make it to our soccer practice tomorrow at 4:00?
>
> B: Sure. I'll come to the practice after the concert finishes.
>
> G: Okay. See you then.

08 위 대화의 빈칸 ⓐ에 알맞은 것은?

① if   ② as
③ since   ④ before
⑤ though

09 위 대화의 밑줄 친 ⓑ를 알맞은 어형으로 바꿔 쓰시오.

➡ _____

10 위 대화의 밑줄 친 ⓒ와 같은 뜻이 되도록 다음 문장의 빈칸에 알맞은 말을 쓰시오.

➡ Make sure you _____ to clap at the real ending.

11 위 대화의 내용과 일치하지 <u>않는</u> 것을 고르시오.

① 소년은 클래식 음악을 듣고 있다.
② 소년은 콘서트에 가기 전에 그 음악에 대해 알고 싶어 한다.
③ 소녀는 콘서트에서 연주하는 음악을 알면 더 재미있을 것이라고 생각한다.
④ 콘서트에서는 음악 연주가 완전히 끝난 후에 박수를 쳐야 한다.
⑤ 소년은 콘서트 때문에 내일 축구 연습에 갈 수 없다.

Grammar

12 다음 빈칸에 들어갈 말로 가장 적절한 것은?

> Do you know _____ ?

① Hammington is from where
② where is Hammington from
③ where Hammington is from
④ is where Hammington from
⑤ from Hammington is where

13 다음 문장의 괄호 안에서 알맞은 말을 고르시오.

(1) This is the reason (why / how) he came here.
(2) Tell me the date on (which / when) you will travel.
(3) Tokyo is a city (where / which) you can easily get lost.
(4) Do you remember the day (when / which) we spent at the beach?
(5) This is (the way how / how) Jake caught the monkey.

14 다음 중 어법상 <u>어색한</u> 것은?

① Do you know when World War II ended?
② Who do you think killed the old woman?
③ I wondered if she would come to the party or not.
④ Tell me if or not you like Jenny.
⑤ I'm not sure whether she is fond of music or not.

15 다음 주어진 단어를 바르게 배열하여 문장을 완성하시오.

(crying, is, know, I, Jane, the, why, reason)

➡ _____

16 다음 중 어법상 바르지 <u>않은</u> 문장의 개수는?

ⓐ I don't know why did he come here.
ⓑ Do you know how dogs swim?
ⓒ I wonder will he come today.
ⓓ Can you tell me which flower he likes better?
ⓔ Do you think where Ann spent her spring vacation?

① 1개 ② 2개 ③ 3개 ④ 4개 ⑤ 5개

17 다음 문장에서 어법상 <u>어색한</u> 부분을 바르게 고쳐 쓰시오.

This is the house which Shakespeare was born.

➡ _____
_____

18 다음 그림을 참고하여 주어진 대화의 빈칸을 완성하시오.

A: Look at this picture. Do you know (1)_____?
B: Yeah, it's Moai.
A: Could you tell me (2)_____?
B: It is in Easter island in Chile.

19 다음 두 문장의 해석을 쓰고 밑줄 친 부분의 어법상 차이를 설명하시오.

(1) This is the park <u>which</u> I used to visit while young.
(2) This is the park <u>where</u> I used to go while young.

(1) 해석: _____
(2) 해석: _____
(3) 어법상 차이: _____
_____

Reading

[20~22] 다음 글을 읽고 물음에 답하시오.

Imagine (A)[you / yourself] at a classical music concert. The orchestra starts ⓐto play one of Mozart's piano (B)[concertos / concerto]. The concert hall is dark and silent. Nobody makes a sound. Everybody looks serious. The audiences only clap after the concerto (C)[will finish / finishes]. This is a familiar scene at concerts today.

20 위 글의 괄호 (A)~(C)에서 문맥이나 어법상 알맞은 낱말을 골라 쓰시오.

➡ (A)_____ (B)_____ (C)_____

21 위 글의 밑줄 친 ⓐto play와 같은 용법으로 쓰인 것을 고르시오.

① She is happy to see you again.
② He must be tired to walk such a long distance.
③ She called you to ask about your plan.
④ They want to take a break after the class.
⑤ We will go to the beach to swim.

22 위 글을 읽고 대답할 수 **없는** 질문은?

① How is the concert hall?
② Is there anyone that makes a sound?
③ Why do the audiences clap?
④ How does everybody look?
⑤ When do the audiences clap?

[23~25] 다음 글을 읽고 물음에 답하시오.

Let's go back (A)_____ time and take a look at one of Mozart's concerts in the 18th century. You are in a bright hall inside a nobleman's house. Mozart is playing the piano. Surprisingly, however, the audiences are eating, ⓐdrinking, and talking freely. They whistle and clap at any time. You are shocked (B)_____ their bad manners, but Mozart ⓑhimself would be surprised by today's quiet audiences. Concerts in Mozart's time were mostly social events. They were good places to meet people. Noise was just part of the concert.

23 위 글의 빈칸 (A)와 (B)에 들어갈 전치사가 바르게 짝지어진 것은?

① on - to   ② by - in
③ in - from   ④ in - by
⑤ on - by

24 위 글의 밑줄 친 ⓐdrinking과 문법적 쓰임이 같은 것을 고르시오.

① His job was driving a taxi.
② She is taking a walk in the park.
③ How about playing outside?
④ My plan is going to America.
⑤ The car was making a loud noise.

➡ ⓐ와 같은 것:_____

25 위 글의 내용과 일치하지 <u>않는</u> 것은?

① 모차르트 시대의 관객들은 연주회장에서 음식을 먹었다.

② 18세기에 관객들은 연주회장에서 술을 마셨다.

③ 모차르트 시대의 관객들은 연주가 끝난 후 박수를 쳤다.

④ 모차르트는 오늘날 연주회장의 관행에 놀랄 것이다.

⑤ 18세기에 소음은 연주회의 한 부분으로 여겨졌다.

27 위 글의 주제로 알맞은 것을 고르시오.

① the area where many big concert halls were built

② the people who went to the concert in the 19th century

③ the reason artists blamed the audience

④ how today's quiet concerts began

⑤ the rule people liked in the 19th century

[28~29] 다음 글을 읽고 물음에 답하시오.

As a result, here we are today, very quiet and serious. We do not know (A)[how / what] concerts will look like in the future (B)[though / because] manners change with time. For now, however, if you want to enjoy classical music concerts, just (C)[forget / remember] this: Enjoy the music, but do not disturb those around you.

[26~27] 다음 글을 읽고 물음에 답하시오.

Today's quiet concerts began in the 19th century ⓐwhen many big concert halls were built. More people, not just noblemen, went to concerts. Artists were no longer dependent on noblemen for money. The artists had more power over their works and started to use their increased power. For example, Wagner blamed the audience for making noise. After some time, a no-clapping-between-movements rule appeared.

28 위 글의 내용과 일치하지 <u>않는</u> 것은?

① 오늘날의 연주회는 조용하다.

② 오늘날의 연주회는 진지하다.

③ 미래의 연주회는 오늘날과 같을 것이다.

④ 예의범절은 시간과 함께 변한다.

⑤ 음악을 즐길 때는 주변 사람들에게 방해가 되지 않아야 한다.

26 위 글의 밑줄 친 ⓐwhen을 대신하여 쓸 수 있는 것은?

① about which   ② in which

③ with which   ④ to what

⑤ during what

29 위 글의 괄호 (A)~(C)에서 문맥이나 어법상 알맞은 낱말을 골라 쓰시오.

➡ (A)_____ (B)_____ (C)_____

[01~02] 다음 빈칸에 알맞은 단어를 고르시오.

출제율 90%

01

Don't _____ me. I have done nothing wrong to you.

① clap   ② blame
③ appear   ④ increase
⑤ disturb

출제율 100%

02

Let me _____ a look at the map.

① let   ② hold
③ allow   ④ take
⑤ make

출제율 90%

03 다음 영영풀이에 해당하는 단어를 쓰시오.

a piece of music for one or more solo instruments playing with an orchestra

➡ _____

출제율 90%

04 다음 빈칸에 들어갈 말이 바르게 짝지어진 것은?

• The photo will lose color _____ time.
• _____ the way, are you free for dinner tomorrow evening?

① at - With   ② on - In
③ with - By   ④ from - At
⑤ out - On

출제율 95%

05 다음 중 〈보기〉에 있는 단어를 사용하여 자연스러운 문장을 만들 수 <u>없는</u> 것은?

┌─── 보기 ───┐
volunteer century classical social
└────────────┘

① We are living in the 21th ____.
② He is slow in ____.
③ She went to a ____ music concert.
④ They ____ at children's center.
⑤ Join a ____ club to make new friends.

[06~09] 다음 대화를 읽고 물음에 답하시오.

G: Yunho! Have you heard about the Christmas concert at the city hall?
B: Yes. I heard that a famous opera singer will be ___ⓐ___ the stage.
G: Oh, then why don't we go on Christmas Day? Can you ___ⓑ___ it?
B: Sure. Do you know what time the concert starts?
G: It starts at 5:30. ©Let's meet at the bus stop at 4:00.
B: Good. Don't forget to dress up.
G: Okay. I won't.

출제율 85%

06 위 대화의 빈칸 ⓐ에 알맞은 말을 쓰시오.

➡ _____

07 위 대화의 빈칸 ⓑ에 알맞은 것은?

① get   ② do
③ arrive   ④ make
⑤ finish

08 위 대화의 밑줄 친 ⓒ와 같은 뜻이 되도록 다음 문장의 빈칸에 알맞은 말을 쓰시오.

> How _____ _____ at the bus stop at 4:00?

09 위 대화의 내용과 일치하지 <u>않는</u> 것은?

① 소년은 크리스마스 콘서트에 대해 알고 있다.
② 콘서트에는 유명한 오페라 가수가 출연한다.
③ 소녀는 콘서트에 가지 않을 것이다.
④ 콘서트는 5시 30분에 열린다.
⑤ 소년은 콘서트에 정장을 차려 입고 갈 것이다.

[10~13] 다음 대화를 읽고 물음에 답하시오.

> G: What are you listening to?
> B: Classical music. I'm going to a concert tomorrow and I'd like to know about the music ⓐ I go. (①)
> G: I guess it's more enjoyable if you know the music. (②)
> B: Actually, I don't want to clap at the wrong time. (③)
> G: Don't you just clap when the music stops? (④)
> B: No. In classical music, one piece of music may have several pauses. (⑤)
> G: I see. Make sure you don't forget to clap at the real ending. ⓑ , can you make it to our soccer practice tomorrow at 4:00?
> B: Sure. I'll come to the practice after the concert finishes.
> G: Okay. See you then.

10 위 대화의 ①~⑤ 중 다음 주어진 문장이 들어갈 알맞은 곳은?

> You should wait and clap at the very end.

①   ②   ③   ④   ⑤

11 위 대화의 빈칸 ⓐ에 알맞은 것은?

① when   ② though
③ before   ④ until
⑤ after

12 위 대화의 빈칸 ⓐ에 알맞은 것은?

① However   ② Therefore
③ Consequently   ④ In the end
⑤ By the way

13 위 대화의 내용으로 보아 대답할 수 <u>없는</u> 것은?

① What is the boy listening to?
② Where is the boy going to tomorrow?
③ Does the boy often go to a concert?
④ When is their soccer practice?
⑤ Will the boy come to the soccer practice tomorrow?

14 다음 빈칸에 들어갈 말로 알맞은 것은?

> I'd like to ask you _____ you're free tonight.

① because   ② that
③ as   ④ if
⑤ what

15 다음 두 문장을 한 문장으로 바르게 연결한 것은?

> • This is the town.
> • I was born here.

① This is the town which I was born.
② This is the town in that I was born.
③ This is the town where I was born.
④ This is the town where I was born here.
⑤ This is where the town I was born.

16 다음 밑줄 친 부분의 쓰임이 어색한 것은?

① Do you know why leaves turn red in autumn?
② Luke's mother knew where he kept the comic books.
③ I wonder that there's an easy way to improve my grade.
④ Do you know how many books your brother has?
⑤ I asked her when she had left her home country.

17 다음 밑줄 친 부분의 쓰임이 나머지 넷과 다른 것은?

① I wonder if my child expresses himself well in English.
② Is it okay if I use your phone to call my mom?
③ Let's wait and see if the weather will be nice.
④ Please tell me if there's anything I can do to help you.
⑤ Alex asked me if I wanted a massage.

[18~20] 다음 글을 읽고 물음에 답하시오.

Let's go back in time and take a look at one of Mozart's concerts in the 18th century. You are in a bright hall inside a nobleman's house. Mozart is playing the piano. Surprisingly, however, the audiences are eating, drinking, and talking freely. They whistle and clap at any time. You are (A)[shock] by their bad manners, but Mozart himself would be surprised by today's quiet audiences. Concerts in Mozart's time were mostly (B)_____ events. They were good places to meet people. Noise was just part of the concert.

18 위 글의 (A)에 주어진 단어의 알맞은 형태를 쓰시오.

➡ _____

19 위 글의 내용을 참고하여 빈칸 (B)에 알맞은 한 단어를 쓰시오

➡ _____

20 위 글에 어울리도록 다음 빈칸 (A)~(C)에 알맞은 단어를 쓰시오.

> Concert halls in Mozart's time were (A)_____ and noisy and the audiences (B)_____ and (C)_____ at any time.

[21~23] 다음 글을 읽고 물음에 답하시오.

Today's (A)[quiet / bright] concerts began in the 19th century ⓐwhen many big concert halls were built. More people, not (B)[because / just] noblemen, went to concerts. Artists were no longer dependent on noblemen for money. The artists had more power over their works and started to use their (C)[increased / increasing] power. For example, Wagner blamed the audience for making noise. After some time, a no-clapping-between-movements rule appeared.

21 *출제율 100%* 위 글의 괄호 (A)~(C)에서 문맥이나 어법상 알맞은 낱말을 골라 쓰시오.

➡ (A)_____ (B)_____ (C)_____

22 *출제율 90%* 위 글의 밑줄 친 ⓐwhen과 같은 용법으로 쓰인 것을 고르시오.

① She was busy when I arrived home.
② When it rains, you should drive carefully.
③ Do you know when she will come here?
④ He doesn't tell me the time when she will arrive.
⑤ She asked me when they would call her.

23 *출제율 95%* 위 글을 읽고 대답할 수 없는 질문은?

① When did the quiet concerts begin?
② Did noblemen go to concerts in the 19th century?
③ How many artists were dependent on noblemen?
④ Who blamed the audience for making noise?
⑤ What kind of rule appeared in the 19th century?

[24~27] 다음 글을 읽고 물음에 답하시오.

As a result, here we are today, very quiet and serious. ⓐWe do not know what will concerts look like in the future because manners change with time. For now, ⓑ_____, if you want (A)[enjoy] classical music concerts, just remember this: (B)Enjoy the music, but do not disturb those around you.

24 *출제율 95%* 위 글의 밑줄 친 ⓐ의 문장에서 어법이 어색한 것을 바로잡아 문장을 다시 쓰시오.

➡ _____
_____

25 *출제율 85%* 위 글의 빈칸 ⓑ에 들어가기에 적절한 한 단어를 쓰시오.

➡ _____

26 *출제율 90%* 위 글의 (A)에 주어진 단어를 어법상 적절한 형태로 쓰시오.

➡ _____

27 *출제율 95%* 위 글의 밑줄 친 (B)를 우리말로 옮기시오.

➡ _____
_____

01 다음 대화의 흐름상 어색한 것을 하나 찾아서 고치시오.

> A: Why don't we go to the library on Monday after school? Can you make it?
> B: Sure, I can. How about on Tuesday?
> A: Okay. Don't forget to bring your library card.
> B: All right. I won't.

➡ _____

[02~04] 다음 대화를 읽고 물음에 답하시오.

> G: You look healthy. What's your secret?
> B: Thanks. Well, I go ⓐ<u>swim</u> every day. You should go with me sometime.
> G: That sound's like fun. ⓑ내가 해야 할 다른 어떤 일이 있니? (any, should)
> B: Don't forget ⓒ(eating, to eat) many kinds of fruits and vegetables, too.

02 위 대화의 밑줄 친 ⓐ를 알맞은 형으로 고치시오.

➡ _____

03 위 대화의 밑줄 친 ⓑ를 주어진 단어를 이용하여 영작하시오. (6 words)

➡ _____

04 위 대화의 ⓒ의 괄호 안에 알맞은 것을 고르시오.

➡ _____

05 다음을 간접의문문을 이용하여 한 문장으로 쓰시오.

(1) • I'll tell you.
  • Where has he been since last Monday?

➡ _____

(2) • I'd like to know.
  • Did you meet her?

➡ _____

(3) • Do you think?
  • Where can I find some fruit?

➡ _____

06 다음 우리말과 일치하도록 빈칸에 알맞은 말을 쓰시오.

> 나는 우리가 수영하러 갔던 그 날을 기억한다.

➡ I remember the day _____ we went swimming.

07 괄호 안에 주어진 어휘를 이용하여 다음 우리말을 영작하시오.

> 다음 기차가 언제 오는지 말해 줄 수 있습니까? (could, the next train) (9 words)

➡ _____

08 다음 우리말을 참고하여 빈칸에 알맞은 단어를 쓰시오.

> 이곳은 내가 종종 공부하는 도서관이다.

➡ This is the library _____ I often study.

09 주어진 두 문장을 한 문장으로 연결하시오.

(1) Do you know? + Does Anna love me?

➡ _____

(2) I don't know. + Why was Kate so surprised?

➡ _____

(3) Cathy will tell me. + Who broke the window yesterday?

➡ _____

(4) Can you imagine? + Which book did Jennifer buy?

➡ _____

[10~12] 다음 글을 읽고 물음에 답하시오.

Imagine (A)_____ at a classical music concert. ①The orchestra starts to play one of Mozart's piano concertos. ② The concert hall is dark and silent. ③ Nobody makes a sound. ④Everybody looks serious. ⑤The audiences only clap after the concerto will finish. This is a familiar scene at concerts today.

10 다음과 같은 뜻의 문장이 되도록 위 글의 빈칸 (A)에 알맞은 단어를 쓰시오.

> • Imagine that you are in a concert hall and the orchestra plays a famous piece of classical music.

➡ _____

11 위 글의 ①~⑤ 중 어법이 어색한 문장을 찾아 쓰고, 올바른 형태로 바로 잡으시오.
➡ 번호: _____
_____
_____

12 What do the audiences do after the concerto is over?

➡ They _____ .

[13~15] 다음 글을 읽고 물음에 답하시오.

(A)Let's go back in time and take a look at one of Mozart's concerts in the 18th century. You are in a bright hall inside a nobleman's house. Mozart is playing the piano. Surprisingly, however, the audiences are eating, drinking, and talking freely. They whistle and clap at any time. You are shocked by their (B)_____ manners, but Mozart himself would be surprised by today's quiet audiences. Concerts in Mozart's time were mostly social events. (C)Mozart 시대의 콘서트는 사람을 만나기 좋은 장소이었다. Noise was just part of the concert.

13 밑줄 친 (A)와 같은 뜻의 문장이 되도록 아래 빈칸에 알맞은 한 단어를 쓰시오.

> • Let's go back in time _____ take a look at one of Mozart's concerts in the 18th century.

14 위 글의 내용으로 보아 빈칸 (B)에 들어가기에 적절한 한 단어를 쓰시오.

➡ _____

15 위 글의 밑줄 친 (C)에 해당하는 문장을 영어로 완성하시오. (주어진 단어 활용)

> (concerts in Mozart's time, places, meet)

➡ _____
_____

01 주어진 어구를 활용하여 〈보기〉와 같이 문장을 쓰시오.

> Tell me … / Did you ask …? / Do you know …? / I wonder … / I don't know … / Can you tell me …? / do you think …?

> ┤ 보기 ├
>
> Did you ask him what he wanted?

(1) _____

(2) _____

(3) _____

(4) _____

(5) _____

(6) _____

(7) _____

02 다음 대화를 읽고 대화의 내용을 요약한 문장을 완성하시오.

> G: Yunho! Have you heard about the Christmas concert at the city hall?
>
> B: Yes. I heard that a famous opera singer will be on the stage.
>
> G: Oh, then why don't we go on Christmas Day? Can you make it?
>
> B: Sure. Do you know what time the concert starts?
>
> G: It starts at 5:30. Let's meet at the bus stop at 4:00.
>
> B: Good. Don't forget to dress up.
>
> G: Okay. I won't.

> The girl asks Yunho (A)_____ he has heard about the Christmas concert at the city hall. He says (B)_____ he heard that a famous opera singer will be on the stage. The girl suggests (C)_____ to the concert with her on Christmas Day. Yunho agrees and asks her what time the concerts starts. The girl says that the concert starts at 5:30. So they will (D)_____ at the bus stop at 4:00. Yunho tells her (E)_____ to forget (F)_____ dress up. The girl says that she won't.

단원별 모의고사

01 다음 짝지어진 단어의 관계가 같도록 빈칸에 알맞은 말을 쓰시오.

> dark : bright : dependent : _____

02 다음 빈칸에 공통으로 알맞은 것은?

> - He has a lot of stress at _____ .
> - This picture is a _____ of great artistic value.

① result ② office
③ work ④ shape
⑤ business

03 다음 영영풀이에 해당하는 것은?

> to disturb someone when they are trying to work, sleep, etc.

① blame ② appear
③ support ④ whistle
⑤ interrupt

04 다음 우리말에 맞게 빈칸에 알맞은 말을 쓰시오.

(1) 그건 그렇고 나는 내 열쇠를 찾을 수 없어.
➡ _____ _____ _____ , I can't find my key.

(2) 방을 좀 볼 수 있을까요?
➡ Can I take _____ _____ _____ your room?

(3) 예술가들은 더 이상 돈 때문에 귀족에게 의존하지 않았다.
➡ Artists were no longer _____ _____ noblemen for money.

[05~08] 다음 대화를 읽고 물음에 답하시오.

G: Yunho! Have you heard about the Christmas concert at the city hall? (①)
B: Yes. I heard that a famous opera singer will be on the stage. (②)
G: Oh, then ___ⓐ___ don't we go on Christmas Day? (③)
B: Sure. Do you know what time the concert starts? (④)
G: It starts at 5:30. Let's meet at the bus stop at 4:00. (⑤)
B: Good. Don't forget to dress ___ⓑ___ .
G: Okay. I won't.

05 위 대화의 ①~⑤ 중 다음 주어진 문장이 들어갈 알맞은 곳은?

> Can you make it?

①   ②   ③   ④   ⑤

06 위 대화의 빈칸 ⓐ에 알맞은 것은?

① How ② Why
③ When ④ What
⑤ Where

07 위 대화의 빈칸 ⓑ에 알맞은 것은?

① up ② on
③ off ④ from
⑤ with

08 위 대화의 내용으로 보아 대답할 수 없는 것은?

① When did the girl hear about the concert?
② Where will the concert be held?
③ Who will be on the stage?
④ What time does the concert start?
⑤ Where and when will the boy and girl meet?

[09~11] 다음 대화를 읽고 물음에 답하시오.

G: You look healthy. (①)
B: Thanks. Well, I go swimming every day. (②) You should go with me sometime. (③)
G: ⓐ그거 재미있을 것 같구나. Any other things I should do? (④)
B: Don't forget ___ⓑ___ many kinds of fruits and vegetables, too. (⑤)

09 위 대화의 ①~⑤ 중 다음 주어진 문장이 들어갈 알맞은 곳은?

> What's your secret?

①　　②　　③　　④　　⑤

10 위 대화의 밑줄 친 ⓐ의 우리말을 주어진 단어를 이용하여 영어로 옮기시오. (that, fun) (4 words)

➡ _____

11 위 대화의 빈칸 ⓑ에 알맞은 것은?

① eat　　② eating　　③ ate
④ to eat　　⑤ to eating

12 다음 대화의 빈칸에 알맞은 것을 고르시오.

A: Let's go see a movie tomorrow.
B: Good idea!
A: _____
B: Okay. Let's meet at 5 o'clock.

① Where can we meet?
② When can you come?
③ How would you like it?
④ Can you make it at 5?
⑤ What time shall we meet?

13 다음 빈칸에 알맞은 말이 바르게 짝지어진 것은?

- This is the place _____ I lost my bag.
- Kate remembers the day _____ we first met.

① where – which　　② where – when
③ how – what　　④ when – where
⑤ what – how

14 다음 문장에서 어법상 어색한 것을 바르게 고쳐 다시 쓰시오.

(1) The girl is asking where is the nearest bus stop.

➡ _____

(2) Do you know will the leaves turn yellow in autumn?

➡ _____

(3) Will you tell me when did you meet her?

➡ _____

15 다음 밑줄 친 부분의 쓰임이 나머지와 다른 하나는?

① I remember the day when Jerry left Paris.
② 2001 was the year when I visited my cousin in the USA.
③ She was washing the dishes when I came home.
④ Do you know the time when the accident happened?
⑤ Christmas season is a time when people feel happy.

16 주어진 어휘를 이용하여 다음 우리말을 영작하시오. (간접의문문을 이용하여 쓸 것.)

(1) 나는 그 소녀가 어디에 살았는지 기억한다.
(remember, live)

➡ _____

(2) Anna는 내게 Angelina를 사랑하는지 물었다.
(ask, love)

➡ _____

17 다음 두 문장이 같은 뜻이 되도록 빈칸에 알맞은 말을 쓰시오.

> This is how we caught the thief.
> = This is the way _____ _____ we caught the thief.

[18~20] 다음 글을 읽고 물음에 답하시오.

Today's quiet concerts began in the 19th century ①which many big concert halls were built. More people, ②not just noblemen, went to concerts. Artists were ③no longer dependent on noblemen for money. The artists had more power over their works and started ④to use their increased power. For example, Wagner ⑤blamed the audience for making noise. After some time, a no-clapping-between-movements rule appeared.

18 위 글에 어울리도록 다음 빈칸 (A)와 (B)에 알맞은 단어를 쓰시오.

> Artists became (A)_____ of the noblemen and a no-clapping-between-movements rule (B)_____ in the 19th century.

19 Why were artists no longer dependent on noblemen for money?

➡ Because many big concerts _____ _____ and more people _____ to concerts in the 19th century.

20 위 글의 밑줄 친 ①~⑤ 중에서 어법상 틀린 것을 찾아 번호를 쓰고, 고치시오.

➡ 번호: _____ 틀린 것: _____
올바른 형태: _____

[21~23] 다음 글을 읽고 물음에 답하시오.

As a result, here we are today, very quiet and serious. We do not know ⓐwhat concerts will look like in the future because manners change (A)_____ time. For now, however, ⓑif you want to enjoy classical music concerts, just remember this: Enjoy the music, but do not disturb those (B)_____ you.

21 위 글의 밑줄 친 ⓐ와 같은 용법으로 쓰인 것을 고르시오.

① She showed me the book which he had bought.
② I know the boy who called you.
③ Do you know the time when she will come?
④ She asked us who could move her desk.
⑤ The air was cool when I opened the door.

22 위 글의 빈칸 (A)와 (B)에 들어갈 전치사가 바르게 짝지어진 것은?

① without – by
② about – around
③ in – from
④ with – around
⑤ with – despite

23 위 글의 밑줄 친 ⓑif와 문법적 쓰임이 같은 것을 고르시오. (2개)

① Do you know if he is ready?
② If you are busy, I will wait.
③ She asked me if I had any questions.
④ I will see if he has enough time.
⑤ He will call you if he needs help.

➡ ⓑ와 같은 것: _____

[24~26] 다음 글을 읽고 물음에 답하시오.

Let's go back in time and take a look at one of Mozart's concerts in the 18th century. You are in a bright hall inside a nobleman's house. Mozart is playing the piano. (A)[Surprise / Surprisingly], however, the audiences are eating, drinking, and talking freely. They whistle and clap at any time. You are shocked by their bad manners, but Mozart (B)[him / himself] would be surprised by today's quiet audiences. Concerts in Mozart's time were (C)[mostly / most] social events. They were good places (D)to meet people. Noise was just part of the concert.

24 위 글의 괄호 (A)~(C)에서 문맥이나 어법상 알맞은 낱말을 골라 쓰시오.

➡ (A)_____ (B)_____ (C)_____

25 위 글의 밑줄 친 (D)to meet와 같은 용법으로 쓰인 것을 고르시오.

① They want to watch the movie.
② He will turn on the TV to see the news.
③ She was happy to receive so many messages.
④ I need a book to read during the night.
⑤ She began to study math.

26 위 글을 읽고 대답할 수 없는 질문은?

① How were the concert halls in the 18th century?
② Where was the concert hall in the 18th century?
③ How many concert halls did they built?
④ What were the audiences doing during the concert?
⑤ What were concerts in Mozart's time?

INSIGHT
on the textbook

교과서 파헤치기

※ 다음 영어를 우리말로 쓰시오.

01	select	22	strange
02	intelligent	23	replace
03	teleport	24	beat
04	burn	25	check
05	translate	26	situation
06	animated	27	closet
07	easily	28	space
08	sense	29	chance
09	freeze	30	dictionary
10	impossible	31	translator
11	amusement	32	unbelievable
12	predict	33	lucky
13	without	34	cloudy
14	machine	35	not just
15	possible	36	don't have to
16	cross	37	in danger
17	danger	38	no longer
18	mean	39	based on
19	off	40	free from
20	perfect	41	by the way
21	through	42	be able to 동사원형
		43	slow down

※ 다음 우리말을 영어로 쓰시오.

01	동영상의, 생기 있는	22	번역하다
02	기회	23	사전
03	구름의, 흐린	24	할인되어
04	가능한	25	옷장
05	행운의	26	완벽한
06	번역가	27	대체하다
07	기계	28	똑똑한
08	건너다	29	~을 통해, ~ 사이로
09	위험	30	상황
10	즐거움, 오락	31	이상한
11	쉽게	32	믿기 어려운, 놀랄만한
12	선택하다	33	확인하다, 점검하다
13	(휴대 전화로) 문자를 보내다	34	공간
14	감지하다	35	그런데, 그건 그렇고
15	의미하다	36	위험에 처한, 위험에 빠진
16	얼리다	37	더 이상 ~하지 않다
17	~ 없이	38	~할 수 있다
18	예측하다	39	~에 근거하여
19	불가능한	40	속도를 늦추다
20	순간 이동하다	41	조심하다
21	불타다	42	~의 염려가 없는
		43	(사전·참고 자료·컴퓨터 등에서 정보를) 찾아보다

※ 다음 영영풀이에 알맞은 단어를 <보기>에서 골라 쓴 후, 우리말 뜻을 쓰시오.

1 _____ : to take the place of: _____

2 _____ : to defeat someone in a game: _____

3 _____ : the best possible: _____

4 _____ : to be destroyed by fire: _____

5 _____ : able to happen or be done: _____

6 _____ : to perceive or realize something: _____

7 _____ : to change words in another language: _____

8 _____ : to go from one side to the other side of an area: _____

9 _____ : having desirable things unexpectedly happen to you: _____

10 _____ : to say that an event will happen in the future: _____

11 _____ : to choose something from a number of things: _____

12 _____ : a large piece of furniture with a door used for storing clothes: _____

13 _____ : when the sky is covered with a lot of clouds: _____

14 _____ : the enjoyment that you get from being entertained: _____

15 _____ : to create the sounds of powerful rhythm with the voice and the hands: _____

16 _____ : a book that contains a list of words and phrases alphabetically with their meanings or their translations in another language: _____

<보기>

dictionary	select	amusement	closet
perfect	beatbox	lucky	translate
beat	replace	sense	burn
cloudy	cross	predict	possible

※ 다음 우리말과 일치하도록 빈칸에 알맞은 말을 쓰시오.

Listen & Speak 1 A

B: _____ _____ _____ _____ a new VR game?

G: That _____ interesting.

Listen & Speak 1 B

1. B: Do you _____ _____ ideas _____ our group _____?

   G: No. _____ _____ you?

   B: I'm _____ we should _____ _____ _____ jobs. _____ do you _____?

   G: That _____ _____ for our project. _____ _____ _____ some information _____ _____ _____.

2. G: The Robot Expo _____ next week. _____ _____ you go _____ me?

   B: Yes, I'd love _____. That _____ _____.

   G: We'll have a _____ _____ _____ _____ engineers.

   B: That'll be _____.

1. B: 우리 조별 프로젝트에 대한 좋은 생각이 있니?
   G: 아니. 너는 어때?
   B: 나는 미래 직업에 대해 이야기하면 좋겠다고 생각하고 있어. 너는 어떻게 생각해?
   G: 우리 프로젝트에 완벽한 것 같아. 인터넷에서 정보를 찾아보자.

2. G: 로봇 박람회가 다음 주에 시작돼. 나와 함께 가는 게 어때?
   B: 응, 가고 싶어. 그거 재미있겠는데.
   G: 우리는 로봇 공학자를 만날 기회가 있을 거야.
   B: 그거 아주 좋겠다.

Listen & Speak 1 C

1. A: I'm _____ _____ _____ a _____.

   B: That sounds _____ _____.

2. A: I'm _____ to _____ a model car.

   B: That _____ _____ _____.

Listen & Speak 2 A

G: Is _____ _____ for you _____ _____ _____ your smartphone?

B: No, it's _____ _____.

Listen & Speak 2 B

1. **G:** This computer _____ nice. _____ _____ is _____?

   M: It's 500 dollars. It's _____ _____ one.

   G: _____ _____ _____ _____ _____ this coupon?

   M: _____ me _____. Yes, you can. So, you'll _____ 30 dollars _____.

   G: _____. I'll _____ it.

2. **B:** We _____ lots of _____ _____ our trip.

   G: We sure _____. We have _____ _____ 500 pictures.

   B: Is _____ _____ _____ _____ an _____ photo album _____ _____ them?

   G: Yes, it's _____. I _____ _____ _____ for that.

Listen & Speak 2 C

1. **A:** _____ _____ _____ for you _____ _____ _____ your eyes _____?

   B: _____. I _____ _____ _____ that.

2. **A:** Is it _____ _____ _____ to _____ _____ Gangwondo _____ bicycle?

   B: _____. I _____ _____ _____.

Real-Life Zone A

G: _____ _____ those words on the board.

B: _____ d o _____ _____? _____ _____ _____ _____ in the _____.

G: What _____ _____ the AI _____?

B: _____ do I _____ it?

G: You _____ your smartphone camera at the words and _____ AI _____ _____. You will _____ _____ _____.

B: Is it _____ _____ _____ _____ _____ those words?

Speaker: Sure. I can _____ any language and _____ it.

B: Wow, that _____ _____. So, AI, _____ do those words _____?

Speaker: They _____ "Dreams _____ _____!"

B: That's _____.

1. G: 이 컴퓨터가 좋아 보이네요. 얼마예요?
   M: 500달러예요. 가장 최신 컴퓨터예요.
   G: 이 쿠폰을 사용하는 것이 가능한가요?
   M: 확인해 볼게요. 네, 사용할 수 있어요. 그러면, 30달러 할인돼요.
   G: 좋아요. 이걸로 살게요.

2. B: 우리는 여행 동안 사진을 많이 찍었어.
   G: 진짜 그랬어. 500장 넘게 있어.
   B: 그 사진들로 동영상 앨범을 만드는 것이 가능하니?
   G: 응, 가능해. 나는 그것을 위한 앱이 있어.

1. A: 눈 감고 문자 메시지 보내는 것이 가능하니?
   B: 물론이지. 할 수 있어.

2. A: 자전거로 강원도를 여행하는 것이 가능하니?
   B: 물론이지. 할 수 있어.

G: 저기 칠판에 있는 글자 좀 봐.
B: 무슨 뜻이지? 사전에서 찾아보자.
G: AI 번역기를 사용하는 게 어때?
B: 어떻게 사용하는 거니?
G: 스마트폰 카메라를 글자 위에 댄 후에 AI에게 번역해 달라고 해 봐. 아마 답을 해 줄 거야.
B: AI가 저런 글자를 읽는 것이 가능해?
Speaker: 물론이에요. 저는 어떤 언어도 읽을 수 있고 번역할 수 있어요.
B: 오, 정말 놀라워. 그럼 AI, 이 글자는 뜻이 뭐니?
Speaker: "꿈은 이루어진다."라는 뜻이에요.
B: 정말 대단하구나.

Step2

※ 다음 우리말에 맞도록 대화를 영어로 쓰시오.

해석

Listen & Speak 1 A

B: _____

G: _____

B: 우리 새로운 VR 게임을 해 보는 게 어때?
G: 그거 재미있겠다.

Listen & Speak 1 B

1. B: _____

   G: _____

   B: _____

   G: _____

   _____

2. G: _____

   B: _____

   G: _____

   B: _____

1. B: 우리 조별 프로젝트에 대한 좋은 생각이 있니?
   G: 아니. 너는 어때?
   B: 나는 미래 직업에 대해 이야기하면 좋겠다고 생각하고 있어. 너는 어떻게 생각해?
   G: 우리 프로젝트에 완벽한 것 같아. 인터넷에서 정보를 찾아보자.

2. G: 로봇 박람회가 다음 주에 시작돼. 나와 함께 가는 게 어때?
   B: 응, 가고 싶어. 그거 재미있겠는데.
   G: 우리는 로봇 공학자를 만날 기회가 있을 거야.
   B: 그거 아주 좋겠다.

Listen & Speak 1 C

1. A: _____

   B: _____

2. A: _____

   B: _____

1. A: 난 드론을 날릴 거야.
   B: 그거 재미있겠다.

2. A: 난 모형 자동차를 조립할 거야.
   B: 그거 재미있겠다.

Listen & Speak 2 A

G: _____

B: _____

G: 네가 스마트폰 없이 사는 것이 가능할까?
B: 아니, 그건 불가능해.

Listen & Speak 2 B

1. G: _____

   M: _____

   G: _____

   M: _____

   G: _____

2. B: _____

   G: _____

   B: _____

   G: _____

1. G: 이 컴퓨터가 좋아 보이네요. 얼마예요?
   M: 500달러예요. 가장 최신 컴퓨터예요.
   G: 이 쿠폰을 사용하는 것이 가능한가요?
   M: 확인해 볼게요. 네, 사용할 수 있어요. 그러면, 30달러 할인돼요.
   G: 좋아요. 이걸로 살게요.

2. B: 우리는 여행 동안 사진을 많이 찍었어.
   G: 진짜 그랬어. 500장 넘게 있어.
   B: 그 사진들로 동영상 앨범을 만드는 것이 가능하니?
   G: 응, 가능해. 나는 그것을 위한 앱이 있어.

Listen & Speak 2 C

1. A: _____

   B: _____

2. A: _____

   B: _____

1. A: 눈 감고 문자 메시지 보내는 것이 가능하니?
   B: 물론이지. 할 수 있어.

2. A: 자전거로 강원도를 여행하는 것이 가능하니?
   B: 물론이지. 할 수 있어.

Real-Life Zone A

G: _____

B: _____

G: _____

B: _____

G: _____

B: _____

Speaker: _____

B: _____

Speaker: _____

B: _____

G: 저기 칠판에 있는 글자 좀 봐.
B: 무슨 뜻이지? 사전에서 찾아보자.
G: AI 번역기를 사용하는 게 어때?
B: 어떻게 사용하는 거니?
G: 스마트폰 카메라를 글자 위에 댄 후에 AI에게 번역해 달라고 해 봐. 아마 답을 해 줄 거야.
B: AI가 저런 글자를 읽는 것이 가능해?
Speaker: 물론이에요. 저는 어떤 언어도 읽을 수 있고 번역할 수 있어요.
B: 오, 정말 놀라워. 그럼 AI, 이 글자는 뜻이 뭐니?
Speaker: "꿈은 이루어진다."라는 뜻이에요.
B: 정말 대단하구나.

※ 다음 우리말과 일치하도록 빈칸에 알맞은 것을 골라 쓰시오.

1 A _____ _____ the _____ Expo
A. AI   B. at   C. Day

2 Jina and Suhan are _____ the _____ AI _____.
A. World   B. Expo   C. at

3 They are _____ the _____ _____.
A. home   B. entering   C. AI

4 Suhan: _____ _____ this! It's a house of the _____.
A. at   B. future   C. look

5 Jina: Let's _____ _____ the bedroom first. Look, _____ a smart _____.
A. into   B. there's   C. go   D. closet

6 Suhan: I'm standing in _____ of this screen on the _____ door and my clothes _____ _____.
A. keep   B. front   C. changing   D. closet

7 Jina: The screen _____ clothes that _____ the _____.
A. suit   B. suggests   C. weather

8 Suhan: That's amazing! We _____ _____ have to _____ about _____ for the weather.
A. longer   B. dressing   C. no   D. worry

9 Jina: Right. Let's _____ _____ _____ the living room.
A. on   B. move   C. to

10 Suhan: Oh, I like _____ _____ _____.
A. speaker   B. music   C. this

11 AI Speaker: I'm _____ _____ a music _____.
A. just   B. speaker   C. not

12 I can do _____ _____ you can _____.
A. than   B. imagine   C. more

13 Jina: It's _____ to _____ that you can _____ us. What can you do?
A. believe   B. hard   C. understand

14 AI Speaker: _____ _____ _____ a movie?
A. watching   B. how   C. about

15 I'll _____ _____ for you.
A. one   B. play

16 Suhan: Look, those _____ windows are _____ _____.
A. getting   B. smart   C. darker

17 I _____ _____ I'm in a movie _____.
A. like   B. theater   C. feel

18 Jina: _____ _____ can you _____?
A. do   B. else   C. what

19 AI Speaker: I can _____, _____. _____, "cats and boots and cats and boots."
A. too   B. comes   C. beatbox   D. here

20 Suhan: You're _____. _____ _____!
A. job   B. good   C. funny

21 Jina: _____! _____ a smart car station _____!
A. outside   B. hurry   C. there's

22 _____ go and _____ _____ that red car.
A. ride   B. let's   C. in

23 Suhan: This car is _____ _____. Let's _____ _____.
A. cool   B. in   C. so   D. get

24 AI Car: Welcome. Are you _____ _____ _____?
A. to   B. ready   C. go

25 Jina: Yes, _____ _____ we _____ now?
A. should   B. what   C. do

26 It's my first _____ to _____ _____ a smart car.
A. ride   B. time   C. in

27 AI Car: You don't _____ _____ do _____.
A. need   B. anything   C. to

28 I will _____ and _____ you _____ the next station.
A. take   B. drive   C. to

29 Suhan: Watch _____! I _____ a cat _____ the street.
A. out   B. crossing   C. see

30 AI Car: Don't _____. I _____ just _____ it.
A. sensed   B. have   C. worry

31 When I _____ _____ situations, I _____ _____ or stop.
A. down   B. dangerous   C. sense   D. slow

32 Jina: _____ _____ you do _____?
A. that   B. how   C. can

33 AI Car: I'm a very _____ _____ car.
A. robotic   B. intelligent

34 I know _____ _____ _____.
A. about   B. all   C. driving

35 I can _____ danger _____ _____ knowledge and _____.
A. on   B. predict   C. experience   D. based

36 Suhan: _____ smart! You think and _____ _____ a person.
A. like   B. how   C. act

37 You _____ really _____ a _____.
A. like   B. human   C. are

---

18 진아: 또 뭘 할 수 있어?

19 인공 지능 스피커: 비트박스도 할 수 있어요. "북치기 박치기 북치기 박치기."

20 수한: 넌 정말 재미있구나. 잘했어!

21 진아: 서둘러! 밖에 스마트 자동차 정류장이 있어.

22 가서 저 빨간 차를 타 보자.

23 수한: 이 차 정말 멋지다. 차에 타자.

24 인공 지능 자동차: 어서 오세요. 갈 준비 됐나요?

25 진아: 응, 우린 이제 뭘 해야 하지?

26 스마트 자동차에 타는 건 처음이야.

27 인공 지능 자동차: 아무 것도 하지 않아도 돼요.

28 제가 운전해서 다음 정류장까지 데려다줄 거니까요.

29 수한: 조심해! 고양이가 길을 건너고 있는 게 보여.

30 인공 지능 자동차: 걱정 말아요. 이미 감지했어요.

31 저는 어떤 위험 상황을 감지하면 속도를 늦추거나 멈춰요.

32 진아: 어떻게 그렇게 할 수 있어?

33 인공 지능 자동차: 전 아주 지능적인 로봇 차예요.

34 저는 운전에 대한 모든 걸 알고 있어요.

35 저는 제 지식과 경험을 바탕으로 위험을 예측할 수 있어요.

36 수한: 정말 똑똑하구나! 사람처럼 생각하고 행동하는구나.

37 정말 인간 같아.

※ 다음 우리말과 일치하도록 빈칸에 알맞은 말을 쓰시오.

1 A Day _____ the _____ _____

2 Jina and Suhan are _____ _____ _____ _____ _____.

3 They _____ _____ the _____ _____.

4 Suhan: Look at this! It's a house _____ _____ _____.

5 Jina: Let's _____ _____ the bedroom first. Look, there's a _____ _____.

6 Suhan: I'm standing in _____ of this screen _____ _____ _____ _____ and my clothes _____ _____.

7 Jina: The screen _____ clothes _____ _____ _____ _____.

8 Suhan: That's amazing! We _____ _____ have to worry about _____ _____ _____ _____ _____.

9 Jina: Right. _____ _____ _____ _____ _____ the living room.

10 Suhan: Oh, I like _____ _____ _____.

11 AI Speaker: _____ _____ _____ a music speaker.

12 I can do _____ _____ you _____ _____.

13 Jina: _____ _____ _____ _____ that you _____ _____ us. What can you do?

14 AI Speaker: _____ _____ _____ a movie?

15 I'll _____ _____ _____ you.

16 Suhan: Look, those smart windows are _____ _____.

17 I _____ _____ I'm in a _____ _____.

1 인공 지능 박람회에서의 하루

2 진아와 수한이가 세계 인공 지능 박람회에 있다.

3 그들은 인공 지능 집으로 들어가고 있다.

4 수한: 이것 봐! 미래의 집이야.

5 진아: 침실 먼저 들어가 보자. 이거 봐, 스마트 옷장이 있어.

6 수한: 옷장 문에 있는 스크린 앞에 서 있으니까 내 옷이 계속해서 바뀌어.

7 진아: 스크린이 날씨에 적합한 옷을 제안하는 거야.

8 수한: 놀라워! 우린 더 이상 날씨 때문에 무슨 옷을 입을지 걱정할 필요가 없겠다.

9 진아: 맞아. 이제 거실로 가 보자.

10 수한: 오, 이 음악 스피커 마음에 들어.

11 인공 지능 스피커: 저는 그냥 음악 스피커가 아니에요.

12 저는 당신이 상상하는 것 이상의 것을 할 수 있어요.

13 진아: 네가 우리를 이해한다니 믿기 어려운 걸! 넌 뭘 할 수 있어?

14 인공 지능 스피커: 영화 보는 건 어때요?

15 하나 틀어 줄게요.

16 수한: 이것 봐, 스마트 창문이 점점 어두워지고 있어.

17 마치 내가 영화관 안에 있는 것 같아.

18 Jina: _____ _____ can you do?

19 AI Speaker: I _____ beatbox, _____ . _____ _____ , "cats and boots and cats and boots."

20 Suhan: You're _____ . _____ _____ !

21 Jina: _____ ! _____ a smart car station _____ !

22 _____ _____ and _____ _____ that red car.

23 Suhan: This car is _____ _____ . Let's _____ _____ .

24 AI Car: Welcome. _____ you _____ _____ _____ ?

25 Jina: Yes, _____ _____ we _____ now?

26 It's _____ _____ _____ _____ in a smart car.

27 AI Car: You _____ _____ _____ do anything.

28 I will drive and _____ _____ _____ the next station.

29 Suhan: _____ _____ ! I see a cat _____ the street.

30 AI Car: _____ worry. I _____ _____ _____ it.

31 When I _____ _____ _____ , I slow _____ or stop.

32 Jina: _____ _____ you _____ that?

33 AI Car: I'm a very _____ _____ car.

34 I know _____ _____ _____ .

35 I can predict danger _____ _____ knowledge and experience.

36 Suhan: _____ smart! You think and act _____ a person.

37 You are really _____ a _____ .

18 진아: 또 뭘 할 수 있어?

19 인공 지능 스피커: 비트박스도 할 수 있어요. "북치기 박치기 북치기 박치기."

20 수한: 넌 정말 재미있구나. 잘했어!

21 진아: 서둘러! 밖에 스마트 자동차 정류장이 있어.

22 가서 저 빨간 차를 타 보자.

23 수한: 이 차 정말 멋지다. 차에 타자.

24 인공 지능 자동차: 어서 오세요. 갈 준비 됐나요?

25 진아: 응, 우린 이제 뭘 해야 하지?

26 스마트 자동차에 타는 건 처음이야.

27 인공 지능 자동차: 아무 것도 하지 않아도 돼요.

28 제가 운전해서 다음 정류장까지 데려다줄 거니까요.

29 수한: 조심해! 고양이가 길을 건너고 있는 게 보여.

30 인공 지능 자동차: 걱정 말아요. 이미 감지했어요.

31 저는 어떤 위험 상황을 감지하면 속도를 늦추거나 멈춰요.

32 진아: 어떻게 그렇게 할 수 있어?

33 인공 지능 자동차: 전 아주 지능적인 로봇 차예요.

34 저는 운전에 대한 모든 걸 알고 있어요.

35 저는 제 지식과 경험을 바탕으로 위험을 예측할 수 있어요.

36 수한: 정말 똑똑하구나! 사람처럼 생각하고 행동하는구나.

37 정말 인간 같아.

※ 다음 문장을 우리말로 쓰시오.

1 A Day at the AI Expo
➡ _____

2 Jina and Suhan are at the World AI Expo.
➡ _____

3 They are entering the AI home.
➡ _____

4 Suhan: Look at this! It's a house of the future.
➡ _____

5 Jina: Let's go into the bedroom first. Look, there's a smart closet.
➡ _____

6 Suhan: I'm standing in front of this screen on the closet door and my clothes keep changing.
➡ _____

7 Jina: The screen suggests clothes that suit the weather.
➡ _____

8 Suhan: That's amazing! We no longer have to worry about dressing for the weather.
➡ _____

9 Jina: Right. Let's move on to the living room.
➡ _____

10 Suhan: Oh, I like this music speaker.
➡ _____

11 AI Speaker: I'm not just a music speaker.
➡ _____

12 I can do more than you can imagine.
➡ _____

13 Jina: It's hard to believe that you can understand us. What can you do?
➡ _____

14 AI Speaker: How about watching a movie?
➡ _____

15 I'll play one for you.
➡ _____

16 Suhan: Look, those smart windows are getting darker.
➡ _____

17 I feel like I'm in a movie theater.
➡ _____

Step3

18 Jina: What else can you do?

➡ _____

19 AI Speaker: I can beatbox, too. Here comes, "cats and boots and cats and boots."

➡ _____

20 Suhan: You're funny. Good job!

➡ _____

21 Jina: Hurry! There's a smart car station outside!

➡ _____

22 Let's go and ride in that red car.

➡ _____

23 Suhan: This car is so cool. Let's get in.

➡ _____

24 AI Car: Welcome. Are you ready to go?

➡ _____

25 Jina: Yes, what should we do now?

➡ _____

26 It's my first time to ride in a smart car.

➡ _____

27 AI Car: You don't need to do anything.

➡ _____

28 I will drive and take you to the next station.

➡ _____

29 Suhan: Watch out! I see a cat crossing the street.

➡ _____

30 AI Car: Don't worry. I have just sensed it.

➡ _____

31 When I sense dangerous situations, I slow down or stop.

➡ _____

32 Jina: How can you do that?

➡ _____

33 AI Car: I'm a very intelligent robotic car.

➡ _____

34 I know all about driving.

➡ _____

35 I can predict danger based on knowledge and experience.

➡ _____

36 Suhan: How smart! You think and act like a person.

➡ _____

37 You are really like a human.

➡ _____

14 **Lesson 7.** Living in the AI World

※ 다음 괄호 안의 단어들을 우리말에 맞도록 바르게 배열하시오.

1 (Day / at / A / AI / the / Expo)
➡ _____

2 (Suhan / and / Jina / at / are / World / the / Expo. / AI)
➡ _____

3 (they / entering / are / AI / the / home.)
➡ _____

4 (Suhan: / at / look / this! // a / it's / of / house / future. / the)
➡ _____

5 (Jina: / go / let's / the / into / first. / bedroom // look, / a / there's / closet. / smart)
➡ _____

6 (Suhan: / standing / I'm / front / in / this / of / screen / the / on / door / closet / and / clothes / my / changing. / keep)
➡ _____
_____

7 (Jina: / screen / the / clothes / suggests / that / the / suit / weather.)
➡ _____

8 (Suhan: / amazing! / that's // we / longer / no / to / have / about / worry / for / dressing / weather. / the)
➡ _____
_____

9 (Jina: / right. // move / let's / to / on / the / room. / living)
➡ _____

10 (Suhan: / oh, / like / I / music / this / speaker.)
➡ _____

11 (AI / Speaker: / not / I'm / a / just / speaker. / music)
➡ _____

12 (I / do / can / than / more / imagine. / can / you)
➡ _____

13 (Jina: / hard / it's / believe / to / you / that / understand / can / us. // what / you / can / do?)
➡ _____

14 (Speaker: / AI / about / how / a / watching / movie?)
➡ _____

15 (play / I'll / for / you. / one)
➡ _____

16 (Suhan: / look, / smart / those / are / windows / darker. / getting)
➡ _____

17 (feel / I / like / in / I'm / movie / theater. / a)
➡ _____

1 인공 지능 박람회에서의 하루

2 진아와 수한이가 세계 인공 지능 박람회에 있다.

3 그들은 인공 지능 집으로 들어가고 있다.

4 수한: 이것 봐! 미래의 집이야.

5 진아: 침실 먼저 들어가 보자. 이거 봐. 스마트 옷장이 있어.

6 수한: 옷장 문에 있는 스크린 앞에 서 있으니까 내 옷이 계속해서 바뀌어.

7 진아: 스크린이 날씨에 적합한 옷을 제안하는 거야.

8 수한: 놀라워! 우린 더 이상 날씨 때문에 무슨 옷을 입을지 걱정할 필요가 없겠다.

9 진아: 맞아. 이제 거실로 가 보자.

10 수한: 오, 이 음악 스피커 마음에 들어.

11 인공 지능 스피커: 저는 그냥 음악 스피커가 아니에요.

12 저는 당신이 상상하는 것 이상의 것을 할 수 있어요.

13 진아: 네가 우리를 이해한다니 믿기 어려운 걸! 넌 뭘 할 수 있어?

14 인공 지능 스피커: 영화 보는 건 어때요?

15 하나 틀어 줄게요.

16 수한: 이것 봐, 스마트 창문이 점점 어두워지고 있어.

17 마치 내가 영화관 안에 있는 것 같아.

18 (Jina: / else / what / do? / you / can)
➡ _____

19 (AI / Speaker: / can / I / too. / beatbox // comes, / here / and / "cats / boots / and / boots." / and / cats)
➡ _____

20 (Suhan: / funny. / you're // job! / good)
➡ _____

21 (Jina: / hurry! / a / there's / car / smart / outside! / station)
➡ _____

22 (go / let's / ride / and / that / in / car. / red)
➡ _____

23 (Suhan: / car / this / cool. / is / so // get / in. / let's)
➡ _____

24 (AI / Car: / welcome. // you / are / to / ready / go?)
➡ _____

25 (Jina: / yes, / should / what / do / we / now?)
➡ _____

26 (my / it's / time / first / ride / to / in / a / car. / smart)
➡ _____

27 (AI / Car: / don't / you / need / do / to / anything.)
➡ _____

28 (will / I / drive / and / you / take / the / to / station. / next)
➡ _____

29 (Suhan: / out! / watch // see / I / cat / a / the / crossing / street.)
➡ _____

30 (Car: / AI / worry. / don't // have / I / sensed / it. / just)
➡ _____

31 (I / when / sense / situations, / dangerous / slow / I / down / stop. / or)
➡ _____

32 (Jina: / can / how / do / that? / you)
➡ _____

33 (Car: / AI / a / I'm / intelligent / very / car. / robotic)
➡ _____

34 (know / I / about / all / driving.)
➡ _____

35 (can / I / danger / predict / on / based / experience. / and / knowledge)
➡ _____

36 (Suhan: / smart! / how // think / you / and / like / act / a / person.)
➡ _____

37 (are / you / like / really / human. / a)
➡ _____

18 진아: 또 뭘 할 수 있어?

19 인공 지능 스피커: 비트박스도 할 수 있어요. "북치기 박치기 북치기 박치기."

20 수한: 넌 정말 재미있구나. 잘했어!

21 진아: 서둘러! 밖에 스마트 자동차 정류장이 있어.

22 가서 저 빨간 차를 타 보자.

23 수한: 이 차 정말 멋지다. 차에 타자.

24 인공 지능 자동차: 어서 오세요. 갈 준비 됐나요?

25 진아: 응, 우린 이제 뭘 해야 하지?

26 스마트 자동차에 타는 건 처음이야.

27 인공 지능 자동차: 아무 것도 하지 않아도 돼요.

28 제가 운전해서 다음 정류장까지 데려다줄 거니까요.

29 수한: 조심해! 고양이가 길을 건너고 있는 게 보여.

30 인공 지능 자동차: 걱정 말아요. 이미 감지했어요.

31 저는 어떤 위험 상황을 감지하면 속도를 늦추거나 멈춰요.

32 진아: 어떻게 그렇게 할 수 있어?

33 인공 지능 자동차: 전 아주 지능적인 로봇 차예요.

34 저는 운전에 대한 모든 걸 알고 있어요.

35 저는 제 지식과 경험을 바탕으로 위험을 예측할 수 있어요.

36 수한: 정말 똑똑하구나! 사람처럼 생각하고 행동하는구나.

37 정말 인간 같아.

※ 다음 우리말을 영어로 쓰시오.

1 ▶ 인공 지능 박람회에서의 하루

➡ _____

2 ▶ 진아와 수한이가 세계 인공 지능 박람회에 있다.

➡ _____

3 ▶ 그들은 인공 지능 집으로 들어가고 있다.

➡ _____

4 ▶ 수한: 이것 봐! 미래의 집이야.

➡ _____

5 ▶ 진아: 침실 먼저 들어가 보자. 이거 봐, 스마트 옷장이 있어.

➡ _____

6 ▶ 수한: 옷장 문에 있는 스크린 앞에 서 있으니까 내 옷이 계속해서 바뀌어.

➡ _____

7 ▶ 진아: 스크린이 날씨에 적합한 옷을 제안하는 거야.

➡ _____

8 ▶ 수한: 놀라워! 우린 더 이상 날씨 때문에 무슨 옷을 입을지 걱정할 필요가 없겠다.

➡ _____

9 ▶ 진아: 맞아. 이제 거실로 가 보자.

➡ _____

10 ▶ 수한: 오, 이 음악 스피커 마음에 들어.

➡ _____

11 ▶ 인공 지능 스피커: 저는 그냥 음악 스피커가 아니에요.

➡ _____

12 ▶ 저는 당신이 상상하는 것 이상의 것을 할 수 있어요.

➡ _____

13 ▶ 진아: 네가 우리를 이해한다니 믿기 어려운 걸! 넌 뭘 할 수 있어?

➡ _____

14 ▶ 인공 지능 스피커: 영화 보는 건 어때요?

➡ _____

15 ▶ 하나 틀어 줄게요.

➡ _____

16 ▶ 수한: 이것 봐, 스마트 창문이 점점 어두워지고 있어.

➡ _____

17 ▶ 마치 내가 영화관 안에 있는 것 같아.

➡ _____

18 진아: 또 뭘 할 수 있어?

➡ _____

19 인공 지능 스피커: 비트박스도 할 수 있어요. "북치기 박치기 북치기 박치기."

➡ _____

20 수한: 넌 정말 재미있구나. 잘했어!

➡ _____

21 진아: 서둘러! 밖에 스마트 자동차 정류장이 있어.

➡ _____

22 가서 저 빨간 차를 타 보자.

➡ _____

23 수한: 이 차 정말 멋지다. 차에 타자.

➡ _____

24 인공 지능 자동차: 어서 오세요. 갈 준비 됐나요?

➡ _____

25 진아: 응, 우린 이제 뭘 해야 하지?

➡ _____

26 스마트 자동차에 타는 건 처음이야.

➡ _____

27 인공 지능 자동차: 아무 것도 하지 않아도 돼요.

➡ _____

28 제가 운전해서 다음 정류장까지 데려다줄 거니까요.

➡ _____

29 수한: 조심해! 고양이가 길을 건너고 있는 게 보여.

➡ _____

30 인공 지능 자동차: 걱정 말아요. 이미 감지했어요.

➡ _____

31 저는 어떤 위험 상황을 감지하면 속도를 늦추거나 멈춰요.

➡ _____

32 진아: 어떻게 그렇게 할 수 있어?

➡ _____

33 인공 지능 자동차: 전 아주 지능적인 로봇 차예요.

➡ _____

34 저는 운전에 대한 모든 걸 알고 있어요.

➡ _____

35 저는 제 지식과 경험을 바탕으로 위험을 예측할 수 있어요.

➡ _____

36 수한: 정말 똑똑하구나! 사람처럼 생각하고 행동하는구나.

➡ _____

37 정말 인간 같아.

➡ _____

※ 다음 우리말과 일치하도록 빈칸에 알맞은 말을 쓰시오.

Before You Read

1. _____ _____
2. AI _____ Human!
3. An AI program _____ _____ a human _____ a *baduk* _____.
4. The AI _____ _____ _____ _____ Lee Sedol, who is _____ _____ _____ _____ *baduk* _____.
5. *Baduk* is a board game, and the rules are _____ _____.
6. Many people _____ it would be impossible _____ _____ _____ _____ _____ a human player.
7. However, the AI _____ _____ _____ _____ Lee's play, and it _____ _____ the game.
8. People _____ _____ that an AI can _____ _____ _____ a human.

Focus on Expressions

1. In 2099, people _____ _____ a flying car _____ _____ the moon.
2. Kids _____ _____ _____ to the moon _____ the _____ _____ _____ is there.
3. _____ _____, horse-riding is _____ _____ _____.
4. They _____ _____ to _____ _____ the horses.

Wrap Up 1-2

1. G: Minseok, there is a _____ _____ machine _____ _____. _____ _____ we _____ it?
2. B: That _____ interesting. We'll _____ _____ _____ easily and fast _____ _____ it.
3. G: I hope so. _____ _____, do you think maybe _____ will be possible _____ _____ _____ _____ humans someday?
4. B: I'm not sure. But we _____ _____ _____ _____ danger _____ _____ robots.
5. G: _____ do you _____?
6. B: Robots can help people _____ _____. Robots can do the dangerous work _____ humans _____ _____ _____.
7. G: You're _____. We should _____ _____ _____ _____ the bright side.

1. 데일리 뉴스
2. AI가 인간을 이기다!
3. 바둑 대국에서 AI 프로그램이 인간을 이겼다.
4. AI가 이세돌과 대국을 벌였는데, 그는 가장 위대한 바둑기사들 중의 한 명이다.
5. 바둑은 보드 게임이고, 그 규칙은 이해하기 어렵다.
6. 많은 사람들은 AI가 인간 기사를 이기는 것은 불가능할 것이라고 믿었다.
7. 그러나, AI는 이세돌의 경기를 예측할 수 있었고, 그리고 마침내 경기에서 이겼다.
8. 사람들은 AI가 인간보다 더 똑똑할 수 있다는 것에 충격을 받았다.

1. 2099년에 사람들은 달에 가기 위해 날아다니는 차를 탑니다.
2. 아이들은 가장 멋진 놀이공원이 그곳에 있기 때문에 달에 가는 것을 좋아합니다.
3. 다른 무엇보다도, 말타기는 그들이 가장 좋아하는 활동입니다.
4. 그들은 말에서 내리기를 원하지 않습니다.

1. G: 민석아, 저쪽에 스마트 음식 주문 자판기가 있어. 가서 해 보지 않을래?
2. B: 재미있겠다. 저걸 사용하면 우린 쉽고 빠르게 주문할 수 있을 거야.
3. G: 그러길 바라. 그건 그렇고, 너는 로봇이 언젠가 인간을 대체할 수 있을 거라고 생각하니?
4. B: 잘 모르겠어. 하지만 우리는 로봇 덕분에 위험이 없어질 거야.
5. G: 무슨 뜻이야?
6. B: 로봇은 위험에 처한 사람들을 도울 수 있어. 로봇이 위험한 일을 할 수 있어서 사람들이 그 일을 하지 않아도 되지.
7. G: 네 말이 맞아. 우리는 항상 좋은 면을 보도록 해야 해.

※ 다음 우리말을 영어로 쓰시오.

Before You Read

1. 데일리 뉴스
➡ _____

2. AI가 인간을 이기다!
➡ _____

3. 바둑 대국에서 AI 프로그램이 인간을 이겼다.
➡ _____

4. AI가 이세돌과 대국을 벌였는데, 그는 가장 위대한 바둑기사들 중의 한 명이다.
➡ _____

5. 바둑은 보드 게임이고, 그 규칙은 이해하기 어렵다.
➡ _____

6. 많은 사람들은 AI가 인간 기사를 이기는 것은 불가능할 것이라고 믿었다.
➡ _____

7. 그러나, AI는 이세돌의 경기를 예측할 수 있었고, 그리고 마침내 경기에서 이겼다.
➡ _____

8. 사람들은 AI가 인간보다 더 똑똑할 수 있다는 것에 충격을 받았다.
➡ _____

Focus on Expressions

1. 2099년에 사람들은 달에 가기 위해 날아다니는 차를 탑니다.
➡ _____

2. 아이들은 가장 멋진 놀이공원이 그곳에 있기 때문에 달에 가는 것을 좋아합니다.
➡ _____

3. 다른 무엇보다도, 말타기는 그들이 가장 좋아하는 활동입니다.
➡ _____

4. 그들은 말에서 내리기를 원하지 않습니다.
➡ _____

Wrap Up 1-2

1. G: 민석아, 저쪽에 스마트 음식 주문 자판기가 있어. 가서 해 보지 않을래?
➡ _____

2. B: 재미있겠다. 저걸 사용하면 우린 쉽고 빠르게 주문할 수 있을 거야.
➡ _____

3. G: 그러길 바라. 그건 그렇고, 너는 로봇이 언젠가 인간을 대체할 수 있을 거라고 생각하니?
➡ _____

4. B: 잘 모르겠어. 하지만 우리는 로봇 덕분에 위험이 없어질 거야.
➡ _____

5. G: 무슨 뜻이야?
➡ _____

6. B: 로봇은 위험에 처한 사람들을 도울 수 있어. 로봇이 위험한 일을 할 수 있어서 사람들이 그 일을 하지 않아도 되지.
➡ _____

7. G: 네 말이 맞아. 우리는 항상 좋은 면을 보도록 해야 해.
➡ _____

※ 다음 영어를 우리말로 쓰시오.

01	collect	
02	affair	
03	official	
04	businessman	
05	suffer	
06	rule	
07	dynasty	
08	explain	
09	unknown	
10	fit	
11	press	
12	through	
13	tourist	
14	independence	
15	community	
16	store	
17	modern	
18	alive	
19	another	
20	movement	
21	village	

22	poem	
23	waste	
24	property	
25	royal	
26	society	
27	found	
28	pottery	
29	support	
30	meaning	
31	taste	
32	interest	
33	architecture	
34	Spanish	
35	in danger	
36	set foot	
37	be known as	
38	care for	
39	fall off	
40	thanks to	
41	be famous for	
42	in need	
43	be in harmony with	

※ 다음 우리말을 영어로 쓰시오.

01	전통	22	통치하다; 규칙, 원칙
02	현대의	23	고통 받다, 시달리다
03	사회, 단체	24	여행객
04	건축	25	운동
05	사업가	26	～을 통하여
06	저장하다, 보관하다	27	적합하다
07	왕조, 시대	28	왕의, 왕실의
08	설명하다	29	또 다른, 다른 하나의
09	의미	30	압박하다
10	도자기	31	마을
11	알려지지 않은	32	지역사회, 주민
12	시	33	낭비하다
13	공무원, 당국	34	자연
14	모으다, 수집하다	35	(사업, 세력 등이) 쇠퇴하다
15	설립하다	36	～으로 가득하다
16	독립	37	～을 돌보다
17	사건, 일	38	～ 덕분에
18	재산	39	수백의, 수많은
19	살아 있는	40	어려움에 처한
20	관심, 흥미	41	～으로 유명하다
21	지원하다	42	～으로 알려지다
		43	～와 조화를 이루다

※ 다음 영영풀이에 알맞은 단어를 <보기>에서 골라 쓴 후, 우리말 뜻을 쓰시오.

1 _____ : not dead: _____

2 _____ : a man who works in business: _____

3 _____ : a family of rulers who rule over a country for a long period of time: _____

4 _____ : a long written story about imaginary people and events: _____

5 _____ : the art of planning, designing and constructing buildings: _____

6 _____ : connected with or belonging to the king or queen of a country: _____

7 _____ : to have the official power to control a country and the people who live there: _____

8 _____ : to give details about something or describe it so that it can be understood: _____

9 _____ : all the things that belong to someone or something that belongs to them: _____

10 _____ : a hard solid substance found in the ground and often used for building houses: _____

11 _____ : the place where someone lives or the town that they come from: _____

12 _____ : to get an institution, company, or organization started, often by providing the necessary money: _____

13 _____ : to bring things or people together from several places or from several people: _____

14 _____ : to put things in a container or other places and leave them there until they are needed: _____

15 _____ : an area of ground, especially one that is used for a particular purpose such as farming or building: _____

16 _____ : all the animals, plants, and other things in the world that are not made by people, and all the events and processes that are not caused by people: _____

보기			
land	store	found	hometown
businessman	architecture	stone	rule
alive	collect	property	nature
royal	novel	explain	dynasty

※ 다음 우리말과 일치하도록 빈칸에 알맞은 말을 쓰시오.

Listen & Speak 1 B-2

G: _____ you know _____ _____ Changdeokgung?

B: Yes, a _____. It's _____ _____ its beautiful garden.

G: I'm _____ _____ go there _____ my Chinese friend.

B: I _____ you'll _____ it.

G: 너는 창덕궁에 대해 아는 것이 있니?

B: 응, 조금. 그것은 아름다운 정원으로 유명해.

G: 난 내 중국인 친구와 함께 그곳에 갈 거야.

B: 그곳이 마음에 들 거야.

Listen & Speak 2 A

B: _____ you _____ this _____?

W: Sure. It's the *Two Sisters* _____ Renoir. He _____ it _____ 1881.

B: 이 그림에 대해 설명을 해 주시겠습니까?

W: 물론이죠. 이 그림은 르누아르의 "두 자매"예요. 그는 1881년에 이 그림을 그렸어요.

Listen & Speak 2 B-1

1. G: Can you _____ _____ _____?

   B: Sure. It _____ _____ _____ Yun Dongju.

   G: What's it _____?

   B: It's _____ him _____ his hometown.

2. B: Could you _____ _____ Helping Hands _____?

   G: It's a _____ _____ in our _____.

   B: Could you _____ me _____ _____ it?

   G: Well, they _____ _____ _____ children in need.

1. G: 이 시를 설명해 줄 수 있니?
   B: 그럼. 그것은 윤동주에 의해 씌어 졌어.
   G: 그것은 무엇에 관한 거니?
   B: 그것은 고향을 그리워하는 작가에 관한 거야.
2. B: '도움의 손길'이 무엇인지 설명해 줄 수 있니?
   G: 그것은 우리 지역 사회에 있는 자 원봉사 단체야.
   B: 그것에 관해 더 말해 줄 수 있니?
   G: 음, 그들은 어려움에 처한 어린이 들을 돌봐.

Listen & Speak 2 C

A: _____ you _____ your plan _____ _____ money?

B: I _____ _____ my money _____ snacks.

A: 돈을 절약할 너의 계획에 대해 설명해 줄 수 있니?

B: 간식에 돈을 낭비하지 않을 거야.

Real-Life Zone A

G: _____ are *hanoks*? Do you know _____ _____ them?

M: *Hanoks* are traditional _____ _____. They _____ _____ to be _____ _____ nature.

G: Could you _____ _____ _____ more about them?

M: *Hanoks* are _____ in the summer and _____ in the winter.

G: 한옥은 무엇이에요? 한옥에 대해 아 는 것이 있으세요?

M: 한옥은 전통적인 한국 가옥이에요. 그것들은 자연과 조화를 이루도록 설 계되었어요.

G: 그것들에 대해 좀 더 설명하실 수 있 어요?

M: 한옥은 여름에는 시원하고 겨울에는 따뜻해요.

W: That _____ interesting. _____ can I _____ these _____
_____?

M: There's a *hanok* village _____ _____.

G: How _____ _____ there and _____ the *hanoks*?

W: Good _____! _____ can we _____ there?

M: You can _____ Bus Number 5 _____ _____ at the bus stop.

Real-Life Zone B

1. **A:** Do you _____ _____ about the Great Wall of China?

   B: Yes. It is _____ _____ the _____ _____ in the world.

   A: Can you _____ _____ it is _____?

   B: It's _____ it is the _____ _____ in the world.

2. **A:** Do you know _____ _____ the _____ *The Old Man and the Sea*?

   B: Yes. It is a _____ _____ _____ Ernest Hemingway.

   A: Can you _____ _____ it is famous?

   B: It's _____ Hemingway _____ the Pulitzer Prize in 1953 _____ this novel.

Real-Life Zone B e.g.

A: Do you _____ _____ _____ the Eiffel Tower?

B: Yes. It _____ _____ _____ 1889 _____ Gustave Eiffel.

A: Can you _____ _____ it is _____?

B: _____ _____ it was the _____ _____ in the world _____ _____ _____.

Wrap Up

B: Do you _____ _____ about a *dol* party?

G: Yes. It's the _____ party for a one-year-old _____.

B: Could you _____ me _____ about it?

G: Well, the family members _____ _____ for the party, and the birthday baby _____ a *hanok*.

B: That _____ _____.

G: The family members _____ _____ and _____ _____ a _____ _____ for the baby. It's a _____ _____.

W: 그거 재미있네요. 이 전통 가옥을 어디에서 볼 수 있어요?

M: 이 근처에 한옥 마을이 있어요.

G: 거기 가서 한옥들을 보는 게 어때요?

W: 좋은 생각이구나! 그곳에 어떻게 갈 수 있죠?

M: 저기 버스 정류장에서 5번 버스를 타시면 돼요.

1. **A:** 중국의 만리장성에 대해 아는 것이 있나요?

   B: 네. 그것은 세계에서 멋진 광경들 중의 하나예요.

   A: 그것이 왜 유명한지 설명해 줄 수 있나요?

   B: 세계에서 가장 긴 성벽이기 때문이죠.

2. **A:** '노인과 바다'라는 소설에 대해 아는 것이 있나요?

   B: 네. 그것은 어니스트 헤밍웨이가 쓴 소설이에요.

   A: 그것이 왜 유명한지 설명해 줄 수 있나요?

   B: 헤밍웨이가 이 책으로 1953년 퓰리쳐상을 받았기 때문이죠.

A: 너는 에펠탑에 대해 아는 것이 있니?

B: 응. 그것은 1889년에 Gustave Eiffel에 의해 세워졌어.

A: 그것이 왜 유명한지 설명할 수 있니?

B: 그것은 그 당시 그 탑이 세계에서 가장 높은 탑이었기 때문이야.

B: 넌 돌잔치에 대해 아는 것이 있니?

G: 응. 그건 한 살 먹은 아기를 위한 생일잔치야.

B: 그것에 대해 더 말해 줄 수 있니?

G: 음, 그 잔치를 위해 가족들이 함께 모이고 생일을 맞은 아기는 한복을 입어.

B: 그거 재미있구나.

G: 가족들은 음식을 함께 나누어 먹고 아기가 오래 살기를 바라. 그건 한국의 전통이야.

대화문 Test

※ 다음 우리말에 맞도록 대화를 영어로 쓰시오.

Listen & Speak 1 B-2

G: _____

B: _____

G: _____

B: _____

G: 너는 창덕궁에 대해 아는 것이 있니?

B: 응, 조금. 그것은 아름다운 정원으로 유명해.

G: 난 내 중국인 친구와 함께 그곳에 갈 거야.

B: 그곳이 마음에 들 거야.

Listen & Speak 2 A

B: _____

W: _____

B: 이 그림에 대해 설명을 해 주시겠습니까?

W: 물론이죠. 이 그림은 르누아루의 "두 자매"예요. 그는 1881년에 이 그림을 그렸어요.

Listen & Speak 2 B-1

1. G: _____

   B: _____

   G: _____

   B: _____

2. B: _____

   G: _____

   B: _____

   G: _____

1. G: 이 시를 설명해 줄 수 있니?
   B: 그럼. 그것은 윤동주에 의해 씌어 졌어.
   G: 그것은 무엇에 관한 거니?
   B: 그것은 고향을 그리워하는 작가에 관한 거야.
2. B: '도움의 손길'이 무엇인지 설명해 줄 수 있니?
   G: 그것은 우리 지역 사회에 있는 자 원봉사 단체야.
   B: 그것에 관해 더 말해 줄 수 있니?
   G: 음, 그들은 어려움에 처한 어린이 들을 돌봐.

Listen & Speak 2 C

A: _____

B: _____

A: 돈을 절약할 너의 계획에 대해 설명해 줄 수 있니?

B: 간식에 돈을 낭비하지 않을 거야.

Real-Life Zone A

G: _____

M: _____

_____

G: _____

M: _____

G: 한옥은 무엇이에요? 한옥에 대해 아 는 것이 있으세요?

M: 한옥은 전통적인 한국 가옥이에요. 그것들은 자연과 조화를 이루도록 설 계되었어요.

G: 그것들에 대해 좀 더 설명하실 수 있 어요?

M: 한옥은 여름에는 시원하고 겨울에는 따뜻해요.

W: _____

M: _____

G: _____

W: _____

M: _____

W: 그거 재미있네요. 이 전통 가옥을 어디에서 볼 수 있어요?
M: 이 근처에 한옥 마을이 있어요.
G: 거기 가서 한옥들을 보는 게 어때요?
W: 좋은 생각이구나! 그곳에 어떻게 갈 수 있죠?
M: 저기 버스 정류장에서 5번 버스를 타시면 돼요.

Real-Life Zone B

1. A: _____

   B: _____

   A: _____

   B: _____

2. A: _____

   B: _____

   A: _____

   B: _____

1. A: 중국의 만리장성에 대해 아는 것이 있나요?
   B: 네. 그것은 세계에서 멋진 광경들 중의 하나예요.
   A: 그것이 왜 유명한지 설명해 줄 수 있나요?
   B: 세계에서 가장 긴 성벽이기 때문이죠.

2. A: '노인과 바다'라는 소설에 대해 아는 것이 있나요?
   B: 네. 그것은 어니스트 헤밍웨이가 쓴 소설이에요.
   A: 그것이 왜 유명한지 설명해 줄 수 있나요?
   B: 헤밍웨이가 이 책으로 1953년 퓰리처상을 받았기 때문이죠.

Real-Life Zone B e.g.

A: _____

B: _____

A: _____

B: _____

A: 너는 에펠탑에 대해 아는 것이 있니?
B: 응. 그것은 1889년에 Gustave Eiffel에 의해 세워졌어.
A: 그것이 왜 유명한지 설명할 수 있니?
B: 그것은 그 당시 그 탑이 세계에서 가장 높은 탑이었기 때문이야.

Wrap Up

B: _____

G: _____

B: _____

G: _____

B: _____

G: _____

B: 넌 돌잔치에 대해 아는 것이 있니?
G: 응. 그건 한 살 먹은 아기를 위한 생일잔치야.
B: 그것에 대해 더 말해 줄 수 있니?
G: 음, 그 잔치를 위해 가족들이 함께 모이고 생일을 맞은 아기는 한복을 입어.
B: 그거 재미있구나.
G: 가족들은 음식을 함께 나누어 먹고 아기가 오래 살기를 바라. 그건 한국의 전통이야.

※ 다음 우리말과 일치하도록 빈칸에 알맞은 것을 골라 쓰시오.

1 The _____ of _____ in _____
    A. Architecture   B. King   C. Gyeongseong

2 _____ you _____ _____ Bukchon?
    A. to   B. been   C. have

3 _____ is a _____ *hanok* _____ in Bukchon.
    A. village   B. beautiful   C. there

4 It is _____ with tourists _____ want to see Korea's _____.
    A. who   B. popular   C. past

5 However, not many people _____ that Bukchon was _____ _____ one man's _____.
    A. created   B. efforts   C. through   D. know

6 That man was Jeong Segwon, _____ _____ the King of Architecture _____ Gyeongseong.
    A. known   B. in   C. as

7 Jeong Segwon was a _____ _____ _____ Geonyangsa in 1920.
    A. founded   B. who   C. businessman

8 At the _____, Korea was _____ by Japan, and the Japanese were changing Gyeongseong to _____ their _____.
    A. ruled   B. fit   C. taste   D. time

9 Many Japanese _____ _____ Gyeongseong were _____ Japanese or _____ houses.
    A. into   B. Western   C. building   D. moving

10 Jeong Segwon _____ to _____ the *hanok* and help the _____ people.
    A. protect   B. suffering   C. wanted

11 He said, "People are _____. We Joseon people should _____ Jongno and not _____ the Japanese _____ foot here."
    A. keep   B. set   C. let   D. power

12 He _____ the land _____ Gyeongbokgung _____ Changdeokgung.
    A. between   B. bought   C. and

13 There he _____ small, _____ *hanoks* for the _____.
    A. people   B. built   C. modern

14 _____ his _____, we now have Bukchon _____ _____ its beautiful *hanoks*.
    A. filled   B. through   C. with   D. efforts

1 경성의 건축왕

2 당신은 북촌에 다녀온 적이 있는가?

3 북촌에는 아름다운 한옥 마을이 있다.

4 그곳은 한국의 과거를 보고 싶어 하는 관광객들에게 인기가 있다.

5 그러나 북촌이 한 사람의 노력으로 만들어졌다는 것을 아는 사람은 많지 않다.

6 그 사람은 경성의 건축왕으로 알려진 정세권이었다.

7 정세권은 1920년에 건양사를 설립한 사업가였다.

8 그 당시 한국은 일본의 지배를 받았고, 일본인들은 경성을 그들의 취향에 맞게 바꾸고 있었다.

9 경성으로 이주하는 많은 일본인들은 일본식이나 서양식 집들을 짓고 있었다.

10 정세권은 한옥을 지키고 고통받는 사람들을 돕기를 원했다.

11 그는 말했다. "사람이 힘이다. 우리 조선 사람들은 종로를 지켜야 하며, 일본인들이 이곳에 발을 붙이지 못하게 해야 한다."

12 그는 경복궁과 창덕궁 사이의 땅을 샀다.

13 거기에 그는 사람들을 위해 작은 현대식 한옥들을 지었다.

14 그의 노력으로 북촌은 현재 아름다운 한옥으로 가득 차 있다.

15 Jeong Segwon helped the _____ _____ in many
_____.

    A. movement   B. ways   C. independence

16 For _____, he built the office building for the Joseon Language
Society and _____ its efforts to _____ the Joseon language
_____.

    A. keep   B. example   C. alive   D. supported

17 When the Joseon Language Affair _____, he was _____ by
the police and _____ a lot.

    A. caught   B. happened   C. suffered

18 Japanese _____ _____ him to _____ Japanese houses.

    A. pressed   B. officials   C. build

19 He said, "I don't know _____ _____ _____ Japanese
houses."

    A. how   B. build   C. to

20 An _____ said, "You _____ how to build *hanoks*, _____
you can _____ Japanese houses, too."

    A. so   B. know   C. official   D. build

21 But he did not do _____ the Japanese _____ him to _____.

    A. what   B. do   C. told

22 The _____ was _____.

    A. high   B. cost

23 His business _____ _____, and he lost his _____.

    A. property   B. off   C. fell

24 However, in _____, thanks _____ Jeong Segwon, the
_____ of Korea _____ live with us today.

    A. still   B. part   C. traditions   D. to

15 정세권은 여러 방법으로 독립운동을 도왔다.

16 예를 들면, 그는 조선어 학회를 위한 회관을 지었고 조선어를 지키려는 그들의 노력을 지원했다.

17 조선어 학회 사건이 발생했을 때 그는 경찰에 잡혀 많은 고통을 겪었다.

18 일본인 관리들은 그에게 일본식 가옥을 지으라고 압박했다.

19 그는 말했다. "나는 일본식 가옥을 지을 줄 모르오."

20 한 관리가 말했다. "당신은 한옥을 지을 줄 아오. 그러니 일본식 가옥도 지을 수 있소."

21 그러나 그는 그 일본인이 그에게 요구한 것을 하지 않았다.

22 그 대가는 컸다.

23 그의 사업은 쇠퇴했고, 그는 재산을 잃었다.

24 그러나 부분적으로나마, 정세권 덕분에 한국의 전통이 오늘날 여전히 우리와 함께 살아 있다.

※ 다음 우리말과 일치하도록 빈칸에 알맞은 말을 쓰시오.

1 _____ _____ of _____ _____ Gyeongseong

2 _____ you _____ _____ Bukchon?

3 _____ _____ a beautiful *hanok* _____ in Bukchon.

4 It is _____ with tourists _____ want to see Korea's _____.

5 _____, not many people _____ that Bukchon _____ _____ _____ one man's _____.

6 That man was Jeong Segwon, _____ _____ the King of _____ in Gyeongseong.

7 Jeong Segwon was a businessman _____ _____ Geonyangsa in 1920.

8 _____ _____ _____, Korea _____ _____ _____ Japan, and the Japanese _____ _____ Gyeongseong to _____ their _____.

9 Many Japanese _____ _____ Gyeongseong _____ _____ _____ or _____ houses.

10 Jeong Segwon _____ _____ _____ the *hanok* and help the _____ people.

11 He said, "People are _____. We Joseon people _____ _____ Jongno and not _____ the Japanese _____ _____ here."

12 He _____ the land _____ Gyeongbokgung _____ Changdeokgung.

13 There he _____ small, _____ *hanoks* for the _____.

14 _____ his _____, we now have Bukchon _____ its beautiful *hanoks*.

---

1 경성의 건축왕

2 당신은 북촌에 다녀온 적이 있는가?

3 북촌에는 아름다운 한옥 마을이 있다.

4 그곳은 한국의 과거를 보고 싶어 하는 관광객들에게 인기가 있다.

5 그러나 북촌이 한 사람의 노력으로 만들어졌다는 것을 아는 사람은 많지 않다.

6 그 사람은 경성의 건축왕으로 알려진 정세권이었다.

7 정세권은 1920년에 건양사를 설립한 사업가였다.

8 그 당시 한국은 일본의 지배를 받았고, 일본인들은 경성을 그들의 취향에 맞게 바꾸고 있었다.

9 경성으로 이주하는 많은 일본인들은 일본식이나 서양식 집들을 짓고 있었다.

10 정세권은 한옥을 지키고 고통받는 사람들을 돕기를 원했다.

11 그는 말했다. "사람이 힘이다. 우리 조선 사람들은 종로를 지켜야 하며, 일본인들이 이곳에 발을 붙이지 못하게 해야 한다."

12 그는 경복궁과 창덕궁 사이의 땅을 샀다.

13 거기에 그는 사람들을 위해 작은 현대식 한옥들을 지었다.

14 그의 노력으로 북촌은 현재 아름다운 한옥으로 가득 차 있다.

15 Jeong Segwon helped the _____ _____ _____ _____ _____.

16 _____ _____, he built the office building for the Joseon Language Society and _____ _____ _____ to _____ the Joseon language _____.

17 When the Joseon Language Affair _____, he _____ _____ _____ the police and _____ _____ _____.

18 Japanese officials _____ him _____ _____ Japanese houses.

19 He said, "I don't know _____ _____ _____ Japanese houses."

20 An _____ said, "You _____ _____ _____ build *hanoks*, _____ you can _____ Japanese houses, _____."

21 But he did not do _____ the Japanese _____ him _____ _____.

22 The _____ was _____.

23 His business _____ _____, and he _____ his _____.

24 However, in _____, _____ _____ Jeong Segwon, the _____ of Korea _____ _____ _____ us today.

15 정세권은 여러 방법으로 독립운동을 도왔다.

16 예를 들면, 그는 조선어 학회를 위한 회관을 지었고 조선어를 지키려는 그들의 노력을 지원했다.

17 조선어 학회 사건이 발생했을 때 그는 경찰에 잡혀 많은 고통을 겪었다.

18 일본인 관리들은 그에게 일본식 가옥을 지으라고 압박했다.

19 그는 말했다. "나는 일본식 가옥을 지울 줄 모르오."

20 한 관리가 말했다. "당신은 한옥을 지울 줄 아오. 그러니 일본식 가옥도 지을 수 있소."

21 그러나 그는 그 일본인이 그에게 요구한 것을 하지 않았다.

22 그 대가는 컸다.

23 그의 사업은 쇠퇴했고, 그는 재산을 잃었다.

24 그러나 부분적으로나마, 정세권 덕분에 한국의 전통이 오늘날 여전히 우리와 살아 있다.

※ 다음 문장을 우리말로 쓰시오.

1 The King of Architecture in Gyeongseong

➡ _____

2 Have you been to Bukchon?

➡ _____

3 There is a beautiful *hanok* village in Bukchon.

➡ _____

4 It is popular with tourists who want to see Korea's past.

➡ _____

5 However, not many people know that Bukchon was created through one man's efforts.

➡ _____

6 That man was Jeong Segwon, known as the King of Architecture in Gyeongseong.

➡ _____

7 Jeong Segwon was a businessman who founded Geonyangsa in 1920.

➡ _____

8 At the time, Korea was ruled by Japan, and the Japanese were changing Gyeongseong to fit their taste.

➡ _____

9 Many Japanese moving into Gyeongseong were building Japanese or Western houses.

➡ _____

10 Jeong Segwon wanted to protect the *hanok* and help the suffering people.

➡ _____

11 He said, "People are power. We Joseon people should keep Jongno and not let the Japanese set foot here."

➡ _____

12 He bought the land between Gyeongbokgung and Changdeokgung.

➡ _____

13 There he built small, modern *hanoks* for the people.

➡ _____

14 Through his efforts, we now have Bukchon filled with its beautiful *hanoks*.

➡ _____

15 Jeong Segwon helped the independence movement in many ways.

➡ _____

16 For example, he built the office building for the Joseon Language Society and supported its efforts to keep the Joseon language alive.

➡ _____

17 When the Joseon Language Affair happened, he was caught by the police and suffered a lot.

➡ _____

18 Japanese officials pressed him to build Japanese houses.

➡ _____

19 He said, "I don't know how to build Japanese houses."

➡ _____

20 An official said, "You know how to build *hanoks*, so you can build Japanese houses, too."

➡ _____

21 But he did not do what the Japanese told him to do.

➡ _____

22 The cost was high.

➡ _____

23 His business fell off, and he lost his property.

➡ _____

24 However, in part, thanks to Jeong Segwon, the traditions of Korea still live with us today.

➡ _____

※ 다음 괄호 안의 단어들을 우리말에 맞도록 바르게 배열하시오.

1 (King / The / Architecture / of / Gyeongseong / in)
➡ _____

2 (you / have / to / been / Bukchon?)
➡ _____

3 (is / there / a / honok / beautiful / Bukchon. / in / village)
➡ _____

4 (is / it / with / popular / who / tourists / to / want / see / past. / Korea's)
➡ _____

5 (not / however, / people / many / know / Bukchon / that / created / was / one / through / efforts. / man's)
➡ _____

6 (man / that / Jeong / was / Segwon, / as / known / King / the / Architecture / of / Gyeongnseong. / in)
➡ _____

7 (Segwon / Jeong / was / businessman / a / who / Geonyangsa / founded / 1920. / in)
➡ _____

8 (the / at / time, / was / Korea / by / ruled / Japan, / and / Japanese / the / changing / were / to / Gyeongseong / fit / taste. / their)
➡ _____

9 (Japanese / many / into / moving / Gyeongseong / were / Japanese / building / or / houses. / Western)
➡ _____

10 (Segwon / Jeong / to / wanted / protect / hanok / the / help / and / suffering / the / people.)
➡ _____

11 (said, / he / "people / power. / are // Joseon / we / people / keep / should / Jongno / not / and / the / let / Japanese / foot / here." / set)
➡ _____

12 (bought / he / land / the / between / Changdeokgung. / and / Gyoengbokgung)
➡ _____

13 (he / there / small, / built / honoks / modern / the / for / people.)
➡ _____

14 (his / through / efforts, / now / we / have / filled / Bukchon / with / beautiful / its / hanoks.)
➡ _____

1 경성의 건축왕

2 당신은 북촌에 다녀온 적이 있는가?

3 북촌에는 아름다운 한옥 마을이 있다.

4 그곳은 한국의 과거를 보고 싶어 하는 관광객들에게 인기가 있다.

5 그러나 북촌이 한 사람의 노력으로 만들어졌다는 것을 아는 사람은 많지 않다.

6 그 사람은 경성의 건축왕으로 알려진 정세권이었다.

7 정세권은 1920년에 건양사를 설립한 사업가였다.

8 그 당시 한국은 일본의 지배를 받았고, 일본인들은 경성을 그들의 취향에 맞게 바꾸고 있었다.

9 경성으로 이주하는 많은 일본인들은 일본식이나 서양식 집들을 짓고 있었다.

10 정세권은 한옥을 지키고 고통받는 사람들을 돕기를 원했다.

11 그는 말했다. "사람이 힘이다. 우리 조선 사람들은 종로를 지켜야 하며, 일본인들이 이곳에 발을 붙이지 못하게 해야 한다."

12 그는 경복궁과 창덕궁 사이의 땅을 샀다.

13 거기에 그는 사람들을 위해 작은 현대식 한옥들을 지었다.

14 그의 노력으로 북촌은 현재 아름다운 한옥으로 가득 차 있다.

15 (Segwon / Jeong / the / helped / movement / independence / in / ways. / many)

➡ _____

16 (example, / for / built / he / office / the / for / building / the / Language / Joseon / Society / and / its / supported / to / efforts / keep / the / language / Joseon / alive.)

➡ _____

_____

17 (the / when / Joseon / Affair / Language / happened, / was / he / by / caught / the / police / suffered / and / lot. / a)

➡ _____

18 (officials / Japanese / him / pressed / build / to / houses. / Japanese)

➡ _____

19 (said, / he / "I / know / don't / to / how / Japanese / build / houses.")

➡ _____

20 (official / an / said, / "you / how / know / to / build / *hanoks*, / you / so / build / can / houses, / Japanese / too.")

➡ _____

_____

21 (he / but / did / do / not / what / Japanese / the / him / told / do. / to)

➡ _____

22 (cost / the / high. / was)

➡ _____

23 (business / his / off, / fell / and / lost / he / property. / his)

➡ _____

24 (however, / part, / in / to / thanks / Segwon, / Jeong / traditions / the / Korea / of / live / still / with / today. / us)

➡ _____

_____

15 정세권은 여러 방법으로 독립운동을 도왔다.

16 예를 들면, 그는 조선어 학회를 위한 회관을 지었고 조선어를 지키려는 그들의 노력을 지원했다.

17 조선어 학회 사건이 발생했을 때 그는 경찰에 잡혀 많은 고통을 겪었다.

18 일본인 관리들은 그에게 일본식 가옥을 지으라고 압박했다.

19 그는 말했다. "나는 일본식 가옥을 지을 줄 모르오."

20 한 관리가 말했다. "당신은 한옥을 지을 줄 아오. 그러니 일본식 가옥도 지을 수 있소."

21 그러나 그는 그 일본인이 그에게 요구한 것을 하지 않았다.

22 그 대가는 컸다.

23 그의 사업은 쇠퇴했고, 그는 재산을 잃었다.

24 그러나 부분적으로나마, 정세권 덕분에 한국의 전통이 오늘날 여전히 우리와 함께 살아 있다.

※ 다음 우리말을 영어로 쓰시오.

1 경성의 건축왕

➡ _____

2 당신은 북촌에 다녀온 적이 있는가?

➡ _____

3 북촌에는 아름다운 한옥 마을이 있다.

➡ _____

4 그곳은 한국의 과거를 보고 싶어 하는 관광객들에게 인기가 있다.

➡ _____

5 그러나 북촌이 한 사람의 노력으로 만들어졌다는 것을 아는 사람은 많지 않다.

➡ _____

6 그 사람은 경성의 건축왕으로 알려진 정세권이었다.

➡ _____

7 정세권은 1920년에 건양사를 설립한 사업가였다.

➡ _____

8 그 당시 한국은 일본의 지배를 받았고, 일본인들은 경성을 그들의 취향에 맞게 바꾸고 있었다.

➡ _____

9 경성으로 이주하는 많은 일본인들은 일본식이나 서양식 집들을 짓고 있었다.

➡ _____

10 정세권은 한옥을 지키고 고통받는 사람들을 돕기를 원했다.

➡ _____

11 그는 말했다. "사람이 힘이다. 우리 조선 사람들은 종로를 지켜야 하며, 일본인들이 이곳에 발을 붙이지 못하게 해야 한다."

➡ _____

_____

12 그는 경복궁과 창덕궁 사이의 땅을 샀다.

➡ _____

13 거기에 그는 사람들을 위해 작은 현대식 한옥들을 지었다.

➡ _____

14 그의 노력으로 북촌은 현재 아름다운 한옥으로 가득 차 있다.

➡ _____

15 정세권은 여러 방법으로 독립운동을 도왔다.

➡ _____

16 예를 들면, 그는 조선어 학회를 위한 회관을 지었고 조선어를 지키려는 그들의 노력을 지원했다.

➡ _____

➡ _____

17 조선어 학회 사건이 발생했을 때 그는 경찰에 잡혀 많은 고통을 겪었다.

➡ _____

18 일본인 관리들은 그에게 일본식 가옥을 지으라고 압박했다.

➡ _____

19 그는 말했다. "나는 일본식 가옥을 지울 줄 모르오."

➡ _____

20 한 관리가 말했다. "당신은 한옥을 지을 줄 아오. 그러니 일본식 가옥도 지을 수 있소."

➡ _____

21 그러나 그는 그 일본인이 그에게 요구한 것을 하지 않았다.

➡ _____

22 그 대가는 컸다.

➡ _____

23 그의 사업은 쇠퇴했고, 그는 재산을 잃었다.

➡ _____

24 그러나 부분적으로나마, 정세권 덕분에 한국의 전통이 오늘날 여전히 우리와 함께 살아 있다.

➡ _____

※ 다음 우리말과 일치하도록 빈칸에 알맞은 말을 쓰시오.

Before You Read

1. _____ _____ _____ the Joseon people _____ _____ the Japanese language.

2. The Joseon people _____ _____ _____ the Joseon language _____.

3. The Joseon people _____ _____ _____ the country.

4. Soon, the _____ _____ _____ _____.

1. 일본 관리들은 조선 사람들에게 일본어를 쓰도록 압박했다.
2. 조선 사람들은 조선어를 살아 있게 지키려고 노력했다.
3. 조선 사람들은 나라를 지키기를 원했다.
4. 이윽고, 독립운동이 일어났다.

Language in Use

1. A woman _____ _____ the building _____ _____ _____ _____.

2. She _____ _____ a new store.

3. Many people _____ _____ _____ to the woman's new store _____ _____ Joe's store.

4. _____ people _____ _____ _____ Joe's store.

5. His food business _____ _____.

1. 한 여인이 Joe의 가게 옆에 있는 건물로 이사 왔다.
2. 그녀는 새로운 가게를 열었다.
3. 많은 사람들이 Joe의 가게 대신에 그 여인의 새 가게로 가기 시작했다.
4. Joe의 가게에 들어오는 사람들은 거의 없었다.
5. 그의 음식 장사는 쇠퇴했다.

Writing Workshop

1. _____ is _____ Yongbok?

2. He lived _____ the _____ _____, and his job _____ _____ fish.

3. _____ he _____ _____, he _____ the Japanese people _____ _____ Ulleungdo.

4. He _____ Japan _____ and said that Ulleungdo and Dokdo _____ _____ _____ Korea.

5. In 1696, the _____ _____ _____ told the Japanese people _____ _____ _____ _____ Ulleugdo and Dokdo.

6. He _____ _____ _____ _____ _____ _____ Ulleungdo and Dokdo.

1. 안용복은 누구인가?
2. 그는 조선왕조 시대에 살았으며, 그의 직업은 물고기를 잡는 것이었다.
3. 그가 물고기를 잡고 있었을 때 그는 일본 사람들이 울릉도 근처에서 물고기를 잡는 것을 보았다.
4. 그는 일본을 두 번 방문해서 울릉도와 독도는 한국에 속해 있다고 말했다.
5. 1696년에 일본인 통치자는 일본인들에게 울릉도와 독도 근처에서 물고기를 잡지 말라고 공식적으로 말했다.
6. 그는 울릉도와 독도를 지키기 위해 최선을 다했다.

※ 다음 우리말을 영어로 쓰시오.

Before You Read

1. 일본 관리들은 조선 사람들에게 일본어를 쓰도록 압박했다.
   ➡ _____

2. 조선 사람들은 조선어를 살아 있게 지키려고 노력했다.
   ➡ _____

3. 조선 사람들은 나라를 지키기를 원했다.
   ➡ _____

4. 이윽고, 독립운동이 일어났다.
   ➡ _____

Language in Use

1. 한 여인이 Joe의 가게 옆에 있는 건물로 이사 왔다.
   ➡ _____

2. 그녀는 새로운 가게를 열었다.
   ➡ _____

3. 많은 사람들이 Joe의 가게 대신에 그 여인의 새 가게로 가기 시작했다.
   ➡ _____

4. Joe의 가게에 들어오는 사람들은 거의 없었다.
   ➡ _____

5. 그의 음식 장사는 쇠퇴했다.
   ➡ _____

Writing Workshop

1. 안용복은 누구인가?
   ➡ _____

2. 그는 조선왕조 시대에 살았으며, 그의 직업은 물고기를 잡는 것이었다.
   ➡ _____

3. 그가 물고기를 잡고 있었을 때 그는 일본 사람들이 울릉도 근처에서 물고기를 잡는 것을 보았다.
   ➡ _____

4. 그는 일본을 두 번 방문해서 울릉도와 독도는 한국에 속해 있다고 말했다.
   ➡ _____

5. 1696년에 일본인 통치자는 일본인들에게 울릉도와 독도 근처에서 물고기를 잡지 말라고 공식적으로 말했다.
   ➡ _____

6. 그는 울릉도와 독도를 지키기 위해 최선을 다했다.
   ➡ _____

※ 다음 영어를 우리말로 쓰시오.

01	blame	22	surprisingly
02	century	23	dependent
03	performance	24	concerto
04	classical	25	trash can
05	actually	26	scene
06	freely	27	increased
07	enjoyable	28	mostly
08	healthy	29	nobleman
09	audience	30	noise
10	disturb	31	orchestra
11	secret	32	correct
12	appear	33	movement
13	work	34	result
14	clap	35	after some time
15	serious	36	as a result
16	between	37	dependent on
17	imagine	38	blame A for B
18	manners	39	for now
19	book fair	40	go back in time
20	memorable	41	at any time
21	familiar	42	take care of
		43	with time

※ 다음 우리말을 영어로 쓰시오.

01	비난하다	
02	박수치다	
03	정지, 멈춤	
04	올바른, 정확한	
05	비밀	
06	심각한, 진지한	
07	방해하다	
08	즐거운, 즐길 수 있는	
09	나타나다	
10	사회적인, 사교적인	
11	놀랍게도	
12	협주곡	
13	관객	
14	익숙한	
15	움직임, (큰 교향곡 따위의) 악장(부분)	
16	사실은	
17	도서 박람회	
18	결과	
19	증가된	
20	밝은	
21	자유롭게	

22	건강한	
23	의존적인, 의존하는	
24	예절	
25	세기	
26	고전의, 클래식 음악의	
27	기억에 남을, 기억할 만한	
28	공연	
29	주로	
30	상상하다	
31	귀족	
32	소음, 잡음	
33	돌려주다, 반납하다	
34	장면	
35	그건 그렇고	
36	~을 살펴 보다	
37	그 결과	
38	우선은, 지금은	
39	아무 때나	
40	B 때문에 A를 비난하다	
41	~에 의존하는	
42	얼마 후	
43	더 이상 ~하지 않는	

※ 다음 영영풀이에 알맞은 단어를 <보기>에서 골라 쓴 후, 우리말 뜻을 쓰시오.

1 _____ : full of light; shining strongly: _____

2 _____ : to start to be seen: _____

3 _____ : to hit your open hands together: _____

4 _____ : a loud or unpleasant sound: _____

5 _____ : to interrupt someone when they are trying to work, sleep, etc.: _____

6 _____ : to make a high sound by blowing air through your lips or teeth: _____

7 _____ : to stop talking or doing something for a short time before continuing: _____

8 _____ : a fact or piece of information that is kept hidden from other people: _____

9 _____ : a man from a family of high social rank; a female member of the nobility: _____

10 _____ : the act of performing a play, concert, or some other form of entertainment: _____

11 _____ : something that is caused by something else that happened or was done before: _____

12 _____ : to think or say that someone or something is responsible for something bad: _____

13 _____ : a piece of music for one or more solo instruments playing with an orchestra: _____

14 _____ : something such as a book, song, or painting that is produced by a writer, musician, artist, etc: _____

15 _____ : a group of musicians who play usually classical music together and who are led by a conductor: _____

16 _____ : to bring something to the place that it came from or the place where it should go: _____

보기			
secret	performance	whistle	clap
noise	disturb	orchestra	concerto
result	work	return	nobleman
blame	pause	appear	bright

※ 다음 우리말과 일치하도록 빈칸에 알맞은 말을 쓰시오.

Listen & Speak 1 B

1. B: Are you _____ _____ _____ to an opera? I have two
    _____ .

   G: Yes, I love opera. _____ is it?

   B: It's _____ Saturday _____ 5:00. Can you _____ _____?

   G: Yes, _____ so much _____ _____ me.

2. B: _____ _____ we go to the new shoe shop _____ _____?

   G: Okay. _____ _____ at 2:00 _____ Saturday?

   B: Can you _____ _____ at 1:00? I _____ _____ _____
    _____ _____ my sister at 3:00.

   G: Sure. _____ you _____.

Listen & Speak 2 B

1. B: We're _____ _____ Hangang this weekend. Do you _____?

   G: Of _____. _____ _____ to bring your camera.

   B: Okay. I _____. I'll _____ some snacks, _____.

   G: _____ great.

2. G: You _____ _____. What's your _____?

   B: Thanks. Well, I _____ _____ _____ _____ _____. You should
    go with me _____.

   G: That _____ _____ fun. _____ _____ things I _____
    _____?

   B: _____ _____ _____ eat _____ _____ of fruits and
    vegetables, _____.

해석

1. B: 너 오페라에 가는 것에 관심이 있
    니? 내게 표가 두 장 있어.
   G: 응, 나 오페라 아주 좋아해. 언제야?
   B: 이번 주 토요일 5시야. 갈 수 있니?
   G: 응. 나한테 물어봐 줘서 정말 고마워.

2. B: 우리 이번 주말에 새로 생긴 신발
    가게에 가는 거 어때?
   G: 좋아. 토요일 2시 어때?
   B: 1시에 가능하니? 난 3시에 여동생
    을 돌봐야 해.
   G: 당연하지. 그때 보자.

1. B: 우리 이번 주말에 한강 가잖아. 기
    억하니?
   G: 물론이지. 카메라 가져 오는 것 잊
    지 마.
   B: 알았어. 잊지 않을게. 나는 약간의
    간식도 가져올게.
   G: 아주 좋아.

2. G: 너 건강해 보여. 비결이 뭐니?
   B: 고마워. 음, 나는 매일 수영하러
    가. 너도 언젠가 나와 함께 가는
    게 좋겠어.
   G: 재밌을 것 같은데. 내가 또 해야
    하는 다른 것들이 있니?
   B: 다양한 종류의 과일과 채소를 먹는
    것도 잊지 마.

Real-Life Zone A

G: What are you _____ _____?

B: Classical music. I'm _____ _____ a concert tomorrow and I'd _____ _____ know about the music _____ I go.

G: I _____ it's _____ enjoyable _____ you know the music.

B: _____, I don't want to _____ at the _____ time.

G: _____ you just _____ _____ the music _____?

B: No. In classical music, one piece of music _____ have several _____. You should _____ and clap at the _____ _____.

G: I _____. _____ _____ you _____ _____ _____ clap at the _____ _____. By the _____, can you _____ _____ to our soccer _____ tomorrow at 4:00?

B: Sure. I'll come to the _____ _____ the concert _____.

G: Okay. _____ you _____.

Real-Life Zone B

A: _____ _____ we go to the library on Monday _____ _____? Can you _____ it?

B: Sorry, but I _____. How _____ _____ Tuesday?

A: Okay. _____ _____ _____ _____ your library card.

B: All _____. I _____.

Wrap Up

G: Yunho! _____ you _____ about the Christmas concert at the city hall?

B: Yes. I _____ _____ a _____ opera singer _____ _____ on the stage.

G: Oh, then _____ _____ we go _____ Christmas Day? Can you _____ _____?

B: Sure. Do you know _____ _____ the concert starts?

G: It starts _____ 5:30. _____ _____ at the bus stop at 4:00.

B: Good. Don't _____ _____ dress _____.

G: Okay. I _____.

G: 무엇을 듣고 있니?
B: 클래식 음악. 나 내일 콘서트에 가는데 가기 전에 음악에 대해 알고 싶어.
G: 음악을 알면 더 즐길 수 있겠지.
B: 사실 박수를 잘못된 때에 치고 싶지 않아.
G: 그냥 음악이 멈추었을 때 박수를 치지 않니?
B: 아니야. 클래식 음악에선 음악 한 곡에 여러 번 멈춤이 있을 수가 있어. 기다렸다가 맨 마지막에 박수를 쳐야 해.
G: 그렇구나. 진짜 마지막에 박수를 치는 것을 잊지 마. 그건 그렇고, 내일 4시 축구 연습에 올 수 있니?
B: 물론이지. 콘서트가 끝난 후 연습에 갈게.
G: 좋아. 그때 보자.

A: 월요일 방과 후에 도서관에 가는 게 어때? 갈 수 있니?
B: 미안하지만, 못 가. 화요일은 어때?
A: 좋아. 도서관 카드 가져오는 걸 잊지 마.
B: 알았어. 잊지 않을게.

G: 윤호야! 너 시청에서 하는 크리스마스 콘서트에 대해 들어 봤어?
B: 응. 유명한 오페라 가수가 무대에 오를 것이라고 들었어.
G: 오, 그러면 크리스마스 날에 가는 게 어때? 갈 수 있니?
B: 물론이지. 너는 콘서트가 언제 시작하는지 아니?
G: 5시 30분에 시작해. 버스 정류장에서 4시에 만나자.
B: 좋아. 옷을 차려입는 것 잊지 마.
G: 알았어. 잊지 않을게.

대화문 Test

※ 다음 우리말에 맞도록 대화를 영어로 쓰시오.

Listen & Speak 1 B

1. B: _____

   G: _____

   B: _____

   G: _____

2. B: _____

   G: _____

   B: _____

   G: _____

Listen & Speak 2 B

1. B: _____

   G: _____

   B: _____

   G: _____

2. G: _____

   B: _____

   G: _____

   B: _____

해석

1. B: 너 오페라에 가는 것에 관심이 있니? 내게 표가 두 장 있어.
   G: 응, 나 오페라 아주 좋아해. 언제야?
   B: 이번 주 토요일 5시야. 갈 수 있니?
   G: 응. 나한테 물어봐 줘서 정말 고마워.

2. B: 우리 이번 주말에 새로 생긴 신발 가게에 가는 거 어때?
   G: 좋아. 토요일 2시 어때?
   B: 1시에 가능하니? 난 3시에 여동생을 돌봐야 해.
   G: 당연하지. 그때 보자.

1. B: 우리 이번 주말에 한강 가잖아. 기억하니?
   G: 물론이지. 카메라 가져 오는 것 잊지 마.
   B: 알았어. 잊지 않을게. 나는 약간의 간식도 가져올게.
   G: 아주 좋아.

2. G: 너 건강해 보여. 비결이 뭐니?
   B: 고마워. 음, 나는 매일 수영하러 가. 너도 언젠가 나와 함께 가는 게 좋겠어.
   G: 재밌을 것 같은데. 내가 또 해야 하는 다른 것들이 있니?
   B: 다양한 종류의 과일과 채소를 먹는 것도 잊지 마.

Real-Life Zone A

G: _____

B: _____
   _____

G: _____

B: _____

G: _____

B: _____
   _____

G: _____
   _____

B: _____

G: _____

G: 무엇을 듣고 있니?

B: 클래식 음악. 나 내일 콘서트에 가는 데 가기 전에 음악에 대해 알고 싶어.

G: 음악을 알면 더 즐길 수 있겠지.

B: 사실 박수를 잘못된 때에 치고 싶지 않아.

G: 그냥 음악이 멈추었을 때 박수를 치지 않니?

B: 아니야. 클래식 음악에선 음악 한 곡에 여러 번 멈춤이 있을 수가 있어. 기다렸다가 맨 마지막에 박수를 쳐야 해.

G: 그렇구나. 진짜 마지막에 박수를 치는 것을 잊지 마. 그건 그렇고, 내일 4시 축구 연습에 올 수 있니?

B: 물론이지. 콘서트가 끝난 후 연습에 갈게.

G: 좋아. 그때 보자.

Real-Life Zone B

A: _____

B: _____

A: _____

B: _____

A: 월요일 방과 후에 도서관에 가는 게 어때? 갈 수 있니?

B: 미안하지만, 못 가. 화요일은 어때?

A: 좋아. 도서관 카드 가져오는 걸 잊지 마.

B: 알았어. 잊지 않을게.

Wrap Up

G: _____

B: _____

G: _____

B: _____

G: _____

B: _____

G: _____

G: 윤호야! 너 시청에서 하는 크리스마스 콘서트에 대해 들어 봤어?

B: 응. 유명한 오페라 가수가 무대에 오를 것이라고 들었어.

G: 오, 그러면 크리스마스 날에 가는 게 어때? 갈 수 있니?

B: 물론이지. 너는 콘서트가 언제 시작하는지 아니?

G: 5시 30분에 시작해. 버스 정류장에서 4시에 만나자.

B: 좋아. 옷을 차려입는 것 잊지 마.

G: 알았어. 잊지 않을게.

Step1

※ 다음 우리말과 일치하도록 빈칸에 알맞은 것을 골라 쓰시오.

1 The _____ of _____ Concert _____

A. Classical   B. History   C. Manners

2 _____ _____ at a _____ music concert.

A. yourself   B. classical   C. imagine

3 The _____ starts to _____ _____ of Mozart's piano _____.

A. one   B. orchestra   C. concertos   D. play

4 The concert _____ is _____ and _____.

A. dark   B. hall   C. silent

5 _____ makes a _____.

A. sound   B. nobody

6 _____ looks _____.

A. serious   B. everybody

7 The _____ only _____ after the concerto _____.

A. clap   B. audiences   C. finishes

8 This is a _____ _____ _____ concerts today.

A. scene   B. at   C. familiar

9 Let's go _____ in time and _____ a _____ at one of Mozart's concerts in the 18th _____.

A. take   B. century   C. back   D. look

10 You are in a _____ hall _____ a _____ house.

A. nobleman's   B. bright   C. inside

11 Mozart is _____ the _____.

A. playing   B. piano

12 _____, however, the _____ are eating, drinking, and _____.

A. audiences   B. freely   C. surprisingly   D. talking

13 They _____ and _____ at any _____.

A. clap   B. time   C. whistle

14 You are _____ by their _____ manners, but Mozart _____ would be _____ by today's quiet audiences.

A. himself   B. shocked   C. bad   D. surprised

15 Concerts in Mozart's _____ were _____ _____ _____.

A. mostly   B. time   C. events   D. social

16 They were _____ _____ _____ people.

A. places   B. meet   C. good   D. to

17 _____ was _____ _____ of the _____.

A. part   B. concert   C. noise   D. just

---

1 클래식 콘서트 관람 예절의 역사

2 당신이 클래식 공연장에 있다고 상상해 보아라.

3 오케스트라가 모차르트의 피아노 협주곡들 중 한 곡을 연주하기 시작한다.

4 콘서트장은 어둡고 조용하다.

5 아무도 소리를 내지 않는다.

6 모두가 진지하게 보인다.

7 청중은 오직 협주곡이 끝난 후에만 손뼉을 친다.

8 이것이 오늘날 콘서트에서 익숙한 장면이다.

9 과거로 거슬러 올라가서 18세기 모차르트의 콘서트들 중 하나를 살펴보자.

10 당신은 한 귀족의 집안 밝은 홀에 있다.

11 모차르트는 피아노를 치고 있다.

12 하지만 놀랍게도, 청중들은 먹고 마시며 자유롭게 대화하고 있다.

13 그들은 아무 때나 휘파람을 불고 박수를 친다.

14 당신은 그들의 나쁜 매너에 충격을 받지만, 모차르트 자신은 오늘날의 조용한 청중에게 놀랄지도 모른다.

15 모차르트 시대의 콘서트는 주로 사교적인 행사였다.

16 콘서트는 사람을 만나기에 좋은 장소였다.

17 소음은 그저 콘서트의 일부였다.

18 Today's _____ concerts began in the 19th _____ _____ many big concert halls were _____.

A. century   B. built   C. quiet   D. when

19 _____ people, _____ _____ _____, went to concerts.

A. noblemen   B. more   C. just   D. not

20 Artists were _____ _____ _____ _____ noblemen for money.

A. on   B. longer   C. dependent   D. no

21 The artists had _____ power over their _____ and started to _____ their _____ power.

A. increased   B. works   C. more   D. use

22 _____ _____, Wagner _____ the audience for making _____.

A. blamed   B. for   C. noise   D. example

23 _____ some _____, a no-clapping-between-movements _____ _____.

A. time   B. appeared   C. after   D. rule

24 _____ a _____, here we are today, very _____ and _____.

A. serious   B. result   C. quiet   D. as

25 We do not know _____ concerts will look _____ in the future _____ manners _____ with time.

A. because   B. like   C. what   D. change

26 For now, _____, if you want to _____ _____ music concerts, just _____ this:

A. classical   B. however   C. remember   D. enjoy

27 _____ the music, but do not _____ those _____ you.

A. disturb   B. enjoy   C. around

18 오늘날의 조용한 콘서트는 많은 대형 공연장이 생긴 19세기에 시작됐다.

19 귀족뿐만 아니라 더 많은 사람들이 콘서트에 갔다.

20 예술가들은 더 이상 돈을 벌기 위해 귀족들에게 의존하지 않았다.

21 예술가들은 자신의 작품에 더 많은 권한이 생겼고 그 힘을 사용하기 시작했다.

22 예를 들어, 바그너는 소음을 낸다는 것 때문에 관객들을 비난했다.

23 얼마 후에 '악장 사이 박수 금지 규칙'이 생겼다.

24 그 결과, 오늘날 우리는, 매우 조용하고 진지하다.

25 예절은 시대에 따라 변하기 때문에 우리는 콘서트가 미래에는 어떤 모습일지 모른다.

26 하지만 지금은 당신이 클래식 음악 공연을 즐기고 싶다면 이것만은 기억해라:

27 음악은 즐기되 당신 주변의 다른 사람들을 방해하지 마라.

※ 다음 우리말과 일치하도록 빈칸에 알맞은 말을 쓰시오.

1 **The** _____ **of** _____ **Concert** _____

2 _____ _____ at a _____ music concert.

3 The _____ starts to _____ _____ _____ Mozart's _____ concertos.

4 The concert _____ is _____ and _____.

5 _____ makes a _____.

6 _____ looks _____.

7 The _____ only _____ after the _____ _____.

8 This is a _____ _____ _____ concerts today.

9 _____ _____ _____ in _____ and _____ a _____ at _____ _____ Mozart's concerts in the 18th century.

10 You are in a _____ hall _____ a _____ house.

11 Mozart is _____ the _____.

12 _____, however, the _____ are eating, drinking, and _____ _____.

13 They _____ and _____ _____ _____ _____.

14 You are _____ _____ their _____ _____, but Mozart _____ would be _____ _____ today's _____ audiences.

15 Concerts in Mozart's time _____ _____ _____ events.

16 They were _____ _____ _____ _____ people.

17 _____ was _____ _____ _____ the concert.

1 클래식 콘서트 관람 예절의 역사

2 당신이 클래식 공연장에 있다고 상상해 보아라.

3 오케스트라가 모차르트의 피아노 협주곡들 중 한 곡을 연주하기 시작한다.

4 콘서트장은 어둡고 조용하다.

5 아무도 소리를 내지 않는다.

6 모두가 진지하게 보인다.

7 청중은 오직 협주곡이 끝난 후에만 손뼉을 친다.

8 이것이 오늘날 콘서트에서 익숙한 장면이다.

9 과거로 거슬러 올라가서 18세기 모차르트의 콘서트들 중 하나를 살펴보자.

10 당신은 한 귀족의 집안 밝은 홀에 있다.

11 모차르트는 피아노를 치고 있다.

12 하지만 놀랍게도, 청중들은 먹고 마시며 자유롭게 대화하고 있다.

13 그들은 아무 때나 휘파람을 불고 박수를 친다.

14 당신은 그들의 나쁜 매너에 충격을 받지만, 모차르트 자신은 오늘날의 조용한 청중에게 놀랄지도 모른다.

15 모차르트 시대의 콘서트는 주로 사교적인 행사였다.

16 콘서트는 사람을 만나기에 좋은 장소였다.

17 소음은 그저 콘서트의 일부였다.

18 Today's _____ concerts began in the 19th _____ _____ many big concert halls _____ _____.

19 More people, _____ _____ _____, went to concerts.

20 Artists were _____ _____ _____ on noblemen _____ _____.

21 The artists had _____ _____ over their _____ and started to _____ their _____ _____.

22 _____ _____, Wagner _____ the audience _____ _____ _____.

23 _____ _____ _____, a no-clapping-between-movements _____ _____.

24 _____ _____ _____, here we are today, very _____ and _____.

25 We do not know _____ _____ will _____ _____ in the future _____ manners _____ _____ _____.

26 _____ _____, _____, if you want to _____ _____ music concerts, _____ _____ this:

27 _____ the music, but _____ _____ _____ _____ _____ you.

18 오늘날의 조용한 콘서트는 많은 대형 공연장이 생긴 19세기에 시작됐다.

19 귀족뿐만 아니라 더 많은 사람들이 콘서트에 갔다.

20 예술가들은 더 이상 돈을 벌기 위해 귀족들에게 의존하지 않았다.

21 예술가들은 자신의 작품에 더 많은 권한이 생겼고 그 힘을 사용하기 시작했다.

22 예를 들어, 바그너는 소음을 낸다는 것 때문에 관객들을 비난했다.

23 얼마 후에 '악장 사이 박수 금지 규칙'이 생겼다.

24 그 결과, 오늘날 우리는, 매우 조용하고 진지하다.

25 예절은 시대에 따라 변하기 때문에 우리는 콘서트가 미래에는 어떤 모습일지 모른다.

26 하지만 지금은 당신이 클래식 음악 공연을 즐기고 싶다면 이것만은 기억해라:

27 음악은 즐기되 당신 주변의 다른 사람들을 방해하지 마라.

※ 다음 문장을 우리말로 쓰시오.

1   The History of Classical Concert Manners

➡ _____

2   Imagine yourself at a classical music concert.

➡ _____

3   The orchestra starts to play one of Mozart's piano concertos.

➡ _____

4   The concert hall is dark and silent.

➡ _____

5   Nobody makes a sound.

➡ _____

6   Everybody looks serious.

➡ _____

7   The audiences only clap after the concerto finishes.

➡ _____

8   This is a familiar scene at concerts today.

➡ _____

9   Let's go back in time and take a look at one of Mozart's concerts in the 18th century.

➡ _____

10   You are in a bright hall inside a nobleman's house.

➡ _____

11   Mozart is playing the piano.

➡ _____

12   Surprisingly, however, the audiences are eating, drinking, and talking freely.

➡ _____

13   They whistle and clap at any time.

➡ _____

14 You are shocked by their bad manners, but Mozart himself would be surprised by today's quiet audiences.

➡ _____

15 Concerts in Mozart's time were mostly social events.

➡ _____

16 They were good places to meet people.

➡ _____

17 Noise was just part of the concert.

➡ _____

18 Today's quiet concerts began in the 19th century when many big concert halls were built.

➡ _____

19 More people, not just noblemen, went to concerts.

➡ _____

20 Artists were no longer dependent on noblemen for money.

➡ _____

21 The artists had more power over their works and started to use their increased power.

➡ _____

22 For example, Wagner blamed the audience for making noise.

➡ _____

23 After some time, a no-clapping-between-movements rule appeared.

➡ _____

24 As a result, here we are today, very quiet and serious.

➡ _____

25 We do not know what concerts will look like in the future because manners change with time.

➡ _____

26 For now, however, if you want to enjoy classical music concerts, just remember this:

➡ _____

27 Enjoy the music, but do not disturb those around you.

➡ _____

Step4

※ 다음 괄호 안의 단어들을 우리말에 맞도록 바르게 배열하시오.

1 (History / The / Classical / of / Manners / Concert)
➡ _____

2 (yourself / imagine / a / at / music / classical / concert.)
➡ _____

3 (orchestra / the / to / starts / one / play / of / piano / Mozart's / concertos.)
➡ _____

4 (concert / the / is / hall / silent. / and / dark)
➡ _____

5 (makes / nobody / sound. / a)
➡ _____

6 (looks / everybody / serious.)
➡ _____

7 (audiences / the / clap / only / the / after / finishes. / concerto)
➡ _____

8 (is / this / a / familiar / at / scene / today. / concerts)
➡ _____

9 (go / let's / back / time / in / and / a / take / look / one / at / Mozart's / of / in / concerts / 18th / the / century.)
➡ _____
_____

10 (are / you / a / in / bright / inside / hall / nobleman's / a / house.)
➡ _____

11 (is / Mozart / the / piano. / playing)
➡ _____

12 (however, / surprisingly, / audiences / the / eating, / are / drinking, / talking / and / freely.)
➡ _____
_____

13 (whistle / they / clap / and / any / at / time.)
➡ _____

14 (are / you / by / shocked / bad / their / manners, / Mozart / but / would / himself / surprised / be / today's / by / audiences. / quiet)
➡ _____
_____

15 (in / concerts / time / Mozart's / mostly / were / events. / social)
➡ _____

16 (were / they / places / good / meet / to / people.)
➡ _____

17 (was / noise / part / just / concert. / the / of)
➡ _____

---

1 클래식 콘서트 관람 예절의 역사

2 당신이 클래식 공연장에 있다고 상상해 보아라.

3 오케스트라가 모차르트의 피아노 협주곡들 중 한 곡을 연주하기 시작한다.

4 콘서트장은 어둡고 조용하다.

5 아무도 소리를 내지 않는다.

6 모두가 진지하게 보인다.

7 청중은 오직 협주곡이 끝난 후에만 손뼉을 친다.

8 이것이 오늘날 콘서트에서 익숙한 장면이다.

9 과거로 거슬러 올라가서 18세기 모차르트의 콘서트들 중 하나를 살펴보자.

10 당신은 한 귀족의 집안 밝은 홀에 있다.

11 모차르트는 피아노를 치고 있다.

12 하지만 놀랍게도, 청중들은 먹고 마시며 자유롭게 대화하고 있다.

13 그들은 아무 때나 휘파람을 불고 박수를 친다.

14 당신은 그들의 나쁜 매너에 충격을 받지만, 모차르트 자신은 오늘날의 조용한 청중에게 놀랄지도 모른다.

15 모차르트 시대의 콘서트는 주로 사교적인 행사였다.

16 콘서트는 사람을 만나기에 좋은 장소였다.

17 소음은 그저 콘서트의 일부였다.

18 (quiet / today's / began / concerts / in / 19th / the / when / century / big / many / halls / concert / built. / were)

➡ _____

19 (people, / more / just / not / noblemen, / to / went / concerts.)

➡ _____

20 (were / artists / longer / no / dependent / noblemen / on / money. / for)

➡ _____

21 (artists / the / more / had / over / power / their / works / and / to / started / use / increased / their / power.)

➡ _____

22 (example, / for / blamed / Wagner / audience / the / making / noise. / for)

➡ _____

23 (some / after / time, / no-clapping-between-movements / a / appeared. / rule)

➡ _____

24 (a / as / result, / we / here / today, / are / quiet / very / serious. / and)

➡ _____

25 (do / we / know / not / concerts / what / will / like / look / the / in / future / manners / because / with / change / time.)

➡ _____

26 (now, / for / however, / you / if / to / want / classical / enjoy / concerts, / music / remember / just / this:)

➡ _____

27 (the / enjoy / music, / do / but / disturb / not / around / you. / those)

➡ _____

18 오늘날의 조용한 콘서트는 많은 대형 공연장이 생긴 19세기에 시작됐다.

19 귀족뿐만 아니라 더 많은 사람들이 콘서트에 갔다.

20 예술가들은 더 이상 돈을 벌기 위해 귀족들에게 의존하지 않았다.

21 예술가들은 자신의 작품에 더 많은 권한이 생겼고 그 힘을 사용하기 시작했다.

22 예를 들어, 바그너는 소음을 낸다는 것 때문에 관객들을 비난했다.

23 얼마 후에 '악장 사이 박수 금지 규칙'이 생겼다.

24 그 결과, 오늘날 우리는, 매우 조용하고 진지하다.

25 예절은 시대에 따라 변하기 때문에 우리는 콘서트가 미래에는 어떤 모습일지 모른다.

26 하지만 지금은 당신이 클래식 음악 공연을 즐기고 싶다면 이것만은 기억해라:

27 음악은 즐기되 당신 주변의 다른 사람들을 방해하지 마라.

※ 다음 우리말을 영어로 쓰시오.

1   클래식 콘서트 관람 예절의 역사
➡ _____

2   당신이 클래식 공연장에 있다고 상상해 보아라.
➡ _____

3   오케스트라가 모차르트의 피아노 협주곡들 중 한 곡을 연주하기 시작한다.
➡ _____

4   콘서트장은 어둡고 조용하다.
➡ _____

5   아무도 소리를 내지 않는다.
➡ _____

6   모두가 진지하게 보인다.
➡ _____

7   청중은 오직 협주곡이 끝난 후에만 손뼉을 친다.
➡ _____

8   이것이 오늘날 콘서트에서 익숙한 장면이다.
➡ _____

9   과거로 거슬러 올라가서 18세기 모차르트의 콘서트들 중 하나를 살펴보자.
➡ _____

10   당신은 한 귀족의 집안 밝은 홀에 있다.
➡ _____

11   모차르트는 피아노를 치고 있다.
➡ _____

12   하지만 놀랍게도, 청중들은 먹고 마시며 자유롭게 대화하고 있다.
➡ _____

13   그들은 아무 때나 휘파람을 불고 박수를 친다.
➡ _____

14   당신은 그들의 나쁜 매너에 충격을 받지만, 모차르트 자신은 오늘날의 조용한 청중에게 놀랄지도 모른다.
➡ _____

15   모차르트 시대의 콘서트는 주로 사교적인 행사였다.
➡ _____

16   콘서트는 사람을 만나기에 좋은 장소였다.
➡ _____

17   소음은 그저 콘서트의 일부였다.
➡ _____

18 오늘날의 조용한 콘서트는 많은 대형 공연장이 생긴 19세기에 시작됐다.

➡ _____

19 귀족뿐만 아니라 더 많은 사람들이 콘서트에 갔다.

➡ _____

20 예술가들은 더 이상 돈을 벌기 위해 귀족들에게 의존하지 않았다.

➡ _____

21 예술가들은 자신의 작품에 더 많은 권한이 생겼고 그 힘을 사용하기 시작했다.

➡ _____

22 예를 들어, 바그너는 소음을 낸다는 것 때문에 관객들을 비난했다.

➡ _____

23 얼마 후에 '악장 사이 박수 금지 규칙'이 생겼다.

➡ _____

24 그 결과, 오늘날 우리는, 매우 조용하고 진지하다.

➡ _____

25 예절은 시대에 따라 변하기 때문에 우리는 콘서트가 미래에는 어떤 모습일지 모른다.

➡ _____

26 하지만 지금은 당신이 클래식 음악 공연을 즐기고 싶다면 이것만은 기억해라.

➡ _____

27 음악은 즐기되 당신 주변의 다른 사람들을 방해하지 마라.

➡ _____

※ 다음 우리말과 일치하도록 빈칸에 알맞은 말을 쓰시오.

Before You Read B

1. A _____ to Good _____ _____

2. _____ a classical music concert can be a _____ _____ if you _____ these tips _____ _____.

3. _____ You _____ In:

4. _____ _____ _____ 20-30 minutes before _____ _____.

5. _____ _____ what music _____ _____ _____.

6. _____ Music _____ _____:

7. _____ _____ your cellphone!

8. _____ quiet. _____ talking, _____, singing _____ _____ the music.

9. _____ _____ until the whole _____ _____ _____.

10. _____ is safe _____ _____ when the audience starts _____.

Writing Workshop

1. Music Concert _____

2. _____ February 2, I went _____ _____ _____ _____ at the Seoul Arts Center _____ Jo Seongu's piano concert _____ _____.

3. It was a great _____ _____ _____ _____ him _____ _____.

4. He _____ Chopin's _____ _____ No. 1.

5. I did not know _____ _____ _____ _____ _____ _____.

6. I liked his _____ _____.

7. I _____ _____ _____ _____ this experience.

Wrap Up 7

1. Reporter: _____ is your new album _____ _____?

2. Justin Otter: It's _____ _____ next month.

3. Reporter: What are _____ _____ _____ _____ the new album?

4. Justin Otter: I'm _____ _____ _____ a concert at the Super Stadium.

5. My hero Michael Johnson _____ _____ _____ his concerts _____ _____ _____ at the place.

1. 콘서트 예절에 대한 안내
2. 당신이 이와 같은 조언들을 명심한다면 클래식 콘서트를 보는 것은 기억에 남는 경험이 될 것이다.
3. 들어가기 전:
4. 콘서트 시간 20-30분 전에 도착하길 계획하라.
5. 어떤 음악이 연주될지 알아보아라.
6. 음악이 연주될 때:
7. 휴대 전화를 꺼라.
8. 조용히 머물러라. 말하거나 휘파람을 불거나 음악에 따라 노래하지 말아라.
9. 전체의 곡이 끝날 때까지 박수치지 말아라.
10. 관객들이 박수 치기 시작할 때 박수를 치는 것이 안전하다.

1. 음악 콘서트 리뷰
2. 2월 2일에 나는 조성우의 피아노 콘서트가 열린 서울아트 센터의 콘서트홀에 갔다.
3. 그가 라이브로 연주하는 것을 듣는 것은 훌륭한 기회였다.
4. 그는 쇼팽의 피아노 협주곡 1번을 연주했다.
5. 나는 클래식 공연이 얼마나 아름다운지 몰랐다.
6. 나는 그의 라이브 공연이 아주 마음에 들었다.
7. 나는 이 경험을 잊지 않을 것이다.

1. 기자: 당신의 새 앨범은 언제 나오나요?
2. 저스틴 오터: 다음 달에 나옵니다.
3. 기자: 새 앨범에 대한 계획은 무엇인가요?
4. 저스틴 오터: 저는 수퍼 스타디움에서 콘서트를 가질 계획입니다.
5. 저의 영웅인 마이클 존슨이 세계 공연 동안 콘서트들 중 하나를 그 장소에서 열었거든요.

※ 다음 우리말을 영어로 쓰시오.

Before You Read B

1. 콘서트 예절에 대한 안내
➡

2. 당신이 이와 같은 조언들을 명심한다면 클래식 콘서트를 보는 것은 기억에 남는 경험이 될 것이다.
➡ _____

3. 들어가기 전:
➡ _____

4. 콘서트 시간 20–30분 전에 도착하길 계획하라.
➡ _____

5. 어떤 음악이 연주될지 알아보아라.
➡ _____

6. 음악이 연주될 때:
➡ _____

7. 휴대 전화를 꺼라.
➡ _____

8. 조용히 머물러라. 말하거나 휘파람을 불거나 음악에 따라 노래하지 말아라.
➡ _____

9. 전체의 곡이 끝날 때까지 박수치지 말아라.
➡ _____

10. 관객들이 박수 치기 시작할 때 박수를 치는 것이 안전하다.
➡ _____

Writing Workshop

1. 음악 콘서트 리뷰
➡ _____

2. 2월 2일에 나는 조성우의 피아노 콘서트가 열린 서울아트 센터의 콘서트홀에 갔다.
➡ _____

3. 그가 라이브로 연주하는 것을 듣는 것은 훌륭한 기회였다.
➡ _____

4. 그는 쇼팽의 피아노 협주곡 1번을 연주했다.
➡ _____

5. 나는 클래식 공연이 얼마나 아름다운지 몰랐다.
➡ _____

6. 나는 그의 라이브 공연이 아주 마음에 들었다.
➡ _____

7. 나는 이 경험을 잊지 않을 것이다.
➡ _____

Wrap Up 7

1. 기자: 당신의 새 앨범은 언제 나오나요?
➡ _____

2. 저스틴 오터: 다음 달에 나옵니다.
➡ _____

3. 기자: 새 앨범에 대한 계획은 무엇인가요?
➡ _____

4. 저스틴 오터: 저는 수퍼 스타디움에서 콘서트를 가질 계획입니다.
➡ _____

5. 저의 영웅인 마이클 존슨이 세계 공연 동안 콘서트들 중 하나를 그 장소에서 열었거든요.
➡ _____

MEMO

MEMO

영어 기출 문제집

적중100

2학기

정답 및 해설

시사 | 송미정

중 2

영어 기출 문제집

적중100

2학기

정답 및 해설

시사 | 송미정

중 2

Living in the AI World

시험대비 실력평가   p.08

01 ③   02 funny   03 ①   04 ③
05 ③   06 ②   07 (1) no longer[more]
(2) don't (h)ave

---

01 ① 동물 중에는 지진을 예측하는 능력을 가진 것이 있다. ② 집의 수도관이 얼지 않기를 희망한다. ③ teleport: 순간 이동하다, 나는 시간과 공간을 통과해 순간 이동할 수 있습니다. ④ 암호를 확인한 다음 다시 시도해 보십시오. ⑤ 나는 아이를 위해 장난감을 골랐다.

02 fun: 재미 funny: 재미있는 / 너의 이야기가 너무 웃겨서 나는 웃음을 멈출 수가 없다.

03 translate: 번역하다 / 불어를 영어로 번역할 수 있는 사람을 아니?

04 beat: 이기다 / 그리스와의 첫 경기에서, 우리나라 팀은 그리스 팀을 이겼다.

05 ③의 like는 '좋아하다'의 의미로 사용하였고, 나머지는 '~와 같이, ~처럼'의 의미로 사용하였다. ① 숲속에서 배우는 것은 재미있을 것 같지 않나요? ② 그 옷을 입으니 완전히 다른 사람처럼 보여요. ③ 왜 그렇게 좋아하시죠? ④ 그것은 약간 체스 게임 같이 보이지 않는가? ⑤ 그들은 사람들처럼 오랫동안 슬퍼한다.

06 strange: 이상한 unusual: 특이한, 이상한 / 실험 후에 사람들에게 어떤 이상한 것을 보았는지 물어봤다.

07 (1) no longe[more]: 더 이상 ~하지 않다 (2) don't have to 동사원형: ~할 필요가 없다(= don't need to, need not)

서술형 시험대비   p.09

01 (1) greedy (2) funny (3) sunny, cloudy (4) lucky
02 (r)eplace
03 By, by
04 (1) translate (2) (p)ossible, finish
    (3) (e)lse (4) (h)ave, perfect
05 (1) in (2) to (3) off
06 (1) I saw him crossing the street.
    (2) He predicted that the GDP would go up.

---

01 (1) greed: 욕심 greedy: 욕심 많은 / Scrooge는 욕심 많은 노인이었다. (2) fun: 재미 funny: 재미있는 / 이야기가 재미있기 때문에 난 이 책을 좋아한다. (3) sun: 태양 sunny: 맑은 cloud: 구름 cloudy: 흐린 / 오늘은 날 씨가 맑았지만 내일은 흐릴 것이

다. 너는 우산을 가져와야 할 것이다. (4) luck: 행운 lucky: 운이 좋은 / 나는 우연히 내가 좋아하는 영화 배우를 만났다. 운이 좋은 날이다! by chance: 우연히

02 replace: 대체하다(= take the place of) / 새로운 세포들이 오래된 세포들을 대신한다.

03 by the way: 그런데, 그건 그렇고 / 그건 그렇고, 아직도 공립 도서관에서 일하시나요? by 동사ing: ~함으로써 / 그것을 함으로써 시간 관리 기술을 배울 수 있습니다.

04 (1) translate: 번역하다 (2) possible: 가능한 Is it possible (for 목적격) to 동사원형 ~?: (…가) ~하는 것이 가능할까? (3) else: 그 밖의 (4) don't have to 동사원형: ~할 필요가 없다(= need not) perfect: 완벽한

05 (1) get in: ~에 타다 / 차에 당장 타, 안 그러면 늦을 거야. (2) get to: ~에 도착하다 / 내가 산 정상에 도착했을 때, 아주 어두워졌다. (3) get off: ~에서 내리다, ~에서 떨어지다 / 우리는 그를 곧 보게 될 것이다. 승객들이 지금 비 행기에서 내리고 있는 중이다.

06 (1) cross: 건너다 (2) predict: 예측하다

 교과서
Conversation

핵심 Check   p.10~11

1 Sounds
2 That sounds good / I think it's exciting
3 Is it possible that
4 Is it possible for him to finish this marathon?
  Can he finish this marathon?
5 Is it possible for you to make a cake?

 교과서 대화문 익히기

📎 **Check(√) True or False**   p.12

1 F   2 T   3 F   4 T

 교과서 확인학습   p.14~15

Listen & Speak 1 A

don't / sounds

Listen & Speak 1 B

1 have any, for, project / What about / talk about future, What, think / sounds perfect, look for

2 begins, Why, with / to, sounds / chance to meet robotics / great

Listen & Speak 1 C

1 going, drone / like fun

2 going, build / like fun

Listen & Speak 2 A

possible, to live without / possible

Listen & Speak 2 B

1 looks, How much / newest / Is it possible to use / check, off / Perfect

2 took, picture during / did, than, it possible to make, out of / have

Listen & Speak 2 C

1 Is it possible, to text with, closed

2 possible for you / by

Real-Life Zone A

at / What, they mean, look them up, dictionary / about using / How / point, translate, get / possible for AI to read / read, translate / unvelievable, mean / amazing

---

시험대비 기본평가   p.16

01 ③   02 ①   03 ②

01 가능 여부를 나타내는 표현들로는 'Is it possible that 주어 동사 ~?', 'Is it possible for 목적격 to 동사원형 ~?', 'Can 주어 동사원형 ~?' 등이 있다.

02 여자아이는 남자아이의 의견을 좋아하면서, 인터넷에서 정보를 찾아보자고 제안하고 있다. sound 형용사: ~하게 들리다

03 로봇 박람회를 같이 가자고 제안하는 말에, (B) 제안을 수락하면서 박람회가 재미있겠다고 자신의 생각을 표현한다. (A) 로봇 공학자를 만날 기회가 있을 거라고 하자 (C) 그러면 좋겠다고 말한다. Why don't you ~?: ~하는 게 어때? exciting: 흥미진진한, 신나는 sound 형용사: ~하게 들리다 chance: 기회 look for: 찾다

시험대비 실력평가   p.17~18

01 ②   02 ④   03 ⑤   04 ④

05 ④   06 ⑤   07 ②   08 ③

09 ④

---

01 sound 형용사: ~하게 들리다 exciting: 흥미진진한, 신나는

02 ① 남자아이는 로봇 박람회를 어떻게 생각하는가? 재미있을 것 같다고 생각한다. ② 그들은 로봇 박람회에서 누구를 만날 수 있을까? 로봇 공학자. ③ 여자아이는 남자아이와 어디를 같이 가기를 원하는가? 로봇 박람회. ④ 로봇 박람회를 가기 위해서 그들은 어디서 만날 것인가? 대화의 내용에 나와 있지 않으므로 대답할 수 없음. ⑤ 언제 로봇 박람회가 시작되는가? 다음 주에.

03 주어진 문장은 글자의 뜻을 물어보고 있는 질문이므로 글자의 뜻을 이야기해 주고 있는 'They mean "Dreams come true!"("꿈은 이루어진다!"라는 뜻이에요.)'라는 대답 앞에 오는 것이 적절하다.

04 사전을 찾지 않고 곧바로 AI 번역기를 사용하였다.

05 주어진 문장은 로봇이 위험에 처한 사람들을 도울 수 있다는 내용으로 ④번 다음 문장인 'Robots can do the dangerous work so humans don't have to.(로봇이 그 위험한 일을 할 수 있어서 사람들이 그 일을 하지 않아도 되지.)'가 주어진 문장을 좀 더 설명한 것으로 볼 수 있다.

06 스마트 음식 주문 자판기를 사용해 보자는 제안에, 쉽고 빠르게 주문을 할 수 있다고 말하고 있으므로, 제안에 대해 긍정하는 내용이 빈칸에 들어가는 것이 적절하다. sound 형용사: ~하게 들리다 interesting: 재미있는, 흥미로운

07 여자아이가 로봇이 인간을 대체할 수 있을 거라고 생각하는지 민석이에게 묻는 질문에 잘 모르겠다고 대답했다.

08 ③ Yes, I can. → Yes, you can. 또는 Is it possible that I keep a pet? → Is it possible that you keep a pet?

09 ④ 영화를 보자는 제안에 반대하는 말을 하고 재미있을 것 같다고 말하는 것은 앞뒤가 맞지 않는다.

서술형 시험대비   p.19

01 Can you

02 Is it possible to use this coupon?

03 She will pay 470 dollars.

04 (A) up (B) about

05 unbelievable

06 Is it possible for you to travel around Gangwondo by bicycle?

01 가능 여부를 나타내는 표현들로는 'Is it possible for 목적격 to 동사원형 ~?', 'Can 주어 동사원형 ~?' 등이 있다.

02 Is it possible (for 목적격) to 동사원형 ~?: (…가) ~하는 것이 가능할까?

03 컴퓨터 가격이 500 달러였는데 30달러 할인되는 쿠폰을 사용하였으므로 470달러를 낼 것이다.

04 (A) look ~ up: (사전·참고 자료·컴퓨터 등에서 정보를) 찾아보다 (B) What about ~?: ~하는 게 어때?

05 unbelievable: 믿기 어려운, 놀랄만한

06 Is it possible (for 목적격) to 동사원형 ~?: (…가) ~하는 것이 가능할까? by bicycle: 자전거로

Grammar

핵심 Check   p.20~21

1 (1) doing   (2) sing   (3) washed
2 (1) to play   (2) to solve   (3) It

시험대비 기본평가   p.22

01 (1) sang → sing(또는 singing)
   (2) to fly → fly(또는 flying)
   (3) choose → to choose
   (4) That → It
02 (1) cry[또는 crying] (2) cleaned
   (3) play(또는 playing) (4) flow(또는 flowing)
03 ④
04 It is necessary for you to take a rest.

01 (1), (2) 지각동사의 목적어가 목적격보어의 행위의 주체가 될 때 목적격보어로 원형부정사나 현재분사를 쓰는 것이 적절하다. (3) 진주어로 to부정사가 적절하다. (4) 가주어로는 that이 아니라 it 을 쓴다.

02 (1) 지각동사의 목적격보어는 목적어와의 관계가 능동일 경우 원형부정사나 현재분사가 쓰인다. (2) 지각동사의 목적격보어는 목적어와의 관계가 수동일 경우 과거분사가 쓰인다. (3) 그들이 경기 하는 것이므로 play 또는 playing이 적절하다. (4) 물이 흐르는 것이므로 능동의 의미를 나타내 는 flow 또는 flowing 이 적절하다.

03 가주어로는 that이 아니라 it을 쓰며 진주어로 to부정사를 이용한다.

04 가주어 it과 진주어 to부정사를 이용하여 문장을 쓴다. 또한 의미상의 주어로 'for+목적격'을 써야 하므로 for를 추가한다.

시험대비 실력평가   p.23~25

01 ⑤   02 ③   03 ①   04 It is
good to ride bicycles for fun on weekends.   05 ④
06 (1) waiting (2) playing (3) played (4) listen (5) It (6) to
swim (7) of   07 ④   08 This → It   09 ③, ④
10 ④   11 him turn[turning] off the stove

16 (1) It is not easy to make her laugh.
   (2) It is my plan to read 10 books during winter vacation.
17 (1) to paint → paint[painting]
   (2) wears → to wear
   (3) of → for
18 (1) Minsu hears a dog bark[barking] whenever he passes by the house.
   (2) I saw a bird fly[flying] high in the sky.
   (3) It is exciting for me to watch baseball games with my friends.
   (4) It is dangerous to put paper near the fire.

01 목적어와의 관계가 능동이므로 지각동사의 목적격보어로 원형부정사 혹은 현재분사가 적절하다. / It을 가주어로 하고 to부정사를 진주어로 쓰는 것이 적절하다.

02 feel은 지각동사이므로 목적격보어로 원형부정사 혹은 현재분사, 과거분사를 취한다. the dog이 his clothes를 끌고 가는 주체가 되므로 pull 또는 pulling이 적절하다.

03 가주어로는 that이 아니라 it을 쓰며 진주어로 to부정사가 적절하다.

04 가주어 it과 진주어로 to부정사를 이용하여 문장을 쓴다.

05 지각동사 feel의 목적격보어로 원형부정사 혹은 현재분사가 적절하다. At times, Nora felt him stare[staring] at her.

06 (1) 지각동사 see의 목적격보어로 원형부정사가 적절하다. (2) 지각동사 hear의 목적격보어로 현재분사가 적절하다. (3) the game이 play되는 것이므로 목적격보어로 수동의 의미를 갖는 과거분사가 적절하다 (4) make는 사역동사이므로 목적격보어로 원형부정사가 적절하다, (5) 가주어로는 that이 아니라 it을 쓴다. (6) 진주어로 to부정사를 쓰는 것이 적절하다. (7) to부정사의 의미상 주어를 나타낼 때 문장에 쓰인 형용사가 사람의 성질을 나타내는 말일 때는 'of+목적격'을 쓴다.

07 지각동사 watch의 목적격보어로 bake나 baking을 쓰는 것이 적절하다.

08 주어로 쓰인 'that'절의 경우에도 보통 가주어 'it'을 쓰고 'that'절을 문장 뒤로 보낸다.

09 목적어와의 관계가 능동이므로 지각동사의 목적격보어로 원형부정사 혹은 현재분사가 적절하다.

10 it을 가주어로 하고 to부정사를 진주어로 쓰는 것이 적절하다.

11 Bill이 난로를 끄는 것을 보았다는 의미이다. 목적어와 목적격보어의 관계가 능동이므로 원형부정사 또는 현재분사로 써야 한다.

12 ② I saw a boy solve[solving] math problems. ③ By the way, do you think it will be possible for robots to replace humans someday? ④ Is it possible to fly through a rainbow?

13 (A) 지각동사의 목적어와 목적격보어의 관계가 능동이므로 현재분사가 적절하다. (B) 지각동사의 목적어와 목적격보어의 관계가 능동이므로 원형부정사가 적절하다. (C) 지각동사의 목적어와 목적격보어의 관계가 수동 (이름이 불리는 것)이므로 과거분사가 적절하다.

14 ②번은 인칭대명사이지만 나머지는 모두 가주어 It이다. 가주어는 해석하지 않지만 인칭대명사는 '그것'이라고 해석한다.

15 주어진 문장과 ③번은 목적격보어로 쓰인 현재분사이다. ① 분사구문 ② 진행형을 만드는 현재분사 ④, ⑤ 동명사

16 it을 가주어로 하고 to부정사를 진주어로 하여 쓰는 것이 적절하다.

17 (1) 지각동사의 목적격보어로 원형부정사나 현재분사가 적절하다. (2) it을 가주어로 하고 to부정사를 진주어로 쓰는 것이 적절하다. (3) to부정사의 의미상 주어로 사람의 성질을 나타내는 형용사가 쓰인 것이 아니므로 'for+목적격'이 적절하다.

18 (1)~(3) 지각동사의 목적격보어로 원형부정사나 현재분사를 이용한다. (4), (5) it을 가주어로 하고 to부정사를 진주어로 하여 'It ~ to부정사' 구문으로 쓰는 것이 적절하다. to부정사의 의미상 주어로 사람의 성질을 나타내는 형용사가 쓰인 것이 아니므로 'for+목적격'이 적절하다.

서술형 시험대비   p.26~27

01 (1) I saw them play[playing] soccer in the playground.
　(2) Barbara felt her heart beat[beating] faster.
　(3) Aaron looked at Sylvia come[coming] with Alex hand in hand.
　(4) A farmer bought 43 sheep at the market and saw them stolen 24 hours later.
　(5) It is hard to take care of a baby.
　(6) It is a lot of fun to go on a picnic.
　(7) It is difficult for me to learn a new language.

02 I heard Sam baking some cookies.

03 (1) It was very difficult to answer the math questions.
　(2) It was a great experience to swim in the blue sea.
　(3) It is good for your health to exercise regularly.
　(4) It is not easy for me to learn English.
　(5) It is true that a friend in need is a friend indeed.

04 (1) to stay (2) pulled (3) sing[singing] (4) take

05 to read 50 novels

06 (1) for me to pass the driver's test
　(2) to watch the view as we went higher and higher
　(3) of you to help that old woman
　(4) that Annabelle didn't tell him a lie

07 make[또는 making]

08 (1) He heard them playing te drums.
　(2) Suhan looked at AI Speaker playing a movie.

09 (1) It is very smart of her to solve that problem.
　(2) It is not safe to swim in this river as it is very deep.

01 (1)~(3) 지각동사의 목적어와 목적격보어의 관계가 능동이므로 목적격보어로 원형부정사 혹은 현재분사가 적절하다 (4) 지각동사의 목적어와 목적격보어의 관계가 수동이므로 과거 분사가 적절하다. (5) It ~ to부정사' 구문으로 쓰는 것이 적절하다. (6) 가주어로는 that이 아니라 it을 쓴다. (7) to부정사의 의미상 주어로 사람의 성질을 나타내는 형용사가 쓰인 것이 아니므로 'for+목적격'이 적절하다.

02 진행형의 문장이므로 목적격보어로 현재분사가 적절하다.

03 (1)~(4) 문장의 주어로 쓰인 to부정사를 뒤로 보내고 대신 주어 자리에 가주어 it을 쓴다. (5) 주어로 쓰인 that절의 경우에도 긴 that절을 뒤로 보내고 주어 자리에 가주어 it을 쓴다.

04 (1) ask는 to부정사를 목적격보어로 받는다. (2) 지각동사의 목적어와 목적격보어의 관계가 수동일 때 목적격보어로 과거분사가 적절하다. (3) 목적어와 목적격보어의 관계가 능동일 때 목적격보어로 원형부정사나 현재분사가 적절하다. (4) 사역동사 make는 원형부정사를 목적격보어로 받는다.

05 가주어로 it이 나와 있으므로 진주어로 to부정사를 쓰는것이 적절하다.

06 (1) '하는데 어려움이 있다'는 것을 '~하기 어렵다'는 문장으로, (2) Watching을 to watch로 바꾸어서, '가주어(it) ~ 진주어(to부정사) …' 구문을 이용하여 쓴다. (4) In fact는 '사실은'이라는 뜻이므로 It is true 다음에 that절을 진주어로 쓴다.

07 지각동사 see의 목적어와 목적격보어의 관계가 능동이므로 목적격보어로 원형부정사나 현재분사가 적절하다.

08 지각동사의 목적어와 목적격보어의 관계가 능동이며, 진행형으로 쓰이고 있으므로 현재분사를 이용한다.

09 (1) to solve의 주어가 she이므로 of her로 의미상의 주어를 나타내야 한다. (2) 전치사 in의 목적어로 this river를 쓴다.

교과서
Reading

확인문제   p.28

1 T　2 F　3 T　4 F

확인문제   p.29

1 T　2 F　3 T　4 F

01 at   02 at the World AI Expo

03 entering   04 of the future   05 go into

06 on the closet door, keep changing

07 that suit the weather

08 no longer, dressing for the weather

09 move on to   10 this music speaker

11 I'm not just   12 more than

13 It's hard to believe   14 How about

15 play one   16 getting darker 17 feel like

18 What else   19 Here comes   20 Good job

21 Hurry   22 ride in   23 so cool, get in

24 ready to go   25 what should   26 my first time

27 don't need to   28 take you to   29 crossing

30 have just sensed

31 sense dangerous situations   32 How

33 intelligent robotic

34 all about driving   35 based on

36 How, like   37 like

1 A Day at the AI Expo

2 Jina and Suhan are at the World AI Expo.

3 They are entering the AI home.

4 Suhan: Look at this! It's a house of the future.

5 Jina: Let's go into the bedroom first. Look, there's a smart closet.

6 Suhan: I'm standing in front of this screen on the closet door and my clothes keep changing.

7 Jina: The screen suggests clothes that suit the weather.

8 Suhan: That's amazing! We no longer have to worry about dressing for the weather.

9 Jina: Right. Let's move on to the living room.

10 Suhan: Oh, I like this music speaker.

11 AI Speaker: I'm not just a music speaker.

12 I can do more than you can imagine.

13 Jina: It's hard to believe that you can understand us. What can you do?

14 AI Speaker: How about watching a movie?

15 I'll play one for you.

16 Suhan: Look, those smart windows are getting darker.

17 I feel like I'm in a movie theater.

18 Jina: What else can you do?

19 AI Speaker: I can beatbox, too. Here comes, "cats

and boots and cats and boots."

20 Suhan: You're funny. Good job!

21 Jina: Hurry! There's a smart car station outside!

22 Let's go and ride in that red car.

23 Suhan: This car is so cool. Let's get in.

24 AI Car: Welcome. Are you ready to go?

25 Jina: Yes, what should we do now?

26 It's my first time to ride in a smart car.

27 AI Car: You don't need to do anything.

28 I will drive and take you to the next station.

29 Suhan: Watch out! I see a cat crossing the street.

30 AI Car: Don't worry. I have just sensed it.

31 When I sense dangerous situations, I slow down or stop.

32 Jina: How can you do that?

33 AI Car: I'm a very intelligent robotic car.

34 I know all about driving.

35 I can predict danger based on knowledge and experience.

36 Suhan: How smart! You think and act like a person.

37 You are really like a human.

01 Jina and Suhan   02 ②, ④, ⑤   03 ②

04 ⑤   05 (A) one (B) What else (C) comes

06 I feel like I'm in a movie theater.   07 ①, ④

08 ②, ⑤   09 ③   10 changing   11 ②, ⑤

12 ④   13 ③   14 ①, ④   15 ⑤

16 (A) music speaker (B) beatbox   17 ①

18 ④   19 ①, ④   20 beaten[beat]

21 it   22 who is one of the greatest baduk players   23 ④

01 '진아'와 '수한'이를 가리킨다.

02 ⓑ와 ②, ④, ⑤번: 현재분사, ①, ③: 동명사

03 '진아'가 침실에 먼저 들어가 보자고 말한다.

04 주어진 문장의 you에 주목한다. ⑤번 앞 문장의 내용을 말한 AI Speaker를 가리키므로 ⑤번이 적절하다.

05 (A) 'a movie'를 지칭하므로 one이 적절하다. 'a+명사'는 one 으로, 'the+명사'는 it으로 받는다. (B) '또 뭘 할 수 있어?'라 고 해야 하므로 What else가 적절하다. (C) "cats and boots and cats and boots."는 비트박스를 하는 한 예에 해당하는 말 이므로 comes 가 적절하다. 비트박스: 사람의 입으로 디제잉 (DJing)의 소리를 흉내 내는 일종의 모사이다.

06 feel like: …한 느낌이 있다

07 '고양이가 길을 건너고 있는게 보인다'고 해야 하므로, 지각동사 see의 목적격보어 자리에 동사원형이나 현재분사가 오는 것이 적절하다.

08 ⓐ와 ②, ⑤번: 멋진, 끝내 주는, ①, ④: (날씨·공기 따위가) 서늘한, 시원한, ③ 차분한, 침착한

09 이 글은 '인공 지능 자동차는 지능적인 로봇 차이기 때문에 운전에 대한 모든 걸 알고 있고 위험을 예측하며 운전할 수 있다'는 내용의 글이므로, 제목으로는 '걱정 말아요! 저는 운전에 대한 모든 걸 알고 있어요.'가 적절하다.

10 keep ~ing: 계속 ~하다

11 worry about = be concerned[worried, anxious] about: ~에 대해 걱정하다, ② be anxious for: 갈망하다, ⑤ be concerned with: …에 관계가 있다, …에 관심이 있다

12 수한이의 옷이 어떻게 계속해서 바뀌는지는 대답할 수 없다. ① They are entering the AI home at the World AI Expo. ② They enter the bedroom first. ③ He is standing in front of the screen on the closet door. ⑤ It suggests clothes that suit the weather.

13 ③은 진아(와 수한)를 가리키고, 나머지는 다 'AI Speaker'를 가리킨다.

14 ⓐ와 ①, ④번: ~처럼(접속사), ② 좋아하다(동사), ③ ~처럼 (전치사), ⑤ 비슷한(형용사)

15 이 글은 AI Speaker가 그냥 음악 스피커가 아니라 사람들이 상상하는 것 이상의 것을 할 수 있다는 내용의 글이므로, 주제로는 '그것의 원래 역할을 하는 외에 AI Speaker가 할 수 있는 것'이 적절하다.

16 AI Speaker는 '음악 스피커'일 뿐만 아니라 영화를 틀어 주고 '비트박스'도 할 수 있다.

17 (A) take+사람+to+장소: ~를 …에 데리고 가다, (C) based on: ~에 근거하여

18 지식과 경험을 바탕으로 '위험을 예측할 수 있다'고 하는 것이 적절하다. ① safety: 안전(함), ⑤ generate: 발생시키다

19 ⓐ와 ②, ③, ⑤: 부사적 용법, ① 형용사적 용법, ④ 명사적 용법

20 'beat'의 과거분사형 beaten과 beat이다.

21 가주어 'it'이 적절하다.

22 one+of+the+복수명사: ~ 중의 하나

23 AI는 이세돌의 경기를 예측할 수 있었고, 그리고 마침내 경기에서 이겼다.

서술형 시험대비   p.38~39

01 entering into → entering

02 We no longer have to worry about dressing for the weather.

03 (a) closet door (b) the weather

04 than

05 What about / Why don't you

06 becoming 또는 growing

07 (1) 영화를 틀어 줄 수 있다.
   (2) 비트박스도 할 수 있다.

08 Intelligence

09 (1) don't have to
   (2) need not

10 AI Car가 이미 고양이가 길을 건너고 있는 것을 감지했고, AI Car는 어떤 위험한 상황을 감지하면 속도를 늦추거나 멈추기 때문이다.

11 a cat crossing the street

12 (A) Suhan (B) his clothes

13 amazed → amazing

14 suggests clothes

01 enter: ~에 들어가다, enter into: (논의·처리 등을) 시작하다

02 no longer: 더 이상 …아닌

03 그것은 스마트 '옷장 문'에 있는 스크린이고 그 앞에 서 있는 사람에게 '날씨'에 적합한 옷을 제안한다.

04 비교급 뒤에 'than'이 적절하다.

05 How about ~ing? = What about ~ing? = Why don't you+동사원형?: ~하는 게 어때?

06 get[become/grow]+형용사의 비교급: 점점 ~해지다

07 인공 지능 스피커는 그냥 음악 스피커가 아니라 당신이 상상하는 것 이상의 것을 할 수 있다고 하면서, 두 가지 예를 설명하고 있다.

08 intelligent의 명사형인 intelligence를 쓰는 것이 적절하다. artificial intelligence = AI: (컴퓨터) 인공 지능

09 don't need to = don't have to = need not: ~할 필요가 없다

10 바로 뒤의 내용을 쓰는 것이 적절하다.

11 '길을 건너고 있는 고양이'를 가리킨다.

12 '수한'이가 실제로 그의 옷을 계속 바꿔 입는 것이 아니다. 그는 단지 옷장 문에 있는 스크린 앞에서 있으면 '그의 옷'이 계속해서 바뀐다.

13 감정을 나타내는 동사는 감정을 유발할 때 현재분사를 쓰는 것이 적절하다.

14 옷장 문에 있는 스크린이 날씨에 적합한 '옷을 제안해주기' 때문이다.

영역별 핵심문제   p.41~45

01 look   02 ①   03 (1) on (2) just
   (3) longer (4) if   04 (1) (b)eat
   (2) (i)ntelligent (3) (r)eplace   05 ④
06 ③   07 ⑤   08 ③   09 for
10 ③   11 ①   12 (A) for (B) Sure
   (C) do   13 ⑤   14 ⑤
15 (1) play(또는 playing)

01 look ~ up: (사전·참고 자료·컴퓨터 등에서 정보를) 찾아보다 / 그는 네가 그것들을 인터넷에서 찾을 충분한 시간을 줄 것이다. look for: 찾다 / 이 고래들은 무리지어 먹이를 찾는다.

02 free from: ~이 없는 / 그녀에게는 걱정거리가 끊이지 않는다.

03 (1) based on: ~에 근거하여 / 그 영화는 유명한 소설에 기반을 두고 있다. (2) not just: 단지 ~뿐이 아니다 / 그것은 단순히 돈의 문제만은 아니다. (3) no longer: 더 이상 ~하지 않는 / 그녀는 더 이상 아이가 아니다. (4) see if 주어 동사: ~인지 아닌지 확인하다 / 문이 잠겨 있는지 가서 확인해 보세요.

04 (1) beat: 이기다 (2) intelligent: 똑똑한 (3) replace: 대체하다

05 (A) '우리는 정말 그랬어.'란 의미로, did는 'took lots of pictures during our trip.'을 의미한다. (B) Is it possible (for 목적격) to 동사원형 ~?: (…가) ~하는 것이 가능할까?

06 사진으로 동영상 앨범을 만드는 것이 가능한지 물어보고 있으므로 가능한지 불가능한지 대답을 해야 한다. 또한 빈칸 뒤에 'I have an app for that.(나는 그것을 위한 앱이 있어.)'라고 말했으므로 가능하다고 대답하는 것이 적절하다.

07 (A) Why don't we ~?: ~하는 게 어때?(제안, 권유) (B) sound 형용사: ~하게 들리다

08 주어진 문장은 상대방의 생각을 물어보는 'What do you think?(너는 어떻게 생각해?)'이다. 그러므로 자신의 생각을 표현한 'That sounds perfect for our project.(우리 프로젝트에 완벽한 것 같아.)' 앞의 질문으로 어울린다.

09 (A) perfect for: ~에 완벽한, ~에 안성맞춤인 (B) look for: 찾다

10 여자아이는 남자아이의 의견이 프로젝트에 완벽하다고 생각한다. disagree: 동의하지 않다

11 로봇 박람회에 같이 가자고 제안하는 말에, 'That sounds exciting.(그거 재미있겠는데.)'이라고 했으므로 빈칸에는 제안에 긍정하는 말이 어울린다.

12 (A) to부정사의 행위에 대하여 행위를 하는 주체가 있을 때 to부정사 앞에 의미상 주어를 넣는다. 의미상의 주어는 일반적으로 'for+목적격'을 사용하며 주절에 사람의 '성질이나 성격 등'을 나타내는 형용사가 쓰였을 경우 'of+목적격'을 사용한다. Is it possible (for 목적격) to 동사원형 ~?: (…가) ~하는 것이 가능할까? (B) 'I can do that.(할 수 있어.)'으로 대답하고 있으므로, 가능하다고 말하는 것이 어울린다. (C) read를 의미하므로 do가 적절하다.

13 첫 문장에는 smell이 나왔으므로 목적격보어로 현재분사가 나와야 한다. 두 번째 문장에서는 지각동사이므로 목적격보어로 동사원형이나 현재분사가 나와야 한다.(사람들이 수영하는 것이므로 능동)

14 가주어로 it이 나와야 하며 진주어로 to부정사가 적절하다.

15 (1)~(3) 지각동사의 목적어가 목적격보어의 행위의 주체가 될 경우 목적격보어로 원형부정사나 현재분사를 쓴다.

16 that이 나오려면 뒤에 주어와 동사가 있는 절이 이어져야 한다. It was interesting to compare their situation and ours.

17 see가 지각동사이므로 목적격보어로 serve나 serving이 적절하다.

18 (1) 지각동사의 목적어와 목적격보어의 관계가 능동일 경우 목적격보어로 원형부정사와 현재분사를 모두 사용할 수 있으나 의미상 그 동작이 진행 중인 것을 나타낼 때에는 주로 현재분사를 사용한다. (2) smell은 목적격보어로 현재분사를 사용한다. (3)~(4) it이 나와 있으므로 '가주어(it) ~ 진주어(to 부정사)' 구문을 이용하여 쓴다.

19 (1), (3) 지각동사의 목적어와 목적격보어가 능동의 관계에 있을 경우 목적격보어로 원형부정사나 현재분사를 쓰고, 수동일 경우 과거분사를 쓴다. (2) smell은 목적격보어로 현재분사를 쓴다. (4) to부정사의 의미상 주어로 사람의 성질을 나타내는 형용사가 쓰인 것이 아니므로 'for+목적격'이 적절하다. (5) for an AI가 의미상의 주어로 나와 있으므로 to beat을 써야 한다. (6) it을 가주어로 하고 to부정사를 진주어로 쓰는 것이 적절하다.

20 주격 관계대명사 'that'이나 'which'가 적절하다.

21 이 글은 인공 지능 집에서 옷장 문에 있는 스크린이 날씨에 적합한 옷을 제안하는 내용의 글이므로, 제목으로는 '옷을 제안하는 스크린'이 적절하다. ⑤ suitable for: …에 알맞은[어울리는]

22 closet: 벽장; 보관 장소로 사용되는 작은 방이나 캐비닛

23 more than you can imagine: 당신이 상상하는 것 이상의 것

24 (A)와 ②번: 가주어, ①, ④: 비인칭 주어 <시간·날짜·거리·날씨 등에 대해 말할 때 동사의 주어 자리에 씀> ③ 가목적어 ⑤ 그것(앞에 이미 언급 되었거나 현재 이야기되고 있는 사물·동물을 가리킴)

25 watch out = look out = be careful: (특히 위험이 있을 때 경고하는 말로) 조심하다

26 ⓑ와 ①번: 완료 용법, ② 경험 용법, ③, ⑤: 계속 용법, ④ 결과 용법

27 앞 문장 '저는 어떤 위험 상황을 감지하면 속도를 늦추거나 멈춰요.'를 가리킨다.

28 "Alpha-Foot"이라고 '불리는' 축구 로봇이라고 해야 하므로, 과거분사로 쓰는 것이 적절하다.

29 ⑤ 위 글은 '학교 신문 기사'이다. ① (책, 연극, 영화 등에 대한) 논평[비평], 감상문, ② 독후감, ③ 수필

단원별 예상문제   p.46~49

01 (b)urn / burn   02 cloudy   03 ②

04 (1) in danger (2) based on   05 (t)ranslator   06 ⑤

07 Is it possible for AI to read those words?

08 dictionary   09 (C) – (D) – (B) – (A)

10 (D) – (A) – (C) – (B)   11 if   12 Is it possible to freeze fire?   13 ②   14 ②

15 ①, ③   16 ②, ⑤   17 ②   18 suits → suit   19 ⑤   20 ④   21 ②

22 ③   23 ②   24 ④

25 (A) robotic car (B) do anything

01 burn: 불타다 / 불에 의해서 파괴되다 / 불을 낮춰, 그렇지 않으면 그게 탈 거야.

02 cloud: 구름 cloudy: 구름이 낀, 흐린

03 ① freeze, freeze: 얼리다 / 얼음 한 판 얼리는 데 하루 종일 걸린다. ② slow, slow down: 속도를 늦추다 / 이것은 노화를 늦추는 데 널리 사용되고 있습니다. ③ texting, text: (휴대전화로) 문자를 보내다 / 친구들과 문자를 주고 받거나 온라인에서 말하는 것을 좋아하나요? ④ point, point (at/toward): 돌리다, 향하게 하다 / 공공장소에서 낯선 사람들을 손가락으로 가리키는 것은 예의 없는 행동이다. ⑤ take, take: 선택하다, 사다 / 어른 표 두 장을 사겠습니다.

04 (1) in danger: 위험에 처한, 위험에 빠진 (2) based on: ~에 근거하여

05 translate: 번역하다 translator: 번역가

06 AI 번역기를 사용하는 방법에 대해 묻고 대답하고 있다.

07 Is it possible (for 목적격) to 동사원형 ~?: (…가) ~하는 것이 가능할까? AI: 인공지능(artificial intelligence)

08 dictionary: 사전 / 알파벳순으로 그것의 의미 또는 다른 언어로의 번역이 있는 일련의 단어와 구를 포함하는 책

11 see if 주어 동사: ~인지 아닌지 확인하다

12 Is it possible (for 목적격) to 동사원형 ~?: (~가) ~하는 것이 가능할까? freeze: 얼리다

13 가주어로는 it을 쓰며 진주어로 to부정사를 이용한다. 또한 의미

상의 주어로 문장에 쓰인 형용사가 사람의 성질을 나타내는 말이 아니므로 'for+목적격'을 쓴다.

14 첫 번째 문장에서는 지각동사의 목적격보어로 원형부정사나 현재분사가 적절하다. 두 번째 문장에서는 it을 가주어로 하고 to부정사를 진주어로 하여 'It ~ to부정사' 구문으로 쓰는 것이 적절하다.

15 ② I heard my name called repeatedly. ④ Mick watched them fight[fighting] each other. ⑤ He was looking at the dog eat[eating] the bones.

16 ① It is necessary to come early in the morning. ③ It is helpful to read many kinds of books. ④ It was really boring for me to memorize English words.

17 (A) worry about: ~에 대해 걱정하다, (B) dress for: … 에 적합한 옷을 입다

18 주격 관계대명사 that의 선행사가 clothes이므로 'suit'로 고치는 것이 적절하다.

19 ⓑ와 ①, ③, ④번: 동명사(목적이나 용도), ②, ⑤번: 현재분사(동작이나 상태, 진행)

20 ⓐ: Suhan(과 Jina), ⓑ, ⓓ, ⓔ: AI Speaker, ⓒ: Suhan과 Jina를 가리킨다.

21 ⓑ와 ②, ④, ⑤번: 명사적 용법, ① 형용사적 용법, ③ 부사적 용법

22 스마트 창문이 점점 어두워지고 있다.

23 ②번 다음 문장의 do that에 주목한다. 주어진 문장의 내용을 받고 있으므로 ②번이 적절하다.

24 이 글은 '인공 지능 자동차는 운전에 대한 모든 걸 알고 운전한다.'는 내용의 글이다.

25 그것은 운전에 대한 모든 걸 알고 있는 아주 지능적인 '로봇차'이다. 사람들은 스마트 자동차에 타고 있는 동안 '아무것도 하지' 않아도 된다.

서술형 실전문제   p.50~51

01 Is that possible → Is it possible

02 I think that is perfect for our project.

03 Is it possible for you to text with your eyes closed?

04 (1) To save energy in our daily lives is important.
   (2) It is important to save energy in our daily lives.
   (1) To feel tired after work is natural.
   (2) It is natural to feel tired after work.

05 riding a horse

06 enter

07 The screen suggests clothes that[which] suit the weather.

08 any longer

09 (A) what (B) How (C) based

10 speed up → slow down

11 What a smart car (you are)!

01 가주어 it은 to부정사를 받고 있는 것이므로 that을 가주어 it 대신에 쓸 수 없다.

02 자신의 의견을 표현하는 말에는 'That sounds ~.', 'I think (that) ~.' 등이 있다.

03 Is it possible (for 목적격) to 동사원형 ~?: (…가) ~하는 것이 가능할까? text: (휴대전화로) 문자를 보내다 with+명사+p.p: ~가 ~된 채로

04 to부정사가 문장의 주어로 쓰일 때 주어 자리에 가주어 it을 두고 to부정사 부분(진주어)을 문장 뒤로 보낸다. 또한 to부정사가 문장의 주어일 때는 단수로 받는다.

05 지각동사의 목적어가 목적격보어의 행위의 주체가 될 때 목적격보어로 원형부정사나 현재분사를 쓴다. 목적격보어 자리에 원형부정사와 현재분사를 모두 사용할 수 있으나 의미상 그 동작이 진행 중인 것을 나타낼 때에는 주로 현재분사를 사용한다.

06 go into = enter: ~에 들어가다

07 주격 관계대명사 that[which]을 사용하는 것이 적절하다.

08 no longer = not ~ any longer: 더 이상 … 아닌

09 (A) 'do'의 목적어가 와야 하므로 what이 적절하다. (B) '어떻게' 그렇게 할 수 있냐고 해야 하므로 How가 적절하다. (C) 지식과 경험을 '바탕으로'라고 해야 하므로 based가 적절하다. based on: ~에 근거하여

10 어떤 위험 상황을 감지하면 '속도를 늦추거나' 멈춘다고 해야 하므로 'slow down'으로 고쳐야 한다. speed up: 속도를 높이다

11 How+형용사[부사]+(주어+동사)! = What+a/an+형용사+명사+(주어+동사)!

창의사고력 서술형 문제 p.52

|모범답안|

01 A: Is it possible to fry an egg on the street[road]?
　B: Yes, I think it's possible. / No, I don't think it's possible.

02 (1) singing (2) a girl eating (3) a boy looking at

03 (A) AI Cook
　(B) vegetables and meat
　(C) a delicious meal
　(D) vegetables and meat

01 Is it possible (for 목적격) to 동사원형 ~?: (…가) ~하는 것이 가능할까? fry an egg: 계란을 부치다

단원별 모의고사 p.53~56

01 getting　02 (1) to　(2) on　(3) of　03 ③

04 Is it possible for you to live without your smartphone?

05 impossible 06 ④　　07 ①　　08 ②

09 (A) interesting (B) to replace

10 (C) from (D) of　　11 ⑤　　12 possible

13 (1) It is good for your health to eat a lot of vegetables.
　(2) It is possible that people may not want to talk to each other anymore.

14 ④　　　15 ⑤

16 (1) Mina smelled onions frying.
　(2) We heard them whispering[whisper] to each other.
　(3) It is interesting to find and create new things.
　(4) It is easy for you to send e-mails.

17 ③　　18 ③　　19 The screen suggests clothes that suit the weather.　　20 ④

21 like　22 that → those　23 ②, ③

24 I can predict danger based on knowledge and experience. 25 ⑤

01 get 비교급: 점점 더 ~해지다 / 이야기는 점점 더 재미있게 된다 get in: ~에 타다 / 그는 택시 앞좌석에 타고 있다

02 (1) face to face: (~와) 서로 얼굴을 맞대고 / 그들은 마주보고 앉아 서로를 바라보고 있다. (2) move on: ~로 이동하다 / 자, 이제 다음 이야기입니다 (3) out of: (원천·출처) ~에서, ~으로부터 / 그들은 옥수수와 콩 같은 식물 재료를 사용하여 플라스틱 제품을 만든다.

03 off: 할인되어 / 개장일에 가구를 구입하시면 25퍼센트 할인해 드립니다.

04 Is it possible (for 목적격) to 동사원형 ~?: (…가) ~하는 것이 가능할까? without: ~ 없이

05 impossible: 불가능한

06 ⓓ는 가주어이며, 나머지는 this computer를 받는 대명사이다.

07 so: 그럼, 그러면

08 ② 현금으로 낼지 카드로 낼지에 대해서는 언급되지 않았다. ① 여자가 가진 쿠폰을 사용할 수 있는가? 사용할 수 있다. ③ 그들은 어디에 있는가? 컴퓨터 가게 ④ 그녀는 얼마나 할인을 받았는가? 30달러 ⑤ 여자는 무엇을 사기를 원하는가? 컴퓨터

09 (A) interesting: 재미있는, 흥미로운 (B) Is it possible for 목적격 to 동사원형 ~?: …가 ~하는 것이 가능할까? replace: 대체하다

10 (C) free from: ~이 없는 (D) because of 명사: ~ 때문에

11 ⓔ dark → bright 로봇이 위험한 일을 할 수 있어서 사람들이 위험이 없어진다는 내용은 좋은 면을 보고 있는 것이다.

12 possible: 가능한 / 일어나거나 발생할 수 있는

13 (1) 문장의 주어로 쓰인 to부정사를 뒤로 보내고 대신 주어 자

리에 가주어 it을 쓴다. (2) 주어로 쓰인 that절의 경우에도 긴 that절을 뒤로 보내고 주어 자리에 가주어 it을 쓴다.

14 지각동사의 목적어와 목적격보어가 능동의 관계에 있을 경우 목적격보어로 원형부정사나 현재분사를 쓴다.

15 to부정사의 의미상 주어로 사람의 성질을 나타내는 형용사가 쓰였으므로 'of+목적격'이 적절하다. It is very kind of you to help us.

16 (1) smell은 목적격보어로 현재분사를 쓴다. (2) 지각동사의 목적어와 목적격보어가 능동의 관계에 있을 경우 목적격보어로 원형부정사나 현재분사를 쓴다. 의미상 그 동작이 진행 중인 것을 나타낼 때에는 주로 현재분사를 사용한다. (3), (4) it을 가주어로 하고 to부정사를 진주어로 쓰는 것이 적절하다. to부정사의 의미상 주어로 사람의 성질을 나타내는 형용사가 쓰인 것이 아니므로 'for+목적격'이 적절하다.

17 ⓑ We heard Yena play(playing) the violin. ⓓ Jeniffer felt him come(coming) closer. ⓖ Is it safe to swim in this river?

18 ⓐ와 ②, ⑤번: 관계대명사, ①, ③, ④: 접속사

19 앞 문장의 내용을 가리킨다.

20 (That's) right.: 그렇습니다, ④ 괜찮아요. ① You got it. 맞습니다. ② You can say that again. 정말 그렇다[(당신 말에) 전적으로 동의한다]. ③ I agree with you. 당신 의견에 동의해요. ⑤ You said it. 맞습니다.

21 (A) like: 좋아하다(동사), (B) like ~처럼(접속사)

22 뒤에 복수명사(smart windows)가 나오기 때문에, 지시형용사도 복수형으로 고치는 것이 적절하다.

23 ⓐ와 ②, ③: 형용사적 용법, ①, ④: 명사적 용법, ⑤ 부사적 용법

24 'on'을 보충하면 된다.

25 인공 지능 자동차는 '자신의' 지식과 경험을 바탕으로 위험을 예측할 수 있다.

Lesson 8

The Unknown Hero

시험대비 실력평가   p.60

01 (1) Chinese   (2) Spanish   02 ③   03 ①

04 ④   05 ②

06 (1) harmony   (2) Thanks

---

01 China: 중국 Chinese: 중국어; 중국의 Spain: 스페인 Spanish: 스페인의; 스페인어

02 ① 내 취미는 우표를 수집하는 것이다. ② 내가 충분히 연습을 하지 않았다는 의미인가요? ③ waste: 낭비하다 / 왜 필요하지도 않은 옷에 돈을 낭비하니? ④ 색깔과 스타일은 개인적인 취향의 문제이다. ⑤ 다른 사람들의 재산을 침해하지 않도록 조심하라.

03 be famous for: ~으로 유명하다 take care of: ~을 돌보다

04 store: 저장하다, 보관하다 / 우리는 창고에 상품을 보관한다.

05 ② loyal: 충실한, 충성스러운 royal: 왕의, 왕실의 ① 우리는 그가 살았는지 죽었는지 모른다. ② 배움에는 왕도가 없다. ③ 나는 또 다른 컴퓨터가 필요하다. ④ 그 도둑은 창문을 통해 들어갔다. ⑤ 그 회사는 유럽 내에 있는 고객들을 지원할 것이다.

06 (1) in harmony with: ~와 조화를 이루어 (2) thanks to: ~ 덕분에

서술형 시험대비   p.61

01 (1) interested   (2) amazed

02 care, take

03 (1) Hundreds   (2) set   (3) filled

04 found

05 (1) At   (2) in   (3) for   (4) as

06 (1) I hope this year will be full of joy.

     (2) I tried the dress on but it didn't fit.

---

01 (1) interest: 흥미, 관심 interested: 흥미가 있는 / Jackson은 미술에 아주 흥미가 있다. (2) amaze: 놀라게 하다 amazed: 놀란 / 우리 모두는 그 뉴스에 놀랐다.

02 care for: ~을 돌보다 take care of: ~을 돌보다 / 그녀는 연로한 부모님을 보살피기 위해 다시 집으로 이사를 했다.

03 (1) hundreds of: 수백의, 수많은 (2) set foot: 발을 들여놓다 (3) be filled with: ~으로 가득 차다

04 found: find(발견하다)의 과거형; 설립하다 / Smith씨는 내년

에 회사를 설립할 것이다. Mike는 방에서 무엇인가 먹을 것을 발견했다.

05 (1) at last: 마침내, 결국 / 결국 우리가 경기에 이겼다. (2) in danger: 위험에 처한 / 그 아이들이 지금 위험에 처해 있다. (3) can't wait for: ~을 몹시 기대하다 / 그는 그 파티를 몹시 기대하고 있다. (4) be known as: ~으로 알려지다 / Ann의 아버지는 위해한 과학자로 알려져 있다.

06 (1) be full of: ~로 가득하다 (2) fit: 맞다 tried the dress on: tried on the dress: 그 드레스를 입어 보았다.

교과서
Conversation

핵심 Check   p.62~63

1 Do you know anything about / Do you know (that)

2 explain / Could, explain

3 Could you explain your plan to save money?

교과서 대화문 익히기

Check(√) True or False   p.64

1 F   2 T   3 T   4 F

교과서 확인학습   p.66~67

Listen & Speak 1 B-2

Do, anything / little, famous for / going to, with / think, like

Listen & Speak 2 A

explain, painting / painted

Listen & Speak 2 B-1

1. explain / was written / about / about, missing

2. explain / volunteer group / tell, more / take care

Listen & Speak 2 C

Could, explain / waste, on

Real-Life Zone A

What, anything about / Korean houses, are

designed, in harmony / a little / cool, warm / sounds,
Where, see / near here / about going, seeing / idea,
How, get / take, over there

Real-Life Zone B

1. know anything / greatest sights / why, famous /
because, longest wall

2. about, novel / short novel / explain why / won, for

Real-Life Zone B e.g.

know anything / was built / explain why / It's
because, tallest tower

Wrap Up

know anything / birthday / tell, more / get together,
wears / interesting / share food, wish for / Korean
tradition

시험대비 기본평가   p.68

01 ④   02 (C) → (B) → (A) → (D)   03 ②

01 Do you know anything about ~?은 어떤 것에 대해 알고
있는지 묻는 표현이다.

02 (C) 창덕궁에 대해 알고 있는 것이 있는지 묻는다. (B) 조금 안
다고 말하면서, 그것은 아름다운 정원으로 유명하다고 대답한
다. (A) 친구와 함께 그곳에 갈 예정이라고 말한다. (D) 그곳이
마음에 들 것이라고 대답한다.

03 'Could you explain ~?'은 어떤 것에 대한 설명을 요청할 때
사용하며 could 대신에 can을 쓸 수 있다.

시험대비 실력평가   p.69~70

01 ②   02 was written   03 ④

04 ④   05 ⑤   06 ①

07 돌잔치를 위해 가족이 함께 모이고 생일을 맞는 아기가
한복을 입는 것

08 share   09 ④   10 written   11 ②

12 He won the Pulitzer Prize.

01 대화의 흐름으로 보아 이 시에 대한 설명을 요청하는 물음이 와야
한다.

02 시가 윤동주에 의해 쓰여진 것이므로 수동태가 되어야 한다.

03 ① 여자아이가 시를 좋아하는지는 알 수 없다. ② 이 시의 제목
은 알 수 없다. ③ 남자아이가 윤동주를 좋아하는지는 알 수 없
다. ④ 이 시는 고향을 그리워하는 작가에 관한 것이다. ⑤ 이
소녀가 이 시에 관심이 있는 이유는 알 수 없다.

04 세종대왕을 아느냐고 물어보는 질문에 모른다고 대답하고 곧바
로 한글을 창제한 왕이라고 말하는 것은 어색하다.

---

05 (C) 에펠탑에 대해 아느냐고 묻는 질문에, (D) 1889년에
Gustave Eiffel에 의해 세워졌다고 대답한다. (B) 그것이 유
명한 이유를 묻자, (A) 그 당시 세계에서 가장 높은 탑이었기 때
문이라고 대답한다.

06 ① 그것에 대해 더 말해 주겠느냐는 표현이 알맞다.

07 That은 지시대명사로 앞 문장의 내용을 받는다.

08 어떤 것을 다른 사람과 함께 가지거나 사용하거나 점거하다:
share: 공유하다, 나눠 갖다

09 ④ 남자아이가 돌잔치에 참석하기를 원하는지는 알 수 없다.

10 수동의 의미이므로 과거분사가 알맞다.

11 ② 유명한 이유를 설명해 달라는 표현이므로 explain이 알맞
다.

서술형 시험대비   p.71

01 in   02 cool   03 interesting

04 Shall   05 how to   06 sight → sights

07 (B) why   (C) because

01 be in harmony with: ~와 조화를 이루다

02 여름에는 시원하고 겨울에는 따뜻하다는 말이 자연스럽다.

03 감정을 나타내는 동사에 '-ing'를 붙이면 '~한 감정을 일으키는'
의 의미가 되고, '-ed'를 붙이면 '~한 감정을 느끼는'의 의미가
된다. interesting: 흥미 있는

04 How about ~ing?는 제안을 나타내는 말로 Shall we ~?로 바
꿔 쓸 수 있다.

05 길을 묻는 표현이다.

06 'one of the 최상급+복수명사'의 구문이다.

07 (B) 이유를 묻는 의문부사 why가 알맞다. (C) It's because
~: ~이기 때문이다

교과서

Grammar

핵심 Check   p.72~73

1 (1) to buy   (2) to be   (3) to be

2 (1) expected, to be

    (2) (c)aused, to (j)ump

    (3) (f)orced, to sign

3 (1) singing

    (2) written

    (3) writing

01 ⑤

02 (1) eating　(2) hidden　(3) talking　(4) invited

03 (1) I want you to clean the windows.

　(2) Timothy got an email sent by a stranger this morning.

　(3) Who are the boys playing soccer on the ground?

　(4) Tell her to buy a comfortable pair of shoes!

04 (1) Jack gave his wife a necklace made of pearls.

　(2) Who is the man cutting the beef sandwiches with a knife?

　(3) Mike advised her to go to bed early.

01　ask의 목적격보어는 to부정사이다.

02　(1) 진행의 의미이므로 현재분사 eating을 쓴다. (2) 수동의 의미이므로 과거분사 hidden을 쓴다. (3) 진행의 의미이므로 현재분사 talking을 쓴다. (4) 수동의 의미이므로 과거분사 invited를 쓴다.

03　(1), (4) want, tell은 to부정사를 목적격보어로 취하는 동사이다. (2) email이 보내지는 것이므로 과거분사가 적절하다. (3) 소년들이 축구를 하는 것이므로 현재분사가 적절하다.

시험대비 실력평가　　　　　　p.75~77

01 ③　　02 ③　　03 ⑤　　04 ②

05 ②　　06 (1) carrying　(2) written　(3) sleeping cat　　07 ①　　08 ①

09 (1) to help　(2) to go　(3) to stay　(4) not to take

10 (1) kick → kicking

　(2) the playing badminton man → the man playing badminton

　(3) baby crying → crying baby

11 ②　　12 ④　　13 ③　　14 ③

15 ⑤　　16 writing, written　　17 ①

18 ④

19 (1) My parents always tell me to do my best in school.

　(2) Good health enabled him to carry out the plan.

20 ③

01　have는 목적어와 목적격보어의 관계가 수동인 경우 목적격보어로 과거분사를 사용하는 동사이다. 신발에 광이 나게 한다는 의미이므로 과거분사를 쓰는 것이 적절하다.

02　① Do you want me to clean your house for you? ② He told Perry to put on a yellow shirt. ④ The doctor advised Ted to stop smoking. ⑤ Ms. Green asked him to carry the boxes.

03　⑤번은 동명사이고 나머지는 다 현재분사이다.

04　현재분사가 뒤에서 앞의 명사를 수식하도록 한다. / expect는 목적격보어로 to부정사를 취한다.

05　첫 번째 문장은 5형식이고 두 번째 문장은 3형식이다. 3형식과 5형식에 쓰이면서, to부정사를 목적격보어와 목적어로 받을 수 있는 동사는 want이다.

06　(1) 현재분사가 뒤에서 앞의 명사를 수식하도록 한다. (2) e-mail이 쓰여진 것이므로 과거분사가 적절하다. (3) 현재분사가 단독으로 쓰일 때는 명사 앞에 와서 명사를 수식한다.

07　warn과 ask는 목적격보어로 to부정사가 오며, to부정사의 부정형은 'not[never]+to 동사원형'이다

08　축구를 하고 있는 것이므로 '수동이나 완료'의 의미로 쓰이는 과거분사가 아니라 '진행'을 나타내는 현재분사를 쓰는 것이 적절하다.

09　(1), (2), (3), (4) ask, allow, order, warn의 목적격보어로 to부정사가 적절하다. to부정사의 부정형은 'not to 동사원형'으로 쓴다.

10　(1) 현재분사가 뒤에서 the boy를 수식하도록 하는 것이 적절하다. (2) 현재분사가 목적어나 부사구를 수반할 때에는 명사 뒤에 와서 앞의 명사를 수식한다. (3) 현재분사가 단독으로 쓰일 때는 명사 앞에 와서 명사를 수식한다.

11　② make는 사역동사이므로 목적격보어로 동사원형이 와야 하며, 나머지는 모두 to부정사가 와야 한다.

12　④ find는 목적격보어로 현재분사를 쓴다. 동사원형은 쓸 수 없다.

13　want는 목적격보어로 to부정사를 쓴다.

14　'전화를 받고 있는'의 의미이므로 현재분사를 쓴다. '저녁식사에 초대된'의 의미이므로 과거분사를 쓴다.

15　allow는 목적격보어로 to부정사를 취한다.

16　'~을 쓰고 있는 소년'이라는 의미이므로 현재분사로 the boy를 수식하고, '한국어로 쓰여진'이라는 의미이므로 과거분사로 the letter를 수식하는 것이 적절하다.

17　make는 목적격보어로 to부정사가 아니라 원형부정사를 쓴다.

18　'태권도를 배우고 있는 여자아이'이므로 현재분사를 이용하여 뒤에서 명사를 수식하도록 해야 한다.

19　(1), (2) tell과 enable은 목적격보어로 to부정사가 온다.

20　③번은 동명사이고 나머지는 모두 현재분사이다.

서술형 시험대비　　　　　　p.78~79

01 (1) helping → to help　(2) go → to go

　(3) left → to leave　(4) excited → exciting

　(5) throws → throwing　(6) to repair → repair

02 (1) beginning　(2) dancing　(3) frightened

(4) taken

03 (1) to come (2) to do (3) expects (4) to go

04 (1) The teacher asked me to close the door.

(2) Mom told me to walk the dog.

(3) Kate climbed the mountain covered with snow.

(4) When are you going to fix the broken window?

(5) Mariko looked at her daughter playing[play] in the park.

05 (1) The business woman running a big company is Sophie.

(2) There is a bridge built long time ago.

06 (1) not to drive so fast

(2) to play the piano for us

07 (1) playing (2) exciting (3) repaired (4) amazing

(5) hit

08 (1) The woman asked the man to carry her bag.

(2) Emma advised me to wait till tomorrow.

(3) Peter told Sylvia to dance with him.

(4) They expected him to participate in the festival.

(5) Good health enabled him to finish the plan.

09 (1) cheering

(2) sliced

10 (1) 현재분사 → 이유: '~하는 중'이라고 해석된다.

(2) 동명사 → 이유: 현재분사로 해석하면 '방이 기다리고 있다는' 것이 되어 어색하며 room의 용도를 나타내어 '대기실'이라는 의미이다.

---

01 (1), (2), (3) ask, want, advise는 목적격보어로 to부정사를 취한다. (4) bowling game이 흥분을 유발하는 것이므로 exciting을 써야 한다. (5) 소년이 공을 던지는 주체이므로 현재분사로 수식하는 것이 적절하다. (6) have는 목적격보어로 원형부정사를 취한다.

02 (1), (2) 분사가 목적어나 부사구를 수반할 때에는 명사 뒤에 와서 앞의 명사를 수식한다. (3) 뉴스에 놀라는 것이므로 과거분사가 적절하다. (4) 사진이 찍히는 것이므로 과거분사가 적절하다.

03 (1), (2), (4) tell, want, allow는 목적격보어로 to부정사를 취한다. (3) hope는 5형식으로 쓰이지 않는다.

04 (1), (2) ask, tell은 목적격보어로 to부정사를 취한다. (3) 눈으로 덮인 것이므로 과거분사를 쓴다. (4) 창문이 깨진 것이므로 과거분사를 쓴다. (5) look at이 지각동사이므로 현재분사나 동사원형을 쓴다.

05 분사가 목적어나 부사구를 수반할 때에는 명사 뒤에 와서 앞의 명사를 수식한다. 이때 명사와 분사 사이에 '관계대명사+be동사'가 생략되어 있다고 볼 수 있다.

06 order와 ask는 목적격보어로 to부정사를 쓰고 부정사의 부정은 not[never]을 앞에 붙인다.

---

07 (1) 배드민턴을 치고 있는 그 소녀는 나의 여동생이다. (2) 나는 너에게 해 줄 흥미진진한 이야기가 있어. (3) 우리는 그 차가 Potter와 Parker에 의해 수리되게 하였다. (4) Jina는 놀라운 농구 선수이다. (5) 너는 그 건물이 덤프트럭에 의해 부딪친 것을 보았니?

08 ask, advise, tell, expect, enable 등은 모두 목적격보어로 to부정사가 와야 한다.

09 (1) 진행의 의미이므로 현재분사를 쓴다. (2) 수동의 의미이므로 과거분사를 쓴다.

교과서
Reading

확인문제   p.80

1 T 2 F 3 T 4 F

확인문제   p.81

1 F 2 T 3 T 4 F 5 T

교과서 확인학습 A   p.82~83

01 Architecture   02 Have, been

03 There is   04 popular, who, past

05 know, was created, efforts

06 known as   07 who founded

08 time, was ruled, fit, taste

09 moving into, Japanese, Western

10 wanted, protect, suffering

11 power, keep, let, set foot

12 between, and

13 modern, people

14 efforts, filled with

15 independence movement, ways

16 example, supported, keep, alive

17 happened, caught, suffered

18 pressed, build

19 how to

20 official, know, so, build   21 what, told

22 cost, high

23 fell, property

24 part, to, traditions, still

1 The King of Architecture in Gyeongseong.

2 Have you been to Bukchon?

3 There is a beautiful *hanok* village in Bukchon.

4 It is popular with tourists who want to see Korea's past.

5 However, not many people know that Bukchon was created through one man's efforts.

6 That man was Jeong Segwon, known as the King of Architecture in Gyeongseong.

7 Jeong Segwon was a businessman who founded Geonyangsa in 1920.

8 At the time, Korea was ruled by Japan, and the Japanese were changing Gyeongseong to fit their taste.

9 Many Japanese moving into Gyeongseong were building Japanese or Western houses.

10 Jeong Segwon wanted to protect the *hanok* and help the suffering people.

11 He said, "People are power. We Joseon people should keep Jongno and not let the Japanese set foot here."

12 He bought the land between Gyeongbokgung and Changdeokgung.

13 There he built small, modern *hanoks* for the people.

14 Through his efforts, we now have Bukchon filled with its beautiful *hanoks*.

15 Jeong Segwon helped the independence movement in many ways.

16 For example, he built the office building for the Joseon Language Society and supported its efforts to keep the Joseon language alive.

17 When the Joseon Language Affair happened, he was caught by the police and suffered a lot.

18 Japanese officials pressed him to build Japanese houses.

19 He said, "I don't know how to build Japanese houses."

20 An official said, "You know how to build hanoks, so you can build Japanese houses, too."

21 But he did not do what the Japanese told him to do.

22 The cost was high.

23 His business fell off, and he lost his property.

24 However, in part, thanks to Jeong Segwon, the traditions of Korea still live with us today.

01 who[that]   02 moved → moving   03 ②

04 우리 조선 사람들은 조선을 지켜야 하며, 일본인들이 이곳에 발을 들여놓지 못하게 해야 한다.

05 ⑤   06 ④

07 It is popular with tourists who want to see Korea's past.

08 known   09 ①   10 ②   11 ③

12 ①   13 ③   14 ⑤   15 ④

16 ③   17 ⑤   18 ②

19 a beautiful hanok village   20 past

21 ②   22 Jeong Segwon was a businessman who founded Geonyangsa in 1920.   23 ⑤

24 ③   25 They were building Japanese or Western houses.

26 ①   27 alive

28 was happened → happened

01 선행사가 사람이고 주격이므로 관계대명사 who나 that을 쓴다.

02 '경성으로 이사 오는 많은 일본인들'의 뜻이 되어야 하므로 능동의 의미를 나타내는 현재분사가 알맞다.

03 문맥상 '한옥을 지키기를 원했다'가 자연스럽다.

04 set foot: 발을 들여놓다

05 정세권은 일본인들이 종로에 발을 들여놓지 않도록 해야 한다고 말했다.

06 ⓐ have been to: ~에 다녀온 적이 있다 ⓑ through: ~을 통하여

07 be popular with: ~에게 인기가 있다

08 수동의 의미이므로 과거분사가 알맞다.

09 in many ways: 여러 방법으로

10 ⓑ, ② 형용사적 용법 ①, ④ 명사적 용법 ③, ⑤ 부사적 용법

11 press는 목적격보어로 to부정사를 취한다.

12 ① 정세권이 왜 독립운동을 도왔는지는 위 글에서 언급되지 않았다.

13 ⓐ와 ②, ③, ④는 선행사를 포함하는 관계대명사이고, ①, ⑤는 의문대명사이다.

14 fall off: 쇠퇴하다 thanks to: ~ 덕분에

15 주어진 문장의 There는 경복궁과 창덕궁 사이의 땅을 가리킨다.

16 목적보어가 원형부정사 set이므로 사역동사 make나 let이 와야 하는데, 문맥상 '일본인들이 발을 들여놓지 않도록 해야 한다'이므로 허용을 나타내는 let이 알맞다.

17 ⓑ, ⑤ ~에 의하여, ~ 때문에 ①, ② ~을 뚫고, ~을 관통하여 ③ ~의 처음부터 끝까지 ④ ~을 사이에 두고

18 filled with: ~으로 가득 찬

19 It은 인칭대명사로 앞에 나온 단수 명사를 받고 있다.

20 현재 이전의 시기와 일어난 일들: past(과거)

21 보기와 ②의 as는 전치사로 '~으로'의 뜻으로 쓰였다.

22 관계대명사 who 대신 that을 써도 좋다.

23 ⓑ, ⑤ 부사적 용법 ①, ③, ④ 명사적 용법 ② 형용사적 용법

24 ① 창의적인 ② 부정적인 ③ 애국적인 ④ 친절한 ⑤ 정렬적인

25 많은 일본인들은 일본식이나 서양식 집을 짓고 있었다.

26 for example: 예를 들면

27 '조선어를 살아 있게 지키다'의 뜻이 되어야 하므로 alive가 알맞다.

28 happen은 자동사이므로 수동태로 쓸 수 없다.

서술형 시험대비 p.90~91

01 He said (that) he didn't know how to build Japanese houses.

02 ⓑ so ⓑ what ⓒ to

03 (A) build (B) property

04 They pressed him to build Japanese houses.

05 to set

06 land

07 (A) and (B) Through (C) with

08 independence

09 For

10 When the Joseon Language Affair happened, he was caught by the police and suffered a lot.

11 (A) to build (B) how

12 It made an effort to keep the Joseon language alive.

13 (A) to (B) with (C) through

14 has

15 known

01 피전달문을 이끄는 접속사 that은 생략할 수 있다.

02 (A) so: 그래서 (B) 선행사를 포함하는 관계대명사 what이 알맞다. (C) thanks to: ~ 덕분에

03 한 일본인 관리의 압력에도 불구하고, 정세권은 일본식 집을 짓지 않았다. 그 결과 그는 그의 재산을 잃었다.

05 let은 목적격보어로 원형부정사를 취하고 allow는 to부정사를 취한다.

06 특히 농사나 건축과 같은 특수한 목적을 위해 사용되는 일정한 지역의 땅: land(땅, 토지)

07 (A) between A and B: A와 B 사이에 (B) through: ~을 통하여, ~으로 (C) filed with: ~으로 가득 찬

08 depend: 의존하다 independence: 독립

09 for example: 예를 들면

10 수동태이므로 'by'를 보충하면 된다.

11 (A) press는 to부정사를 목적격보어로 취한다. (B) build의 목적어인 Japanese가 있으므로 what은 올 수 없다.

13 (A) have been to: ~에 다녀오다 (B) be popular with: ~에게 인기가 있다 (C) through: ~으로, ~을 통해

14 There is ~ 구문은 have[has] 동사를 써서 바꿔 쓸 수 있다.

15 수동의 뜻을 나타내므로 과거분사로 고쳐야 한다.

영역별 핵심문제 p.93~97

01 (1) French (2) architect

02 (1) interested (2) part (3) modern 03 ②

04 ① 05 ⑤ 06 (D) → (A) → (C) → (B)

07 ④ 08 ①

09 They are designed to be in harmony with nature.

10 ③ 11 ④ 12 ③

13 (1) give → to give
  (2) to wait → wait
  (3) to repair → repair
  (4) played → play[playing]
  (5) writing → written

14 ④ 15 ④ 16 ⑤

17 (1) Lucy's dad wants her to be a police officer.
  (2) My mother asked me to buy some milk on my way home.
  (3) The teacher told the students to bring some water.
  (4) She got her two sons to divide a cake exactly in half.

18 (1) We like to walk[walking] on fallen leaves.
  (2) He hit the flying ball.

19 (1) 해석: Jane은 얇게 썰어진 치즈를 좋아한다.
  (2) 해석: Jane은 치즈를 얇게 써는 것을 좋아한다.
  (3) 어법상 차이: sliced는 '썰어진 (치즈)'라는 의미의 과거분사로 cheese를 수식하고, slicing은 '(치즈를) 써는 것'이라는 의미로 동명사로 쓰였다.

20 ③ 21 ② 22 ruler 23 ③

24 여러분은 이런 종류의 항아리를 본 적이 있나요?

25 painted

26 They used it for storing rice.

27 Why 28 national 29 ③, ⑤ 30 body

31 Western 32 ② 33 ⑤

01 (1) 나라와 언어명의 관계이다. (2) 명사와 그 명사의 행위자의 관계이다.

02 (1) be interested in: ~에 관심이 있다 (2) part: 부분 (3) modern: 현대의

03 be famous for: ~으로 유명하다

04 상상의 사람들과 사건들에 관해 쓴 긴 이야기: novel(소설)

05 설명을 요청하는 문장이 되어야 한다.

06 (D) 설명 요청→ (A) 설명 → (C) 더 자세한 설명 요청 → (B) 대답

07 ⓓ You should. → You shouldn't. 뒤에 이어지는 문장이 책이 재미있지 않았다는 뜻이므로 책을 사지 말라는 대답이 자연스럽다.

08 한옥에 대해 알고 있는지 묻는 문장이므로 ①이 적절하다.

09 They가 가리키는 것이 traditional Korean houses이므로 수동태의 문장이 되어야 한다.

10 어떤 장소에 가는 방법을 묻는 표현이므로 How가 알맞다.

11 남자는 전통 마을이 이곳에서 가깝다고 대답했다.

12 주어진 문장의 밑줄 친 부분은 동명사이다. 따라서 '~하는 중인'이라는 의미의 현재분사로 쓰인 ③번이 답이다.

13 (1) ask의 목적격보어로 to부정사가 와야 한다. (2), (3) make, have는 사역동사이므로 목적격보어로 동사원형이 와야 한다. (4) 지각동사의 목적격보어이므로 동사원형이나 현재분사를 쓴다. (5) '쓰인'의 뜻으로 수동의 의미이므로 과거분사를 쓴다.

14 ask의 목적격보어로 to부정사가 적절하다.

15 ④ '웃고 있는'의 의미가 알맞으므로 현재분사 smiling을 쓴다.

16 (A) '고장난 카메라'라는 의미이므로 과거분사를 쓰는 것이 적절하다. (B) 사물을 수식하는 것이므로 현재분사를 쓰는 것이 적절하다.(C) '잠긴 문'이라는 의미이므로 과거분사를 쓰는 것이 적절하다.

17 (1) want, (2) ask, (3) tell, (4) get 등의 동사는 목적격보어로 to부정사가 와야 한다.

18 (1) 낙엽은 떨어진 잎을 말하는 것이므로 'fallen leaves'라고 쓸 수 있다. (2) '날아오는 공'이므로 현재분사로 ball을 수식하도록 문장을 만든다.

19 like는 동명사를 목적어로 취할 수 있는 동사이며, 위 문장에서 치즈는 slice의 주체가 될 수 없으므로 slicing이 현재분사라고 볼 수 없다.

20 글의 흐름상 그가 일본인들이 울릉도 근처에서 고기 잡는 것을 보았다는 문장 다음에 이어져야 하므로 ③번이 적절하다.

21 ⓐ, ② 동명사 ①, ③, ④, ⑤ 현재분사

22 나라를 다스리는 사람: ruler(통치자)

23 안용복이 고기를 잘 잡았는지는 위 글의 내용에서 알 수 없다.

24 pot: 항아리, 냄비

25 꽃들이 그려진 것이므로 수동의 뜻을 나타내는 과거분사가 적절하다.

26 쌀을 저장하기 위해 사용했다.

27 How about ~ing?=Why don't you ~?: ~하는 게 어때?

28 nation의 형용사형은 national이다.

29 ⓒ, ③, ⑤ 관계대명사 ① 진주어 ② 동사의 목적어가 되는 명사

절을 이끄는 접속사이다. ④ It ... that 강조구문

30 사람의 머리, 팔, 다리를 포함한 육체의 모든 부분: body(몸, 신체)

31 West의 형용사형은 Western이다.

32 set foot: 발을 들여놓다

33 ⑤ 정세권이 어떻게 종로를 지켰는지는 대답할 수 없다.

단원별 예상문제 p.98~101

01 ④	02 in	03 ⑤	04 ③
05 돌잔치	06 ②	07 tradition	08 ④
09 on the land between Gyeongbokgung and Changdeokgung			
10 Gyeongseong		11 movement	12 ③
13 ③	14 (1) to help, comes	(2) to feed	
15 ②	16 ②	17 ⑤	
18 (A) happened (B) to build (C) what			19 ③
20 ③	21 wearing		
22 (A) painted (B) holding		23 ④	24 has
25 ③	26 created → was created		
27 ⑤	28 ①		

01 take care of=care for: ~을 돌보다

02 in danger: 위험에 빠진 / 그는 생명의 위험을 느꼈다. be interested in: ~에 흥미가 있다 / Jake는 체스에 흥미가 있다.

03 ① meaning: 의미 / 이 단어의 의미가 뭐죠? ② explain: 설명하다 / 먼저, 경기 규칙을 설명해 드리겠습니다. ③ waste: 낭비하다 / 왜 필요하지도 않은 옷에 돈을 낭비했니? ④ abroad: 해외에 / 나는 해외로 여행할 계획이다. ⑤ unknown: 알려지지 않은 / 그 소년은 무슨 알려지지 않은 이유 때문에 별들을 세느라 애를 쓰고 있었다.

04 신체 또는 마음의 고통을 느끼다: suffer(시달리다, 고통 받다)

05 It은 인칭대명사로 앞에 나온 a dol party를 받는다.

06 wish for: ~을 바라다

07 오랫동안 존재해 온 관습이나 믿음: tradition(전통)

08 ④ 몇 명의 가족이 돌잔치를 위해 모이는지는 대답할 수 없다.

09 there는 앞에 나온 장소의 부사구를 받는다.

10 it은 인칭대명사로 앞에 나온 단수명사를 받는다.

11 move의 명사형은 movement이다.

12 ③ 경복궁과 창덕궁 사이에 많은 한옥이 있는지는 위 글에서 알 수 없다.

13 '책을 읽는' 소녀이므로 현재분사로, '깨진 유리창'이므로 과거분사로 각각 수식하는 것이 적절하다.

14 때의 부사절에서는 현재시제를 사용하여 미래를 나타내며 ask와 tell은 목적격보어로 to부정사가 나온다.

15 ② '~라고 이름 지어진'이라는 의미이므로 과거분사로 수식한다.

16 ② ask의 목적격보어로 to부정사가 적절하다.

17 tell의 목적격보어로 to부정사가 적절하다.

18 (A) happen은 자동사이므로 수동태로 쓸 수 없다. (B) press는 목적격보어로 to부정사를 취한다. (C) 선행사를 포함하는 관계대명사가 알맞다.

19 '대가는 컸다'의 뜻으로 cost가 주어일 때는 형용사 high가 적절하다.

20 ③ 정세권은 일본식 집을 짓기를 원하지 않았다.

21 능동의 의미이므로 현재분사가 적절하다.

22 (A) 수동의 의미이므로 과거분사가 적절하다. (B) 능동의 의미이므로 현재분사가 적절하다.

23 위 글의 주제는 행복해 하는 Johnsy이므로 희망에 찬 분위기가 적절하다.

24 There is[are] ~ 구문은 have[has] 동사를 써서 바꿔 쓸 수 있다.

25 be popular with: ~에게 인기가 있다

26 문맥상 수동태가 적절하다.

27 주어진 문장은 음식 사업이 쇠퇴했다는 뜻이므로 사람들이 가게에 오지 않았다는 말 다음에 와야 한다.

28 문맥상 사람들이 가게에 거의 오지 않았다는 말이므로 Few가 적절하다.

서술형 실전문제
p.102~103

01 I don't know much about it and I'm interested in it. → I don't know much about it but I'm interested in it.

02 Yes, I know a little about Changdeokgung.

03 to Changdeokgung

04 explain

05 (1) to tell   (2) to study   (3) (to) push

06 (1) named   (2) talking

07 (1) not to be   (2) not to give

08 (1) This is the only book written by him.
   (2) The boy living in this house is Andy.
   (3) The teacher told us to gather at the gym.
   (4) Jiho asked Dohun to clean the window.

09 during

10 to not fish → not to fish

11 He was a fisherman.

12 storing

13 현대적인 옹기

01 나는 그것에 대해 많이 알지 못하며 그것에 흥미가 있다고 말하는 것은 어색하다.

02 a little: 조금

03 there는 앞에 나온 장소를 나타내는 부사구를 가리킨다.

---

04 Could you explain ~?은 설명을 요청하는 표현이다.

05 ask, encourage, help는 to부정사를 목적격보어로 취하는 동사이다. help는 동사원형을 쓸 수도 있다.

06 (1) '~라고 이름 지어진'이라는 의미이므로 과거분사로 수식한다. (2) 로봇이 말하는 주체가 되므로 현재분사로 수식한다.

07 ask와 encourage는 목적격보어로 to부정사를 쓰고 부정사의 부정은 not을 to ~ 앞에 붙인다.

08 (1) 과거분사 written은 명사 book 뒤에서 수식한다. (2) 현재분사 living은 명사 boy 뒤에서 수식한다. (3) tell의 목적격보어로 to부정사가 나온다. (4) ask의 목적격보어로 to부정사가 나온다.

09 '~ 중에, ~ 동안에'의 뜻으로 특정한 기간을 나타내는 명사가 올 때는 during을 쓴다.

10 to부정사의 부정은 to부정사 앞에 not을 붙인다.

11 안용복의 직업은 물고기를 잡는 것이라고 했다.

12 전치사의 목적어이므로 동명사형이 되어야 한다.

13 it은 인칭대명사로 앞에 언급된 a modern onggi를 가리킨다.

창의사고력 서술형 문제
p.104

|모범답안|

01 (1) Dad wants me to come home early.
   (2) My classmates asked me to be quiet in class.
   (3) She told him to fix the computer.
   (4) She didn't allow us to play the piano.
   (5) I advised her to go home early after the concert.
   (6) The teacher forced the students to attend the classes.
   (7) We persuaded him to come to Ann's birthday party.

02 (A) between
   (B) building
   (C) moving
   (D) taste
   (E) protect
   (F) independence
   (G) example
   (H) building

단원별 모의고사
p.105~108

01 ②   02 ⑤   03 ④

04 한 살 먹은 아기를 위한 생일 잔치

05 wears   06 ④   07 ③   08 ④

09 경복궁과 창덕궁 사이에 있는 땅에

10 You are also helping the independence movement in many ways.

01 hundreds of: 수백의, 수많은 / 허리케인 시즌만 되면 수백 명의 사람들이 목숨을 잃습니다. thanks to: ~ 덕분에 / 그녀의 발명 덕분에 많은 사람들이 좀 더 나은 생활을 하고 있다.

02 '살아 있는'의 뜻으로 living은 한정적 용법, alive는 서술적 용법으로 쓰인다. other는 뒤에 복수 명사가 오고, another는 단수 명사가 온다.

03 ④ stone: 돌

04 it은 앞 문장의 the birthday party for a one-year-old baby를 받는다.

05 옷, 신발, 장갑과 같은 것을 여러분의 신체 또는 신체의 부분에 걸치다: wear(입다, 신다, 쓰다)

06 ④ 돌잔치에 가족들이 어떤 음식을 먹는지는 알 수 없다.

07 (C) 만리장성에 대해 아는 것이 있냐고 묻는다. (A) 그렇다고 대답한다. (B) 그것이 유명한 이유를 다시 묻는다. (D) 세계에서 가장 긴 벽이기 때문이라고 대답한다.

08 일본인들이 경성에 와서 그들의 취향에 맞게 경성을 바꾼다는 문장 다음에 와야 한다.

09 there는 on the land between Gyeongbokgung and Changdeokgung을 가리킨다.

10 also는 보통 be동사와 일반동사 사이에 위치한다. 여러 방법으로: in many ways

11 ③ Jeong이 일본식 집을 짓는 법을 모르는지는 위 대화의 내용으로 보아 알 수 없다.

12 make는 사역동사로 동사원형을 목적격보어로 취한다. 나머지는 모두 to부정사를 목적격보어로 취하는 동사들로 to do가 들어가야 한다.

13 모두 '~을 사용하는'이라는 의미의 현재분사가 쓰이지만 ④번에는 과거분사 used가 쓰여 '중고차'라는 의미를 만든다.

14 cause, expect, ask, want, tell 모두 목적격보어로 to부정사가 나와야 한다. ceremony: 식, 의식

15 분사가 명사 뒤에서 명사를 꾸며줄 때, 분사 앞에는 '주격 관계대명사+be동사'가 생략되었다고 볼 수 있다.

16 충격을 느끼는 것이므로 과거분사로 주어를 설명하는 것이 적절하다.

17 빈칸에는 to부정사를 목적격보어로 취할 수 있는 동사가 들어가야 한다.

18 ⓐ, ② 경험 ①, ④ 계속 ③ 완료 ⑤ 결과

19 보기와 ③ ~으로 ① ~할 때 ② ~하는 대로, ~처럼 ④ ~이기 때문에 ⑤ ~함에 따라, ~할수록

20 문맥상 수동태가 되어야 한다.

21 문맥상 결과를 나타내는 접속사 so가 적절하다.

22 앞 문장과 대조되는 내용이 나오므로 상반을 나타내는 접속부사 however가 알맞다.

23 어떤 사람이 돈을 벌기 위해 하는 일: job(직업)

24 동사를 수식하므로 official의 부사형이 와야 한다.

25 ④ 안용복은 일본을 두 번 방문했다.

Lesson 9

Manners Make the Man

1 (1) make it / fine   (2) about going / problem
2 (1) Don't forget to   (2) Remember to   (3) Make sure
  to   (4) won't

시험대비 실력평가   p.112

01 tourist   02 ④   03 ④   04 ③
05 ⑤   06 ②
07 (1) bright   (2) freely   (3) concerto

---

01 도서관 : 사서 / 관광 : 관광객
02 increase: 증가하다
03 disturb: 방해하다(=interrupt)
04 누군가 또는 무언가가 어떤 나쁜 일에 책임이 있다고 생각하거
  나 말하다를 가리키는 단어는 'blame(비난하다)'이다.
05 <보기>와 ⑤는 '작품'이라는 의미로 쓰였고, 나머지는 '일, 직
  장'이라는 의미로 쓰였다.
06 be on time: 제시간에 오다 / take a look at: ~을 보다
07 (1) bright: 밝은 (2) freely: 자유롭게 (3) concerto: 협주곡

교과서 대화문 익히기

Check(√) True or False   p.116

1 F   2 T   3 T   4 F

서술형 시험대비   p.113

01 (1) artist   (2) scientist   (3) novelist   (4) tourist
02 clap
03 (1) blame   (2) audience   (3) serious   (4) mostly
04 (C)onsequently
05 (1) no longer   (2) dependent on   (3) at any time
06 (1) I need a small trash can.
   (2) Noise was just part of the concert.
   (3) Concerts in Mozart's time were mostly social
     events.

---

01 (1) artist: 예술가 (2) scientist: 과학자 (3) novelist: 소설가
  (4) tourist: 관광객
02 두 손뼉을 마주 치다: clap(박수치다)
03 (1) blame: 비난하다 (2) audience: 청중 (3) serious: 심각한
  (4) mostly: 주로
04 as a result: 그 결과(=consequently)
05 (1) no longer: 더 이상 ~ 않다 (2) dependent on: ~에 의
  존하는 (3) at any time: 아무 때나
06 (1) trash can: 쓰레기통 (2) part of: ~의 일부 (3) mostly:
  주로 / social: 사교적인

교과서 확인학습   p.118~119

Listen & Speak 1 B
1. interested in, tickets / When / this, at, make it /
   thanks, asking
2. Why don't, this / What about / make it, have to / See

Listen & Speak 2 B
1. going to, remember / Don't forget / won't / Sounds
2. look, secret / go swimming, sometime / sounds like,
   Any other / forget to, many kinds

Real-Life Zone A
listening to / going to, like to, before / guess, more, if /
clap, wrong / when, stops / may, pauses, wait, very
end / see, Make sure, forget to, real ending, way, make
it, practice, after, finishes, See

Real-Life Zone B
Why don't, after, make / can't, about / Don't forget /
right, won't

Wrap Up
Have, heard, that, will be, why don't, make it / what
time / at, Let's meet / forget to / won't

시험대비 기본평가   p.120

01 ④   02 (C) → (B) → (D) → (A)   03 ②

01 갈 수 있느냐고 묻는 표현이 와야 한다.

02 (C) 주말에 신발 가게에 가겠느냐고 묻는다. (B) 좋다고 말하면서, 토요일 2시에 가자고 제안한다. (D) 1시에 갈 수 있느냐고 묻는다. (A) 좋다고 대답한다.

03 'Don't forget to ~.'는 어떤 일을 잊지 말고 하라고 상기시키는 표현이다.

01 healthy
02 Are there any other things that[which] I should do?   03 ①   04 Remember 05 ⑤
06 ③, ④
07 ②   08 ①   09 ③   10 ④
11 I'll come to the practice after the concert finishes.
12 ②

01 health의 형용사형이 와야 한다. healthy: 건강한

02 앞에 Are there가 생략된 문장이다. things 다음에는 관계대명사 목적격 that이나 which가 생략되었다.

03 ① 소녀는 소년에게 건강해 보이는 비결을 묻고 있다.

04 Remember는 '기억하다'의 뜻이므로 Don't forget과 의미가 같다.

05 (C) 월요일에 도서관에 가자는 제안에, (D) 월요일 대신 화요일에 가자고 대답한다. (A) 좋다고 말하며 도서관 카드를 가져오라고 말하자, (B) 알겠다고 대답한다.

06 Can you make it at ~?은 약속 시간을 정할 때 쓰는 표현이다.

07 listen to: ~을 듣다

08 before: ~하기 전에 if: ~한다면

09 ⓑ와 ③의 may는 '~일지도 모르다'의 뜻으로 약한 추측을 나타낸다.

10 make it to: ~에 오다

11 때를 나타내는 부사절은 미래의 일을 나타낼 때 현재형을 쓴다.

12 ② 소년이 종종 잘못된 때에 박수를 치는지는 알 수 없다.

01 that   02 let's
03 Do you know what time the concert starts?
04 Don't forget to dress up.
05 They will meet at the bus stop at 4:00.
06 How → Why
07 Shall

01 heard의 목적어가 되는 명사절을 이끄는 접속사 that이 필요하다.

02 why don't we ~?는 제안을 나타내는 말로 let's ~로 바꾸어 쓸 수 있다.

03 간접의문문으로 바꾼다. 간접의문문은 '의문사+주어+동사'의 어순이 된다.

04 dress up: 옷을 차려 입다

06 Why don't we ~?: ~하는 게 어때?

07 How about ~?은 Shall we ~?나 Let's ~로 바꿔 쓸 수 있다.

[교과서]
Grammar

1 (1) when (2) where (3) why (4) how / the way
2 (1) what you bought
  (2) if[whether] you like
  (3) Who do you think will

01 ②
02 (1) when (2) where (3) when (4) why
03 ①
04 (1) where (2) when (3) why (4) how

01 간접의문문은 '의문사+주어+동사'의 형태로 다른 문장 안에서 목적어 역할을 한다.

02 (1) 선행사 the month는 때를 나타내므로 관계부사 when을 쓴다. (2) 선행사 the restaurant는 장소를 나타내므로 관계부사 where를 쓴다. (3) 선행사 the day는 때를 나타내므로 관계부사 when을 쓴다. (4) 선행사 the reason은 이유를 나타내므로 관계부사 why를 쓴다.

03 간접의문문의 어순은 '의문사+주어+동사'이며 의문사가 없는 경우는 'if[whether]+주어+동사'로 쓴다.

04 (1) 선행사가 장소이므로 관계부사 where (2) 선행사가 때이므로 관계부사 when (3) 선행사가 이유이므로 관계부사 why (4) 방법을 나타내므로 관계부사 how

01 ⑤   02 ①   03 ⑤

04 (1) where   (2) the way   (3) for which

05 (1) Do you know who that tall guy over there is?

  (2) Tell me who made this chocolate cake.

  (3) I wonder if[whether] Marianne got married.

  (4) Where do you think Snow White is?

06 ②   07 ⑤   08 ①

09 (1) I know who won the race.

  (2) Do you know when the bus will come?

  (3) The man is asking her how long it takes to get to TIG Market.

  (4) Who do you think will win the game?

  (5) What do you guess she wants to buy?

10 ①

11 (1) when does the show start → when the show starts

  (2) that does the bag have → if[whether] the bag has

  (3) Do you think who → Who do you think

12 ②, ④   13 ⑤

14 (1) I know how she solved the problem.

  (2) I know (the reason) why Jerry was angry.

  (3) This is the library where I often stop by on my way home.

15 ④   16 ④   17 ③, ⑤

18 (1) How long does it take to reach the top?

  (2) Was the thief a man or a woman?

  (3) What is the secret of his success?

01 간접의문문은 '의문사+주어+동사'의 어순이다. It으로 받고 있으므로 단수가 적절하다.

02 선행사가 때(the day)를 나타내므로 때의 관계부사 when 또는 '전치사+관계대명사'인 on which가 와야 하는데, on이 빈칸 앞에 있으므로 which가 적절하다.

03 간접의문문의 어순은 '의문사+주어+동사'의 형태임에 유의한다.

04 (1) 선행사가 장소이므로 관계부사로 where를 써야 한다. which를 쓰려면 staying 다음에 전치사 in[at]이 있어야 한다. (2) the way와 관계부사 how는 함께 쓸 수 없다. (3) 관계부사 why 대신에 for which를 쓸 수 있다.

05 간접의문문의 어순은 '의문사+주어+동사'이며 의문사가 없는 경우는 'if[whether]+주어+동사'로 쓴다. 의문사가 주어인 경우에는 의문사가 주어 역할을 동시에 하므로 직접의문문처럼 '의문사+동사'의 어순임에 유의해야 한다. think 동사가 주절에 있을 경우 간접의문문의 의문사를 문장 맨 앞에 써야 함에도 유의한다.

06 나머지는 모두 '언제'를 뜻하는 의문부사인 반면 ②는 관계부사이다.

07 의문사가 없는 간접의문문의 어순은 'if[whether]+주어+동사'이지만, if를 쓸 경우 or not을 바로 붙여 쓰지 않는다.

08 (1) 선행사가 이유이므로 관계부사로 why를 써야 한다. (2) the way와 관계부사 how는 함께 쓸 수 없다. how 대신 the way를 써도 좋다.

09 간접의문문의 어순은 '의문사+주어+동사'이며 의문사가 없는 경우는 'if[whether]+주어+동사'로 쓴다. think나 guess 동사가 주절에 있을 경우 간접의문문의 의문사를 문장 맨 앞으로 배치한다.

10 ①은 때를 나타내는 선행사를 취하는 관계부사 when을 쓰고 나머지는 모두 where를 쓴다.

11 (1) 간접의문문의 어순은 '의문사+주어+동사'이다. (2) 의문사가 필요 없는 자리이므로 'if[whether]+주어+동사'로 써야 한다. (3) think 동사가 주절에 있을 경우 간접의문문의 의문사를 문장 맨 앞에 써야 한다.

12 관계부사 where 대신 to which를 써도 좋다.

13 간접의문문의 어순은 '의문사+주어+동사'이다.

14 (1) how 대신 the way를 써도 좋다. (2) 선행사가 이유이므로 관계부사 why가 적절하다. (3) 선행사가 장소이므로 관계부사 where가 적절하다.

15 주어진 문장과 ④에서 when은 관계부사로 쓰였고, 나머지는 모두 접속사로 쓰였다.

16 올바른 문장은 This is the house where I live with my parents.이다.

17 선행사가 계절이므로 관계부사 when 대신 in which를 써도 좋다.

18 간접의문문의 어순은 '의문사+주어+동사'이며 의문사가 없는 경우는 'if[whether]+주어+동사'로 쓴다. (3)에서 believe 동사가 주절에 있을 경우 간접의문문의 의문사를 문장 맨 앞으로 배치한다.

01 (1) Tell me what you want for Christmas.

  (2) She asks me how much sugar there is in the bottle.

  (3) Do you know where Greece is on the map?

  (4) I wonder if[whether] he is a singer.

  (5) I have no idea if[whether] he will join us soon.

  (6) Where do you think your soul goes after you die?

02 (1) This is the house where[in which] I was born.

(2) December 25th is the day when[on which] Christmas is celebrated.

(3) There is a small bed where[on which] I always sleep.

(4) This is the way[how] I solved the problem.

03 (1) I ate　(2) she left　(3) he is　(4) if

04 (1) why　(2) which[that]　(3) the way 또는 how
(4) when

05 (1) The doctor will ask you what you ate for breakfast.

(2) Please let us know if[whether] you are able to attend the meeting.

(3) What do you suppose they are thinking?

06 (1) where　(2) why　(3) when

07 (1) Daniel told us how he became a singer.

(2) It is doubtful whether he will come or not.

08 (1) Do you remember the day when you first saw your little sister?

(2) A park is a place where people take a walk.

(3) Mariel wants to know whether he is going to meet Asako.

09 (1) Nobody knows. Why did Lauren leave the office early?

(2) It is difficult to understand. What does the teacher say?

(3) Steve didn't tell me. When did the movie begin?

(4) Do you think? What is the most typical Korean dish?

(5) They wonder. Can they borrow some books today?

01 간접의문문의 어순은 '의문사+주어+동사'이며 의문사가 없는 경우는 'if[whether]+주어+동사'로 쓴다. think 동사가 주절에 있을 경우 간접의문문의 의문사를 문장 맨 앞으로 배치한다.

02 (1) the house를 수식하는 관계부사는 where를 쓴다. '전치사+관계대명사'로 바꿔 써도 좋다. (2) the day를 수식하는 관계부사는 when을 쓴다. (3) a small bed를 수식하는 관계부사는 where를 쓴다. (4) the way how는 쓸 수 없다. the way나 how를 별개로 써야 한다.

03 (1), (2), (3) 간접의문문의 어순은 '의문사+주어+동사'이다. (4) I konw 뒤에는 that절, know 뒤에는 if[whether]절이 온다.

04 (1) 선행사가 이유를 나타내는 말이므로 why를 써야 한다. (2) 관계사절에 전치사 in이 쓰였으므로 where를 which[that]로 써야 한다. (3) the way와 how를 같이 쓸 수 없으므로 the way 또는 how만을 써야 한다. (4) 선행사가 때를 나타내는 말

이므로 when을 써야 한다.

05 (1), (2), (3) 간접의문문의 어순은 '의문사+주어+동사'이며 의문사가 없는 경우는 'if[whether]+주어+동사'로 쓴다. suppose 동사가 주절에 있을 경우 간접의문문의 의문사를 문장 맨 앞으로 배치한다.

06 (1) 선행사가 장소이므로 where를 쓴다. (2) 선행사가 이유이므로 why를 쓴다. (3) 선행사가 때이므로 when을 쓴다.

08 (1) when은 선행사 the day 뒤에 쓰여 수식한다. (2) 관계부사 where는 장소를 나타내는 선행사 a place를 수식한다. (3) whether가 이끄는 명사절이 know의 목적어가 된다.

09 간접의문문의 어순은 '의문사+주어+동사'이며 의문사가 없는 경우는 'if[whether]+주어+동사'로 쓴다. think 동사가 주절에 있을 경우 간접의문문의 의문사를 문장 맨 앞으로 배치한다.

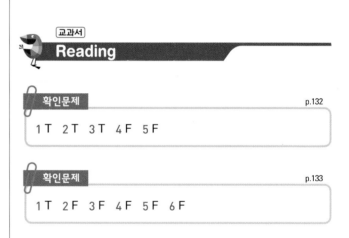

교과서 Reading

확인문제　　　　　　　　p.132

1 T　2 T　3 T　4 F　5 F

확인문제　　　　　　　　p.133

1 T　2 F　3 F　4 F　5 F　6 F

교과서 확인학습 A　　　p.134~135

01 Classical, Manners

02 Imagine yourself, classical

03 orchestra, play one, piano

04 hall, dark, silent

05 Nobody, sound

06 Everybody, serious

07 audiences, clap, finishes

08 familiar scene at

09 go back, time, take, look

10 bright, inside, nobleman's

11 playing, piano

12 Surprisingly, audiences, talking freely

13 whistle, clap

14 shocked, bad, himself, surprised, quiet

15 were mostly social

16 good places to meet

17 just part

18 quiet, century when, were built

19 not just noblemen

20 no longer dependent

21 more power, use, increased

22 For example, blamed, for

23 After, rule appeared

24 As a result, quiet

25 what concerts, look like, because, change

26 however, enjoy classical, just remember

27 Enjoy, disturb those

23 After some time, a no-clapping-between-movements rule appeared.

24 As a result, here we are today, very quiet and serious.

25 We do not know what concerts will look like in the future because manners change with time.

26 For now, however, if you want to enjoy classical music concerts, just remember this:

27 Enjoy the music, but do not disturb those around you.

교과서 확인학습 B
p.136~137

1 The History of Classical Concert Manners

2 Imagine yourself at a classical music concert.

3 The orchestra starts to play one of Mozart's piano concertos.

4 The concert hall is dark and silent.

5 Nobody makes a sound.

6 Everybody looks serious.

7 The audiences only clap after the concerto finishes.

8 This is a familiar scene at concerts today.

9 Let's go back in time and take a look at one of Mozart's concerts in the 18th century.

10 You are in a bright hall inside a nobleman's house.

11 Mozart is playing the piano.

12 Surprisingly, however, the audiences are eating, drinking, and talking freely.

13 They whistle and clap at any time.

14 You are shocked by their bad manners, but Mozart himself would be surprised by today's quiet audiences.

15 Concerts in Mozart's time were mostly social events.

16 They were good places to meet people.

17 Noise was just part of the concert.

18 Today's quiet concerts began in the 19th century when many big concert halls were built.

19 More people, not just noblemen, went to concerts.

20 Artists were no longer dependent on noblemen for money.

21 The artists had more power over their works and started to use their increased power.

22 For example, Wagner blamed the audience for making noise.

시험대비 실력평가
p.138~141

01 ①, ④, ⑤

02 The concert hall is dark and silent. Nobody makes a sound. Everybody looks serious. The audiences only clap after the concerto finishes.

03 ①   04 ③

05 today's quiet audiences 06 ②, ⑤

07 in which   08 ②   09 ①, ②, ④

10 (A) what   (B) manners   (C) those

11 ①   12 ②   13 ①, ②, ⑤

14 concerto → concertos   15 ⑤   16 ④

17 ①, ④   18 ④   19 ④

20 built → were built   21 ①

22 ④   23 ②

01 ⓐ와 ①, ④, ⑤번: 명사적 용법, ② 부사적 용법, ③번: 형용사적 용법

02 'This가 가리키는 것은 오늘날의 연주회 장면이다.

03 오늘날의 연주회장은 어둡고 조용하다.

04 ⓐ take a look at ~을 보다, ⓒ be surprised by[at] ~에 놀라다

05 모차르트는 오늘날의 조용한 관객에 의해서 놀라게 될 것이다.

06 ⓑ와 ①, ③, ④번: 진행 시제를 나타내는 현재분사, ②, ⑤: 동명사

07 관계부사 when = 전치사+which

08 이 글은 오늘날의 조용한 콘서트가 어떻게 시작되었는지 그 유래를 설명하고 있다.

09 ① 19세기에 큰 연주회장이 많이 지어졌다. ② 예술가들이 돈에 대하여 귀족에게서 독립했다. ④ 바그너는 소음을 내는 청중을 싫어했다. (③ 그들의 작품이 더 우수했는지는 알 수 없다.) ⑤ 악장사이 박수 안 치는 규칙을 누가 만들었는지는 알 수 없다.

10 (A) look like의 목적어가 되는 의문대명사 what이 적절하다. (B) "예의범절"이라는 뜻은 manners이다. manner는 "방법"

이라는 뜻이다. (C) "~하는 사람들"이라는 뜻은 복수를 나타내어 those를 쓴다.

11 연주회장에서의 예의범절이 현재는 과거와 달라졌고 미래에는 어떻게 변할지 알 수 없지만, 그것과 상관없이 현재의 바람직한 관람 태도를 나타내는 대조의 표현이 적절하다.

12 연주회장에서 지켜야 하는 것은 주변 사람들에게 피해를 주지 않는 것이기 때문에 "주변의"를 가리키는 around가 적절하다.

13 ⓐ와 ③, ④: 재귀 용법, ①, ②, ⑤번: 강조 용법

14 "~ 중에서 하나"라는 뜻일 때는 "one of the/소유격+복수명사"의 형태를 가지기 때문에 concerto를 concertos로 바꾸어야 한다.

15 ⑤ 왜 오케스트라가 모차르트의 피아노 콘체르토를 연주했는지는 이 글에서 소개되지 않았다.

16 ④ 이 글은 오늘날과 다르게 Mozart 시대의 콘서트가 어떠했는지를 보여준다. 따라서 글의 주제는 "Mozart 시대의 콘서트는 어떠했는가?"이다.

17 ⓐ와 ②, ③, ⑤번: 형용사적 용법, ① 명사적 용법, ④ 부사적 용법

18 ④ 그 당시의 연주회에서는 관객이 아무 때나 박수치고, 휘파람을 불었다.

19 ④: "A를 ~ 때문에 비난하다"는 의미일 때는 "blame A for ~"라고 한다.

20 부사절의 주어 many big concert halls는 짓는 입장이 아니라 지어지는 위치에 있기 때문에 수동태가 되어서 "were builit"가 되어야 한다.

21 오늘날의 조용한 콘서트는 19세기에 시작되었다.

22 "~처럼 보이다"는 "look like"이다. look after 돌보다, look into 조사하다, look at 보다, look out 밖을 내다보다

23 (A) 오늘날의 연주회는 조용하므로 quiet (B) 문장을 연결할 때는 접속사가 있어야 한다. because of는 뒤에 명사(구)가 온다. (C) 연주회에서는 남에게 방해가 되지 않아야 하므로 disturb

🦉 서술형 시험대비   p.142~143

01 번호: ⑤   틀린 것: look   올바른 형태: looks

02 audience

03 콘서트장은 어둡고 조용하다. 아무도 소리를 내지 않는다. 모두가 진지해 보인다. 청중은 오직 협주곡이 끝난 후에만 손뼉을 친다.

04 take

05 nobleman

06 freely

07 noise

08 weren't

09 (A) be built   (B) power

10 what

11 ⓐ because   ⓑ those

12 음악은 즐기되 주변의 다른 사람들을 방해하지 마라.

13 Nobody

14 Everybody[Everyone] looks serious.

15 (A) dark   (B) silent   (C) clap

01 ⑤ 주어 Everybody는 단수 취급하기 때문에 단수 동사 looks가 되어야 한다.

02 "공공장소에서 하는 연설이나 공연을 보고, 듣는 사람의 무리"는 "관객, 청중"을 나타낸다.

03 This는 보통 앞 문장을 가리키지만 여기서는 앞에 주어진 콘서트 장소에 대한 설명 전체를 가리킨다.

04 접속사 and로 연결되는 병렬 구조에서 동사원형 go와 같은 형태인 take가 되어야 한다.

05 "사회적으로 높은 계층에 있으며 공작 등과 같은 호칭을 가지는 사람"은 "귀족"이다.

06 동사 eat, drink, talk를 수식하는 단어는 부사가 되어야 한다.

07 바그너는 소음을 내는 것 때문에 관객을 비난했다.

08 "더 이상 ~하지 않는"에 해당하는 의미의 "no longer"는 "not ~ any longer"로 바꾸어 쓸 수 있다.

09 19세기에는 많은 대규모 공연장이 건설되고, 예술가들은 자신의 작품에 대해 더 많은 권력을 가지게 되었다.

10 전치사 like의 목적어 역할을 하는 의문대명사 what이 적절하다.

11 ⓐ 절과 절을 연결하는 접속사 because가 적절하다. ⓑ "~하는 사람들"이라는 의미로 지시대명사 those가 적절하다.

12 주어진 문장에서 this가 가리키는 것은 뒤에 이어지는 문장을 가리킨다.

13 콘서트장은 조용하기 때문에 "누구도 소음을 내지 않는다."고 해야 한다.

14 "~해 보이다"에 해당하는 동사는 look이다.

15 오늘날의 연주회장은 어둡고 조용하며, 관객은 협주곡이 끝난 후에만 박수를 친다.

🦉 영역별 핵심문제   p.145~149

01 unfamiliar   **02** ⑤   **03** ④

04 (1) at any time   (2) for now   (3) As a result

05 ⑤   **06** (D) → (A) → (C) → (B)   **07** ②

08 ①   **09** Actually   **10** remember   **11** ⑤

12 ③

13 (1) why   (2) which   (3) where   (4) which   (5) how

14 ④   **15** I know the reason why Jane is

crying.　16 ③

17 This is the house where Shakespeare was born.
/ This is the house in which Shakespeare was born.

18 (1) what it is　(2) where it is

19 (1) 해석: 이곳은 내가 어렸을 때 방문하고 했던 공원이다.
(2) 해석: 이곳은 내가 어렸을 때 가곤 했던 공원이다.
(3) 어법상 차이: (1) which는 관계대명사이다. (2) where는 관계부사이다.

20 (A) yourself　(B) concertos　(C) finishes

| 21 ④ | 22 ③ | 23 ④ | 24 ②, ⑤ |
| 25 ③ | 26 ② | 27 ④ | 28 ③ |

29 (A) what　(B) because　(C) remember

01 주어진 단어의 관계는 반의어 관계이다. appear (나타나다) : disappear (사라지다) = familiar (친숙한) : unfamiliar (친숙하지 않은)

02 어떤 것을 원래 있던 곳이나 가야 할 곳으로 가져가다를 나타내는 말은 return(돌려주다, 반납하다)이다.

03 dependent: 의존적인

04 (1) at any time: 아무 때나 (2) for now: 지금은 (3) as a result: 그 결과

05 How about ~ing?: ~하는 것은 어때?

06 (D) 오페라에 관심 있느냐고 질문 → (A) 그렇다고 대답하며 오페라가 언제 있느냐고 질문 → (C) 토요일이라고 대답하며 갈 수 있느냐고 질문 → (B) 갈 수 있다고 대답

07 ⓑ bringing → to bring (미래의 일은 'forget+to부정사'의 형을 쓴다.)

08 글의 흐름상 조건을 나타내는 접속사 if가 알맞다.

09 actual의 부사형이 와야 한다.

10 not forget은 remember와 같은 뜻이다.

11 ⑤ 소년은 콘서트가 끝난 후에 연습하러 갈 것이라고 말했다.

12 간접의문문의 어순은 '의문사+주어+동사'의 형태임에 유의한다.

13 (1) 선행사가 이유이므로 why를 쓴다. (2) 선행사가 the date(날짜)이므로 관계부사 when이나 '전치사+관계대명사'인 on which가 와야 한다. 전치사 on이 있기 때문에 which를 써야 한다. (3) 선행사가 장소이므로 where를 쓴다. (4) 선행사 the day가 spent의 목적어이므로 관계대명사 which를 쓴다. (5) the way나 how를 써야 한다.

14 의문사가 없는 간접의문문의 어순은 'if[whether]+주어+동사'이며 if는 or not과 붙여 쓰지 않는다.

15 이유를 나타내는 관계부사와 선행사의 위치에 주의한다.

16 ⓐ why he came here ⓒ 의문사가 없으므로 if he will

come ⓔ 주절의 동사가 think이므로 Where do you think Ann spent her spring vacation?

17 the house를 수식하는 관계부사 where나 '전치사+대명사'인 in which를 쓴다.

18 간접의문문의 어순은 '의문사+주어+동사'이며 (1)에는 무엇인지를 묻는 표현이, (2)에는 장소를 묻는 표현이 들어가는 것이 적절하다.

19 (1)은 선행사 the park이 visit의 목적어이므로 관계대명사 which가 와야 한다. (2)는 go to the park의 관계이므로 관계부사 where가 와야 한다.

20 (A) 명령문은 주어 You가 생략된 것이기 때문에 목적어는 재귀대명사 yourself가 되어야 한다. (B) "one of the 복수명사"가 되어야 하기 때문에 concertos가 되어야 한다. (C) 시간의 부사절에서는 미래 대신 현재를 쓴다.

21 ⓐ와 ④번: 부정사의 명사적 용법 ①, ②, ③, ⑤ 부정사의 부사적 용법

22 본문에는 관객이 박수를 치는 이유에 대하여서는 언급이 없다.

23 (A) "시간상으로, 시간에서"의 의미로 "in time", (B) "~에 의해서"의 의미로 행위자를 나타낼 때는 by

24 ⓐ와 ②, ⑤: 현재분사, ①, ③, ④: 동명사

25 모차르트 시대에는 연주회장에서 아무 때나 박수를 치고 휘파람을 불었다.

26 관계부사는 "전치사+which"로 바꾸어 쓸 수 있다. the 19th century를 선행사로 하는 관계부사 when은 in which로 바꾸어 쓸 수 있다.

27 이 글은 19세기에 예술가들에 대한 권한이 증가하면서 조용한 연주회가 시작된 과정을 소개하고 있다.

28 예절이 변하기 때문에 미래의 연주회가 어떠할 지는 알 수 없다.

29 (A) look like의 목적어가 될 수 있는 의문대명사 what이 적절하다. (B) 내용상 이유를 나타내는 접속사 because가 적절하다. (C) 음악을 즐기기 위해서 지켜야 할 예의범절은 "기억하라"고 해야 한다.

단원별 예상문제　p.150~153

01 ②	02 ④	03 concerto	04 ③
05 ②	06 on	07 ④	
08 about meeting		09 ③	10 ⑤
11 ③	12 ⑤	13 ③	14 ④
15 ③	16 ③	17 ②	

18 shocked　19 social

20 (A) bright　(B) whistled　(C) clapped

21 (A) quiet　(B) just　(C) increased

22 ④　　23 ③

24 We do not know what concerts will look like in

01 blame: 비난하다

02 take a look at: ～을 보다

03 오케스트라와 연주하는 하나 이상의 독주 악기를 위한 음악: concerto(협주곡)

04 with time: 시간이 지남에 따라 / by the way: 그건 그렇고

05 ① century: 세기 / 우리는 21세기에 살고 있다. ② movement: 움직임 / 그는 움직임이 느리다. ③ classical: 클래식의 / 그녀는 클래식 공연에 갔다. ④ volunteer: 자원봉사하다 / 그들은 어린이 센터에서 자원봉사를 한다. ⑤ social: 사교적인 / 새로운 친구를 사귀기 위해 사교 모임에 가입하라.

06 be on the stage: 무대에 서다

07 크리스마스에 갈 수 있느냐고 묻고 있으므로 make it이 알맞다.

08 Let's ～는 How about ~ing?로 바꿔 쓸 수 있다.

09 ③ 소녀는 소년에게 콘서트에 가자고 제안했다.

10 기다렸다가 맨 마지막에 박수를 쳐야 한다는 뜻이므로 클래식 음악에서는 한 곡에 여러 번 멈춤이 있다는 말 다음에 와야 한다.

11 글의 흐름상 콘서트에 가기 전에 클래식 음악에 대해 알고 싶다는 말이 알맞다.

12 '그런데'의 뜻으로 화제를 바꿀 때 쓰는 by the way가 알맞다.

13 ③ 소년이 종종 콘서트에 가는지는 알 수 없다.

14 의문사가 없는 간접의문문은 'if[whether]+주어+동사'로 쓴다.

15 선행사 the town 뒤에 관계부사 where를 쓴다.

16 I wonder 다음에는 if나 whether로 시작하는 간접의문문이 온다.

17 ②번은 조건절에 쓰인 if이지만 나머지는 모두 간접의문문을 이끌고 있다.

18 shock은 "충격을 주다"의 의미로 그 당시의 방식에 주어가 놀라게 되는 수동의 입장이기 때문에 과거분사가 되어야 한다.

19 이어지는 문장에서 사람들을 만나기에 좋은 장소라고 하는 것으로 보아 "사교적인"에 해당하는 social이 적절하다.

20 Mozart 시대의 연주회장은 밝고, 소음이 많았으며 아무 때나 휘파람을 불고 박수를 쳤다.

21 (A) 오늘날의 공연장의 분위기를 나타내는 것은 quiet이다. (B) "～뿐만 아니라"의 뜻으로는 "not just"가 적절하다. (C) "증가된"의 의미로 수동의 의미를 포함하는 것은 과거분사 increased이다.

22 ⓐ와 ④번: 관계부사 ①, ②: 접속사, ③, ⑤: 의문부사(간접의문)

23 ③ 얼마나 많은 예술가들이 귀족에게 의존했는지에 대한 언급은 없다.

24 what으로 시작하는 부분은 간접의문문으로 간접의문문은 "의문사+주어+동사"의 어순이다.

25 앞뒤의 내용이 대조적이기 때문에 however가 적절하다.

26 동사 want의 목적어는 to부정사이다.

27 those around you= people who are around you

서술형 실전문제

01 Sure, I can. → Sorry, but I can't.

02 swimming

03 Any other things I should do?

04 to eat

05 (1) I'll tell you where he has been since last Monday.
(2) I'd like to know if[whether] you met her.
(3) Where do you think I can find some fruit?

06 when

07 Could you tell me when the next train comes?

08 where

09 (1) Do you know if[whether] Anna loves me?
(2) I don't know why Kate was so surprised.
(3) Cathy will tell me who broke the window yesterday.
(4) Which book can you imagine Jennifer bought?

10 yourself

11 ⑤ The audiences only clap after the concerto will finish. → The audiences only clap after the concerto finishes.

12 clap

13 to

14 bad

15 Concerts in Mozart's time were good places to meet people.

01 월요일에 도서관에 가자는 제안에 화요일이 어떠냐고 묻고 있으므로 Sure, I can.은 어색하다.

02 go swimming: 수영하러 가다

03 문장 앞에 Are there와 관계대명사 목적격 that이나 which가 생략되었다.

04 문맥상 미래의 일을 나타내는 to부정사가 와야 한다.

05 간접의문문의 어순은 '의문사+주어+동사'이며 의문사가 없는 경우는 'if[whether]+주어+동사'로 쓴다. think 동사가 주절에 있을 경우 간접의문문의 의문사를 문장 맨 앞으로 배치한다.

06 선행사가 때를 나타내므로 관계부사 when을 쓴다.

07 간접의문문의 어순은 '의문사+주어+동사'이다.

08 선행사가 장소를 나타내므로 장소의 관계부사 where를 써야 한다.

09 간접의문문의 어순은 '의문사+주어+동사'이며 의문사가 없는 경우는 'if[whether]+주어+동사'로 쓴다. 의문사가 주어인 경우에는 직접의문문처럼 '의문사+동사'의 어순임에 유의해야 하며 imagine 동사가 주절에 있을 경우 간접의문문의 의문사를 문장 맨 앞에 써야 함에도 유의한다.

10 "자신이 ~한 상황에 있다는 것을 상상해 보라"는 의미로 목적어는 자신을 가리키는 재귀 대명사가 적절하다.

11 시간이나 조건의 부사절에서는 미래의 의미에 해당하는 경우에도 현재시제를 사용한다.

12 클래식 연주회에서 협주곡이 끝나면 위 글에 따르면 청중이 하는 일은 박수를 치는 것이다.

13 and 이하를 목적을 나타내는 to부정사의 부사적 용법으로 바꾸어 쓸 수 있다.

14 Mozart 시대의 콘서트를 감상하는 방식은 오늘날의 관점에서 보았을 때는 "나쁜 예의 범절"에 해당할 수 있다.

15 모차르트 시대의 연주회 = concerts in Mozart's time, 사람들을 만나기 좋은 장소 = good places to meet people

🐰 창의사고력 서술형 문제 p.156

|모범답안|

01 (1) Tell me whom you will vote for?

(2) Did you ask Ann why she was absent?

(3) Do you know who fixed the computer?

(4) I wonder if Max can play the piano.

(5) I don't know when he went to the concert.

(6) Can you tell me which flower he likes better?

(7) Which do you think she chose?

02 (A) if[whether]

(B) that

(C) going

(D) meet

(E) not

(F) to

💿 단원별 모의고사 p.157~160

01 independent 02 ③ 03 ⑤

04 (1) By the way (2) a look at (3) dependent on

---

05 ③ 06 ② 07 ① 08 ①

09 ① 10 That sounds like fun.

11 ④ 12 ④ 13 ②

14 (1) The girl is asking where the nearest bus stop is.

(2) Do you know if[whether] the leaves will turn yellow in autumn?

(3) Will you tell me when you met her?

15 ③

16 (1) I remember where the girl lived.

(2) Anna asked me if[whether] I loved Angelina.

17 in which 18 (A) independent (B) appeared

19 were built, went

20 번호: ① 틀린 것: which 올바른 형태: when

21 ④ 22 ④ 23 ②, ⑤

24 (A) Surprisingly (B) himself (C) mostly

25 ④ 26 ③

01 두 단어는 반의어 관계이다. dark (어두운) : bright (밝은) / dependent (의존적인) : independent (독립적인)

02 work: 직장, 작품

03 일을 하거나 잠을 자려고 할 때 누군가를 방해하다: interrupt (방해하다)

04 (1) by the way: 그건 그렇고 (2) take a look at: ~을 보다 (3) dependent on: ~에 의존하는

05 갈 수 있느냐고 묻는 말이므로 크리스마스에 가자고 제안하는 말 다음에 와야 한다.

06 Why don't we ~?: ~하는 게 어때?

07 dress up: 옷을 차려 입다

08 ① 그 소녀가 언제 콘서트에 대해 들었는지는 알 수 없다.

09 문맥상 소년이 건강해 보이는 비결을 묻는 말이므로 You look healthy. 다음에 와야 한다.

10 fun은 명사이므로 like와 함께 쓰여야 한다.

11 forget+동명사: ~한 것을 잊다 / forget+to부정사: ~할 것을 잊다

12 B가 동의하고 5시에 만나자고 말했으므로 약속 시간을 정하는 표현인 ④가 알맞다.

13 선행사가 장소인 관계부사는 where, 때인 관계부사는 when이다.

14 (1), (2), (3) 간접의문문의 어순은 '의문사+주어+동사'이며, 의문사가 없는 경우는 'if[whether]+주어+동사'로 쓴다.

15 ③은 '~할 때'를 뜻하는 접속사인 반면에 나머지는 모두 관계부사이다.

16 (1), (2) 간접의문문의 어순은 '의문사+주어+동사'이며 의문사가 없는 경우는 'if[whether]+주어+동사'로 쓴다.

17 the way how는 쓸 수 없지만, how를 in which로 바꿔 쓸 수 있다.

18 19세기에 많은 사람들이 공연장을 찾게 되면서 예술가들이 귀족으로부터 독립적이 되고 작품 중간에 박수를 치지 않는 규칙이 생겨났다.

19 19세기에 큰 연주회장이 지어지고, 많은 사람들이 연주회장에 가게 되면서 예술가들이 귀족에게 의존하지 않을 수 있게 되었다.

20 ① the 19th century를 선행사로 하는 관계부사 when이 들어가야 한다.

21 ⓐ와 ④번: 간접의문문, ①, ②: 관계대명사절 ③: 관계부사절, ⑤ 접속사절

22 (A) 시간이 흐름에 따라 = with time, (B) 너의 주변에 = around you

23 ⓑ와 ②, ⑤: 부사절을 유도하는 접속사 if, ①, ③, ④: 간접의문문을 유도하는 접속사 if

24 (A) 문장 전체를 수식하는 부사 Surprisingly가 적절하다. (B) 강조 용법의 재귀대명사를 쓸 수 있는 위치이다. (C) "주로"의 의미로 부사 mostly가 적절하다.

25 (D)와 ④번: 부정사의 형용사적 용법, ①, ⑤번: 부정사의 명사적 용법, ②, ③: 부정사의 부사적 용법

26 위 글에서 18세기 연주회는 오늘날과 달랐다는 것을 알 수 있지만, 얼마나 많은 연주회장을 지었는지는 알 수 없다.

교과서 파헤치기

단어 TEST Step 1   p.40

01 선택하다	02 똑똑한	03 순간 이동하다
04 불타다	05 번역하다	06 동영상의, 생기 있는
07 쉽게	08 감지하다	09 얼리다
10 불가능한	11 즐거움, 오락	12 예측하다
13 ~ 없이	14 기계	15 가능한
16 건너다	17 위험	18 의미하다
19 할인되어	20 완벽한	21 ~을 통해, ~ 사이로
22 이상한	23 대체하다	24 이기다
25 확인하다, 점검하다		26 상황
27 옷장	28 공간	29 기회
30 사전	31 번역가	32 믿기 어려운, 놀랄만한
33 행운의	34 구름의, 흐린	35 단지 ~뿐이 아니다
36 ~할 필요가 없다	37 위험에 처한, 위험에 빠진	
38 더 이상 ~하지 않다	39 ~에 근거하여	40 ~의 염려가 없는
41 그런데, 그건 그렇고	42 ~할 수 있다	43 속도를 늦추다

단어 TEST Step 2   p.41

01 animated	02 chance	03 cloudy
04 possible	05 lucky	06 translator
07 machine	08 cross	09 danger
10 amusement	11 easily	12 select
13 text	14 sense	15 mean
16 freeze	17 without	18 predict
19 impossible	20 teleport	21 burn
22 translate	23 dictionary	24 off
25 closet	26 perfect	27 replace
28 intelligent	29 through	30 situation
31 strange	32 unbelievable	33 check
34 space	35 by the way	36 in danger
37 no longer	38 be able to 동사원형	
39 based on	40 slow down	41 watch out
42 free from	43 look ~ up	

단어 TEST Step 3   p.42

1 replace, 대체하다   2 beat, 이기다
3 perfect, 완벽한   4 burn, 불타다   5 possible, 가능한
6 sense, 감지하다   7 translate, 번역하다
8 cross, 건너다   9 lucky, 행운의   10 predict, 예측하다
11 select, 선택하다   12 closet, 옷장

13 cloudy, 구름의, 흐린   14 amusement, 즐거움, 오락
15 beatbox, 비트박스를 하다   16 dictionary, 사전

대화문 TEST Step 1   p.43~44

Listen & Speak 1 A

Why don't we try, prefer

Listen & Speak 1 B

1 have any, for, project / What about / thinking, talk about future, What, think / sounds perfect, Let's look for, on the Internet
2 begins, Why don't, with / to, sounds exciting / chance to meet robotics / great

Listen & Speak 1 C

1 going to fly, drone / like fun
2 going, build / sounds like fun

Listen & Speak 2 A

it possible, to live without / not possible

Listen & Speak 2 B

1 looks, How much, it / the newest / Is it possible to use / Let, check, get, off / Perfect, take
2 took, pictures during / did, more than / it possible to make, animated, out of / possible, have an app

Listen & Speak 2 C

1 Is it possible, to text with, closed / Sure, can do
2 possible for you, travel around, by / Sure, can do that

Real-Life Zone A

Look at / What, they mean, Let's look them up, dictionary / about using, translator / How, use / point, ask, to translate, get an answer / possible for AI to read / read, translate / sounds unvelievable, what, mean / mean, come true / amazing

대화문 TEST Step 2   p.45~46

Listen & Speak 1 A

B: Why don't we try a new VR game?
G: That sounds interesting.

Listen & Speak 1 B

1 B: Do you have any ideas for our group project?
   G: No. What about you?
   B: I'm thinking we should talk about future jobs. What do you think?
   G: That sounds perfect for our project. Let's look for some information on the Internet.

2 G: The Robot Expo begins next week. Why don't you go with me?

B: Yes, I'd love to. That sounds exciting.

G: We'll have a chance to meet robotics engineers.

B: That'll be great.

Listen & Speak 1 C

1 A: I'm going to fly a drone.

B: That sounds like fun.

2 A: I'm going to build a model car.

B: That sounds like fun.

Listen & Speak 2 A

G: Is it possible for you to live without your smartphone?

B: No, it's not possible.

Listen & Speak 2 B

1 G: This computer looks nice. How much is it?

M: It's 500 dollars. It's the newest one.

G: Is it possible to use this coupon?

M: Let me check. Yes, you can. So, you'll get 30 dollars off.

G: Perfect. I'll take it.

2 B: We took lots of pictures during our trip.

G: We sure did. We have more than 500 pictures.

B: Is it possible to make an animated photo album out of them?

G: Yes, it's possible. I have an app for that.

Listen & Speak 2 C

1 A: Is it possible for you to text with your eyes closed?

B: Sure. I can do that.

2 A: Is it possible for you to travel around Gangwondo by bicycle?

B: Sure. I can do that.

Real-Life Zone A

G: Look at those words on the board.

B: What do they mean? Let's look them up in the dictionary.

G: What about using the AI translator?

B: How do I use it?

G: You point your smartphone camera at the words and ask AI to translate. You will get an answer.

B: Is it possible for AI to read those words?

Speaker: Sure. I can read any language and translate it.

B: Wow, that sounds unbelievable. So, AI, what do those words mean?

Speaker: They mean "Dreams come true!"

B: That's amazing.

01 Day at, AI   02 at, World, Expo

03 entering, AI home   04 Look at, future

05 go into, there's, closet

06 front, closet, keep changing

07 suggests, suit, weather

08 no longer, worry, dressing

09 move on to   10 this music speaker

11 not just, speaker

12 more than, imagine

13 hard, believe, understand

14 How about watching   15 play one

16 smart, getting darker

17 feel like, theater   18 What else, do

19 beatbox, too, Here comes

20 funny, Good job

21 Hurry, There's, outside   22 Let's, ride in

23 so cool, get in   24 ready to go

25 what should, do   26 time, ride in

27 need to, anything   28 drive, take, to

29 out, see, crossing

30 worry, have, sensed

31 sense dangerous, slow down   32 How can, that

33 intelligent robotic

34 all about driving

35 predict, based on, experience   36 How, act like

37 are, like, human

01 at, AI Expo   02 at the World AI Expo

03 are entering, AI home   04 on the future

05 go into, smart closet

06 front, on the closet door, keep changing

07 suggests, that suit the weather

08 no longer, dressing for the weather

09 Let's move on to

10 this music speaker

11 I'm not just

12 more than, can imagine

13 It's hard to believe, can understand

14 How about watching   15 play one for

16 getting darker

17 feel like, movie theater   18 What else

19 can, too, Here comes

20 funny, Good job

21 Hurry, There's, outside

22 Let's go, ride in   23 so cool, get in

24 Are, ready to go   25 what should, do

26 my first time to ride   27 don't need to

28 take you to   29 Watch out, crossing

30 Don't, have just sensed

31 sense dangerous situations, down

32 How can, do   33 intelligent robotic

34 all about driving   35 based on

36 How, like   37 like, human

32 진아: 어떻게 그렇게 할 수 있어?

33 인공 지능 자동차: 전 아주 지능적인 로봇 차예요.

34 저는 운전에 대한 모든 걸 알고 있어요.

35 저는 제 지식과 경험을 바탕으로 위험을 예측할 수 있어요

36 수한: 정말 똑똑하구나! 사람처럼 생각하고 행동하는구나.

37 정말 인간 같아.

1 A Day at the AI Expo

2 Jina and Suhan are at the World AI Expo.

3 They are entering the AI home.

4 Suhan: Look at this! It's a house of the future.

5 Jina: Let's go into the bedroom first. Look, there's a smart closet.

6 Suhan: I'm standing in front of this screen on the closet door and my clothes keep changing.

7 Jina: The screen suggests clothes that suit the weather.

8 Suhan: That's amazing! We no longer have to worry about dressing for the weather.

9 Jina: Right. Let's move on to the living room.

10 Suhan: Oh, I like this music speaker.

11 AI Speaker: I'm not just a music speaker.

12 I can do more than you can imagine.

13 Jina: It's hard to believe that you can understand us. What can you do?

14 AI Speaker: How about watching a movie?

15 I'll play one for you.

16 Suhan: Look, those smart windows are getting darker.

17 I feel like I'm in a movie theater.

18 Jina: What else can you do?

19 AI Speaker: I can beatbox, too. Here comes, "cats and boots and cats and boots."

20 Suhan: You're funny. Good job!

21 Jina: Hurry! There's a smart car station outside!

22 Let's go and ride in that red car.

23 Suhan: This car is so cool. Let's get in.

24 AI Car: Welcome. Are you ready to go?

25 Jina: Yes, what should we do now?

26 It's my first time to ride in a smart car.

27 AI Car: You don't need to do anything.

28 I will drive and take you to the next station.

29 Suhan: Watch out! I see a cat crossing the street.

30 AI Car: Don't worry. I have just sensed it.

31 When I sense dangerous situations, I slow down or stop.

1 인공 지능 박람회에서의 하루

2 진아와 수한이가 세계 인공 지능 박람회에 있다.

3 그들은 인공 지능 집으로 들어가고 있다.

4 수한: 이것 봐! 미래의 집이야.

5 진아: 침실 먼저 들어가 보자. 이거 봐, 스마트 옷장이 있어.

6 수한: 옷장 문에 있는 스크린 앞에 서 있으니까 내 옷이 계속해서 바뀌어.

7 진아: 스크린이 날씨에 적합한 옷을 제안하는 거야.

8 수한: 놀라워! 우린 더 이상 날씨 때문에 무슨 옷을 입을지 걱정할 필요가 없겠다.

9 진아: 맞아. 이제 거실로 가 보자.

10 수한: 오, 이 음악 스피커 마음에 들어.

11 인공 지능 스피커: 저는 그냥 음악 스피커가 아니에요.

12 저는 당신이 상상하는 것 이상의 것을 할 수 있어요.

13 진아: 네가 우리를 이해한다니 믿기 어려운 걸! 넌 뭘 할 수 있어?

14 인공 지능 스피커: 영화 보는 건 어때요?

15 하나 틀어 줄게요.

16 수한: 이것 봐, 스마트 창문이 점점 어두워지고 있어.

17 마치 내가 영화관 안에 있는 것 같아.

18 진아: 또 뭘 할 수 있어?

19 인공 지능 스피커: 비트박스도 할 수 있어요. "북치기 박치기 북치기 박치기."

20 수한: 넌 정말 재미있구나. 잘했어!

21 진아: 서둘러! 밖에 스마트 자동차 정류장이 있어.

22 가서 저 빨간 차를 타 보자.

23 수한: 이 차 정말 멋지다. 차에 타자.

24 인공 지능 자동차: 어서 오세요. 갈 준비 됐나요?

25 진아: 응, 우린 이제 뭘 해야 하지?

26 스마트 자동차에 타는 건 처음이야.

27 인공 지능 자동차: 아무 것도 하지 않아도 돼요.

28 제가 운전해서 다음 정류장까지 데려다줄 거니까요.

29 수한: 조심해! 고양이가 길을 건너고 있는 게 보여.

30 인공 지능 자동차: 걱정 말아요. 이미 감지했어요.

31 저는 어떤 위험 상황을 감지하면 속도를 늦추거나 멈춰요.

32 Jina: How can you do that?

33 AI Car: I'm a very intelligent robotic car.

34 I know all about driving.

35 I can predict danger based on knowledge and experience.

36 Suhan: How smart! You think and act like a person.

37 You are really like a human.

Before You Read

1. DAILY NEWS

2. Beats

3. has beaten, in, match

4. had a match with, one of the greatest, players

5. difficult to understand

6. believed, for an AI to beat

7. was able to predict, finally won

8. are shocked, be more intelligent than

Focus on Expressions

1. get in, to get to

2. love to go, because, greatest amusement park

3. Above all, their favorite activity

4. don't want, get off

Wrap Up 1-2

1. smart food-ordering, over there, Why don't, try

2. sounds, be able to order, by using

3. By the way, for robots to replace

4. will be free from, because of

5. What, mean

6. in danger, so, don't have to

7. right, always try to look on

Before You Read

1. DAILY NEWS

2. AI Beats Human!

3. An AI program has beaten a human in a *baduk* match.

4. The AI had a match with Lee Sedol, who is one of the greatest *baduk* players.

5. *Baduk* is a board game, and the rules are difficult to understand.

6. Many people believed it would be impossible for an AI to beat a human player.

7. However, the AI was able to predict Lee's play, and it finally won the game.

8. People are shocked that an AI can be more intelligent than a human.

Focus on Expressions

1. In 2099, people get in a flying car to get to the moon.

2. Kids love to go to the moon because the greatest amusement park is there.

3. Above all, horse-riding is their favorite activity.

4. They don't want to get off the horses.

Wrap Up 1-2

1. G: Minseok, there is a smart food-ordering machine over there. Why don't we try it?

2. B: That sounds interesting. We'll be able to order easily and fast by using it.

3. G: I hope so. By the way, do you think maybe it will be possible for robots to replace humans someday?

4. B: I'm not sure. But we will be free from danger because of robots.

5. G: What do you mean?

6. B: Robots can help people in danger. Robots can do the dangerous work so humans don't have to.

7. G: You're right. We should always try to look on the bright side.

10 stone, 돌, 석조　11 hometown, 고향

12 found, 설립하다　13 collect, 모으다, 수집하다

14 store, 저장하다　15 land, 토지, 땅　16 nature, 자연

단어 TEST Step 1　p.21

01 모으다, 수집하다　02 사건, 일　03 공무원, 당국

04 사업가　05 고통 받다, 시달리다

06 통치하다; 규칙, 원칙　07 왕조, 시대

08 설명하다　09 알려지지 않은

10 적합하다　11 압박하다　12 ~을 통하여

13 여행객　14 독립　15 지역사회, 주민

16 저장하다, 보관하다　17 현대의

18 살아 있는　19 또 다른, 다른 하나의

20 운동　21 마을　22 시

23 낭비하다　24 재산　25 왕의, 왕실의

26 사회, 단체　27 설립하다　28 도자기

29 지원하다　30 의미　31 맛, 취향

32 관심, 흥미　33 건축　34 스페인의

35 위험에 빠진　36 발을 들여놓다　37 ~으로 알려지다

38 ~을 돌보다　39 (사업, 세력 등이) 쇠퇴하다

40 ~ 덕분에　41 ~으로 유명하다　42 어려움에 처한

43 ~와 조화를 이루다

단어 TEST Step 2　p.22

01 tradition　02 modern　03 society

04 architecture　05 businessman　06 store

07 dynasty　08 explain　09 meaning

10 pottery　11 unknown　12 poem

13 official　14 collect　15 found

16 independence　17 affair　18 property

19 alive　20 interest　21 support

22 rule　23 suffer　24 tourist

25 movement　26 through　27 fit

28 royal　29 another　30 press

31 village　32 community　33 waste

34 nature　35 fall off　36 be filled with

37 care for　38 thanks to　39 hundreds of

40 in need　41 be famous for　42 be known as

43 be in harmony with

단어 TEST Step 3　p.23

1 alive, 살아 있는　2 businessman, 사업가, 실업가

3 dynasty, 왕조　4 novel, 소설

5 architecture, 건축, 건축학　6 royal, 왕의, 왕실의

7 rule, 통치하다　8 explain, 설명하다　9 property, 재산

대화문 TEST Step 1　p.24~25

Listen & Speak 1 B-2

Do, anything about / little, famous for / going to, with / think, like

Listen & Speak 2 A

Could, explain, painting / by, painted, in

Listen & Speak 2 B-1

1 explain this poem / was written by / about / about, missing

2 explain what, is / volunteer group, community / tell, more about / take care of

Listen & Speak 2 C

Could, explain, to save / won't waste, on

Real-Life Zone A

What, anything about / Korean houses, are designed, in harmony with / explain a little / cool, warm / sounds, Where, see, traditional houses / near here / about going, seeing / idea, How, get / take, over there

Real-Life Zone B

1 know anything / one of, greatest sights / explain why, famous / because, longest wall

2 anything about, novel / short novel written by / explain why / because, won, for

Real-Life Zone B e.g.

know anything about / was built in, by / explain why, famous / It's because, tallest tower, at that time

Wrap Up

know anything / birthday, baby / tell, more / get together, wears / sounds interesting / share food, wish for, long life / Korean tradition

대화문 TEST Step 2　p.26~27

Listen & Speak 1 B-2

G: Do you know anything about Changdeokgung?

B: Yes, a little. It's famous for its beautiful garden.

G: I'm going to go there with my Chinese friend.

B: I think you'll like it.

Listen & Speak 2 A

B: Could you explain this painting?

W: Sure. It's the *Two Sisters* by Renoir. He painted it in 1881.

1 G: Can you explain this poem?

  B: Sure. It was written by Yun Dongju.

  G: What's it about?

  B: It's about him missing his hometown.

2 B: Could you explain what Helping Hands is?

  G: It's a volunteer group in our community.

  B: Could you tell me more about it?

  G: Well, they take care of children in need.

A: Could you explain your plan to save money?

B: I won't waste my money on snacks.

G: What are *hanoks*? Do you know anything about them?

M: *Hanoks* are traditional Korean houses. They are designed to be in harmony with nature.

G: Could you explain a little more about them?

M: *Hanoks* are cool in the summer and warm in the winter.

W: That sounds interesting. Where can I see these traditional houses?

M: There's a *hanok* village near here.

G: How about going there and seeing the *hanoks*?

W: Good idea! How can we get there?

M: You can take Bus Number 5 over there at the bus stop.

1 A: Do you know anything about the Great Wall of China?

  B: Yes. It is one of the greatest sights in the world.

  A: Can you explain why it is famous?

  B: It's because it is the longest wall in the world.

2 A: Do you know anything about the novel *The Old Man and the Sea*?

  B: Yes. It is a short novel written by Ernest Hemingway.

  A: Can you explain why it is famous?

  B: It's because Hemingway won the Pulitzer Prize in 1953 for this novel.

A: Do you know anything about the Eiffel Tower?

B: Yes. It was built in 1889 by Gustave Eiffel.

A: Can you explain why it is famous?

B: It's because it was the tallest tower in the world at that time.

B: Do you know anything about a *dol* party?

G: Yes. It's the birthday party for a one-year-old baby.

B: Could you tell me more about it?

G: Well, the family members get together for the party, and the birthday baby wears a *hanok*.

B: That sounds interesting.

G: The family members share food and wish for a long life for the baby. It's a Korean tradition.

01 King, Architecture, Gyeongseong

02 Have, been to

03 There, beautiful, village

04 popular, who, past

05 know, created through, efforts

06 known as, in

07 businessman who founded

08 time, ruled, fit, taste

09 moving into, building, Western

10 wanted, protect, suffering

11 power, keep, let, set

12 bought, between, and

13 built, modern, people

14 Through, efforts, filled with

15 independence movement, ways

16 example, supported, keep, alive

17 happened, caught, suffered

18 officials pressed, build

19 how to build

20 official, know, so, build

21 what, told, do   22 cost, high

23 fell off, property

24 part, to, traditions, still

01 The King, Architecture in   02 Have, been to

03 There is, village

04 popular, who, past

05 However, know, was created through, efforts

06 known as, Architecture   07 who founded

08 At the time, was ruled by, were changing, fit, taste

09 moving into, were building Japanese, Western

10 wanted to protect, suffering

11 power, should keep, let, set, foot

12 bought, between, and

13 built, modern, people

14 Through, efforts, filled with

15 independence movement in many ways

16 For example, supported its efforts, keep, alive

17 happened, was caught by, suffered a lot

18 pressed, to build　　　　　19 how to build

20 official, know how to, so, build, too

21 what, told, to do　　　　　22 cost, high

23 fell off, lost, property

24 part, thanks to, traditions, still live with

1 경성의 건축왕

2 당신은 북촌에 다녀온 적이 있는가?

3 북촌에는 아름다운 한옥 마을이 있다.

4 그곳은 한국의 과거를 보고 싶어 하는 관광객들에게 인기가 있다.

5 그러나 북촌이 한 사람의 노력으로 만들어졌다는 것을 아는 사람은 많지 않다.

6 그 사람은 경성의 건축왕으로 알려진 정세권이었다.

7 정세권은 1920년에 건양사를 설립한 사업가였다.

8 그 당시 한국은 일본의 지배를 받았고, 일본인들은 경성을 그들의 취향에 맞게 바꾸고 있었다.

9 경성으로 이주하는 많은 일본인들은 일본식이나 서양식 집들을 짓고 있었다.

10 정세권은 한옥을 지키고 고통받는 사람들을 돕기를 원했다.

11 그는 말했다. "사람이 힘이다. 우리 조선 사람들은 종로를 지켜야 하며, 일본인들이 이곳에 발을 붙이지 못하게 해야 한다."

12 그는 경복궁과 창덕궁 사이의 땅을 샀다.

13 거기에 그는 사람들을 위해 작은 현대식 한옥들을 지었다.

14 그의 노력으로 북촌은 현재 아름다운 한옥으로 가득 차 있다.

15 정세권은 여러 방법으로 독립운동을 도왔다.

16 예를 들면, 그는 조선어 학회를 위한 회관을 지었고 조선어를 지키려는 그들의 노력을 지원했다.

17 조선어 학회 사건이 발생했을 때 그는 경찰에 잡혀 많은 고통을 겪었다.

18 일본인 관리들은 그에게 일본식 가옥을 지으라고 압박했다.

19 그는 말했다. "나는 일본식 가옥을 지을 줄 모르오."

20 한 관리가 말했다. "당신은 한옥을 지을 줄 아오. 그러니 일본식 가옥도 지을 수 있소."

21 그러나 그는 그 일본인이 그에게 요구한 것을 하지 않았다.

22 그 대가는 컸다.

23 그의 사업은 쇠퇴했고, 그는 재산을 잃었다.

24 그러나 부분적으로나마, 정세권 덕분에 한국의 전통이 오늘날 여전히 우리와 함께 살아 있다.

1 The King of Architecture in Gyeongseong.

2 Have you been to Bukchon?

3 There is a beautiful *hanok* village in Bukchon.

4 It is popular with tourists who want to see Korea's past.

5 However, not many people know that Bukchon was created through one man's efforts.

6 That man was Jeong Segwon, known as the King of Architecture in Gyeongseong.

7 Jeong Segwon was a businessman who founded Geonyangsa in 1920.

8 At the time, Korea was ruled by Japan, and the Japanese were changing Gyeongseong to fit their taste.

9 Many Japanese moving into Gyeongseong were building Japanese or Western houses.

10 Jeong Segwon wanted to protect the *hanok* and help the suffering people.

11 He said, "People are power. We Joseon people should keep Jongno and not let the Japanese set foot here."

12 He bought the land between Gyeongbokgung and Changdeokgung.

13 There he built small, modern *hanoks* for the people.

14 Through his efforts, we now have Bukchon filled with its beautiful *hanoks*.

15 Jeong Segwon helped the independence movement in many ways.

16 For example, he built the office building for the Joseon Language Society and supported its efforts to keep the Joseon language alive.

17 When the Joseon Language Affair happened, he was caught by the police and suffered a lot.

18 Japanese officials pressed him to build Japanese houses.

19 He said, "I don't know how to build Japanese houses."

20 An official said, "You know how to build *hanoks*, so you can build Japanese houses, too."

21 But he did not do what the Japanese told him to do.

22 The cost was high.

23 His business fell off, and.he lost his property.

24 However, in part, thanks to Jeong Segwon, the traditions of Korea still live with us today.

Before You Read

1. Japanese officials pressed, to use

2. tried to keep, alive

3. wanted to protect

4. independence movement rose up

Language in Use

1. moved into, next to Joe's store

2. opened up

3. started to go, instead of

4. Few, set foot in

5. fell off

Writing Workshop

1. Who, An

2. during, Joseon Dynasty, was catching

3. When, was fishing, saw, fishing near

4. visited, twice, were part of

5. Japanese ruler officially, not to fish near

6. did his best to protect

Dokdo.

6. He did his best to protect Ulleungdo and Dokdo.

Before You Read

1. Japanese officials pressed the Joseon people to use the Japanese language.

2. The Joseon people tried to keep the Joseon language alive.

3. The Joseon people wanted to protect the country.

4. Soon, the independence movement rose up.

Language in Use

1. A woman moved into the building next to Joe's store.

2. She opened up a new store.

3. Many people started to go to the woman's new store instead of Joe's store.

4. Few people set foot in Joe's store.

5. His food business fell off.

Writing Workshop

1. Who is An Yongbok?

2. He lived during the Joseon Dynasty, and his job was catching fish.

3. When he was fishing, he saw the Japanese people fishing near Ulleungdo.

4. He visited Japan twice and said that Ulleungdo and Dokdo were part of Korea.

5. In 1696, the Japanese ruler officially told the Japanese people not to fish near Ulleugdo and

단어 TEST Step 1　　　　　　　　　　　　　p.40

01 비난하다	02 세기, 100년	03 공연
04 고전의, 클래식 음악의		05 사실은
06 자유롭게	07 즐거운, 즐길 수 있는	
08 건강한	09 관객	10 방해하다
11 비밀	12 나타나다	13 작품
14 박수치다	15 심각한, 진지한	
16 (위치가) ~ 사이[중간]에		17 상상하다
18 예절	19 도서 박람회	
20 기억에 남을, 기억할 만한		21 익숙한
22 놀랍게도	23 의존적인, 의존하는	
24 협주곡	25 쓰레기통	26 장면
27 증가된	28 주로	29 귀족
30 소음, 잡음	31 오케스트라	32 올바른, 정확한
33 움직임, (큰 교향곡 따위의) 악장(부분)		34 결과
35 얼마 후	36 그 결과	37 ~에 의존하는
38 B 때문에 A를 비난하다		
39 우선은, 현재로는, 지금은		
40 과거로 거슬러 올라가다		41 아무 때나
42 ~을 돌보다	43 시간이 지남에 따라	

단어 TEST Step 2　　　　　　　　　　　　　p.41

01 blame	02 clap	03 pause
04 correct	05 secret	06 serious
07 disturb	08 enjoyable	09 appear
10 social	11 surprisingly	12 concerto
13 audience	14 familiar	15 movement
16 actually	17 book fair	18 result
19 increased	20 bright	21 freely
22 healthy	23 dependent	24 manners
25 century	26 classical	27 memorable
28 performance	29 mostly	30 imagine
31 nobleman	32 noise	33 return
34 scene	35 by the way	36 take a look at
37 as a result	38 for now	39 at any time
40 blame A for B	41 dependent on	42 after some time
43 no longer		

단어 TEST Step 3　　　　　　　　　　　　　p.42

1 bright, 밝은　　2 appear, 나타나다　　3 clap, 박수치다
4 noise, 소음, 잡음　　5 disturb, 방해하다

6 whistle, 휘파람을 불다　　7 pause, 정지하다, 멈추다
8 secret, 비밀　　9 nobleman, 귀족
10 performance, 공연　　11 result, 결과
12 blame, 비난하다　　13 concerto, 협주곡
14 work, 작품　　15 orchestra, 오케스트라
16 return, 돌려주다, 반납하다

대화문 TEST Step 1　　　　　　　　　　　　p.43~44

Listen & Speak 1 B

1 interested in going, tickets / When / this, at, make it
/ thanks, for asking
2 Why don't, this weekend / What about, on / make it,
have to take care of / See, then

Listen & Speak 2 B

1 going to, remember / course, Don't forget / won't,
bring, too / Sounds
2 look healthy, secret / go swimming every day,
sometime / sounds like, Any other, should do / Don't
forget to, many kinds, too

Real-Life Zone A

listening to / going to, like to, before / guess, more, if /
Actually, clap, wrong / Don't, clap when, stops / may,
pauses, wait, very end / see, Make sure, don't forget
to, real ending, way, make it, practice / practice after,
finishes / See, then

Real-Life Zone B

Why don't, after school, make / can't, about on / Don't
forget to bring / right, won't

Wrap Up

Have, heard / heard that, famous, will be / why don't,
on, make it / what time / at, Let's meet / forget to, up /
won't

대화문 TEST Step 2　　　　　　　　　　　　p.45~46

Listen & Speak 1 B

1 B: Are you interested in going to an opera? I have
　　two tickets.
　G: Yes, I love opera. When is it?
　B: It's this Saturday at 5:00. Can you make it?
　G: Yes, thanks so much for asking me.
2 B: Why don't we go to the new shoe shop this
　　weekend?
　G: Okay. What about at 2:00 on Saturday?
　B: Can you make it at 1:00? I have to take care of my
　　sister at 3:00.

G: Sure. See you then.

Listen & Speak 2 B

1 B: We're going to Hangang this weekend. Do you remember?

G: Of course. Don't forget to bring your camera.

B: Okay. I won't. I'll bring some snacks, too.

G: Sounds great.

2 G: You look healthy. What's your secret?

B: Thanks. Well, I go swimming every day. You should go with me sometime.

G: That sounds like fun. Any other things I should do?

B: Don't forget to eat many kinds of fruits and vegetables, too.

Real-Life Zone A

G: What are you listening to?

B: Classical music. I'm going to a concert tomorrow and I'd like to know about the music before I go.

G: I guess it's more enjoyable if you know the music.

B: Actually, I don't want to clap at the wrong time.

G: Don't you just clap when the music stops?

B: No. In classical music, one piece of music may have several pauses. You should wait and clap at the very end.

G: I see. Make sure you don't forget to clap at the real ending. By the way, can you make it to our soccer practice tomorrow at 4:00?

B: Sure. I'll come to the practice after the concert finishes.

G: Okay. See you then.

Real-Life Zone B

A: Why don't we go to the library on Monday after school? Can you make it?

B: Sorry, but I can't. How about on Tuesday?

A: Okay. Don't forget to bring your library card.

B: All right. I won't.

Wrap Up

G: Yunho! Have you heard about the Christmas concert at the city hall?

B: Yes. I heard that a famous opera singer will be on the stage.

G: Oh, then why don't we go on Christmas Day? Can you make it?

B: Sure. Do you know what time the concert starts?

G: It starts at 5:30. Let's meet at the bus stop at 4:00.

B: Good. Don't forget to dress up.

G: Okay. I won't.

01 History, Classical, Manners
02 Imagine yourself, classical
03 orchestra, play one, concertos
04 hall, dark, silent
05 Nobody, sound
06 Everybody, serious
07 audiences, clap, finishes
08 familiar scene at
09 back, take, look, century
10 bright, inside, nobleman's
11 playing, piano
12 Surprisingly, audiences, talking freely
13 whistle, clap, time
14 shocked, bad, himself, surprised
15 time, mostly social events
16 good places to meet
17 Noise, just part, concert
18 quiet, century when, built
19 More, not just noblemen
20 no longer dependent on
21 more, works, use, increased
22 For example, blamed, noise
23 After, time, rule appeared
24 As, result, quiet, serious
25 what, like, because, change
26 however, enjoy classical, remember
27 Enjoy, disturb, around

01 History, Classical, Manners
02 Imagine yourself, classical
03 orchestra, play one of, piano
04 hall, dark, silent
05 Nobody, sound
06 Everybody, serious
07 audiences, clap, concerto finishes
08 familiar scene at
09 Let's go back, time, take, look, one of
10 bright, inside, nobleman's
11 playing, piano
12 Surprisingly, audiences, talking freely
13 whistle, clap at any time
14 shocked by, bad manners, himself, surprised by, quiet
15 were mostly social

16 good places to meet

17 Noise, just part of

18 quiet, century when, were built

19 not just noblemen

20 no longer dependent, for money

21 more power, works, use, increased power

22 For example, blamed, for making noise

23 After some time, rule appeared

24 As a result, quiet, serious

25 what concerts, look like, because, change with time

26 For now, however, enjoy classical, just remember

27 Enjoy, do not disturb those around

1 클래식 콘서트 관람 예절의 역사

2 당신이 클래식 공연장에 있다고 상상해 보아라.

3 오케스트라가 모차르트의 피아노 협주곡들 중 한 곡을 연주하기 시작한다.

4 콘서트장은 어둡고 조용하다.

5 아무도 소리를 내지 않는다.

6 모두가 진지하게 보인다.

7 청중은 오직 협주곡이 끝난 후에만 손뼉을 친다.

8 이것이 오늘날 콘서트에서 익숙한 장면이다.

9 과거로 거슬러 올라가서 18세기 모차르트의 콘서트들 중 하나를 살펴보자.

10 당신은 한 귀족의 집안 밝은 홀에 있다.

11 모차르트는 피아노를 치고 있다.

12 하지만 놀랍게도, 청중들은 먹고 마시며 자유롭게 대화하고 있다.

13 그들은 아무 때나 휘파람을 불고 박수를 친다.

14 당신은 그들의 나쁜 매너에 충격을 받지만, 모차르트 자신은 오늘날의 조용한 청중에게 놀랄지도 모른다.

15 모차르트 시대의 콘서트는 주로 사교적인 행사였다.

16 콘서트는 사람을 만나기에 좋은 장소였다.

17 소음은 그저 콘서트의 일부였다.

18 오늘날의 조용한 콘서트는 많은 대형 공연장이 생긴 19세기에 시작됐다.

19 귀족뿐만 아니라 더 많은 사람들이 콘서트에 갔다.

20 예술가들은 더 이상 돈을 벌기 위해 귀족들에게 의존하지 않았다.

21 예술가들은 자신의 작품에 더 많은 권한이 생겼고 그 힘을 사용하기 시작했다.

22 예를 들어, 바그너는 소음을 낸다는 것 때문에 관객들을 비난했다.

23 얼마 후에 '악장 사이 박수 금지 규칙'이 생겼다.

24 그 결과, 오늘날 우리는, 매우 조용하고 진지하다.

25 예절은 시대에 따라 변하기 때문에 우리는 콘서트가 미래에는 어떤 모습일지 모른다.

26 하지만 지금은 당신이 래식 음악 공연을 즐기고 싶다면 이것만은 기억해라.

27 음악은 즐기되 당신 주변의 다른 사람들을 방해하지 마라.

1 The History of Classical Concert Manners

2 Imagine yourself at a classical music concert.

3 The orchestra starts to play one of Mozart's piano concertos.

4 The concert hall is dark and silent.

5 Nobody makes a sound.

6 Everybody looks serious.

7 The audiences only clap after the concerto finishes.

8 This is a familiar scene at concerts today.

9 Let's go back in time and take a look at one of Mozart's concerts in the 18th century.

10 You are in a bright hall inside a nobleman's house.

11 Mozart is playing the piano.

12 Surprisingly, however, the audiences are eating, drinking, and talking freely.

13 They whistle and clap at any time.

14 You are shocked by their bad manners, but Mozart himself would be surprised by today's quiet audiences.

15 Concerts in Mozart's time were mostly social events.

16 They were good places to meet people.

17 Noise was just part of the concert.

18 Today's quiet concerts began in the 19th century when many big concert halls were built.

19 More people, not just noblemen, went to concerts.

20 Artists were no longer dependent on noblemen for money.

21 The artists had more power over their works and started to use their increased power.

22 For example, Wagner blamed the audience for making noise.

23 After some time, a no-clapping-between-movements rule appeared.

24 As a result, here we are today, very quiet and serious.

25 We do not know what concerts will look like in the

future because manners change with time.

26 For now, however, if you want to enjoy classical music concerts, just remember this:

27 Enjoy the music, but do not disturb those around you.

구석구석지문 TEST Step 1 p.57

Before I Read B

1. Guide, Concert Manners
2. Watching, memorable experience, keep, in mind
3. Before, Go
4. Plan to arrive, concert time
5. Find out, will be played
6. When, Is Playing
7. Turn off
8. Stay, No, whistling, along to
9. Don't clap, piece is over
10. It, to clap, clapping

Writing Workshop

1. Review
2. On, to a concert hall, where, was held
3. opportunity to listen to, play live
4. played, Piano Concerto
5. how beautiful the classical music was
6. live performance
7. will not forget

Wrap Up 7

1. When, coming out
2. coming out
3. your plans for
4. planning to have
5. held one of, during his world tour

구석구석지문 TEST Step 2 p.58

Before I Read B

1. A Guide to Good Concert Manners
2. Watching a classical music concert can be a memorable experience if you keep these tips in mind.
3. Before You Go In:
4. Plan to arrive 20-30 minutes before concert time.
5. Find out what music will be played.
6. When Music Is Playing :
7. Turn off your cellphone!

8. Stay quiet. No talking, whistling, singing along to the music.
9. Don't clap until the whole piece is over.
10. It is safe to clap when the audience starts clapping.

Writing Workshop

1. Music Concert Review
2. On February 2, I went to a concert hall at the Seoul Arts Center where Jo Seongu's piano concert was held.
3. It was a great opportunity to listen to him play live .
4. He played Chopin's Piano Concerto No. 1.
5. I did not know how beautiful the classical music was .
6. I liked his live performance.
7. I will not forget this experience.

Wrap Up 7

1. Reporter: When is your new album coming out?
2. Justin Otter: It's coming out next month.
3. Reporter: What are your plans for the new album?
4. Justin Otter: I'm planning to have a concert at the Super Stadium.
5. My hero Michael Johnson held one of his concerts during his world tour at the place.

MEMO

MEMO